Molecular Biology

A Complete Course

With More Than 125 Diagrams

Molecular Biology

A Complete Course

With More Than 125 Diagrams

Ram Naresh Singh

Former Professor, Molecular Biology Unit,
Tata Institute of Fundamental Research,
Homi Bhabha Road, Mumbai - 400 005, India

CBS

CBS PUBLISHERS & DISTRIBUTORS PVT. LTD.

New Delhi • Bangalore • Pune • Cochin • Chennai (India)

ISBN : 978-81-239-1606-4

First Edition : 2008
Reprint : 2012

Published by Satish Kumar Jain and produced by V.K. Jain for
CBS Publishers & Distributors Pvt. Ltd.,
CBS Plaza, 4819/XI Prahlad Street, 24 Ansari Road, Daryaganj,
New Delhi - 110002, India. • Website: www.cbspd.com
e-mail: delhi@cbspd.com, cbspubs@airtelmail.in
Ph.: 23289259, 23266861, 23266867 • Fax: 011-23243014

Branches:

- ***Bengaluru:*** Seema House, 2975, 17th Cross, K.R. Road, Bansankari 2nd Stage, Bengaluru - 560070 Ph.: +91-80-26771678/79 • E-mail: cbsbng@gmail.com, bangalore@cbspd.com
- ***Pune:*** Bhuruk Prestige, Sr. No. 52/12/2+1+3/2, Narhe, Haveli (Near Katraj-Dehu Road By-pass), Pune - 411051 Ph.: +91-20-64704058/59, 32342277 • E-mail: pune@cbspd.com
- ***Kochi:*** 36/14, Kalluvilakam, Lissie Hospital Road, Kochi - 682018, Kerala • Ph.: +91-484-4059061-65 Fax: +91-484-4059065 • E-mail: cochin@cbspd.com
- ***Chennai:*** 20, West Park Road, Shenoy Nagar, Chennai - 600030 Ph.: +91-44-26260666, 26208620 E-mail: chennai@cbspd.com

Printed at :
India Binding House, Noida (UP)

Preface

Molecular Biology has revolutionized the traditional descriptive science of Biology. Its advent has opened a vast vista of precise information and mechanics of cellular processes. In totality, Molecular Biology deals with the elucidation of the basic mechanisms through which the molecules exert their specific action in or on the living cells. The potential and power of Molecular Biology has become more evident after the development of the Recombinant DNA Technology, Genetic Engineering and Stem Cell research.

Looking at the importance of the subject, some excellent books have been published (Appendix 3). These books serve the purpose of textbook, as well as a reference book. Then why write another textbook on Molecular Biology? I had tried to answer this question in my earlier book '*Basics of Molecular Biology*'. I shall recapitulate those reasons for the readers of this book '*Molecular Biology*'.

Rarely is the study of Molecular Biology done in isolation by a student. In fact, in addition to Molecular Biology, the student invariably is asked to master other subjects. The available books on Molecular Biology are indeed powerhouses for information, but extend over 700-1500 pages. A student barely has time to go through the book once, let alone master the contents of the book. An up-to-date, leaner, simpler and precise textbook on the subject would be invaluable to students in this field.

This need has made me write '*Molecular Biology*' in the following format:

1. Keep the book as close to the basics as possible so that students may learn without having to first assimilate complex terminology.
2. Stress the essential facts and avoid overloading the book with estoric details, only of interest to a minute proportion of the scientific community.
3. Illustrate the book with line diagrams, which are easy to understand, memorize and reproduce at a later date. This is invariably useful while

explaining a difficult concept to others as well as during examinations. Complex three-dimensional colour figures have been avoided.

4. Keep the text within the reach of the student. Owning the textbook and not the photocopy version has been a major focus; hence the text has been formatted to keep printing costs at a minimum.

Molecular Biology is a rapidly advancing science. This makes it necessary to update and revise the knowledge as and when possible. Keeping this view in mind chapters on: (i) Non-coding RNAs, (ii) Mitochondria, (iii) Chloroplasts, (iv) Protein Filaments, (v) Vesicular Transport and Protein Recycling, (vi) Stem Cells and (vii) Chemical Genetics have been especially written. In addition the chapters on Genetic Recombination; Retroviruses and Retroposons; Recombinant DNA and Genetic Engineering have been written with additional current knowledge. Most of the diagrams in these chapters are made by the author through computer graphics.

This book although was originally conceived for students of B.Sc., and M.Sc., yet the individuals with a background in the sciences as well as students at other levels, may benefit from its simplistic approach. Those who wish to go deeper in the subject, a few articles or books are listed at the end of each chapter as '***Further reading***'. Some experiments marked with an asterisk (*) in the book, are quite suitable for doing in a laboratory under the guidance of a teacher. Although I have striven to keep the text abreast of newer developments, I apologize for the occasional omission of scientific minutae. *Molecular Biology* is intended to give the reader a sound foundation and a flavour of the subject as it stands today. Its primary purpose is to be an initial stepping stone towards greater heights.

Ram Naresh Singh
E-mail: nareshkusum@yahoo.com
nareshkusumsingh@gmail.com

Acknowledgements

I express my sincere thanks to Mr. Mankatti and Mr. Wadke for the painstaking help in making some illustrations. Mr. N.P. Mankatti has meticulously made some diagrams on a computer, and Mr. V.B. Wadke has taken pains in making some free-hand drawings for the book.

I would like to share some pleasant experiences with readers. When children were young, I taught them many things on many occasions. When the time came for me to learn many things in computer graphics, children came forward in a big way to teach me so many things on different occasions. I appreciate their patience and perseverance in teaching me. I express my indebtedness on this account to Dr. Harshwardhan Thaker, Dr. Ila Singh and Dr. Aalok Singh.

I express my indebtedness to my wife Mrs. Kusum Singh, for her encouragement and active support not only during the preparation of this book, but throughout the last 45 years in research and teaching.

Lastly but not the least, I thank the Publishers of the book for being patient with me and doing an excellent job.

Molecular Biology – A Complete Course, brings the subject to the current level in an easy style useful for students and general readers. Feedbacks from students, teachers and general readers are most welcome.

Ram Naresh Singh
E-mail: nareshkusum@yahoo.com
nareshkusumsingh@gmail.com

Contents

CHAPTER 1

Molecular Biology and the Living Cell

Molecular Biology is concerned with the elucidation of the basic mechanisms by which the molecules exert their specific action in or on the living cell. Naturally, two questions arise:

1. How do we distinguish between a living system and a non-living object?
2. What is a living cell?

To answer the first question, let us look into some of the properties exhibited by living systems. A living system:

(i) Has the capacity of self-reproduction of its own kind.

(ii) Has an organization.

(iii) Exists over a period of time.

(iv) Exhibits growth and development.

(v) Shows existence of a metabolism, where many sets of chemical reactions synthesize some molecules, while other molecules are degraded.

(vi) Responds to physical and chemical stimuli. The physical stimulus could be through light, heat, sound, touch, acceleration, or gravity etc., while chemical stimuli act on the living system when the substances are presented along with fluids such as air or water. Response to any of the stimuli is also known as *behaviour* shown by the living system.

(vii) Exhibits capacity to undergo hereditary change or mutation.

Often crystals show all the above-mentioned properties except number vii, the capacity to undergo hereditary change and hence are usually excluded from the living systems. Viruses in mature state lack perceptible metabolism, yet need cellular metabolism for reproduction and can as well mutate. On these prominent criteria viruses may be favoured as living beings.

(viii) Most of the living systems are made of membrane-bound compartments, known as *cells*.

Animal cells are mostly surrounded by a *plasma membrane*. Whereas plant cells, usually have a *cell wall* around them and viruses have a *protein coat*. The *Cell Theory* or the cellular nature of the living systems was first proposed by Schleiden and Schwann. They also proposed that cells form from other cells. The microscopic observations of cells were made by Leevenhoek.

A cell having a well-defined nucleus is known as an *eucaryotic cell*, while organisms such as bacteria, where nucleus is not well demarcated are classified as *prokaryotic cell* or *procaryotes*. In *Greek* language *caryon* means *nucleus*.

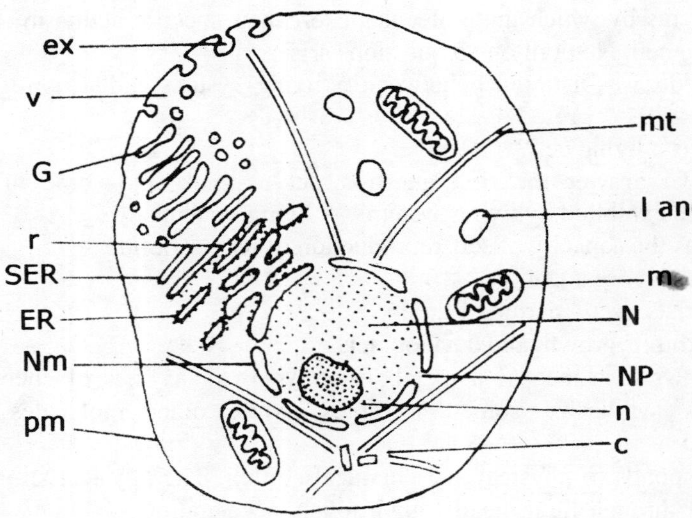

Fig.1.1. Line diagram of a typical animal cell. c = centrosome containing a pair of centrioles perpendicular to each other; ER = rough endoplasmic reticulum; ex = exocytosis; G = Golgi body; l = lysosome; m = mitochondrion;. mt = microtubule; N = nucleus; Nm = nuclear membrane; Np = nuclear pore; n = nucleolus; p = peroxisome; pm = plasma membrane; r = ribosomes; SER = smooth endoplasmic reticulum; v = vesicle.

Nucleus within the cell is typically a spherical or an ellipsoidal organelle of 3-10 μm diameter, which is surrounded by 2 layers of membrane, known as nuclear membranes, (Nm). The fluid content of the nucleus communicates with that of the surrounding cytoplasm through nuclear pores, (NP). Most of the hereditary material *deoxyribonucleic acid* (DNA) of the organism along with basic proteins, *histones* is organized in chromosomes located in the nucleus. In addition to chromosomes, the cellular organelles like mitochondria and chloroplasts also contain DNA.

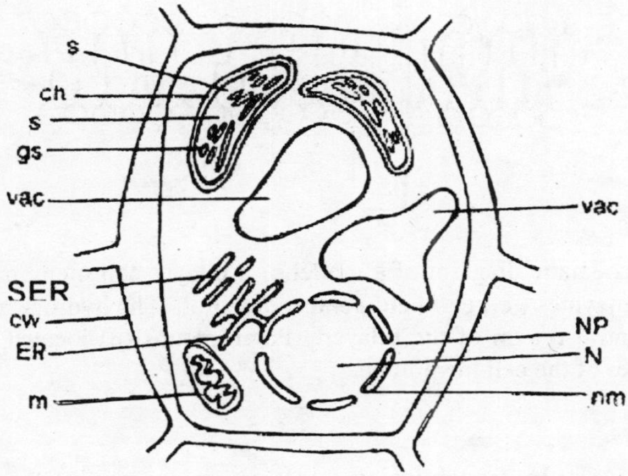

Fig. 1.2. Line diagram showing features of a plant cell, in addition to those present in an animal cell shown in Fig. 1.1. ch = chloroplast; cw = cell wall; gs = granna stacks; ER = rough endoplasmic reticulum; m = mitochondrion; N = nucleus; nm = nuclear membrane; NP = nuclear pore; s = stroma containing ribosomes and DNA; SER = smooth endoplasmic reticulum; vac=vacuole.

Nucleolus measuring less than 1 μm in diameter, exists within the nucleus and is known to be the site of *ribosomal ribonucleic acid* (rRNA) synthesis. A cell prior to cell division may show 2 *nuclei* or even 2 *nucleoli* within a nucleus.

Endoplasmic reticulum. There are two types of *endoplasmic reticula*: rough and smooth. *Rough endoplasmic reticulum* (ER) occurs in the cytoplasm in the form of sheets embedded on its outer surface with *ribosomes* involved in protein synthesis. Whereas, the *smooth endoplasmic reticulum* (smooth ER) is more tubular, lacks attached ribosomes and is *involved in lipid metabolism*.

Plasma membrane. *Phospholipid* molecules make continuous sheet of 5–8 nm thick plasma membrane (pm), as outer boundary of the cell. The plasma membrane has several types of proteins embedded in it, which function as pumps and channels for specific ions or molecules.

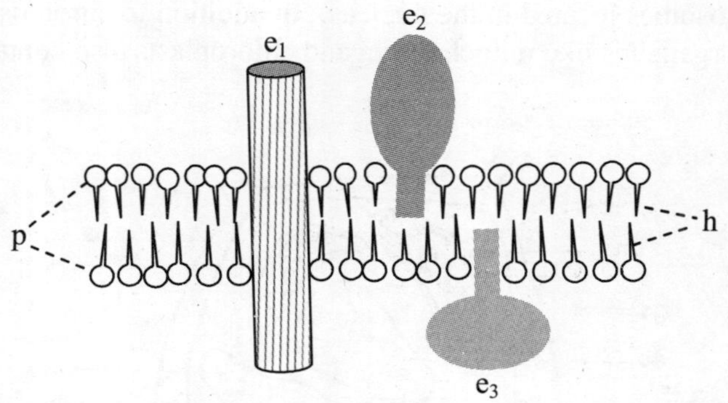

Fig. 1. 3. Schematic diagram of a model of a bilayer cell membrane with large proteins or enzymes (e_1, e_2, e_3 etc.) embedded in it. The hydrocarbon chains (h) form the central region of the bilayer. Polar groups (p) located on inner and outer surfaces of the cell membrane.

Golgi bodies. In transmission electron micrographs they appear as membrane-bound sacks, stacked together and vesicles bud off from them. *These vesicles transport molecules from Golgi body to cell surface or other parts of the cell. Golgi body is involved in modifying, sorting, packaging molecules usually for secretion or transport to other parts of the cell.*

Lysosomes are membrane-bound vesicles of 0.2 - 0.5 μm diameter containing hydrolytic enzymes for intracellular digestion.

Peroxisomes are other membrane-bound vesicles, containing oxidative enzymes that make and degrade hydrogen peroxide.

Mitochondria synthesize adenosine triphosphate (ATP), by the reaction of oxygen and food molecules. The terminal stage of oxidation occurs at the inner membrane folded into *cristae*. Mitochondrion may vary in size and shape but usually they are 0.5μm wide and 1-3 μm long.

Microtubules are cylindrical hollow tubes formed from 13 linear proto-filaments each composed of alternative α and β *tubulins* and bunched together with the same polarity so that one end has + and the other end has – (*minus*) polarity. *These tubules help maintain the cell-shape, as* *well as in the movement of chromosomes and cell division.*

Centrosomes are the main microtubule-organizing centre of the cell. Each *centrosome* has *a pair of centrioles*, arranged at *right angles* to each other in a configuration resembling **L**. They are hollow cylinders 400 nm long and 150 nm in diameter.

Additional Organelles in Plant Cells

In addition to the organelles present in the eucaryotic animal cells, some plant cells have *plastids*, and *vacuoles*. Depending upon structure and function, plastids can be divided into various types, like *chloroplast*, *chromoplast* and *leucoplast*.

Chloroplasts are approximately 5 μm long spindle-shaped plastids containing chlorophyll. They are double-membrane bound organelles, containing stacked-membrane structures known as grana and thylakoid along with DNA and ribosomes. The photosynthetic system contains chlorophyll pigment.

Vacuole is a large membrane-bound vesicle (*tonoplast*), usually containing remnant products after digestion.

Cell Wall of Plants usually contains fibrils of cellulose cemented with other polysaccharides. They are 0.1-10 μm thick.

In addition to these cell organelles, the cell contains a very large number and variety of molecules falling in to main categories of proteins, nucleic acids, saccharides and traces of metal ions, all soluble in the cellular fluid *protoplasm*.

The essential cell-organelles are usually common amongst most types of cells. However, the types of cell in a vertebrate-body could be as large as 200. On the other side protozoa (particularly ciliates) have very intricate and complex cells.

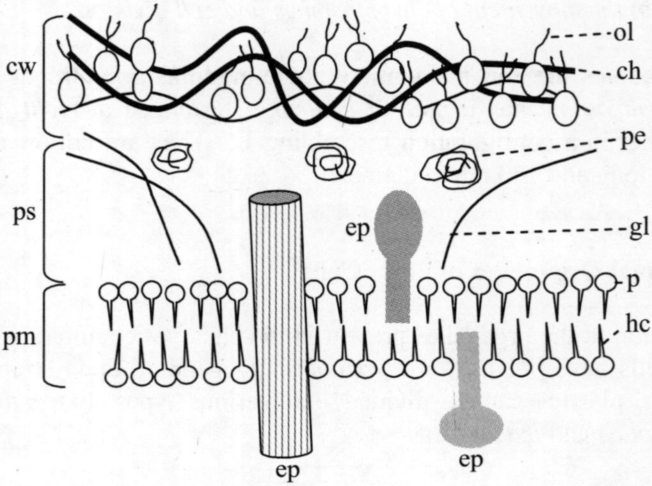

Fig. 1.4. The cell wall of yeast consists of a matrix of intertwined polysccharides, glucan and chitin. On the outer side of this matrix are embedded mannoproteins with oligo-saccharide (sugar) molecules. ch = chitin filaments; cw = cell wall; ep = embedded protein or integral protein; gl = glucan; hc = hydrocarbon chains; ol = oligosaccharides with mannoproteins; p = polar groups of plasma membrane; pe = periplasmic enzyme; pm = plasma membrane; ps = periplasmic space.

Further reading

Alberts, B., Bray, D., Lewis, J., Raff, M., Roberts, K., and Watson, J.D. *Molecular Biology of the Cell.* Garland Publishing Inc., New York, Third Edition, p.1294 (1994).

Darwin, C. On the Origin of Species, (1859). Reprinted Penguin, New York, 1984.

CHAPTER 2

Cell Division: Mitosis and Meiosis

Unicellular organisms such as bacteria multiply by the binary division of the cell, where a cell grows and divides medially to give rise to 2 almost identical cells. However, when the cell division gives rise to one cell smaller than the other, it is known as budding. Budding phenomenon is shown by yeast and some bacteria such as *Corynebacteria*.

Fig. 2.1: (a) A cell udergoing binary fission to give two daughter cells. (b) A cell budding to give rise to a daughter cell.

Multicellular organisms and some unicellular organisms like yeast or fungi have more than one type of cells. These cells can be classified into two broad categories: *somatic cells* and *germ line cells*. The germ line cells form gametes. The somatic cells multiply by the process of *mitotic cell division* (or *mitosis*). ***Mitosis*** is the replication and division of nucleus prior to and during the cell multiplication. Though the process of mitosis is a continuous process, yet for the sake of convenience of description, it has been divided into 4 steps: *prophase, metaphase, anaphase* and *telophase*. *Interphase* is the interval between two successive mitotic events.

The nucleus of an un-dividing cell or resting cell upon staining with basic dyes shows reticular (net-like) structure with 1 or 2 nucleoli rich in RNA, and surrounded by nuclear double membrane. The resting cell indeed may have a lot of metabolic activity.

Prophase: Nucleoli disappear on the onset of prophase. Reticular structure changes its appearance to densely staining threads - *chromosomes* (chromo = colour, soma = body; in *Greek*). These chromosomes form thick and short spirals and split into *two chromatids*, all along the length except at a place known as *centromere*. *At the end of prophase of mitosis the nuclear membrane disappears and chromosomes are in contact with cytoplasm.*

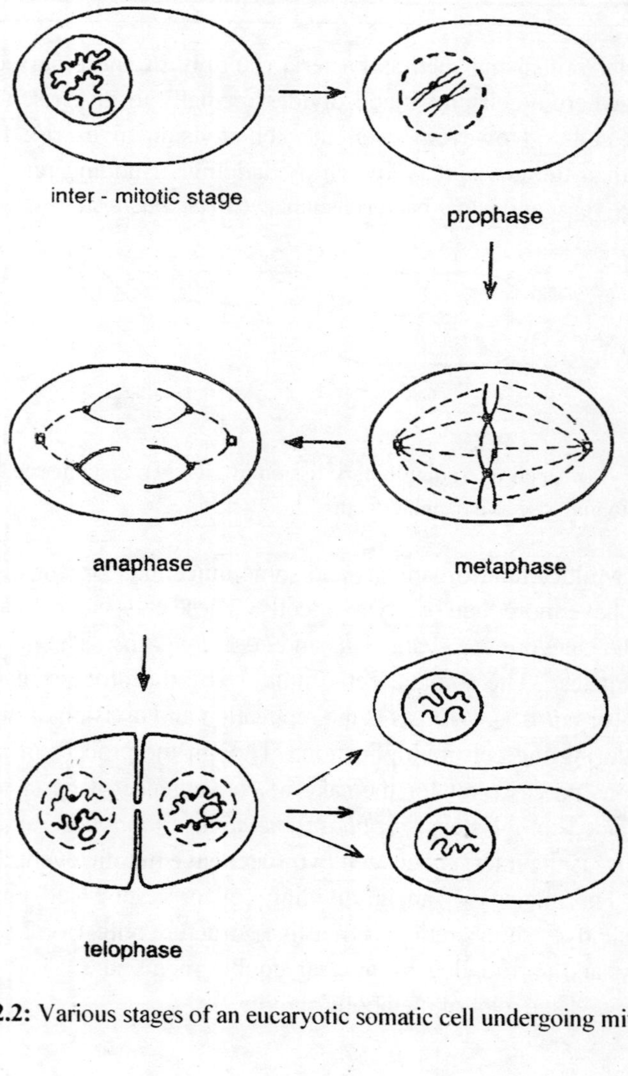

Fig. 2.2: Various stages of an eucaryotic somatic cell undergoing mitosis.

Metaphase: The *spindle-fibres* appear to radiate from two *centrioles* (2 *poles*). All chromosomes are aligned on the *equatorial plate* or *equatorial plane.*

Anaphase: *The centromere of each chromosome divides.* The two daughter chromatids separate. The daughter centromeres with chromatids attached appear to migrate along the spindle fibres, towards opposite poles. Thus two identical sets of chromatids are generated near the two opposite poles of the cell.

Telophase: A new nuclear membrane ellipsoid is formed around the each set of chromosomes. Chromosomes elongate into thread-like structures and new nucleoli appear. A new cell wall or membrane appears near the equatorial plane, completing the cell division.

Mitosis ensures that each of the two daughter cells acquire sets of chromosomes identical to those of the parent cell. If we observe the *chromosomes during metaphase*, it becomes evident that:

a. Chromosomes have typical individual shape, and can be identified by their appearance.

b. Somatic cells of a species have a constant number of chromosomes, while different species have different, though a fixed number of chromosomes.

c. In a somatic cell usually each chromosome is represented by two copies, one coming from the male and the other from the female parents.

In contrast to the diploid somatic cells, the *gametes* (gamos = marriage, *Greek*) or the *germ cells*, have half the diploid number of chromosomes and are termed *as haploid cells.* The *haploid number of chromosomes* (n), in man is 23, mice 20, tomato 12, maize 10, *Aspergillus* 8, *Drosophila* 3-6, and mosquito 6. Most of the bacteria, algae, fungi, and protozoa are haploid organisms and if they form zygotes, they undergo reductive divisions soon in the following few divisions. In mosses the diploid stage is a minor phase of the plant. *Only in ferns, higher plants and animals the diploid becomes a prominent phase, where cells have 2n number of chromosomes.*

Cells having two sets of chromosomes are known as *diploid*. There are exceptions to the rule. For example somatic cells of most of the male *Hymenoptera* are *haploid* and many plant cells have more than 2 sets of chromosomes, hence termed as *polyploid*. *Polyploidy* is quite common in plants.

MEIOSIS

Another type of cell division *meiosis* (meios = less, *Greek*) is known to occur in the *germ line cells* of sexually reproducing organisms. The diploid cell having 2 sets of chromosomes divides twice through stages called *meiosis I* and *meiosis II*, to give rise to 4 granddaughter cells, *while the chromosomes divide only once*. This results in each granddaughter cell having a set of only half the number of chromosomes of the original cell.

In *prophase* of *meiosis I* chromosomes appear as thin, long threads, which unlike the chromosomes in mitosis appear single. Homologous chromosomes are attracted to each other and form pair or *synapse*, i.e. they form intimate contact all along their lengths. Such *homologous pairs* of chromosomes are called *bivalents*, which proceed to shorten and thicken. The attraction between a pair abruptly subsides and each chromosome divides into *2 chromatids* so that a four stranded structure *tetrad* attached at its own centromere results. *Centromere does not divide*. During the tetrad formation, a very important phenomenon called *crossing over* occurs. *Any 2 homologous chromatids exchange segments in a reciprocal manner*. The crossing over causes a chromatid to become partly paternal and partly maternal and the other is a mirror image of this chromatid. Chromatids, which do not exchange segments, remain *parental type*. By its position and frequency both, the crossing over phenomenon is correlated to *genetic recombination* of paternal and maternal characters. The site of crossing over on the tetrad is known as *chiasma* (chiasma = cross, *Greek*), because of its X-shaped appearance.

In **metaphase** *nucleolus and the nuclear membrane disappear and the spindle is formed*. *Undivided centromeres* attached with two chromatids are aligned by spindle fibres on the equatorial plane.

In the anaphase of meiosis centromeres do not divide, so that homologous paternal and maternal chromosomes separate. In addition, some chromatids will be recombinant due to crossing over.

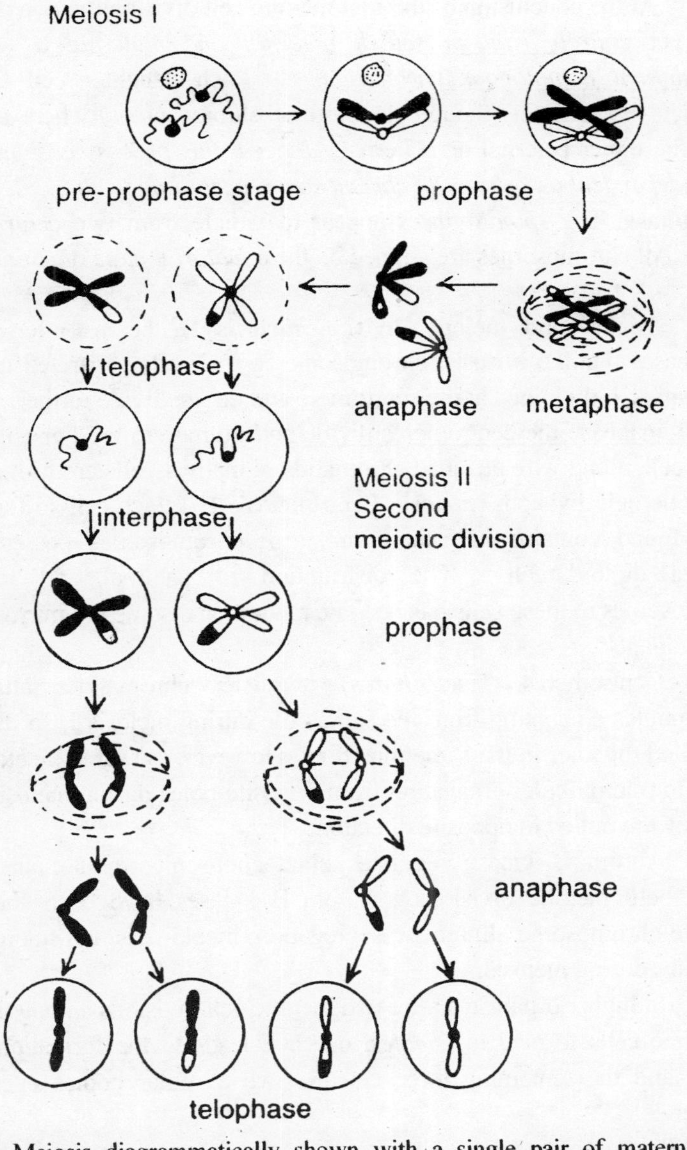

Fig.2.3: Meiosis diagrammatically shown with a single pair of maternal and paternal homologous chromosomes. Maternal chromosome is solid filled in the diagram to distinguish it from paternal chromosome. Only nucleus of the cell is depicted at each stage.

At the conclusion of the fiist meiotic cell division the two daughter cells get *entirely random set of paternal and maternal as well as recombinant homologous chromosomes*. Each daughter cell has one complete haploid set (though doublet) of chromosomes, where any one could be either paternal or maternal. *Indeed, this process is segregation and independent assortment of chromosomes according to chance.*

Metaphase: The *spindle-fibres* appear to radiate from two *centrioles* (2 *poles*). All chromosomes are aligned on the *equatorial plate* or *equatorial plane*.

The second meiotic division **meiosis II**, begins after a brief interphase. Unlike **mitosis**, chromosomes are already separated into two chromatids, only joined at the centromere and do *not* divide further. During second anaphase the centromeres divide and migrate to the opposite poles of the cell, along with attached chromatids. Finally 4 cells are formed after 2 meiotic cell divisions, **meiosis I** and **meiosis II**. Each cell so formed is haploid and contains half the number of chromosomes possessed by original diploid cell. The distribution of paternal and maternal chromosomes in these cells has become random and some are mirror image recombinants.

Centromeres (*kinetochores*) of sister chromatides attach to microtubules emanating from the same pole during meiosis I, so that they are pulled together in the same direction. However, the same kinetochores attach to microtubules emanating from opposite poles during meiosis II, so that they are pulled in opposite directions.

Aurora B kinase regulates kinetochore-microtubule attachment during both meiotic divisions. Aurora B kinases have been shown to regulate chromosome alignment, segregation, cytokinesis and microtubule dynamics during meiosis.

In higher organisms after two meiotic cell divisions among the four germ line cells formed in *females*, one cell leads to the formation of an oocyte and the remaining three cells known as polar bodies eventually degenerate.

Parthenogenesis, a form of asexual reproduction occurring commonly in insects and some arthropods and is known to occur rarely in most vertebrates except mammals. Amongst vertebrates parthenogenetic births have been recorded in species of snakes, lizards and sharks. It is a *'last-resort tactic'* that female uses when she cannot find another mate. In such a situation the secondary oocyte that contains half the complement of female chromosomes and normally becomes egg. fuses with another cell known as the secondary polar body containing identical genetic material. Thus a diploid embryo is produced that undergoes development to a full animal. It ensures the survival of the species in the absence of males but the genetic diversity is lost; making the species more susceptible to diseases and stressful situations.

Further reading

Gelfand, V.I., Scholey, J.M. Every motion has its motor. *Nature*, *359*: 480 (1992).

McIntosh, J.R., Koonce, M.P. Mitosis. *Science*, *246*: 622 (1989).

Moens, P.B. Meiosis. Academic Press, New York, (1987).

Monje-Casas, F., Prabhu, V.R.., Lee, B.H., Boselli, M.,and Amon, A. Kinetochore orientation during meiosis is controlled by Aurora B and the monopolin complex. *Cell*, *128*: 477-490 (2007).

Kaitna, S., Pasierbek, P., Jantsch, M., Loidl, J., and Glotzer, M. The Aurora B kinases AIR-2 regulates kinetochores during mitosis and is required for separation of homologous chromosomes during meiosis. *Curr. Biol.*,*12*: 798-812 (2002).

CHAPTER 3

Mendel's Laws of Inheritance

Living things usually have the capacity to reproduce offsprings similar to themselves. But the offsprings may not be exactly like parents. There may be some differences between parents and offsprings, and amongst various offsprings. These differences are known as character or trait differences or variations, and help in the study of the *heredity* of the living thing or an organism. *Heredity* studied in all its aspects is the science of genetics. Genetics relies heavily on the character or trait differences between organisms. The character or trait difference could be *physical*, such as colour of the eye or hair, shape of wings, shape of the seed, yield of seeds, height of the plant etc., or *biochemical* such as ability to ferment a particular sugar, grow at a higher or lower temperature, inability to grow without providing a particular chemical additive in the food etc. Such character differences should usually be stable over generations and one could possibly establish *pure breeding lines* for the character under study.

Mendel published his outstanding experiments on the **laws of inheritance** in 1865. Mendel's predecessors had failed earlier, whereas he succeeded for 4 main reasons. Mendel studied:

(i) pure breeding lines of peas, as parents,

(ii) examined only a single clear-cut character difference at a time, and

(iii) quantitatively recorded the number of progeny of different types.

(iv) In addition, Mendel studied 7 well-defined pairs of characters of pea, such as colour of the seed yellow or green; colour of the flower purple or white; shape of the seed round or wrinkled; height of the plant tall or dwarf etc. The determinant of each pair of character happened to be located on a different chromosome.

In a pea plant, the flower is usually self-fertilized. The male organ stamen sheds pollen on the female organ stigma, within the same flower. The self-pollination can be prevented by cutting-off the stamen (known as emasculation), before it sheds pollen. Such emasculated flowers may be cross-fertilized manually by dusting pollen from another variety of pea flower, on the stigma of first.

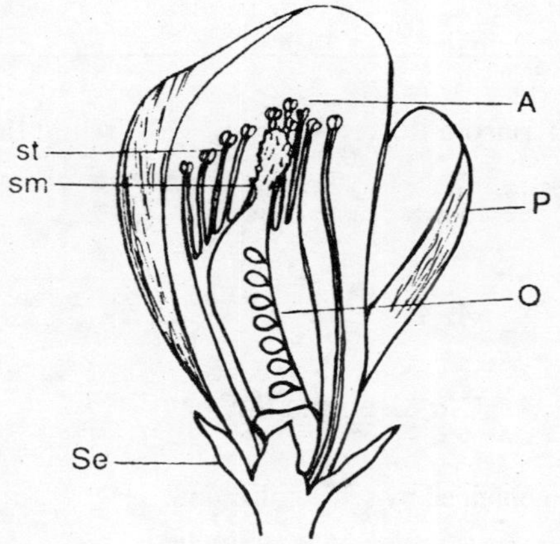

Fig. 3.1. Schematic diagram of a pea flower depicting prominent parts.

A = Anther ; O = Ovary with several ovules; P = Petals; sm = Stigma; Se = Sepals; st = Stamen (9+1).

In the first series of experiments, Mendel crossed two pea plants which differed in a single character, say purple flower versus white flower. The resulting seeds were sowed and the expression of the character-differences in the hybrid or first generation (F_1 = *first filial generation*) of plants were recorded.

Mendel observed that all the plants of F_1 generation resembled only one parent. For instance, when one parent had purple flowers and the other white, the flowers of F_1 plants were all purple. Thus purple pigmentation was found to be a *dominant character* over white. Similarly, when other characteristics were examined such asthe shape of the seed, round was found dominant over wrinkled seeds. Yellow seed colour was found dominant over green.

In the next set of experiments, Mendel crossed two hybrids of F_1 generation or allowed them self fertilization and count the distribution of a pair of character in second generation (F_2 = *second filial generation*). Mendel found that, whichever of the 7 pairs of characters he studied, approximately three-quarters of the F_2 generation plants showed a dominant character and the character shown by the remaining number of (quarter) plants was termed as *recessive*. This approximate 3 : 1 ratio between dominant and recessive traits was confirmed later by several workers in many different systems (Fig.3.2).

Phenotype : purple flower   white flower

Genotype : *AA*   *aa*

Gametes: *A*, *A*   *a*, *a*

X

F_1 hybrid   *Aa*   purple flower

F_2 generation obtained by self fertilization:

Male gametes

Female gametes	*A*	*a*
A	*AA*	*Aa*
a	*Aa*	*aa*

Fig. 3.2. Schematic diagram showing Mendel's Principle of Gene Segregation, giving rise to 3 : 1 ratio of dominant to recessive trait in F_2 generation. The ratio of purple and white flower population was 3 : 1.

The conceptual importance of Mendel's experiments is the reappearance of the recessive trait in the F_2 generation. This showed that *the recessive trait is neither lost nor blended with the dominant character in* F_1 *hybrids, but are preserved intact and can be recovered in* F_2 *generation.* Mendel argued that the two potentialities such as ability to yield purple or white flowers inherited by the hybrid from two pure breeding parents *must be due to two physical determinants*. *These physical determinants or particulate factors can be separated or segregated in* F_2 *generation.* This is known as the ***Mendel's Law of Segregation*** or ***Principle of Segregation***.

The particulate factors of Mendel are now known as *genes*. *Genes* that determine the purple pigment or white colour of the flower are homologous to one another in F_1 hybrid are now called *allelic genes* or *alleles* (allelo = each other, *Greek*).

After determining the existence of allelic pairs of genes that determine the difference of characters, Mendel proposed a general theory. Assuming that the two allelic genes *A* and *a* determine the purple or white colour of the flowers, where *A* is dominant and *a* is recessive. The genetic constitution or *genotype* of one *pure breeding line* (in this case purple flowered plant) will be *AA* and the other pure breeding line (white flower bearing plant) will be *aa*. Gametes formed from such lines will be *A* and *a* respectively. The genotype of hybrid in F_1 will be *Aa*. The gene *A* being dominant on gene *a*, the hybrid *Aa* will have the appearance or *phenotype* (phenomei = I appear, *Greek*) will be purple.

It could be observed from the diagram (Fig.3.2) that there are 2 types of purple flowers. One those have genotype *AA* and are of pure breeding line and the other with genotype *Aa* those are hybrid. Outward appearances or phenotypes of both types of flowers are similar. Whether their genotype is *AA* or *Aa* can be decided by setting up a cross with double recessive pure breeding line *aa* (white flowers). A cross with double recessive is also known as Back Cross where each gene has full potential of its expression (Fig.3.3).

A back cross can establish whether the parent crossed to the double recessive is a pure breeding homozygous or a heterozygous (hybrid) for the genes under consideration.

With respect to a particular gene, the genetic constitution of a diploid cell could be *AA*, *Aa* or *aa*. When two alleles present in the cell are identical such as *AA* or *aa* the cell is homozygous for these genes. Otherwise *aA* or *Aa* cell is known as heterozygous for these genes. Many a times the *dominance of an allele is not complete, rather partial.* In such cases the phenotype of the heterozygote (*Aa*) is in between those displayed by homozygotes *AA* and *aa*. Flower colour in snap-dragon (*Antirrhinum*) and sickle-cell anaemia in humans are good examples of *partial dominance* of alleles as well as functional inter-relationship of alleles. A schematic diagram shows the partial dominance in snap dragon (Fig.3.4).

AA X *aa* double recessive

Gametes *A* , *A* *a* , *a*

		Gametes 1st parent	
		A	*A*
Gametes 2nd parent	*a*	*Aa*	*Aa*
	a	*Aa*	*Aa*

When the 1st parent is a pure breeding, homozygous AA the progeny of back cross will be all Aa , purple flowers.

If the 1st parent is a hybrid in a back cross:

Aa X *aa* double recessive

Gametes *A, a* *a, a*

		Gametes 1st parent	
		A	*a*
Gametes 2nd parent	*a*	*Aa*	*aa*
	a	*Aa*	*aa*

Half of the population of flowers in the progeny will have genotype *Aa* with phenotype purple flowers, and the other half of the population will have genotype *aa* with phenotype white flowers.

Fig. 3.3. Schematic diagram of a Back Cross

Sickle-cell anaemia disease is due to alteration of a gene controlling the synthesis of haemoglobin in humans. Whenever the partial pressure of oxygen in blood or tissues drops such haemoglobin crystallizes and blood cells assumes sickle like shape. Chilling to lower temperatures or breathing in rarefied atmosphere such as high mountains can trigger such precipitation. Red blood cells of heterozygous adult contain normal and abnormal haemoglobins in equal proportions. Besides this disadvantage however, sickle-cell trait offers survival advantage in malaria-endemic region as it makes them immune to infection with malarial parasite as is in some regions of Africa and South-East Asia.

Phenotypes	Red flower		White flower
Genotypes	*AA*	X	*aa*
Gametes	*A*, *A*		*a*, *a*

		Gametes 1st parent	
		A	*A*
Gametes 2nd parent	*A*	*Aa*	*Aa*
	a	*Aa*	*Aa*

All offsprings are heterozygous *Aa* and give rise to pink flowers, a colour intermediate between red and white.

Fig. 3.4. Schematic diagram showing the partial dominance of an allele for flower colour in snap dragon and the intermediate phenotype *pink* of the heterozygotic flowers instead of red.

Law of independent assortment of genes

Mendel after examining how the single traits are inherited, studied inheritance when parents differed by more than one trait. Mendel selected two pure breeding lines of pea plant. Parent 1 yielded yellow and round seeds and the parent 2 produced green and wrinkled seeds. It was established during the single trait inheritance studies that genes for yellow and green colours behave as alleles where yellow is dominant. Similarly genes for the shape of the seed round and wrinkled are alleles where round is dominant. Like earlier experiment, he crossed them by cutting the stamens and dusting the pollen from other plant.

Mendel, as expected found all F1 seeds as yellow and round. These seeds were planted to give F1 plants, which were allowed to fertilize themselves. The F2 generation seeds were examined and counted or scored for each trait. It was observed that in addition to two parental types, *yellow round* and *green wrinkled*; two recombinant types *yellow wrinkled* and *green round* also appeared. The approximate ratios observed in such experiments were:

yellow round : yellow wrinkled : green round : green wrinkled :: 9:3:3:1.

In genetics, by convention the genotypes of dominant traits such as yellow and round are denoted by capital letters *A* and *B*. By convention, the corresponding recessive alleles green and wrinkle, are denoted in small case *a* and *b* respectively. Each independent pair of character segregate in the ratio of 3 : 1. Segregations of the two pairs of traits occur totally independent of each other. Since parents are pure breeding lines and according to Mendel the trait is controlled by two alleles, the genotypes and phenotypes of the experiments may be diagrammatically represented as:

Phenotypes	Yellow Round		green wrinkled
Genotypes	*AB/AB*	X	*ab/ab*
Gametes	*AB, AB*		*ab, ab*
F_1	*AB/ab*	Yellow round hybrid seeds	

Plants were allowed to grow from such seeds and the flowers have gametes (in the form of pollen and ovum) formed from recombination and meiosis have genotypes *AB*, *Ab*, *aB* and *ab*.

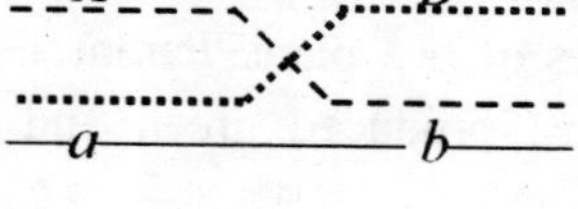

The flowers are allowed to carry out self-fertilisation and the seeds of F_2 generation are formed.

The genotypes of various progenies obtained can be deduced diagrammatically as:

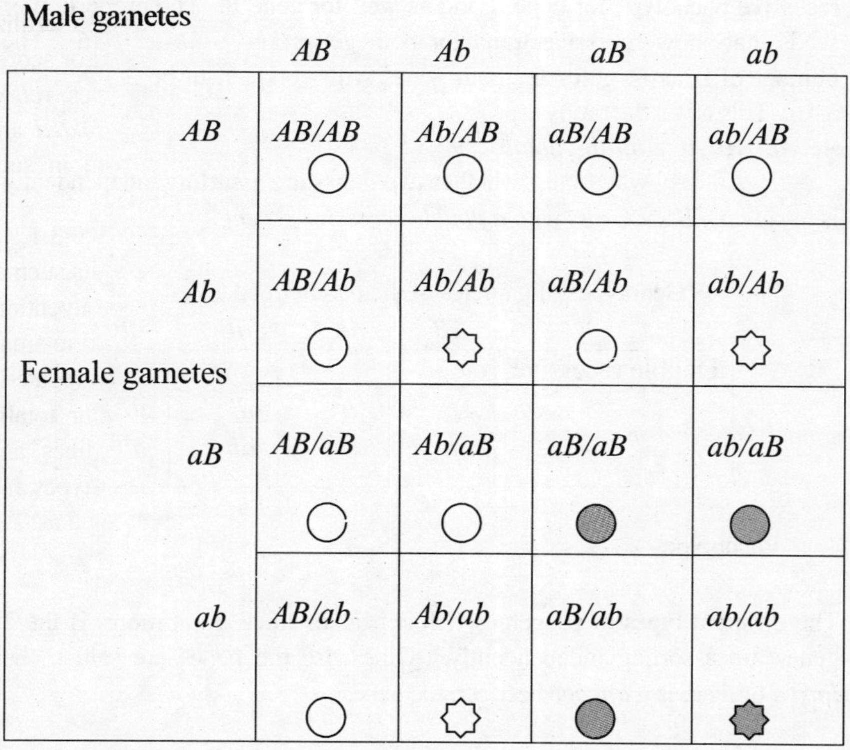

Fig.3.5. Genotypes and phenotypes of the progenies in a dihybrid cross according to Mendel's law of independent assortment of genes.

Phenotypes:

= Yellow round seeds.

= Yellow wrinkled seeds.

= Green round seeds.

= Green wrinkled seeds.

Expected genotypes and phenotypes can also be worked out arithmetically, when two pairs of genes segregate independently. Since 3/4 of the total number of seeds are expected to be showing dominant trait for gene *A* and similar proportion for dominant trait of gene *B*. If events occur independently, then the seeds having both dominant traits will be 3/4 X 3/4 = 9/16. Similarly 1/4 of the total numbers of seeds is expected to show recessive phenotype for gene *A* and as well for gene *B*. The proportion of seeds that show recessive traits for both genes 1/4 X 1/4 = 1/16. The number of heterozygotes for both genes will work out to be 3/4 X 1/4 = 3/16. This gives the ratios as:
AB/AB : *Ab/Ab* : *aB/aB* : *ab/ab* :: 9 : 3 : 3 : 1.

An easy way to test whether two genes are assorting independently is to *set up a Back Cross with a double recessive parent.*

Genotypes of gametes of the parent to be tested

	AB	*Ab*	*aB*	*ab*
Double recessive *ab*	*AB*/*ab*	*Ab*/*ab*	*aB*/*ab*	*ab*/*ab*
Phenotypes	1 :	1 :	1 :	1

The different types of progenies will appear in equal porportions, if the 2 genes are assorting independently. Otherwise the genes are said to be *linked* or there is a *linkage* between the genes.

Meiosis and the independent assortment of genes

If we look at the mechanism of distribution of genes during meiosis, it will be clear that the very process of random alignment of tetrads on the equatorial plane and the subsequent separation to either poles by spindle fibres ensures random assortment of genes located on different chromosomes. If the genes are located on the same chromosome, it is expected that they will not assort independently. Examples of such genes are many and they are known as linked genes.

Exceptions to the Mendel's Laws of inheritance

1. By 1900 many cases were reported where pairs of genes do not assort independently in gametes, rather they tend to be together or show *linkage*.
2. Cytoplasmic genes such as those present in mitochondria (e.g. of yeast) or chloroplasts show *no* Mendelian inheritance.

Further reading

Birky, C.W., Jr. Transmission genetics of mitochondria and chloroplasts. *Annu. Rev. Genet. 12*: 471 (1978).

von Heijne, G. Why mitochondria need a genome? *FEBS Lett. 198*: 1 (1986).

CHAPTER 4

Deoxyribonucleic Acid (DNA)

Four years after Mendel published his results on garden pea and proposed the laws of inheritance, Miescher in 1869 isolated from the nuclei of pus cells a substance that he called `*nuclein*'. It was later found that nuclein had the properties of an acid and thereafter became known as nucleic acid. Histochemical techniques and chemical analysis showed that living cells may have two types of nucleic acids:

(1) Deoxyribonucleic acid or DNA and

(2) Ribonucleic acid or (RNA).

(A) It was found that the DNA is associated with chromosomes in the nucleus, whereas RNA is present in the nucleus and cytoplasm.

(B) Somatic cells of any given species possess a constant amount of DNA per cell. The amount of RNA varies according to the metabolic activity of the cell.

(C) In any species the amount of DNA in the haploid or germ line cell is half of the diploid somatic cell. In polyploid cells (usually in plants), the amount of DNA is a multiple of the DNA complement found in the haploid cell.

Transfer of hereditary characters by nucleic acids

It was established by 3 definitive experiments with bacteria or viruses that nucleic acids mediate transfer of genetic traits.

1. **Avery, Macleod and McCarty** showed in 1944 that the purified samples of high molecular weight DNA from smooth colony forming virulent *Pneumococci* could transform the rough colony forming non-virulent *Pneumococci* to a virulent smooth colony former. This transforming capacity of DNA was destroyed by an enzyme called *deoxyribonuclease*, which degraded DNA into smaller pieces of

nucleotides. *Proteases* which degrade proteins had no effect on the *transforming activity* of DNA. *This experiment showed that the hereditary information is carried by DNA.*

2. **Hershey and Chase** in 1952 labelled the protein coat of a virulent bacteriophage T2 by radioactive sulphur S^{35}, and its DNA by radioactive phosphorus P^{32}. They infected *Escherichia coli* cells with such double-labelled phage particles. After a few minutes, the adsorbed phage particles were detached from bacteria by violent agitation in a mixer-blender. It was shown that P^{32} labelled DNA had entered the bacterial cells and ultimately produced more phage particles inside the bacterium. Whereas, the S^{35} labelled protein remained mainly outside of the cells. This experiment showed that the *hereditary information needed to produce virus particles rested with DNA and not protein.*

3. **Reconstituted virus particles by Frankel-Conrat and Williams.** Several viruses infecting animals, plants or bacteria have RNA encased in a protein coat. Tobacco mosaic virus (TMV) has a helical RNA surrounded by baton-shaped protein units arranged perpendicular to the long axis of helix, so that the gross structure of the virus appears rod-shaped. RNA and protein of this virus can be chemically separated. The RNA was found to be infective but not the protein. The enzyme ribonuclease destroyed the infectivity of RNA by chewing it down to small pieces. **Frankel-Conrat and Williams** in 1955, reconstituted morphologically intact and virulent TMV by mixing purified viral RNA and protein in a test tube.

Many strains of TMV are known whose protein molecules can be distinguished by amino acid composition or by serology. Frankel-Conrat and Singer fractionated two such strains of TMV. They mixed RNA from virus 1 to the protein of virus 2 and *vice versa.* When tobacco plant was infected by such *re-constituted virus particles*, it was found that progeny virions have proteins of the same types as that of the original particle from which RNA was extracted. The protein formed differed from the protein of reconstituted infective virions. *The experiment showed that the specificity of the protein synthesized is determined by RNA of the infecting virus and not by its protein.*

Chemical analysis of DNA

Chargaff performed the chemical analysis of DNA in 1955 from a large number of sources. Degradation of DNA either by an acid or an enzyme showed that it is composed of three types of molecules:

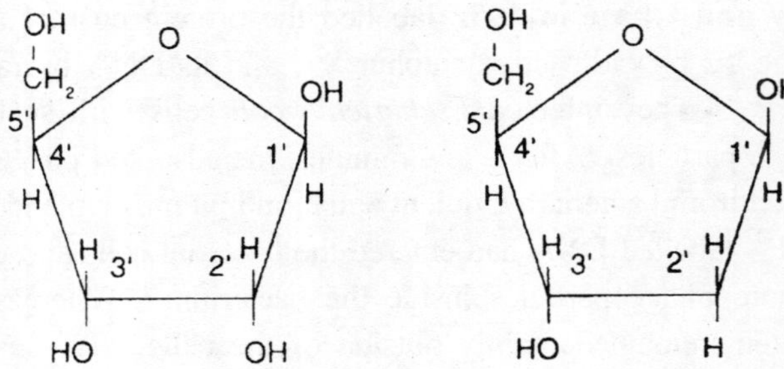

D-ribose 2-deoxy-D-ribose

(i) pentose sugar 2-deoxy-D-ribose.

(ii) phosphoric acid, H_3PO_4 which imparts acidic properties to DNA.

(iii) nitrogenous bases such as purines with double ring-structures and pyrimidines with single ring-structures. Adenine (A) and Guanine (G) are purines, whereas Thymine (T), Cytosine (C) and Uracil (U) are pyrimidines.

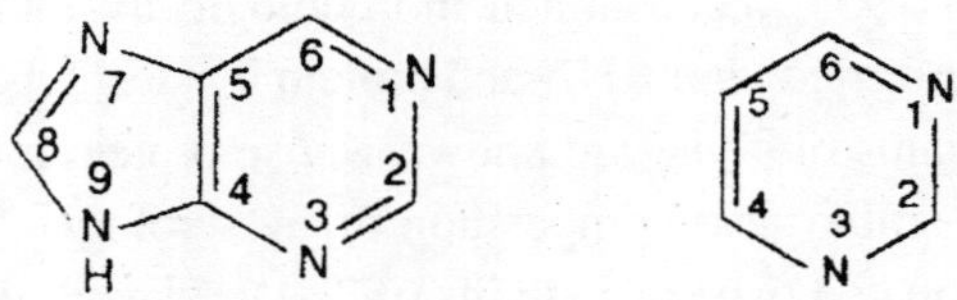

Purine Pyrimidine

Any of these bases can combine with the pentose sugar to form a glycosidic compound, better known as nucleoside. A phosphate group when attached to the sugar of the nucleoside forms a nucleotide. Thus four nucleotides deoxyadenylic acid, deoxyguanidylic acid, deoxythymidylic acid or deoxycytidylic acid are formed depending upon the base adenine, guanine, thymine or cytosine respectively forms bond with deoxyribose. Sugar residues of nucleotides join together through phosphate group such that C3' position is linked with C5' position of the next molecule. These 3'-5'-3'-5'-

linkages yield a long chain DNA polymer or a *polynucleotide*. The phosphate bond could also form in a sequence 5'-3'-5'-3'-. These two possibilities give directionality or *polarity* to the individual polynucleotide chain.

The chemical analysis of DNA revealed 3 additional features:

1. The DNA from different living systems contains equivalent number of purine and pyrimidine bases, such that (A + G) = (T + C).

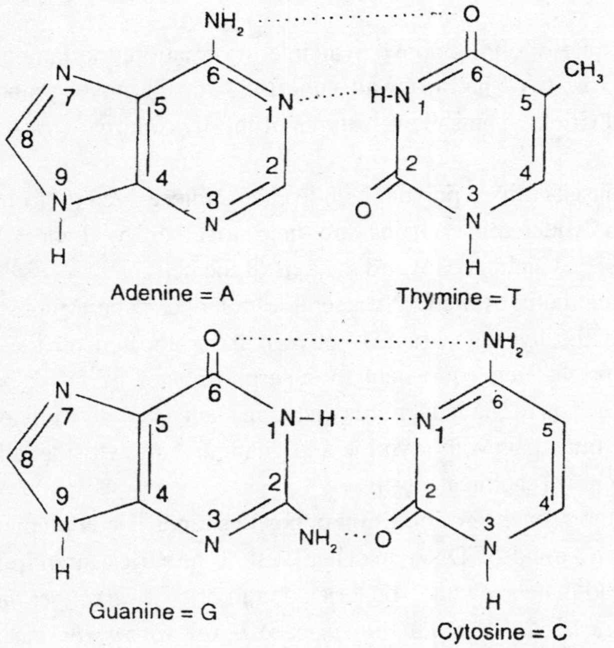

2. In addition there is equivalence between numbers of adenine and thymine as well as guanine and cytosine, so that A = T and G = C.
3. The base ratio (A + T)/ (G + C) varies widely in living systems, but is constant for a species.

X-Ray diffraction analysis of DNA

The arrangement of the individual component of the polynucleotide was deduced by X-ray diffraction analysis, with the following main findings.

(i) Purines and pyrimidines are positioned at right angles to the long axis of the polynucleotide chain. In addition they are stacked like a pile of coins. The distance between central plane of the adjacent bases being 3.4 Angstroms (Å).

(ii) The polynucleotide chain of DNA molecule is wound in the shape of a helix. Each complete turn of the helix measures 34 Å.

(iii) X-ray diffraction data further showed that a DNA molecule contains more than one polynucleotide chain arranged helically.

Watson and Crick double helix model of DNA

In spite of all the above available information, the famous *Double Helix Model of DNA* had to await until 1953 for the novel proposition of Watson and Crick. The salient features of the *Watson and Crick Model of DNA* are:

1. DNA consists of two polynucleotide chains interwoven to form a helix.
2. Two polynucleotide chains are held together by hydrogen bonds between bases, which face toward the axis of the helix.
3. The double helix of the DNA resembles a ladder, where rungs could be imagined as the hydrogen bonds between bases located on the opposite strands. Uprights are equivalent to superphosphates of DNA backbone. The opposite ends of the ladder are twisted in such a way to form a spiral.
4. Adenine must pair with thymine and guanine with cytosine, all in most stable tautomeric (chemical) forms.
5. Though the sequence of bases on opposite strands is complementary i.e. A on Watson strand of DNA matched with T on Crick strand and G on Watson strand matches with C on Crick strand or *vice versa*; yet *there is no theoretical restriction on the sequence of bases so far as one chain is concerned.* The neighbouring base could be any of the four bases such that -A-A-, -A-G-, -A-T-or -A-C- with equal probability.
6. The two polynucleotide chains of a helix run in opposite directions 3'→ 5' and 5'→ 3' (Fig.4.3).

Replication of DNA

According to the Watson and Crick model of DNA, the primary requisite of replication of DNA is that both strands of DNA must unwind at least partly for the matching of bases on the parent strand with those on the daughter strand.

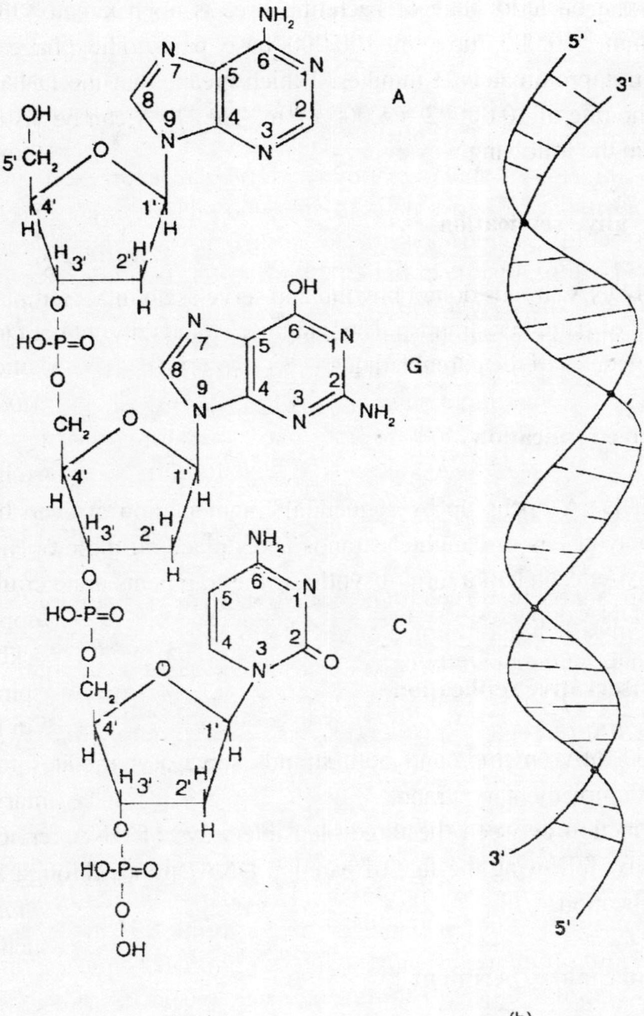

Fig. 4.1. (a) A polynucleotide chain of DNA, showing the arrangement of sugar and phosphate molecules forming the backbone of DNA and attachment of bases to the sugar molecules. The sequence of bases on the polynucleotide imparts uniqueness to a stretch of DNA. (b) A right- handed double helix model of DNA proposed by Watson and Crick. The polynucleotide chains are inter-twined in opposite directions (polarity). Each turn of DNA is 34 Ångstrom long and contains 10 bases, 3.4 Ångstrom apart. Adenine (A), pairs with thymine (T) and guanine (G), pairs with cytosine (C). The thickness of the double helix is 20 Ångstroms.

The DNA of a bacteriophage or bacterial virus is approximately 34 μm long containing 10,000 turns or 100,000 base pairs. The phage DNA duplicates in approximately 2 minutes. Which means that the DNA must unwind at the rate of 10,000/ 2 = 5,000 r.p.m. The DNA can be visualized to replicate in the following ways:

1. Conservative replication

The parental DNA strands do not unwind and serve as an intact template for the synthesis of daughter strands. The daughter strands do not contain any atoms or molecules of the parent strands.

2. Dispersive replication

The parental DNA opens up by sequential fragmentation at every half a turn and the synthesis of daughter strands takes place on these opened up fragments. After each half a turn of synthesis the fragments unite crosswise to form two DNA duplexes.

3. Semiconservative replication

The parental DNA unwinds and both strands serve as templates for the synthesis of complementary strands.

Distinction between the three plausible ways of DNA replication can be done by following the fate of parental DNA strands through a few cycles of replication.

Meselson and Stahl experiment

Meselson and Stahl first labelled the DNA of *Escherichia coli* bacteria by growing them for 7–8 generations in a medium containing heavy isotope of nitrogen N^{15} (*non radioactive, heavy isotope of nitrogen*) as a sole source of nitrogen. This way most of the normally occurring N^{14} atoms in the cells, including those in both strands of the DNA duplex were replaced by heavy N^{15}. An aliquot of bacterial culture was removed (time 0), for DNA extraction.

Thereafter large excess of N^{14} (in the form of ammonium salt) was added to the culture medium so that now on mostly N^{14} atoms will be incorporated in newly synthesized DNA. At intervals equal to half the generation time of *E. coli* the samples from the culture were removed for DNA extraction.

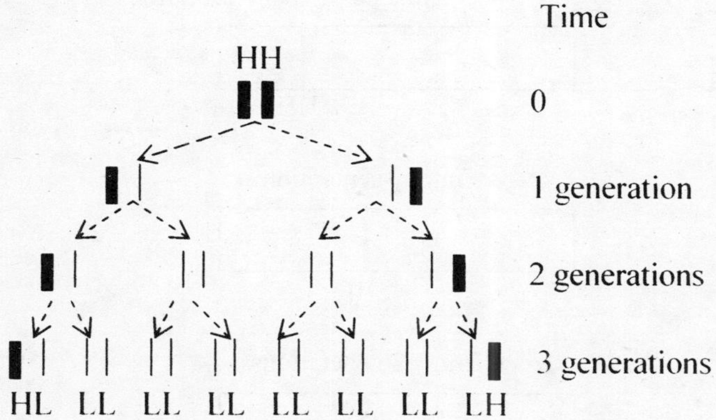

Fig. 4.2. The scheme showing the formation of hybrid HL (heavy strand H and light strand L) DNA duplex and the light (both strands light LL) DNA from initially both strands labelled heavy HH DNA by N^{15} label. Thick vertical line ▌ denotes single strand of N^{15} labelled heavy DNA of *E. coli* and the other vertical line | denotes N^{14} containing light density single strand of DNA.

Such DNA samples were analyzed by caesium chloride density-gradient centrifugation in an Analytical Ultracentrifuge, where DNA-band can be analyzed by photography using ultraviolet light absorption.

To begin with (at 0 time), the DNA sample showed only one band of heavy DNA, where both strands are labelled with heavy isotope of nitrogen N^{15}. For convenience such a DNA could be denoted as HH. After one generation, the heavy DNA band disappears and another band of DNA having density halfway between heavy and light densities appears. The intermediate density DNA, denoted as HL is likely to contain heavy and light DNA in equal proportions. At the end of second generation the intermediate density DNA is conserved but another band of light DNA denoted as LL appears. The LL DNA increases in amount in subsequent generations while HL DNA remains constant.

These experimental observations fit well with the *semi-conservative replication of DNA*, where the parental DNA unwinds and both strands serve as templates for the synthesis of complementary strands. Two DNA molecules so produced are hybrids: each containing one original parental strand and one newly synthesized complementary strand.

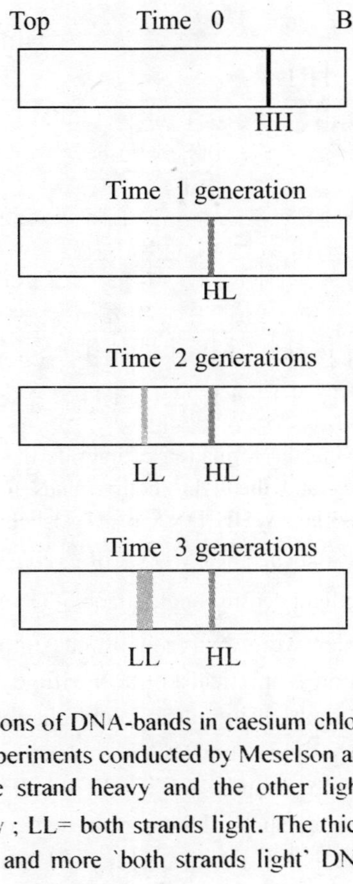

Fig. 4.3. The positions of DNA-bands in caesium chloride (CsCl) density gradient centrifugation in experiments conducted by Meselson and Stahl. HH = both strands heavy ; HL = one strand heavy and the other light called hybrid density or intermediate density ; LL= both strands light. The thickness of LL band increases with time as more and more `both strands light` DNA is formed in subsequent generations.

Cell Machinery Required for DNA Replication

The replication of DNA would require at least 3 steps: *initiation* of replication on the DNA template, *elongation* of synthesized DNA chain, and *termination* of replication. All these steps will require a host of enzymes and molecules in the cell (*in vivo*) or in a test tube (*in vitro*).

An enzyme that can make new DNA molecules from a DNA template is known as DNA polymerase. Three types of DNA polymerases are known in *E. coli*. DNA polymerases I and II repair the damaged DNA, while DNA polymerase III is a replicase and is involved in *de novo* synthesis of new strands of DNA.

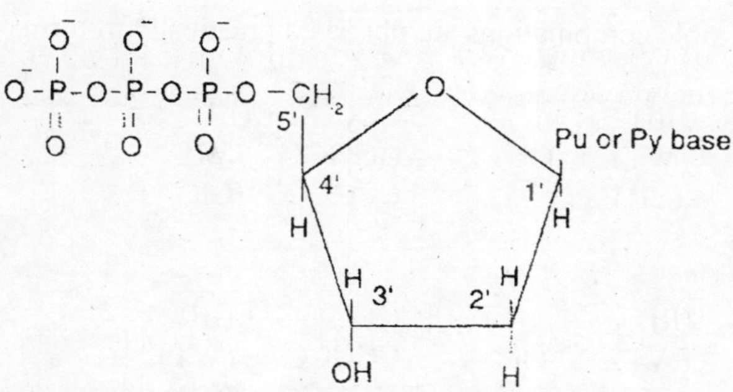

5´-2 deoxyribonucleotides

For *in vitro* DNA systhesis (i) a mixture of all the four 5'-triphosphates namely A-p-p-p; G-p-p-p; T-p-p-p and C-p-p-p (ii) purified DNA polymerase prepared from cell free extracts of *E. coli*, (iii) a high molecular weight DNA to serve as a primer and (iv) Mg ++ ions are required. The synthesis continues until one of the nucleotides gets exhausted. Also the synthesis does not occur with nucleoside 5'-diphosphates nor if *any* 5'-triphosphate is absent in the mixture. The DNA polymerase promotes formation of 3'-5' phospho-diester linkages.

The replication of DNA is covered further in the **Chapter 19**.

Triple stranded DNA

Either purine rich or pyrimidine rich Watson or Crick strands of DNA are prone to forming triple stranded DNA structures nonenzymatically. The incoming third strand of DNA normally occupies the wider groove of DNA double helix.

5'---------Py rich---------3' Third incoming strand (III)
5'———Pu rich———3' Watson strand (WT)
3'———Py rich———5' Crick strand (CR)

Or

5'----------Pu rich----------3' (III)
5 '———Py rich——— 3' (WT)
3'———Pu rich——— 5' (CR)

All four possible combinations are observed practically to form:

5' TT T TT-	(III)		5'CCCCC-	(III)
5' AAAAA	(WT)	Or	5'GGGGG	(WT)
3' TTT TT	(CR)		3'CCCCC	(CR)

5'AAAAA-	(III)		5'GGGGG	(III)
5' TTT TT	(WT)	Or	5'CCCCC	(WT)
3' AAAAA	(CR)		3'GGGGG	(CR)

The polarity of the incoming third strand is the same as that of complementary common strand and not as expected that of opposite polarity. Such triple stranded DNA structures form on annealing. These structures are not very stable and above all ***no recombination*** is possible between the third strand and the strand with homologous base sequences as they happen to have opposite polarity. Such triple stranded DNA structures have been known for the last 45 years.

Rao and his colleagues have found in 1993 that the triple stranded DNA structures can also form under the influence of protein *rec A*. However, they differ in 3 respects from the molecules formed by annealing.

1. The polarity of incoming third strand is opposite of the complementary common strand.
2. The incoming third strand and the strand with homologous sequences have same polarity and therefore both can recombine and exhibit genetic recombination.
3. The triple stranded DNA formed in the presence of *rec A* is more stable than those formed by annealing.

3'----------Mixed Sequence ---------- 5' (III) strand
5'——— Complementary ——— 3' (WT) strand
3'——— Homologous ———5' (CR) strand

Triple stranded DNA structures formed under the influence of protein *rec A*.

Further reading

Avery, O.T., Macleod, C.M. and McCarty, M. Studies on the chemical nature of the substance inducing transformation of pneumococcal types. *J. Exptl. Med. 79*: 137 (1944).

Hershey, A.D., and Chase, M. Independent functions of viral protein and nucleic acid in growth of bacteriophage. *J. Gen. Physiol. 36*: 39 (1952).

Chargaff, E. Isolation and composition of the deoxypentose nucleic acids and the corresponding nucleoproteins. *In* The Nucleic Acids I. (eds. E. Chargaff and J.N. Davidson), Academic Press, New York, p.307 (1955).

Watson, J.D.,and Crick, F.H.C. Genetic implications of the structure of deoxyribonucleic acid. *Nature*, London, *171*: 964 (1953).

Meselson, M., and Stahl, F.W. The replication of DNA in *Escherichia coli*. *Proc. Natl. Acad. Sci.*, Washington, *44*: 671 (1958).

Rao, B.J., Chiu, S.K., and Radding, C.M. A base-triplet model for homologous recognition promoted by *rec A* protein. *In* Structural Biology, State of the Art. Adenine Press, New York, p. 21 (1993).

CHAPTER 5

Mutations and Mutagenesis

Heritable changes between parents and their progenies are called mutations. Usually mutations are due to alterations in parents' genetic material that is often DNA, except in some viruses whose genetic material is RNA.

Progress in the science of Genetics could not have occurred, if there were no mutations and they were not studied. In the hypothetical absence of mutations, there would have been hardly any variety in living systems. They would have looked alike. In turn they would not have varied degree of resistance to different calamities and all could have been wiped out by one stroke of nature. Variety is the essence of life, and mutations play a very crucial role in our lives.

Mutations can be classified into 2 broad categories: *spontaneous* and *induced*.

Spontaneous mutations

Spontaneous mutations occur due to natural causes such as:

1. Error introduced in the genetic material during its replication.
2. Error during the formation of gametes, i.e. during *meiosis*.
3. Back ground levels of ionizing radiations such as cosmic radiations, ultra violet radiation, γ rays, α and β particles from naturally occurring radioactive substances such as thorium, uranium or from transuranium elements and radon gas.

The rate of mutations varies from organism to organism and even varies for different genes of the same organism. The rate of spontaneous mutations ranges between 10^{-8} (low) to 10^{-4} (high) per cell per generation.

Types of mutations

There are several types of mutations, depending upon the kind and extent of change produced in the genetic material.

1. **Point mutations**

   The point mutation causes change of a single base in the genetic material. It could be a base substitution. When a purine (A or G) is replaced by purine (G or A respectively); and a pyrimidine (T or C) replaced by a pyrimidine (C or T respectively), it is called a *transition mutation*. However, if a purine is replaced by pyrimidine or *vice versa* it is called a *transversion mutation*.

   Transition
   Pu → Pu
   or
   Py→ Py.

   Pu ↔ Py
   Transversion.

   A point mutation could also be an *addition or deletion of a base*. Addition or deletion of a base in the structural gene could produce a *frame shift mutation* that changes the reading frame in the messenger RNA.

2. **Deletions** could be of a single base as referred above or it could be of a stretch of DNA.
3. **Inversions** involve a stretch of chromosome or DNA that is reinserted in the chromosome, so that sequences of bases or genes are *reversed*.
4. In **translocations** a piece of DNA has moved from its original place and got inserted in another place on the same or a different chromosome.

Induced mutations

In addition to the spontaneous mutations occurring at their own pace, many a times it is desirable to induce mutations for a particular character or trait. These mutations can be induced either by ionizing radiations or by chemical mutagens.

Ultra violet radiation in the wavelength 250-256 nm, X-rays, γ rays, β electron beam, neutrons, α particles are known mutagens. Beside giving general guidelines, it is not possible to predict the type of mutation that will occur by application of radiations. However, **chemical mutagens** usually give results on the predicted lines. Some of the prominent types of chemical mutagens are given below.

1. **Base analogue mutagens**, such as 5-bromouracil (Bu); 5-bromodeoxyuridine (BudR); 2-aminopurine (AP) *can replace bases during the DNA replication.*

I II III Generation

A-T → **A**-Bu → G-**Bu** → **G**-C

Transition of A-T pair to G-C by Bu treatment. | line represents newly replicated DNA strand and the ▮ line represents pre-existing DNA strand in each round of replication. Three rounds of replication (I→ III), are at least needed to change an AT pair to a GC pair effectively.

When G pairs erroneously with Bu:

I II III Generation

G-C → **G**-Bu →A-**Bu** →**A**-T

Three rounds of replication after Bu incorporation changes a GC pair to an AT pair. Similar schemes can be written for BudR and AP actions on DNA.

1. ***Chemicals such as nitrous acid (HNO_2) and hydroxyl amine***
2. ***(NH_2OH) alter the bases of non-replicating DNA.***

Nitrous acid oxidatively deaminates the bases e.g adenine to hypoxanthine, which on subsequent replication pairs with cytosine C. Therefore an AT pair of bases on the DNA is converted to GC pair

HNO_2 treatment

I II round of DNA replication

T—A → HX— C—G—C

Hydroxyl amine (NH_2OH) treatment converts NH_2 group at position 6 into OH in cytosine base. In this modified form during subsequent replication of DNA, it pairs with A instead of G. This results in conversion of a GC pair into AT pair, in second round of DNA replication.

3. Chemicals whose action removes DNA bases

Such chemicals are mostly alkylating agents like sulphur or nitrogen mustard gases, ethylene oxide, ethylethane sulphonate (EES), ethylmethane sulphonate (EMS), which act specifically at N7 position of guanine. The 7-alkyl guanine is released from DNA even at 37° C and neutral pH.

Chemical	*Change*	*Type of change*
Bu	AT↔ GC	Two way transition
AP	AT↔GC	Two way transition
HNO_2	AT↔GC	Two way transition
NH_2OH	GC→AT	One way transition
EES	GC→AT GC→TA GC→CG	One way transition Transversion Transversion

Mutagenisis with acridine dyes

On treatment with acridine dye such as proflavin, the DNA of phages allows intercalation (sandwiching) of acridine molecules in between the bases. The sandwiched acridine molecule produces slight distortion in the DNA double helix. In the next round of replication this results either a deletion of a base or an addition of any of the 4 bases. Acridine dye proflavin has been extensively used to get frame shift mutations in phages of T series.

Plasmids and viruses as mutagens

Certain transposable elements and phages like μ can drastically alter the structure or sequences of the genome, thereby causing mutant phenotypes. This has been described in **Chapter 22**.

Theories about mutations

Before the modern concepts about mutations crystallized, Lamarck tried to explain variations found in the living species by enunciating:

1. Acquired traits are inherited.
2. Bacterial variations resulted from adaptation, i.e. environment provided an inheritable alteration in the organism exposed to it. This theory was known as *Lamarck's doctrine of the inheritance of acquired characteristics* or in brief these views were known as **Lamarckism**.

Over the years many beautiful experiments have been done, and most of them do not favour Lamarckism.

Luria and Delbrück proposed **mutation hypothesis** to explain variations in the genetic traits. According to the mutation hypothesis, *a mutation* (such as resistance to a drug or a phage in case of bacteria) *has a finite probability of spontaneously occurring per cell per generation. The contact of the drug or phage is not needed for the bacteria to develop resistance for them. On exposure to the drug or phages the resistant bacteria survive and are selected, whereas the sensitive ones die.*

Newcombe experiment*

Newcombe did a simple experiment. Two sets of petri dishes were plated with bacteria sensitive to phage T1. These plates were incubated for confluent growth of bacteria. One set was sprayed with T1 phages. In the other set of plates, the bacteria were re-spread with a spreader, thereby colonies are spread all over the plate. Subsequent to this, phage was sprayed on these plates. On both sets of plates the sensitive bacteria will lyse and only the resistant bacteria would grow. If the resistance to the phage in bacteria developed *after* coming in contact with the phage

T1, then the number of resistant colonies would be same on both sets of plates as the total number of bacteria on undisturbed and re-spread plates is almost the same. If the resistant colonies were formed before the phage was sprayed, then they would be spread over the re-spreaded plates. And these plates would show far more resistant colonies than the undisturbed plates. Newcombe did find about 100 times more resistant colonies on the re-spread petri dishes than the undisturbed plates. This experiment very elegantly showed that the mutations arise spontaneously and the resistant bacteria existed even before the application of phage. Exposure to the drug or phage is not a pre-condition for spontaneous mutation to occur.

Replica plating*

Lederberg and Lederberg developed a novel and simple technique of creating replicas of colonies growing on petri dishes. This technique is used all over the world by innumerable scientists working with mutants or clones of micro-organisms.

A sterilized piece of pile-cloth such as velvet or velveteen is placed on a cylindrical block measuring a few mm less than the diameter of the petri dish on which well separated colonies of bacteria are grown. The pile cloth is stretched and firmly held to the cylinder by a metal collar. The petri dish, with bacterial colonies facing down is pressed against the pile-cloth, so that some bacteria from each colony are transferred to the velvet piles. A new petri dish with agar medium is pressed against the velvet in the likewise manner. The impressions of bacterial colonies transferred to velvet are taken on the new petri dish. In this manner six or seven impressions can be taken. The orientation of taking impression is marked on each petri dish, so that when the colonies grow in each petri dish, they could be compared. The piles of the velvet or velveteen work as thousands of inoculating needles. This is called replica plating of colonies.

Lederberg and Lederberg developed this technique to test the development of resistance to T1 phage in *E. coli*. To begin with, a confluent growth of *E. coli* sensitive bacteria was grown on a petri dish. This plate was replica plated twice. The replica plated plates were sprayed with T1 phage. Most of the bacteria on the plate lysed and only a few colonies grew which were found to be T1 resistant. The distribution pattern of resistant colonies looked similar on two successive replica plates. Corresponding to a resistant colony, the approximate location on the original plate is cut out, re-suspended and a small aliquot

re-plated. Greater numbers of resistant colonies were found on second set of replica plates. Again the corresponding area was cut out from the original plate of this step and plated after dilution. These steps are repeated a few more times until all the colonies growing on petri dishes are resistant to phage T1. This experiment showed that phage resistant bacteria can form in a population which has not seen the phage T1.
In addition, it proved that mutations arise spontaneously and exit even before being exposed to a drug or a virus.

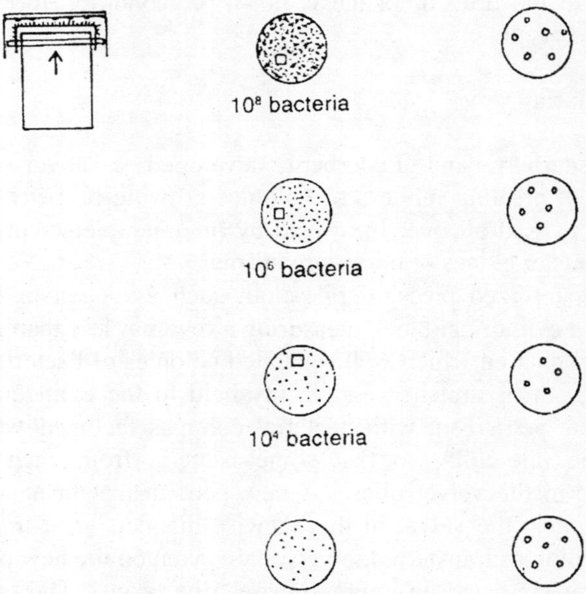

Fig.5.1. Replica plating used successively.

SIB selection method of getting mutants without exposing the culture directly to the drug*

Replica plating though conveniently shows the existence of spontaneous mutations even before selection is applied, but it does not pickup all mutations in a culture. Cavalli-Sforza and Lederberg developed a method of indirect selection of mutations in a growing fluid culture. The logic of this method is as follows. If the spontaneous rate of mutation is expected to be around 10^{-6}, a small aliquot of the culture is inoculated in several independent tubes such that the probability of having a mutant in any tube is 0.1. This can be achieved by inoculating say 10^5 bacteria in each tube. The cultures are allowed to grow in all tubes. A small aliquot of culture is taken from each tube and assayed individually by challenging with the drug for which the resistant mutant is sought. The original tubes with cultures are carefully stored until the results are known. The tube containing the highest proportion of mutant is retained and the others are discarded. From this culture tube, many independent cultures are set up again by inoculating 10^5 bacteria to each tube. The probability of getting a mutant cell in a tube is 0.1. The cultures are again allowed to grow to sufficient titre. The tubes are stored carefully and small aliquots are tested for the proportion of drug resistance cell in the culture. The tube containing the highest proportion of mutants is retained and the rest are discarded. The process is repeated likewise several times until the culture tube has a pure population of mutant in it. If by mistake the tube with highest proportion of mutant is not selected then the process reverts to a few steps backwards, but can be continued onwards.

Ames test for mutagenicity*

Ames test uses a histidine requiring strain of *Salmonella* bacteria. This strain is also defective in DNA repair mechanism, so that whatever mutations arise are not repaired or corrected. The appropriate concentration of the substance to be tested for mutagenicity is mixed with this culture of *Salmonella* in the presence of homogenized rat liver cell extract. Rat-liver cell-extract is added to simulate the biochemical processing that is likely to occur in a living animal. Aliquots of the mixture containing *Salmonella* bacteria, liver extract, and the test substance are incubated for a length of time, then plated out on an agar medium lacking histidine. Plates are incubated at 37 °C for 2 days. The colony-count of histidine independent bacteria over the control indicates mutagenicity of the substance tested.

Rate of mutation

The rate of mutation can be determined by many formulae, derived in different ways.
Some useful and convenient ones are given here.

The rate of mutation m is = $\log_e 2 \cdot (M_2 - M_1)/(N_2 - N_1)$, where M_2 and M_1 are number of mutants (titre) or say resistant bacteria and N_2 and N_1 are the number (titre) of the viable cells at times 2 and 1 respectively. This expression was developed by Beale and Newcombe.

The other expression deduced by Catcheside is

$$m = 2 \log_e 2 \frac{\frac{M_2}{N_2} - \frac{M_1}{N_1}}{g}$$

where g is the number of generations between time points 2 and 1 when the observations were recorded. M_2 and M_1 represent the number of mutants and N_2 and N_1 denote the number of viable population at the two time points 2 and 1.

The proportion of mutants in a growing population is usually not high enough, so that the mutations keep increasing until the proportion of mutants becomes large enough, when their rate of *back-mutation* becomes significant.

Generation Number	0	1	2	3	4	5
Total number of Bacteria	N	2N	4N	8N	16N	32N
Number of old Mutants			4mN +	16mN +	48mN +	128mN +
Number of new Mutants		2mN	4mN	8mN	16mN	32mN
Proportion of mutant in total bacteria		m	2m	3m	4m	5m

For RNA viruses the *rate of point mutation* is around 10^{-4} per base per generation. It is between 10^{-5} to 10^{-8} per base pair per generation for different microbes and 10^{-9} per base pair per cellular generation for human cells. Roughly mutation frequencies increase with increasing population sizes and decreasing information content of the genome, which results in surprisingly stable mutation rate of *1/300 non-neutral mutations per genome per generation.* However, mutation rates vary even within and across a genome. Recent studies with human genome revealed hot spots and cold spots for mutations that stretch over hundreds of kilobases.

Further reading

Cavalli-Sforza, L.L., and Lederberg, J. Isolation of preadaptive mutants in bacteria by sib selection. *Genetics, 41*: 367 (1956).

Drake,J.W. The distribution of rates of spontaneous mutation over viruses, prokaryotes and eukaryotes. *Ann. N.Y. Acad Sci. 870*: 100-107 (1999)

Newcombe, H.B. Origin of bacterial variants. *Nature*, London, *164*: 150 (1949).

Lederberg, J., and Lederberg, E.M. Replica plating and indirect selection of bacterial mutants. *J. Bacteriol. 63*: 399 (1952).

Rando,O.J., and Verstrepen, K.J. Timescales of genetic and epigenetic inheritance. *Cell, 128*: 655-668 (2007)

Watson, J.D., Crick, F.H.C. The structure of DNA. *Cold. Spr. Harb. Symp. Quant. Biol. 18*: 123 (1953).

CHAPTER 6

Genetic Transformation

Transformation is a mode of transfer of genetic information mediated by the molecules of DNA. The DNA from donor cells either obtained by chemical extraction* or by natural lysis of cells or DNA extruded by growing cells may penetrate into the cells of the same or related species under favourable conditions. The incoming DNA can replace the homologous nucleotide sequence of the recipient genome. If the nucleotide sequence of the incoming donor DNA partly differs from the nucleotide sequence of the homologous region of the recipient genome, then new genetic information will be provided to the '*transformed*' cell and its progeny. The ability of cells to get transformed depends upon both genetic and environmental factors. *A cell capable of taking up DNA from outside and thereby get transformed is known as competent cell.*

In 1928 Griffith observed that the vaccine of heat killed virulent Pneumococci could convert an avirulent Pneumococcal strain into a virulent one. He achieved this by giving a sub-cutaneous injection of a mixture of heat-killed Pneumococci and live avirulant organism. Later similar transformation was shown to occur *in vitro*, and by the cell-free extract of the donor strain.

After several years in 1944, Avery and two of his colleagues MacLeod and McCarty demonstrated that the substance responsible for the transformation of avirulent strain to a virulent one is deoxyribonucleic acid (DNA). Since then, the occurrence of genetic transformation has been shown to occur in more than 50 bacterial species.

---

*The DNA can be isolated by methods described by Marmur (1961) or Kirby (1957), after rupturing the cells. Cells can be ruptured by enzymes, detergents, ultrasonics, subjecting them to very high and low pressure changes or grinding them with acid purified sand.

Transformation can affect almost any character, whose inheritance by a recipient strain is detectable e.g. presence or absence of capsule, inability to grow without the supplement of any amino acid or vitamin, resistance to a drug or a chemical, ability to ferment a sugar, inability to attach a phage.

The competent state: development and maintenance

A cell is capable of DNA uptake during its competent state. The competent state is found to be transitory and its duration is confined to only a part of the cell cycle. The time of appearance of maximal competence in different bacterial systems like *Bacillus subtilis* and *Pneumococcus* is variable and is dependent on the conditions of growth. The competence is maximal in early exponential phase if *B. subtilis* spores are used to initiate the culture, otherwise in late logarithmic phase when actively growing cells are used to initiate the culture. Competence similarly becomes maximal in the early exponential phase in *Rhizobium* and late exponential phase in *Haemophilus influenzae*. A synchronized culture of *Pneumococcus* displays periodic appearance of maximal competence during logarithmic phase of growth, commensurate with division time. The average duration of competence in *Pneumococcus* is 15 minutes, whereas *B. subtilis* cells can remain competent for 3-4 hours (Fig.6.1).

In a culture, the rate of appearance of competence far exceeds the growth rate of cell-population by several orders of magnitude. This rapid appearance of competence is mediated by a protein, which can induce competence in non-competent cells of *Pneumococcus*, *Streptococcus*, or *B. subtilis*. In *Haemophilus*, a low molecular weight metabolite in the supernate of highly competent culture can induce competence in poorly competent cells, and competent cells lose competence on washing. The competent cells of *Pneumococcus* on treatment with trypsin (a protein degrading enzyme) lose transformability. Trypsin treatment alters or removes some specific surface molecules from the cells, which can be made competent again by a short duration of growth and re-addition of competence factor.

On heating for 5 minutes at $50^{o}C$, competent cells of *B. subtilis* cease to be competent, but only a slight loss in the number of transformants occurs if heating is done after DNA uptake by the cells. Cells that had lost competence, did not regain competence for at least several hours, though

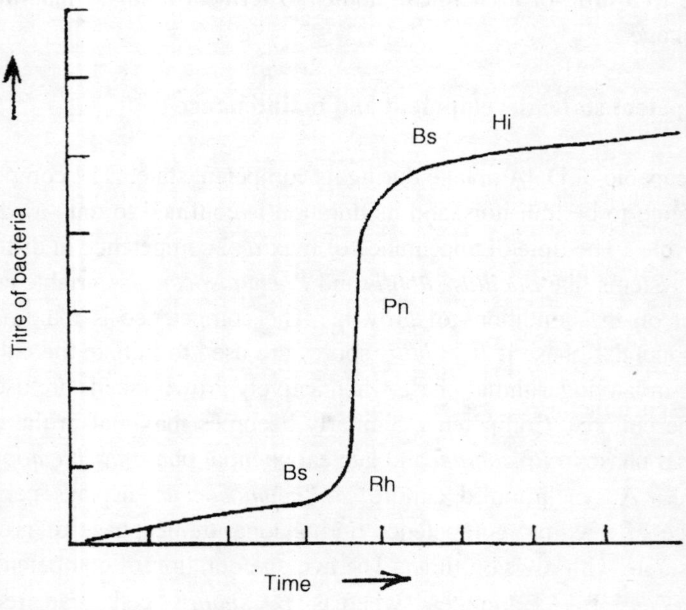

Figure: 6.1. The period of appearance of the maximal competence in different bacteria related to growth curve. Bs — *Bacillus subtilis*; Hi — *Haemophilus influenzae*; Pn — *Pneumococcus*; Rh — *Rhizobium*.

other non-competent cells in population continue to become competent. These studies suggest that the heat labile factor needed for acquisition of competence is synthesized only once during the period a cell remains competent.

The development and maintenance of competence is sensitive to the inhibition of syntheses of protein and ribonucleic acid (RNA). Concentrations of actinomycin D as low as 0.06 μg/ml cause 70% decrease in transformation frequency and 0.25 μg/ml result in complete loss of competence in *B. subtilis*. Puromycin inhibits development of competence and also destroys competence in cells, which have acquired it. However, puromycin does not affect the uptake of DNA by cells, which retain their competence. Similarly chloramphenicol blocks the appearance of competence in *B. subtilis*. In *Streptocococcus*, *H. influenzae* and *Pneumococcus* similar results have been reported. Inhibition of DNA synthesis in *B. subtilis* by thymine starvation or in *Pneumococcus* by 5-fluorodexoyuridine had little effect on competence.

Metabolic factors like inosine, nicotinamide adenine dinucleotide (NAD), glycerol, and uracil supress the development of competence in *H. influenzae*. It is possible to initiate competence even in their presence if the oxygen tension in the culture is temporarily reduced for one hour. This suggests that *the initiation of competence occurs by removal from the medium of a repressing substance rather than the addition of an inducer.*

Competence factors and their mode of action

The competence factors of *B. subtilis*, *Streptococcus* and *Pneumococcus* are all sensitive to heat inactivation and proteolytic enzymes and appear to be components of cell wall. However, the competence factor of *H. influenzae* is refractive to proteolytic enzymes and is relatively heat stable. A nuclease was found to be associated with the competence factors of *Pneumococcus* and *B. subtilis* suggesting that *the competence factor itself is a nuclease or it acts in combination with the nuclease for the uptake of DNA.*

The interaction between cells and *competence factor* (CF) may be visualized to occur at least in two phases. The first phase:

incompetent cell + CF → incompetent cell (CF)

does not require protein synthesis and is insensitive to subtilisin. The second phase:

incompetent cell (CF) + protein synthesis → competent cell.

This step is sensitive to inhibition of protein and RNA syntheses, indicating that *synthesis of a new protein is needed for the acquistion of competence by the cell.*

Cell wall changes accompanying acquisition of competence

Bacterial cells are usually impermeable to the molecules of the size and charge, characteristic of DNA and without the modification of cell wall it may not be possible for DNA to enter the cell. Strains of *B. subtilis* showing poor and high competence are known to have quantitative chemical differences in their cell wall preparations. At least some residual amount of cell wall is essential for uptake of DNA molecules by the cells and for the production of a transformed colony. In *B. subtilis*, protoplasts take up 1/50th as much DNA as bacilli. *Protoplasts perhaps have no DNA affinity sites on their surface.*

Physiological properties of competent cells

A large variety of experiments show that the competent cells of *B. subtilis* are in a state of *biosynthetic latency*, compared to growing non-competent cells.

1. Competent cells appear to be non-dividing and exhibit a delay of 3-5 hours in the expression of newly transformed genes as well as the beginning of cell division.
2. During the later stages of competence development, the competent cells of *B. subtilis* are more resistant to killing action of penicillin and to thymine-less death.
3. Competent cells synthesize cellular macromolecules at a much slower than normal rate.
4. However, the biosynthetic latency of competent cells does not seem to affect the rapid physical and genetic integration of incoming DNA with the host DNA.
5. In *B. subtilis* competent cells, approximately 5% of DNA bases are single stranded. These bases are ionized at pH 11 and can be titrated with caesium ions.
6. The competent cells of *B. subtilis* are unable to respond to photoreactivation after ultraviolet irradiation, indicating defect in DNA repair system.

Genetic loci affecting competence

The ability of cells to become competent and participate in genetic transformation is affected by a number of genes. Some non-sporulating mutants of *B. subtilis* retain competence, while others lose competence. The development of competence possibly requires some `early' functions common with sporulation.

Two types of mutations, which affect competence, are known in *Pneumococcus* and *Streptococcus*. One results in inability of cell to produce competence factor (CF) and the other renders the cell incapable of reacting with added competence factor. The mutants of the former type are designated as $(CF)^-$ and the latter type are known as $(CF\ site)^-$. The three known streptococcal strains Challis, Wicky and Blackburn could be designated as $(CF)^+$ $(CF\ site)^+$; $(CF)^-$ $(CF\ site)^+$ and $(CF)^-$ $(CF\ site)^-$ respectively.

More than 70 competence mutants *com*$^-$ were isolated after nitrosoguanidine treatment of *H. influenzae*. The prominent among them are, mutants which could take up and get transformed by denatured DNA but not by native DNA.

DNA adsorption and uptake by competent culture

The main physical characteristic of DNA on which its adsorption and uptake by competent cells is known to depend is its size. However, only homologous or very closely related donor DNA can become integrated into the recipient genome. DNA uptake ceases and no transformation occurs when the molecular weight of DNA preparation is reduced to 5×10^5 by hydrodynamic shearing or ultrasonic vibrations. The transformation efficiency diminishes by a factor of 10,000 over the size range 10^7 to 3×10^5 Daltons. The higher limit of DNA size effective in transformation is still uncertain. Though the heterologous *transduction* between the strains 168 and W 23 of *B. subtilis* by phage PBS1 is almost nil, *yet heterologous transformation occurs easily*. The difference in size between transducing and transforming DNA fragments seems to be an important factor distinguishing the two processes.

DNA labelled with P^{32} loses biological activity as a consequence of P^{32} disintegration to S^{32} However, it appears that P^{32} disintegration between markers in a linkage group does not always destroy the linkage of genes in *Pneumococcus*.

Single stranded DNA and transformation

The hydrogen bonded structure of the double-helix of individual DNA molecules can be disrupted by heating at approximately 100°C for a few minutes, followed by rapid cooling. Competent cells of *B. subtilis* can be successfully transformed with such heat denatured, single stranded DNA in the presence of ethylenediamine tetra-acetic acid (EDTA). EDTA complexes with divalent cations such as Ca(II) and Mg(II), which otherwise probably enhance the activity of a strand-specific nuclease synthesized and excreted by competent cells in the culture medium. Under optimal conditions (pH 6.1), the efficiency of transformation by single stranded DNA is approximately 50% that of native double stranded DNA. In *B. subtilis* cultures *the competence for both single and double stranded DNA increases and decreases simultaneously*. Competition between single and double stranded DNA for uptake can be shown to occur, and the same cell can be doubly transformed by DNA molecules of both configurations. *Diplococcus pneumonia* can also accept single stranded DNA and get transformed at low efficiency of 0.5% compared to that of native DNA.

Synthetic poly<u>deoxy</u>ribonucleotides are known to be taken up by competent cells of *B. subtilis*, but no competition was observed with tranforming DNA. *Poly<u>ribo</u>nucleotides are <u>not</u> taken up by B. subtilis cells. The pH and ionic strength of the medium and the extent of fragmentation of DNA affect the quantitative adsorption of DNA by the cell suggesting that the initial interaction of DNA with the cell is ionic.*

Binding of DNA by competent cells

Binding of DNA with the competent cells takes place in two distinguishable steps – *reversible binding* and *irreversible binding*. The competent cells, which have been exposed to P^{32}-labelled DNA for a few minutes and washed in cold medium, release part of the incorporated radioactivity on rewarming or by deoxyribonuclease (DNAse) treatment. This uptake is known as reversible uptake of DNA. A few minutes later the adsorbed DNA becomes insensitive to DNase and the uptake becomes irreversible. *The irreversible fixation of one genome equivalent DNA per bacterium is required for maximal transformation of one character.*

The transforming DNA, which has become DNase insensitive during transformation, has not necessarily passed across the cell membrane. It seems to be localized for 6 to 10 minutes in extramembranal – periplasmic space under the cell wall. During these 6 to 10 minutes up to 75% reversal of transformation in *B. subtilis* can be achieved by treatment with cyanide. Irreversible uptake of DNA by competent cells of *B. subtilis* is also prevented on inhibition of oxidative phosphorylation by 2, 4-dinitrophenol, sodium azide or iodoacetate. *For transport of DNA inside the cell across the membrane a rate-limiting, energy dependent step seems to be involved.* Energy sources like glucose were found to be essential for uptake. This suggests an enzymatically active transport mechanism for DNA uptake.

When the uptake of DNA by *B. subtilis* competent cells was terminated by DNase, a contact time of 1 minute at 37°C and 2.5 minutes at 29°C between DNA and competent cells was found necessary before the appearance of any transformants could be detected. *The time lag was independent of DNA concentration, genetic marker studied, presence of homologous DNA,* and shearing and cross linking of transforming DNA. No such lag was observed, when the cells were not treated with DNase, but merely washed to stop further attachment of DNA molecules. The time lag in appearance of double transformants was related to their map distance. *These results indicate that the DNA molecules enter the competent cells in a length wise manner. The minimum effective length of DNA that participate in genetic recombination in B. subtilis, calculated from these experiments to be equal to 5,000 nucleotide pairs of molecular weight approximately* 3×10^6. DNA enters *H. influenzae* and *Pneumococcus* also in a linear and progressive fashion.

When tritium labelled cell bound DNA was autoradiographed, more than 90% of silver grains were found in the vicinit;y of the tip or close to the middle of the *B. subtilis* cells. Ultrathin sections of these cells, when observed in transmission electron microscope showed significant increase in the number of membraneous invaginations called '*mesosomes*' in these cells. The silver grians were mostly localized near the outer surface of mesosomes. These studies suggest that *in B. subtilis specific penetration sites for DNA are located near the tip or close to the middle of the cell.*

Penetration of the plasma membrane by DNA

Inhibition of transformation by rabbit gamma globulin containing antibodies specific for single-stranded DNA can occur even after the absorbed transforming DNA becomes insensitive to DNase. This finding suggest that the transforming DNA is complexed in a deoxyribnulease insensitive form to the surface of the cell and *prior to transport across the membrane is converted to single stranded state*. The insensitivity of newly acquired DNA to DNase does not necessarily mean that the DNA is in intracellular compartment.

Eclipse of the transforming activity of the donor DNA and its recovery from eclipse

In *Pneumococcus*, the donor DNA soon after irreversible fixation to competent cells, loses transiently (eclipse) its biological activity. By giving P^{32}-labelled DNA to competent cells of *Pneumococci*, it was observed that *one half of the radioactivity fixed by the cells was present in the form of high molecular weight single stranded DNA. The other half was in the form of degraded acid soluble material. This suggested the mechanism of DNA uptake by competent cells, in which the entering DNA molecule meets a molecule of nuclease on cell membrane, which drags one strand of DNA into the cell, while the other strand is degraded.* The initial products of entry in *Pneumococcus* are single stranded DNA and 5'-deoxynucleotides. In *B. subtilis*, three kinds of products derived from donor DNA were observed during transformation. These products were 5'-mononucleotides, single strand fragments (SSF) of molecular weight 1-2 x 10^5, and double strand fragments (DSF) with initial molecular weight of 9 x 10^6. On the basis of this a scheme of transformation was suggested for *B. subtilis*. *Donor DNA attaches to the competent cells and is converted to duplex fragments by double-strand endonulease cleavage. DSF still accessible to external nuclease, attach to the cell membrane in the periplasm. One strand of each DSF is degraded to 5'-mononucleotides by the action of a surface localized exonuclease and the other strand penetrates the membrane and becomes available for pairing with the homologous region of the recipient chromosome. Conversion of DNA to these three kinds of products, explains the eclipse phenomenon in B. subtilis.*

In *B. subtilis*, the DNA regains its transforming activity from eclipse as a function of incubation time. Within 10 minutes, most of the donor DNA is found to be covalently and genetically linked to the DNA of the recipient cell, but the biochemical expression of the genetic characters takes place 45 minutes to 3 hours after uptake of DNA by the competent cells. In *Hemophilus* the mechanism seems to be at least temporally different as no single stranded DNA could be detected in the cells and the donor DNA was recovered as high molecular weight double-stranded material. In spite of the fact that double stranded transforming DNA is converted to single-stranded form on entry into competent cells, *B. subtilis* DNA cross linked by exposure to low pH or two-arm nitrogen mustard, retains transforming activity, if the molecule contains one cross link. Even covalently cross-linked *B. subtilis* DNA produced by reaction with nitrous acid is active in transformation. In view of the above findings the question remains whether the passage of donor DNA through a single stranded stage is obligatory for transformation in *B. subtilis* or the cells have some alternative mechanism of DNA uptake when exposed to cross linked DNA.

Transformation of *Escherichia coli* and yeast

In 1970 the establishment of transformation in *E. coli* has opened up the vast area of *recombinant DNA technology* or *genetic engineering*. It was discovered that at high concentration of Ca (II) ions in the medium, exogenous DNA with its own replication gene could efficiently transform the cell. Linear DNA was found to transform with lesser efficiency. The uptake of DNA by many types of bacteria under high concentrations of Ca (II) ions has opened up enormous potentials of recombinant DNA possibilities. Similarly the success of transformation in yeast has opened up the field of gene manipulation in eucaryotic cells. Over the years, the well-planned experiments with phages and plasmids of bacteria have paid rich dividends.

A general method of transformation for *E. coli* and yeast has been developed by Klebe and colleagues by using polyethylene glycol (PEG), where the removal of yeast cell wall is not needed. The efficiency of transformation in *E.coli* was found to be around $10^6 - 10^7$ transformants / μg of DNA.

In another method Dower and co-workers observed that *E. coli* cells can be transformed to very high efficiency by subjecting a mixture of cells and DNA to a brief but intense electric field of exponential decay waveform (electroporation). Up to 10^9 -- 10^{10} transformants / μg DNA could be obtained by this method. The frequency of transformation is directly proportional to transforming DNA concentration over six orders of magnitude.

Integration of donor DNA into the recipient genome

When the donor DNA carries one drug resistance and the recipient strain another drug resistance marker, 15 minutes after DNA uptake in *Pneumococcus* and 30 minutes after uptake in *Hemophilus*, the re-extracted DNA can transmit resistance for both drugs to another sensitive strain with maximum efficiency. The donor and recipient markers show identical increase after one generation. However, the number of transformants was found to increase only after two or three generations. This shows that the number of transformed nuclei may double at the first generation but the increase in the number of transformed cells will be apparent only when by nuclear segregation, cells are produced in which all nuclei possess transformed genes.

In summary the competence factor C made by competent culture, is secreted in the cell medium. The competence factor C interacts with receptor R on the surface of the same cell or other cells in the culture. This interaction through several unclear steps, ultimately exposes a DNA-binding protein and a nuclease on the surface of membrane. If provided, the double stranded high molecular weight donor DNA, gets anchored to the competent cell at several of its uptake sites. The donor DNA is cut into double stranded pieces and progressively nicked. The nuclease at the uptake site degrades one strand of DNA-duplex to nucleotides, which are released in the medium. The other intact strand on entry in the cell gets associated with a competence specific protein (p). This single strand DNA-protein complex recombines with recipient (host cellular) DNA and replaces one strand on the recipient DNA (endogenote) by donor DNA (exogenote) through recombination (Fig.6.2). The DNA ligase seals the ends of incoming DNA with the recipient and establishes transformation event of the cell.

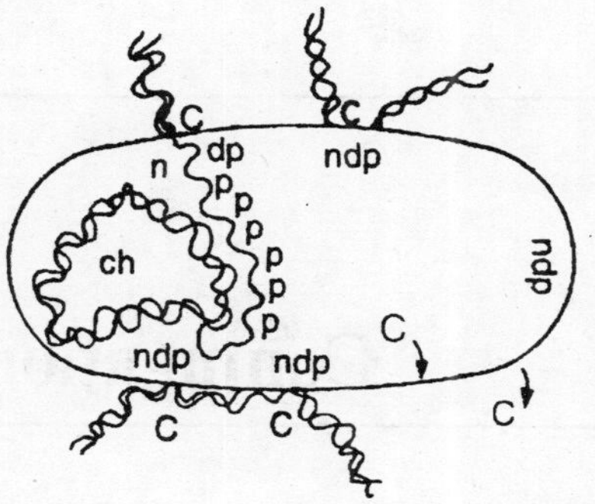

Fig. 6.2. A summary diagram showing some prominent steps leading to the uptake of exogenous transforming DNA by the competent cell (and) undergoing transformation. C — competence factor ; ch — chromosome; n — nuclease; dp — DNA binding protein ; p — protein binding single stranded DNA.

Further reading

Dower, W.J., Miller, J.F., and Ragsdale, C.W. High efficiency transformation of *Escherichia coli* by high voltage electroporation. *Nucleic Acids Research, 16*: 6127-6145 (1988).

Fox, M.S., and Allen, M.K. On the mechanism of deoxyribonucleate integration in Pneumoccal transformation. *Proc. Natl. Acad. Sci.*, Washington, *52*: 412 (1964).

Kirby, K.S. A new method for the isolation of deoxyribonucleic acids. Evidence on the nature of bonds between deoxyribonucleic acid and protein. *Biochem. J. 66*: 495 (1957).

Klebe, R.J., Harriss, J.V., Sharp, Z.D., and Douglas, M.G. A general method for polyethylene-glycol-induced genetic transformation of bacteria and yeast. *Gene, 25*: 333-341 (1983).

Marmur, J. A procedure for the isolation of deoxyribonucleic acid from micro-organisms. *J. Mol. Biol. 3*: 208 (1961).

Singh, R.N. Number of deoxyribonucleic acid uptake sites in competent cells of *Bacillus subtilis*. *J. Bacteriol. 110*: 266 (1972).

CHAPTER 7

Conjugation in Bacteria

Conjugation in bacteria involves actual copulation between sexually differentiated male and female bacterial-cells. This is followed by transfer of a part or the whole chromosome from male to the female bacterium.

The ability of the male bacterium to transfer chromosome to a female bacterium is promoted by the presence of a plasmid or sex factor *F'* in the male bacterium. This plasmid or sex factor *F* is usually a piece of extrachromosomal DNA.

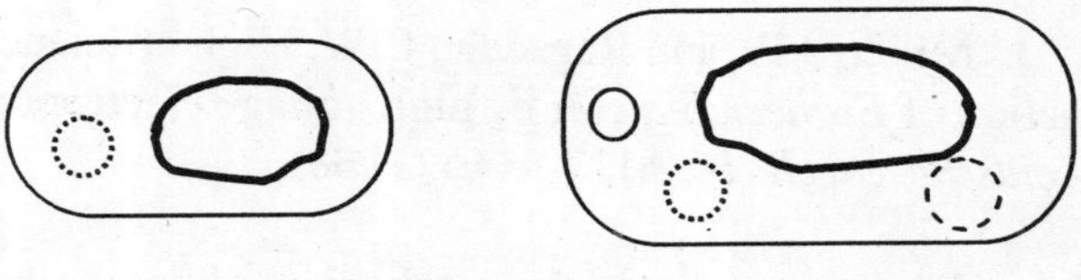

Fig.7.1. Bacteria harbouring plasmid/s.

On mixing growing cultures of $F+$ bacteria with F^- bacteria, the $F+$ character (plasmid) is transmitted from $F+$ to F^- cells with efficiency ranging between 5 – 95%. A majority of bacteria in the mixed culture may become donors in an hour, by acquiring *F* plasmid from $F+$ cells. However, the mixture of bacteria yields on an average only 1 chromosomal recombinant per million bacteria. *It shows that the sex factor F is transmitted to the female cells independently of the bacterial chromosome.*

Some Properties of the Sex Factor *F*

1. One arm of a U-tube is filled with $F+$ bacteria and the other arm of the U-tube separated by a membrane filter having 0.2 μm diameter pores, is filled with F^- bacteria. By movement of a piston in the arm, the culture filtrate can be mixed, but cells cannot pass through the membrane filter. In such a set up the transfer of sex factor to F^- cells does not take place,

indicating that cell to cell contact is necessary for the transfer of sex factor. This is dissimilar to transformation, where DNA molecules can pass through membrane filter and cell contact is not necessary for transfer of genetic information. It is also dissimilar to transduction, where virus vector can pass through the pores of the membrane filter.

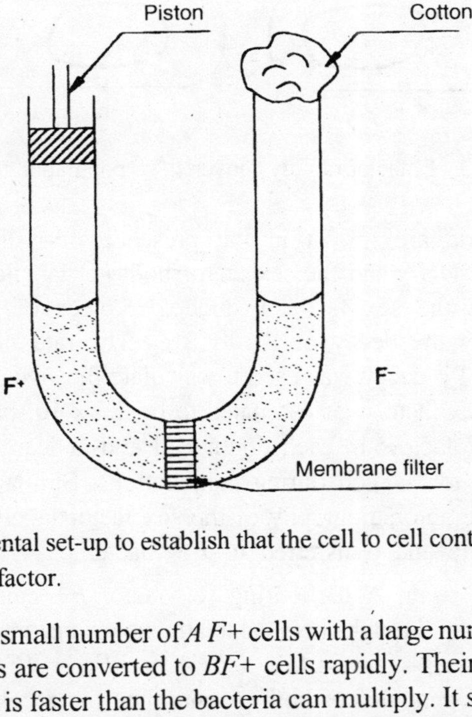

Fig. 7.2. Experimental set-up to establish that the cell to cell contact is necessary for the transfer of *F'* factor.

2. On mixing a small number of *A F*+ cells with a large number of *BF*⁻ cells, the *BF*⁻ cells are converted to *BF*+ cells rapidly. Their conversion from *BF*⁻ to *BF*+ is faster than the bacteria can multiply. It shows that the sex factor can multiply autonomously and faster than bacterial chromosome as well as the cell division. Sex factor spreads like an epidemic in the *BF*⁻ population.
3. The treatment of F^+ population with acridine orange can cure them of sex factor plasmid and make cells *FÉ*. Low concentrations of acridine orange do not prevent growth of bacterial culture.
4. Sex factor can also be lost spontaneously or by irradiation with ultra violet or ionizing radiation. *F*+ bacteria grown to saturation in nutrient broth or agar surface lose donor character and behave as *F*⁻ phenocopies. The *F*+ character can be regained by subculture of *F*⁻ phenocopies in a fresh medium.

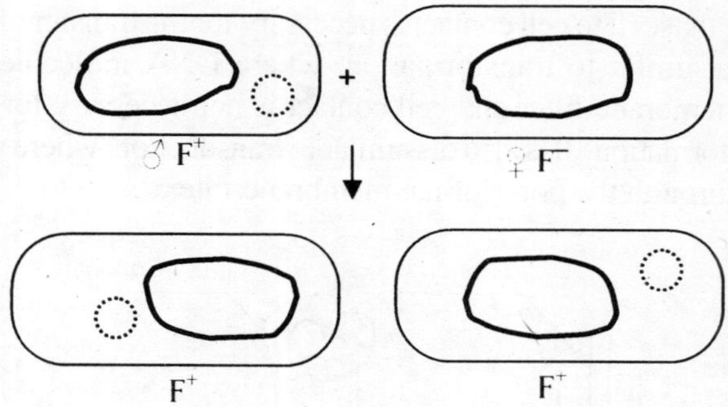

Fig. 7.3. F' factor rapidly converts *F É* population to *F* '

5. If *F+* bacteria are grown in the presence of radioactive P^{32}, the chromosomal DNA and the sex factor both get labelled by P^{32}. This indicates that the sex factor is indeed a piece of DNA, which is inactivated by the decay of P^{32} to S^{32}. The rate of inactivation of sex factor by P^{32} decay was used to calculate the size of the sex factor. The size of sex factor was estimated to be 2.5 x 10^5 base pairs. There are many sex factors in each donor cell and at least one such factor is transferred to F^- cell during conjugation. Similar estimates were arrived by the autoradiography of the sex factor labelled with tritiated (H^3) thymidine and transferred to F^- bacteria.
6. The bacterial strain A harbouring sex factor *F+* can lose sex factor spontaneously or through chemical treatment and become AF^- permitting reciprocal crosses such as *AF+* x BF^- or *BF+* x AF^-. If the zygote contained full genomes of both parents then the recombinants formed in both crosses should have been same. But it was found that the recombinants formed in *AF+* x BF^- and *BF+* x AF^- crosses are not the same. Results could be explained by *one-way partial transfer of genetic information from F+ to* F^- *bacterium.*

The high frequency recombination, *Hfr* donors

1. The donor strains named *Hfr* giving 1,000 fold more frequency of recombination than *F+* strain, were isolated from *F+* bacteria.
2. *Hfr* donors behave as '*super males*' in transfer of chromosome to F^- females. But in *Hfr* x F^- cross, a majority of F^- bacteria remain

F^- and only a few are converted to $F+$ status. These bacterial cells converted to $F+$ state can behave as *Hfr* (*high frequency recombination)* donors.

3. Comparison of the results obtained from $F+$ x F^- cross and *Hfr* x F^- cross show that $F+$ bacteria can transfer any segment of their chromosome to F^- at a low frequency (approximately 0.01%), whereas, *Hfr* donor transfers chromosome from a fixed point (called *origin*) in a linear sequential manner in a fixed direction (clockwise or anti-clockwise) at 1,000 times greater frequency (1 – 45%).
4. Conjugation experiments with *Hfr* donor suggest that *Hfr* strain is formed from $F+$ bacteria by alteration in the state of the sex factor. *The sex factor gets integrated in to the chromosome of F^- bacterium to convert it to Hfr. By this integration to chromosome the sex factor does not remain as infective as the free plasmid (sex factor) that existed in the cytoplasm of the bacterium.*
5. The integration of $F+$ factor to a circular bacterial chromosome can in principle form two types of *Hfr*. One having origin at *A* and transferring genes to F^- female in the sequence *ABCD*.......*XYZF+* (*clockwise*). The other *Hfr* strain having origin at *Z* and transferring genes in the reverse order *ZYX*............*DCBAF+* (*anti-clockwise*). In addition different *Hfr* strains may differ in the position of the origin such as *BCDE*.....*XYZAF+* or *CDEF*..........*XYZABF+*.

Spontaneous random breakage of chromosome and mapping of genes by recombination data

During *Hfr* x F^- mating the genes nearer the origin O are transferred to F^- with higher frequency than those farther from O. The frequency of transfer of genes decreases with *increasing* distance from O. *The transfer of the sex factor takes place at the end and is least frequent compared to other genes on the donor chromosome.* This is mainly due to the random breakage of *Hfr* donor chromosome during transfer to F^- female.

Interrupted mating experiments and mapping of genes in time units*

From conjugation experiments the sequence of genes and distances between genes on the chromosome can be determined by interrupting the mating after lapse of different times. The mating between bacteria can be interrupted, by agitating the culture vigorously in a mixer-blender at 40,000 revolutions per minute. Such an agitation disrupts the chromosome involved in transfer process but does not affect the viability of bacterial cells, so that they can be assayed for the transfer of different marker genes. If not broken by chance in approximately 90 minutes the entire chromosome of the *Hfr* donor could transfer to F^- at 37° C.

Chromosomes in *Hfr*, *F+* and F^- bacteria are circular structures as shown by autoradiography and genetic linkage data.

By growing an *Hfr* strain to saturation density, it can be converted to F^- phenocopy. This phenocopy F^- when mated with another type of *Hfr* donor can give rise to a chromosome with two sex factors inserted in the same chromosome at different locations. When such double males are mated to F^- recipient, they behave as if they have two chromosomes, which are transferred independently. However, in one mating event a bacterium receives genes nearer to one origin only and not both.

There are 3 slightly varying methods of doing a conjugation experiment. These methods give data in 3 different ways. All these 3 sets of data can be utilised to find sequential order of genes and distances between them. The mapping of genes from all 3 methods is consistent.

Uninterrupted mating*

Cultures of *Hfr* donor and recipient bacteria bearing appropriate genetic markers are grown at 37° C in broth. Aliquots of both cultures are mixed and thereafter samples are removed at various intervals, diluted about 1,000 times with pre-warmed (37 ° C) broth. After allowing time for the gene to be transferred to the recipient, the bacteria were plated for assay of recombinants.

The purpose of 1,000 fold dilution is to prevent further formation of conjugating pairs of bacteria. The pairs already formed continue to mate, so that the graph obtained by plotting the number of recombinants versus time, indicating the rate at which mating pairs of bacteria are formed. The types of data obtained are shown in Fig. 7.4 by continuous lines.

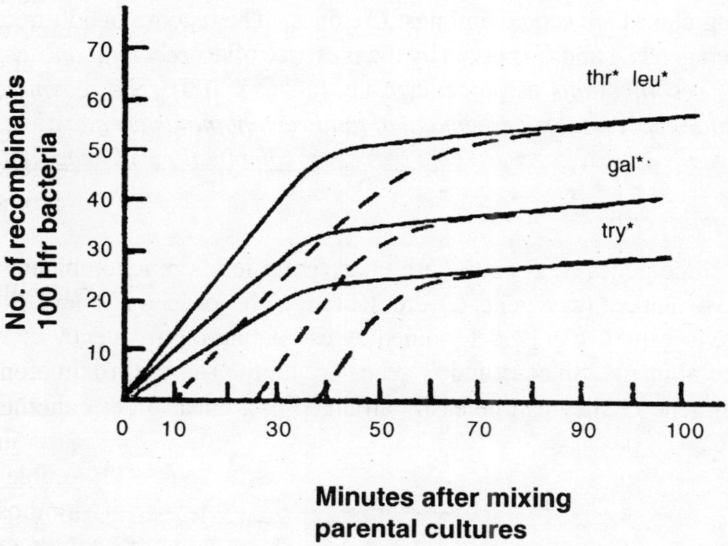

Fig. 7.4. Forr ion of recombinants in a conjugation experiment

Interrupted mating or mapping in time units

The samples are vigorously agitated at > 40,000 rpm in a mixer-blender for 3 minutes before diluting and plating. The agitation separates the mating pairs as well as interrupts further entry of donor DNA. Each gene enters the recipient cell at a specific time after the formation of mating pairs. Therefore various genes can be sequentially arranged according to their times of entry into the recipients. This corresponds well with the order of genes: *thr+ leu+ gal+ try+* on the bacterial chromosome. These 2 methods are good for measuring fairly long, genetic distances (2 time units) on bacterial chromosome.

Mapping by recombination

For genes separated by less than 2 time units these 2 methods are inaccurate. The recombination analysis, whereas is quite precise and works up to *intra-cistronic level.*

Two point cross

For the determination of the distance between two linked genes *A* and *C*, more distal *Hfr* wild type allele *C* is selected. By replica plating the recipient allele carrying clones are scored amongst *C* clones. The recombination frequency between genes *A* and *C* is given by the presence of *aC recombinants* amongst total *C recombinants* as percentage i.e. (aC/C x 100). *The recombination frequency expressed as percentage of total recombinants is equivalent to the distance between two genes.* <u>*One percent recombination is 1 map unit*</u>.

Three point cross

When three genes *A*, *B* and *C* are under consideration, recombinants for a selective marker (say gene *C*) are scored. The order of *A* and *B* genes relative to gene *C* can be determined by estimating the frequency of *Ac* and *Bc* recombinants. Since *A* and *B* genes are on the same (proximal) side of a distal gene *C*, they can be easily arranged in a linear order either as *ABC* or *BAC*.

—*A*——*B*——*C*——	—*B*——*A*————*C*—
—*a*——*b*——*c*——	—*b*——*a*————*c*—
(Possibility I)	*(Possibility II)*

However to determine the correct distance between any two genes say *B* and *C* (*cf. Possibility I*), the recombinants *Ac* arising by crossover in the interval *AB* should be subtracted from the total, *ABc* – *Abc*, because *Bc* recombinants can arise in two ways, by crossover in the interval *AB* or interval *BC*. For determination of distance between *B* and *C* genes the determination of crossovers in *BC* interval is really needed. Similar correction will be required if the order of genes is found to be *BAC*. If recombinants for all the marker genes could be selected the resolution of the system is greatly increased and can be even extended to the *measurement of intra-cistronic distances*.

Conjugation has been studied in great detail in *E. coli K-12*. It is known to occur in other strains of *E. coli* and several other species of bacteria as well.

The rate of transfer of chromosome by *Hfr* donor to the recipient is very much dependant on temperature. At 37° C the complete chromosome of *Hfr* is transferred in 90 minutes. At 32° C the time taken for complete chromosome transfer is almost double. Corrections of genetic and physical measurements of DNA can be obtained by conjugation experiments.

Whole chromosome	= 3.15×10^6 b.p.
	= 90 time units.
1 time unit	= 20 recombinant units.
Map length of chromosome	= 1800 map units.
1 recombinant unit	= 1750 nucleotide pairs long.

Different *Hfr* strains transfer proximal part of their chromosome at high frequency. The *Hfr* chromosome tends to break randomly during mating. This reduces the probability of transfer of distal genes. Distal-most genes located at the tail end of *Hfr* chromosome enter the recipient at about 110 to 120 minutes after the mating pairs are formed. Recombinants for these genes arise at the frequency of 0.1 per 100 *Hfr* bacteria i.e. 1 in 1,000 *Hfr* transfer the distal genes successfully.

In an *Hfr* strain transferring genes in the order OABCD.........*XYZ*, the recipient cells receiving terminal gene *Z* will yield highest proportion of *Hfr* recombinants. Similarly in another *Hfr* strain transferring genes in a sequence *OZYXWVU...CBA*, *Hfr* state will be attained by cells acquiring the terminal gene *A*. A large number of *Hfr* strains are now known with different points of origin and transferring genes in either clockwise (*Hfr C*) or anti-clockwise (*Hfr H*) sequence.

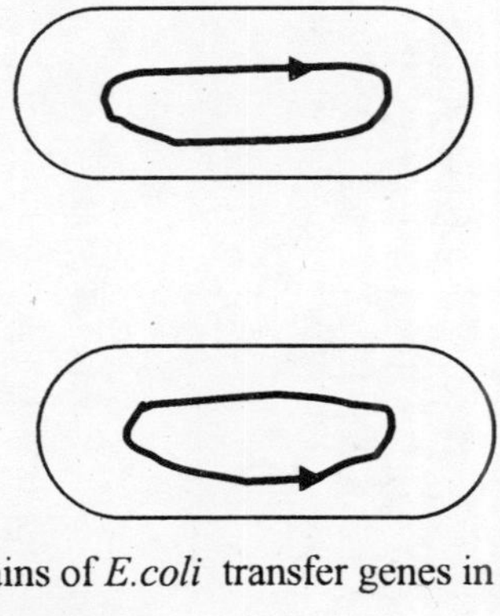

Fig. 7.5. *Hfr* strains of *E.coli* transfer genes in clockwise or anti-clockwise sequence.

During mating the entering DNA randomly breaks amongst different mating pairs. This causes the percentage-recombinants for a gene to be higher if it is closer to the point of entry or origin compared to the distal gene. Therefore the genes can be organized in a linear order such as *thr+ leu+ gal+ try+* on the *E. coli* chromosome by this method.

Further reading

Lederberg, J., and Tatum, E.L. Gene recombination in *E. coli. Nature*, london, *158*: 558 (1946).

Hayes, W. The mechanism of genetic recombination *in E. coli. Cold Spr. Harb. Symp. Quant. Biol. 18*: 75 (1953).

Siddiqi, O., and Fox, M.S. The integration of donor DNA in bacterial conjugation. *J. Mol. Biol. 77*: 101 (1973).

CHAPTER 8

Sexduction

The *sex factor* is a small autonomous stretch of DNA, which has a specific location on host bacterial chromosome. At times the sex factor undergoes recombination with the host chromosome leading to an exchange of a segment between the sex factor and the bacterial chromosome. This results in a sex factor containing a tiny part of the bacterial chromosome. Such a sex factor is called *F-prime* or *F'* or *substituted sex factor*. Bacteria harbouring *F'* factor are known as *intermediate donor* (*I*) ranging in efficiency between *Hfr* (high efficiency) and *F* (low efficiency), two types of male bacteria. These intermediate donors carrying sex factors were discovered by Adelberg and Burns in 1959.

The process of genetic transfer by means of *F-prime (F')* factors is called *F-duction* or *sexduction. F' factor may incorporate as much as 1% of the bacterial chromosome or 4 consecutive auxotrophic genes. If this joint structure contains genes for conjugation and replication, it can be transferred to recipient bacteria and propagated.*

The segment of bacterial chromosome carried by a sex factor has nearly perfect homology with the recipient chromosome. This facilitates the pairing and recombination between them. This also results in higher frequency of insertion as well as release of substituted sex factor (*F'*) than that of wild type sex factor (*F*), so that a cell will alternate rapidly between *Hfr* and *F+* states. The population of such bacteria can transfer autonomous sex factor and chromosome at high frequency (Fig. 8.1).

Selection of sex factor associated with a gene of interest from bacteria

A streptomycin sensitive *Hfr* strain containing a distal z+ gene is mated with *streptomycin resistant recipient*, containing the recessive allele (*z*-) of the gene. The mating is interrupted after 1 hour. During this time only half

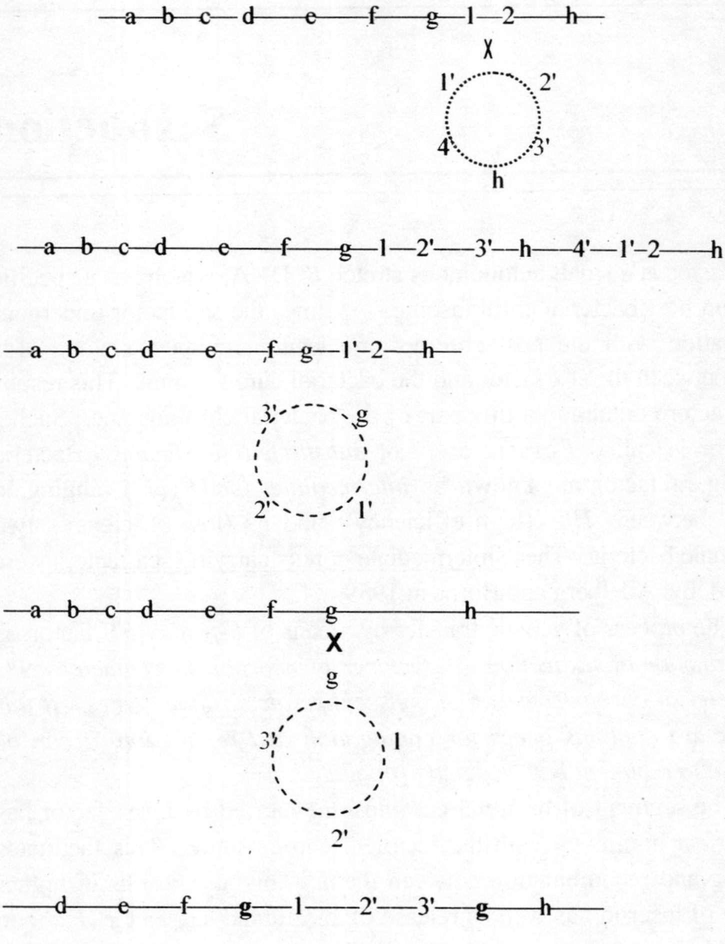

Fig. 8.1. Campbell's model showing a circular prophage picking up a small region of bacterial chromosome by a rare illegitimate pairing. Similar mechanisms could form a sex factor, which carries bacterial chromosomal segment. A part of the sex factor is retained on the bacterial chromosome. F-prime factors carrying different regions of bacterial chromosomes have been isolated.

of the chromosome would have been transferred. *Hfr* donor bacteria are killed by application of streptomycin. The mating was interrupted before the *z+* gene could transfer as a chromosomal marker. Therefore any *z+* survivors will be those cells which received rare *F'–z+* factors These rare *z+* bacteria having coloured colonies, differ from true recombinants in 2 ways.

1. They are unstable for *z+* trait and give rise to *z–* progeny at the rate of 1/1,000 per cell, per generation.

2. They are intermediate donors with respect to *Hfr* and *F+*. They transfer proximal chromosomal genes, sex factor and *z+* gene together with great efficiency to *z–* recipients. Sex factor and the gene behave as a single unit in replication and transfer. *Indeed, they are heterogenotes of the kind z– / F— z. This is one of the important characteristics of sexduction.* The transfer of such a sex factor carrying a recessive allele (F—z_1-) to recipient cell carrying another allele (z_2) of the same mutant phenotype give rise to heterogenotes of the type z_2– / F'—z_1^- (Fig. 8.2)

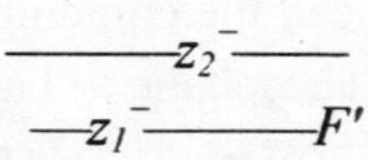

Fig. 8.2. Complementation test by sexduction. Mutant phenotype if z_1 and z_2 are in the same functional gene, and wild type if they are in different genes.

The *partial diploids* will show mutant phenotype if z_1 and z_2 are in the same functional unit and wild type if they are in different functional units. *Sexduction can provide a reliable method of performing genetic complementation test in bacteria and establish dominance or recessiveness of closely located genes.*

Further reading

Adelberg, E.A., and Burns, S.N. A variant sex factor in *Escherichia coli*. *Genetics*, *44*: 497 (1959).

CHAPTER 9

Bacterial Viruses

Bacteriophages or phages (pronounced as f-ages or also as faages) are viruses, which thrive on specific bacteria. Phages share 3 important properties with viruses:

1. Infectivity.
2. Absence of metabolic-machinary of their own, so that they are dependant on host for their reproduction.
3. They possess usually only one type of nucleic acid. Bacterial viruses usually contain DNA, whereas animal viruses have DNA and some like HIV or plant viruses like TMV have RNA as genetic material.

Bacteriophages were independently discovered by Twort in England and d'Herelle in France. Phages became fundamental tool in biological research and served as model virus largely due to the persuasive efforts of Delbrück , who convinced the contemporary research workers to study a few phages in detail. The phage – bacterium system has some unique advantages over the other host – virus systems, such as:

1. Unlike most of the viruses, every phage particle has a probablity close to 1 of infecting a specific bacterium.
2. The infectious particles can be counted by the plaques (clearing) they produce on a lawn of bacteria.
3. The kinetics of infection process can be studied quantitatively.
4. Genetic constitution of both phages and bacteria are amenable to analysis.

On the basis of interaction with host bacteria, different types of phages have been classified into two main groups: (1) *virulent*, and (2) *temperate*. Virulent phages usually lyse (rupture) the bacteria after infecting them. They follow lytic cycle. Whereas, in the *temperate phages*, each particle can either follow a lytic cycle or establish a symbiotic relation with bacterium so that it is propagated with the bacterium in subsequent generations. Bacteria, carrying a *temperate phage* are known as *lysogenic bacteria* and the phage in such a state is known as a *prophage*. *Whether a temperate phage will cause lysis of bacteria or make it lysogenic, largely depends on the physiological state of bacteria.*

Seven virulent phages of T-series and the λ phage (Lambda phage) have been studied in great detail.

Table 9.1. Properties of some prominent phages of T series.

Autonomous virulent phages

Phage Name	Bacterial Chromosome on infection	Bacterial Metabolism	Hydroxymethyl Cytosine in DNA
T2;T4; T6	Rapidly destroyed	Ceases	Yes
T5	Rapidly destroyed	Ceases	No

Dependent virulent phages

T1;T3;T7 Serologi-cally and genetically *unrelated*	Intact DNA needed	Continues	No

The electron microscopy of T2 phage preparations stained either with 1% phosphotungstic acid solution (*negative stain*) or 1% uranyl acetate (*positive stain*), showed it similar to a tadpole in shape. The head is 1,000 Å long bi-pyramidal hexagonal prism of 650 Å width. A straight tail 1,000 Å long and 250 Å wide is attached to the head. The tail has an outer covering like a hollow cylinder, which can contract and reveal a core of 70Å diameter. The core is also hollow tube of inner diameter 25 Å. The proximal end of the tail is attached to the head, while the distal end has a hexagonal base plate with 6 spikes. In addition, the base plate bears 6 tail fibres each 1,300 Å long and 20 Å wide with one bend near the middle.

The phages of T series, temperate phages P1, P2, P22 and lambda (λ) phage have basically similar structures with some variations. For example phages P5 and λ have thinner tail with a single spike and are devoid of tail fibres.

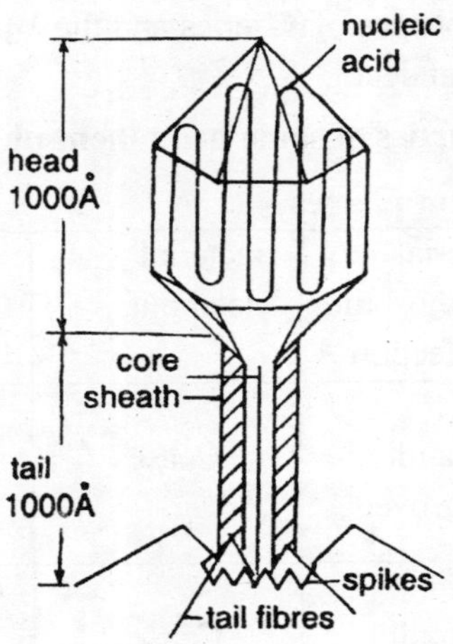

Fig. 9.1. Schematic diagram of T4 bacteriophage.

The heads of T2 and T4 phages contain DNA a little more than a complete genome. The chromosomes of a phage population are not identical, rather they are *a circular permutations of 'one another'. The individual phage chromosome is formed by cutting off a fixed length of DNA, a little longer than complete genome from a long DNA molecule of appropriate sequence.*

Genomes

ABCDEFGHIJABCDEFGHIJABCDEFGHIJABCDEF

Chromosomes

The T4 DNA replicates as a long polymer. Indeed, chromosome deletions, increase the redundancy at the ends of chromosomes in the phage population, such as:

Genomes

ABEFGHIJABEFGHIJABEFGHIJABEFGHIJABEFGHIJ

Chromosomes.

The hypothesis that phages pack a 'headful' of DNA seems to be most plausible.

In addition to these comparatively large phages smaller phages of different shapes resembling animal or plant viruses are known.

Single strand DNA phage φX 174 (*phi*X 174)

The phage ϕX 174 discovered by Sinsheimer in 1962 has 12 subunits located at the vertices of an icosahedron of 200 Å diameter, devoid of any tail. The ϕX 174 phage contains a single stranded DNA. Two sets of experiments indicated that phage ϕX174 has DNA in single stranded form.

1. In a double stranded DNA the ratio of purines to pyrimidines is 1 as adenine usually pairs with thymine, whereas guanine pairs with cytosine. In the DNA of ϕX174, adenine, thymine, guanine and cytosine are present in the ratios of 1 : 1.33 : 0.98 : 0.75 respectively.

2. When labelled with radioactive P^{32}, inactivation or lethality of double stranded DNA of phages such as T2 or T4 occurs on an average at the rate of 10 disintegrations of P^{32} to S^{32} per molecule. This is probably because the damage at nearby sites on both strands of DNA molecule is required for knocking off its ability to replicate. Whereas, each disintegration of P^{32} incorporated in the DNA of ϕX174 or similar phage S13 is lethal.

The DNA of phage ϕX174 is 4,500 nucleotide long and has a molecular weight 1.6x 10^6 Daltons. It is expected to harbour only a few genes. The DNA is present in the form of a continuous loop with supercoiled structure. The host bacterium *E coli C* continues to synthesize DNA, RNA and protein during the 8-minute latent period of infection by ϕX174. The bacterium lyses after 20 minutes to liberate several hundred phage particles.

Replication of the phage ϕX 174 DNA: stamping machine model

The infecting single stranded circular DNA is converted to a double stranded *replicative form* RF by host enzymes. The host polymerase replicates RF DNA in to 2 progeny duplexes. These duplexes are utilized for making m-RNA of base sequence similar to parental single stranded DNA. The mRNA so synthesized is used for making viral proteins. The parental RF DNA is the sole template used for synthesis of all single stranded ϕX174 DNA. This mechanism of DNA replication resembles a *'stamping machine'* (Fig.9.2).

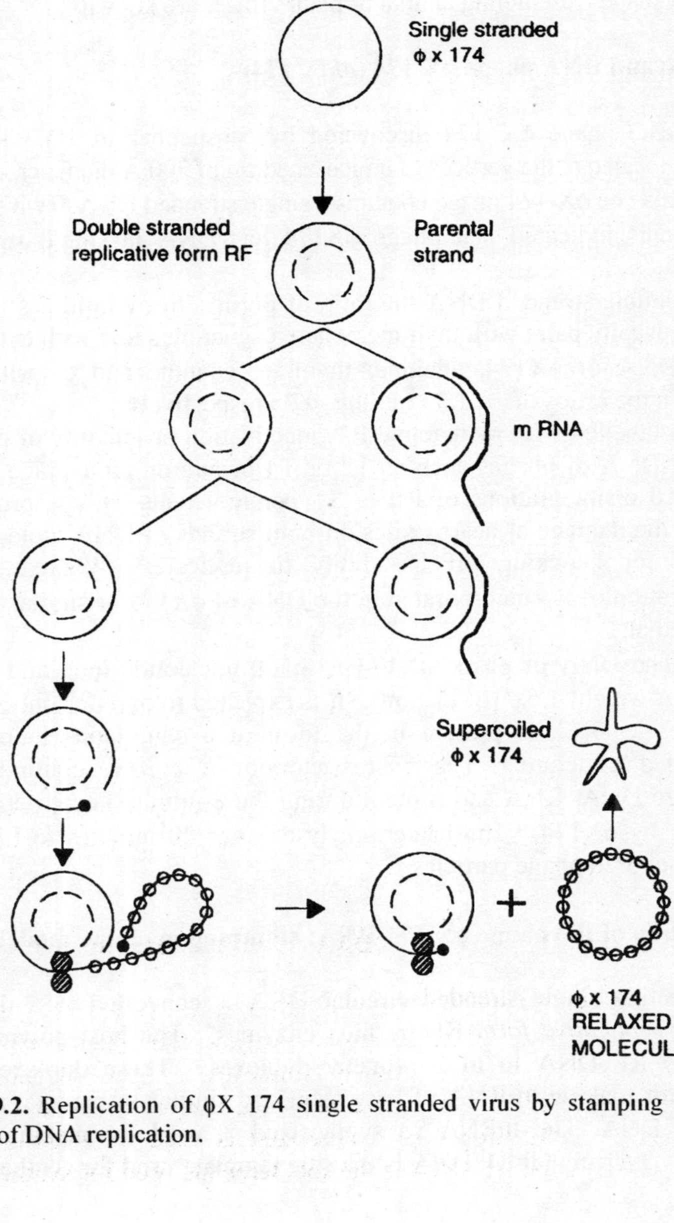

Fig. 9.2. Replication of ϕX 174 single stranded virus by stamping machine model of DNA replication.

Filamentous phages

The filamentous phages such as f 1 contain single-stranded DNA. The filamentous phages fl, fd and M13 are male specific in *E. coli* but not so in *Pseudomonas*. They could be about 800 Å long and 60 Å in diameter. The DNA of these phages have approximate molecular weight $2x10^6$ Daltons and they can get attached to terminal end of the sex pilus of bacterium. They can be distinguished from sex-fimbriae when viewed through an electron microscope. During infection the protein tube of the filamentous phage remains out of bacterium. The time taken for the phage DNA to enter the bacterium could be as small as 20 sec to as large as several minutes; depending upon the length of sex pilus through which it is entering the bacterium. A peculiar feature of infection by filamentous phages is that the bacteria do not lyse. The progeny filamentous phages are longitudinally extruded out of bacterial cell at several places on the cell wall.

RNA containing bacteriophages

A group of RNA containing viruses such as ms2, f 2 to f 7, f r, M12, μ2, γ17 and β specifically attach to sex fimbriae or pili of male *E. coli K-12* bacteria. All these RNA containing viruses are antigenically related but not identical. The Qβ phage containing RNA is antigenically different. RNA phages can get adsorbed to sex-fimbriae but not to filamentous phages. The RNA *coli*-phages infect not only *E. coli* but also bacteria of other genera such as *Salmonella, Shigella* and *Proteus.*

The RNA coli-phages are polyhedral and are 200 Å in diameter. The genome consists of 3,500 ribonucleotides and the protein coat is constructed from 150 identical units.

There is an eclipse period of 15 minutes on infection. On infecting bacteria the RNA virus serves as a messanger RNA to syntesize its own RNA polymerases. The single stranded RNA is converted to double stranded form, which serves as a template for the progeny RNA molecules. The progeny RNA molecules serve as messanger RNA for synthesis of protein coat. Lysis occurs more effectively if mated at 45°C for 25 minutes. *The burst size is approximately 20,000 virions/ bacterium. An appreciable proportion of virus population is non-viable.* As such, no genetic recombination has been observed among RNA phages. But functional and genetic analysis through the study of their temperature sensitive mutants, conditional lethals and complementation tests have been possible. By complementation tests of conditional lethals such as ambers and temperature sensitive mutations, the presence of 6 genes was established in phage M13.

Constituents of a Phage

A T2 phage particle (or virion) weighs approximately $5x10^{13}$ gm and contains 40% DNA and 60% protein. A lambda virion weighs almost half of T2 virion and contains DNA and protein in equal proportions. The DNA may be released from the phage-capsid *via* tail by giving an osmotic shock to the phages, by transferring them from high concentration of ≥ 2M salt solution, to water. The release of DNA molecule can be visualized by an electron microscope. Kleinschmidt developed a method of spreading DNA (which is acidic) in a molecular layer of basic protein such as lysozyme or cytochrome C. The technique is extremely simple and elegant. A suspension of phage particles containing preferably more than 10^{12} phages /ml is made in 2M salt solution and 0.1% lysozyme. A drop of this suspension is allowed to roll down from a clean and wet glass slide inclined at 45° on a water surface. As soon as the phages touch water surface, the DNA is released in the denatured lysozyme layer. Beautiful rosette structure of DNA coils with empty phage-ghost at the centre can be visualized by picking them on a polyvinylformal-coated grid. These specimens are stained with 1 % uranyl acetate solution at 60° C for 5 minutes. Usually a magnification 5,000 to 10,000 X is sufficient for viewing the DNA. At less than 10^{12} titre of phages, it takes lot of time to locate the phage particles in the electron microscope field, because they are too sparsely distributed on the grid. *The ghost phage particles, which have oozed out DNA, can still adsorb to specific bacteria, but cannot cause infection.*

Experiment by Hershey and Chase

Two types of culture of the phage T2 were grown. One culture containing radioactive P^{32} that specifically labels DNA and the other culture containing radioactive S^{35} that labels proteins of the phage. These labelled phages were utilized individually or together to infect *E. coli* cells. The bacteria, together with adsorbed phage particles were separated from the culture medium by centrifugation. The phages sticking out of the bacteria were sheared off in a high-speed blender, keeping the bacteria intact and viable. The radioactivity was assayed in each fraction of supernatant liquid. The results showed that P^{32} label (in the form of DNA) got ingested in the bacteria. However, S^{35} radioactivity mostly remained outside with the phage-ghosts. Only 3 % of S^{35} radioactivity present as internal proteins (polyamines) and associated with DNA, entered the cell. This experiment elegantly showed that infection of bacteria with phages is a genetic phenomenon, where DNA (or RNA in the case of RNA phages) is the carrier of information to the next progeny of phages.

Mechanics of infection by the phage

The presence of Ca (II) and Mg (II) ions is necessary for the attachment of T4 and λ to *E. coli*. These cations probably neutralize the negative charge of the cell surface. Similarly L-tryptophan is needed as an adsorption co-factor for T4 and T6 in synthetic medium. The role of L-tryptophan appears to be to release tail fibres, which are wound around the sheath. Initially the tail fibres of the phage get attached to the bacterium. The base plate makes a firm contact with the wall of the bacterium. The phage enzyme (lysozyme) is released and makes a hole in the rigid cell wall. The molecules released by this lytic activity trigger the contraction of the phage tail-sheath, leading to the penetration of the core in the cell wall and the DNA is discharged inside the bacterial cell. The nature of forces involved in pumping 5×10^{5} Å long and 20 Å wide DNA through 1,000 Å long 25 Å wide tube in a minute are not yet understood.

Two sets of experiments were developed by Ellis and Delbruck, which helped in quantification of results of phage infection.

One step growth experiment*

The kinetics of phage multiplication in a bacterial population could be studied through this experiment. An aliquot of phage suspension is added to freshly growing broth culture of sensitive bacteria. A few minutes are allowed to elapse for phage particles to adsorb to the bacteria. The unadsorbed phages are either inactivated by phage antiserum or removed by centrifugation. The bacteria phage complex is highly diluted in broth maintained at 37 °C. Samples are withdrawn at intervals and assayed for the number of plaque forming units by top layer plating.

The plaque-count for the first 25 minutes remains constant. During the latent period each plaque indicates a phage-infected bacterium, which lyses after plating and liberates progeny phages. *Therefore each plaque represents a bacterium infected with phage,* and not a single phage particle. After the latent period, infected bacteria start lysing and within 10 minutes the phage titre reaches maximum and forms a plateau. At this stage the phage particles are not localized inside the bacteria, rather they are suspended in the broth. *The plaque count represents at this time the number of free phage particles, each virion generating a plaque.*

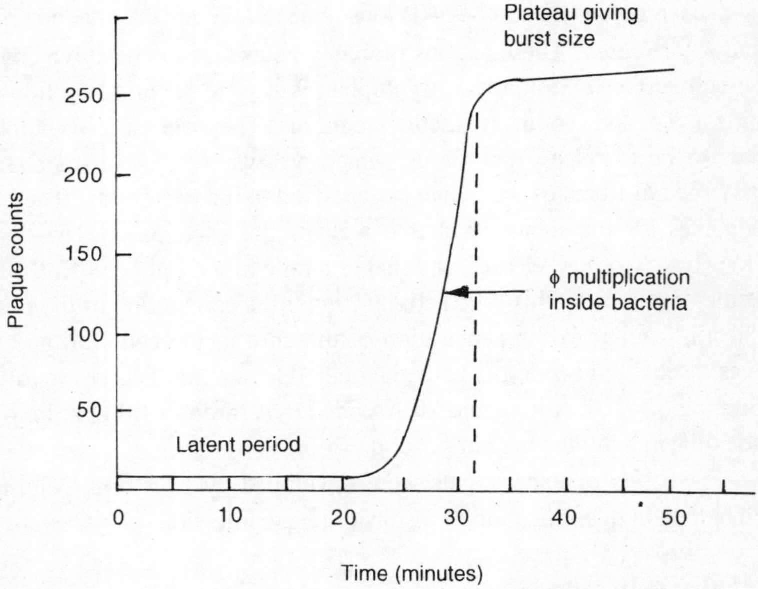

Fig. 9.3. Plot for one step growth experiment with a bacteriophage.

From such an experiment, the average yield of *phage particles per infected bacterium* (<u>*burst size*</u>) can be estimated. The plaque count during the latent period gives the number of phage-infected bacteria and the plaque count along the plateau gives the total number of phage particles generated.

$$\text{Therefore the } \textit{burst size} = \frac{\text{The plaque titre at the plateau.}}{\text{The plaque titre during latent period.}}$$

The burst size can be increased by delaying the lysis of bacteria. Chloramphenicol or 5-methyltryptophan added during the middle of the latent period delays lysis by inhibiting protein synthesis. The phage DNA synthesis continues uninhibited. Shortly after the drug is removed by dilution or centrifugation the lysis begins, greatly increasing the burst size.

Similar results were obtained when cultures of *E. coli* were infected with wild type (*r*+) phages T2, T4, or T6. If after infection the culture is not diluted, then the latent period is greatly prolonged. This phenomenon is called *lysis inhibition.* The plaques formed by *r*+ phages, are small and have a turbid halo. Mutants of these wild type phages arise, which form large clear plaques designated as '*r*' type because they cause rapid lysis and do not show lysis inhibition.

Benzer analyzed in great detail the r+ and r_{II} (pronounced r-two) mutations. The power of selection of r_{II} system is enormous because of the fact that the r_{II} phages form *r* type plaques on *E. coli B*, *r*+ type small plaques with turbid halo on *E. coli K* non-lysogenic strain and do not form <u>any</u> plaques on *E. coli K12 λ* lysogenic strain. Therefore a very large number of r_{II} phage particles can be plated on *E. coli K12 λ* lysogenic strain and only true recombinants or revertants *r*+ can be estimated with ease.

Table 9.2. The phenotype of *r* mutations of phage T4 isolated on *E. coli B*.

Phage strain	*E. coli B*	*E. coli K12* Nonlysogenic	*E. coli K12* λ-lysogenic
wild type	wild	wild	wild
r_I	*r*	*r*	*r*
r_{II}	*r*	wild	—
r_{III}	*r*	wild	wild

wild = r+ small plaques with turbid halo; *r* = large clear plaques;
— = no growth.

Applications of bacteriophages

It has been recognized in recent years that bacteriophages can be used:

1. For the detection of pathogenic bacteria.
2. For treatment of wounds infested with multiple drug resistance bacteria.
3. As vehicles for delivery of protein or DNA or protein plus DNA vaccines, known as phage-display vaccination.
4. As tools for screening libraries of proteins, peptides or antibodies known as phage-display libraries.
5. For gene delivery, where the phage coat protects DNA from degradation after injection in the organism. The attached molecular tag on phage coat enables targeting of particular cell-types, a requirement for effective gene therapy.
6. The ease of manipulation and production makes phages a favourable candidate for use in research, therapeutics, biotechnology and medical fields.

Further reading

Clark, J.R., and March, J.B. Bacteriophages and biotechnology: vaccines, gene therapy and antibacterials. *Trends in Biotechnology*, *24*: 212-218 (2006).

Ellis, E.L., and Delbruck, M. The growth of bacteriophage. *J. Gen Physiol. 22*: 365 (1939).

Benzer, S. Fine structure of a genetic region in bacteriophage. *Proc. Natl. Acad. Sci.*, Washington, *41*: 344 (1955).

Sinsheimer, R.L. Single-stranded DNA. *Sci. Am. 207*: 109 (1962).

CHAPTER 10

Temperate Bacteriophages and Lysogeny

A few strains of bacteria appear to harbour bacteriophages in some intracellular form. Free phages were always found to be present extracellularly in the cultures of these bacteria. It is also not possible to cure bacteria from these phages, by any of the following methods.

1. Serial propagation of single cell lines.
2. Treatment of such bacteria with phage-specific anti-sera.

or

3. In the case of sporulating bacteria, by heating the spores to temperatures known to inactivate phages.

These bacteria harbouring *temperate phages* in *non-infectious* form are called *lysogenic* and the *latent temperate bacteriophage* carried by lysogenic bacteria is known as *prophage*. *These bacteria are usually immune to lytic infection by closely related phages.*

Lysogeny is quite common and widespread in many species of bacteria. In addition a bacterium may carry more than one type of prophage at a time. As many as 5 different types of prophages in a strain of Staphylococcus are known to be present..

The detection of lysogenic state usually depends on the discovery of a sensitive indicator strain of bacteria on which the harboured phage can form plaques. For example the *E. coli K12* strain was used in laboratories several years without realizing that it is lysogenic harbouring a prophage λ. Accidently it was found that cultures of the strain produced plaques when plated along with radiation induced auxotrophic mutant of *E. coli K12*, which by chance was also cured of the phage λ by irradiation.

Tests for lysogeny

The existence of lysogeny can be established and the phage assayed on a sensitive indicator bacterial strain in the following ways.

1. A high dilution of suspected lysogenic bacteria is plated with excess of indicator bacteria. A confluent lawn of indicator bacteria forms on growth. Free phage particles form normal turbid plaques. Colonies of lysogenic bacteria are surrounded by a halo of lysis formed by freshly generated phage particles during the growth of lysogenic bacteria. Such colony centre plaques are very typical of the existence of a lysogenic state in the tested strain of bacteria.

2. Phage particles can be separated from the suspected lysogenic bacteria by filtration through membrane filter or by taking the supernatant liquid after centrifugation. To kill any contaminating bacteria the phage suspension is shaken with a few drops of chloroform. The phage is then assayed on the indicator bacteria for formation of plaques.

3. When a lysogenic culture grown in rich medium is irradiated with ultra violet rays, the bacteria tends to lyse after 1 or 2 generations.

Pseudo-lysogeny

In pseudo-lysogeny the phage particles are present in the bacterial culture as free particles but are not carried inside individual bacteria. For different reasons such cases are known.

1. When phage T7 infects *Shigella dysenteriae*, the lysis of initially infected bacteria releases an enzyme. This enzyme destroyed the receptors for phage on the remaining cells and makes them resistant. On sub-culturing the resistant bacteria, the enzyme is diluted out and the process of infection is re-initiated and stopped.
2. When phage T3 infects *E. coli B* or a virulent mutant of phage P22 infects *Salmonella*, the phage is propagated for many generations inside some cells they infect, while lysis is partially repressed in a proportion of them. The bacteria responsible for persistence of phage are known as *carriers of phage* or in *a carrier state*.

In both types of *pseudo-lysogeny*, phage-free bacterial clones can be obtained by promoting growth in the presence of phage-antiserum or by repeated sub-culture of single colonies. Any bacterium in a lysogenic culture has a small probability of 10^{-2} to 10^{-5} per cell per generation of liberating phages by lysis. Usually the ratio of floating phage particles in a bacterial culture remains constant. However, environmental condition of the experiment can alter the ratio profoundly.

Many effective lysis inducing agents are known, such as X-rays, γ-rays, hydrogen peroxide, organic peroxides, nitrogen mustard, DNA synthesis inhibitors, e.g. fluorodeoxyuridine, Mitomycin C or thymine starvation. However, not all lysogenic bacteria can be induced to lyse. The lysis depends on the genetic constitution of prophage rather than of bacterium. A strain of bacteria may be prone to lysis induction when lysogenized with one type of phage but not with the other. The example for the latter type is phage P2 of *Shigella that can lysogenize E. coli is not inducible.* Indication that in lysogeny the prophage is associated with the bacterial chromosome came from conjugation experiments of Lederberg, Lederberg and Wollman. Genetic crosses were made between *E. coli K12 F+ λ* lysogenic with *E. coli K12 F^-* non-lysogenic, in which the lysogeny could be scored like any other gene. The locus for lysogeny, was found to be very closely linked to the *gal* gene on the bacterial chromosome. This locus for lysogeny could be the prophage itself or another bacterial gene necessary to maintain the prophage. Distinction between these two possibilities was made by Appleyard by setting up crosses in which both parents were lysogenized with a different mutant of phage λ. The segregation of prophages among recombinants was studied and both prophages were found to be closely linked to their parental *gal* alleles, in relation to lysogeny or non-lysogeny. These experiments showed that *the determinant of lysogeny is the prophage and it occupies a specific site on bacterial chromosome as well as it is inherited like a bacterial gene.*

Using *Hfr* males Jacob and Wollman mapped the prophage locations of 14 different temperate phages of *E. coli.* Only 7 were inducible and others were non-inducible. *However, lysogenization with one strain did not give immunity to lytic infection by any other phage.* Each prophage was found to be located at different but specific position on the bacterial chromosome. However, in the case of a non-inducible phage *P2*, Bertani showed that *it has 3 alternative prophage sites occupied in order of preference on the bacterial chromosome.*

Campbell's model of circular phage-chromosome insertion in the bacterial chromosome

Campbell proposed a simple model where a circular phage-chromosome could integrate as a linear structure in the bacterial chromosome by a single reciprocal recombination.

Salient features of the Campbell's model

1. The continuity of prophage and bacterial chromosome was further established by single deletion events, which encroach in both structures together.
2. *A logical prediction of this model is that the insertion of a second phage should be easier since the resident prophage and two attachment sites offer increased regions of homology. However, this does not happen and double lysogeny is more difficult to establish than single lysogeny.* This anomaly could be due to synthesis of a repressor by the resident prophage, which does not encourage subsequent infections.
3. An important feature of the Campbell's model is the circularity of the phage chromosome. Hershey, Burgi and Ingraham first showed that the linear molecule of DNA present in λ virions has complementary cohesive ends, which can hydrogen bond to form a circle.

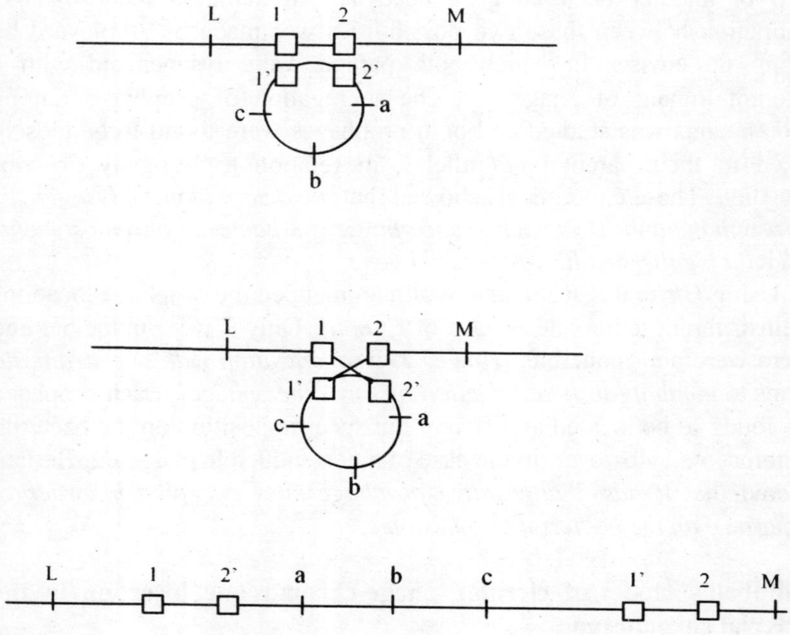

Fig. 10.1. Integration of a prophage in bacterial chromosome by a reciprocal recombination, as proposed by Campbell's model.

4. Genetically homologous regions between the phage and bacterial chromosome (region 1, 2) are duplicated at each end of the prophage.
5. Insertion of prophage in bacterial chromosome should increase the distance between markers on either side of prophage or reduce the linkage between such markers.
6. Pairing again of the homologous regions of prophage and bacterial chromosome followed by a reciprocal recombination leads to the release of phage genome, a plausible mechanism of phage induction.

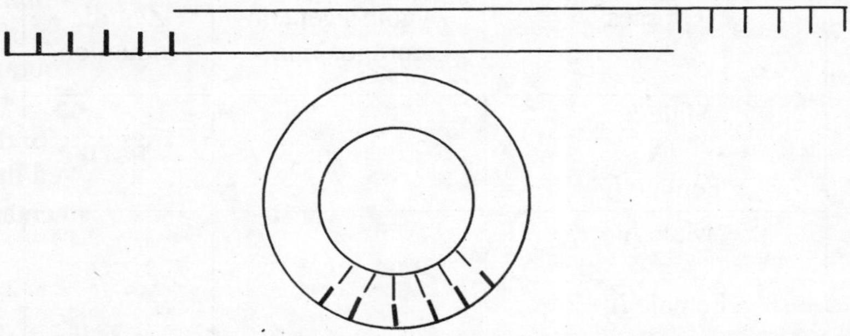

Fig. 10.2. The cohesive ends of the phage λ, help it to form a circular molecule from a linear structure and *vice versa*.

Half molecules of λ can be obtained by subjecting λ-DNA preparation to very high revolution (50,000 r.p.m.) shear-breakage in a mixer blender. The right and left half of λ-DNA differ in buoyant density and can be separated by density gradient centrifugation. It was found that only right and left half adhere to each other, and do not stick to themselves.

The circular nature of λ-DNA has since been established by Kleinschmidt's technique of DNA visualization through electron microscope. Presence of cohesive sites in temperate bacteriophages seems to be quite common feature.

It is unlikely that the association of λ-prophage with bacterial chromosome is held by hydrogen bonds alone. The formation of covalent bond between them seems to be essential for circularity of bacterial chromosome as well.

Zygotic induction and the genetic control of phage function with the help of a cytoplasmic repressor

The outcome of a conjugation experiment between lysogenic and non-lysogenic strains of *E. coli* is very much dependent on whether the male operator or female or both parents carry prophage. *If the inducible prophage such as λ is carried by Hfr, it will enter in to vegetative state soon after entry in the female bacteria. After a latent period the zygote formed by conjugation lyses and releases infective phages. Jacob and Wollman designated this phenomenon as zygotic induction.*

Table 10.1. Relation between zygotic induction and presence of prophage in male or female parent during *E. coli* conjugation.

Crosses	Zygote's genetic composition	Zygotic Induction
Male *ly*+ X Female ly^-	$ly+ / ly^-$	Present
Male ly^- x Female *ly*+	$ly- / ly+$	Absent
Male ly_1+ X Female ly_2+	ly_1+ / ly_2+	Absent

Genetically marked lysogenic prophage = $ly+$; ly_1+; ly_2+ .
Absence of lysogeny = ly^-.

It is observed that the transition from prophage to vegetative phage occurs only when the prophage is introduced in to the cytoplasm of a non-immunized (*prophage absent*) bacterium, either by means of conjugation or by transduction.experiment.

Jacob, Monod and Wollman opined that lytic infection by phage, lysogeny and immunity of bacteria are all dependent on the functional activity of the phage genome mediated by the cytoplasmic repressor molecules. The synthesis of repressor is determined by the ***regulator gene* (*R*)**, which may or may not be linked to genes controlled by repressor. *The site of action of repressor is not structural genes, rather it binds to an adjacent region on the chromosome, called* ***operator***. The function of gene is to switch off or on the activity of structural gene. If the repressor binds to the operator gene, the RNA polymerase cannot bind to the DNA and no transcription of mRNA takes place on the structural genes. In turn the synthesis of proteins determined by structural genes is also switched off. If the repressor molecules do not bind to operator because (1) either operator or repressor gene has mutated (2) repressor molecules have been inactivated say by ultra violet (uv) irradiation, then the phage genes are expressed and the lysis is induced.

These possibilities are diagrammatically depicted as under.

1. ***Normal phage***: the repressor binds to the operator *o* region, inactive structural genes *S*, cell immune to similar re-infection. No lysis occurs.

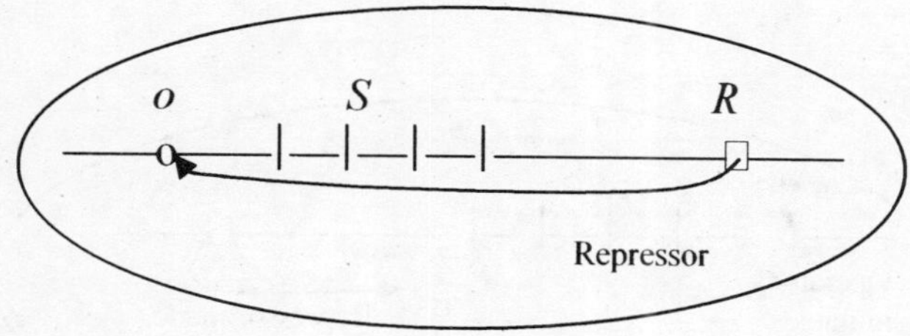

2. ***Induction by uv irradiation***: Repressor is inactivated by uv , operator site *o* is free, RNA polymerase can transcribe mRNA on structural genes *S* , phage synthesized, lysis of cell releases temperate phages

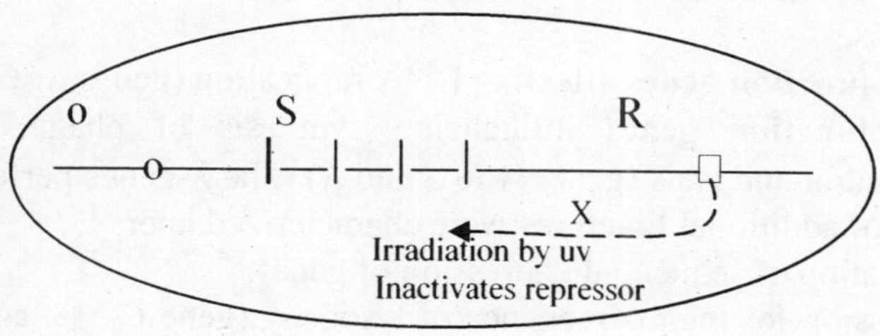

3. ***Mutation in the repressor gene***: The repressor either altered or not produced at all., therefore no repressor binds to operator *o*, structural genes *S* are permanently active, lysis sets in.

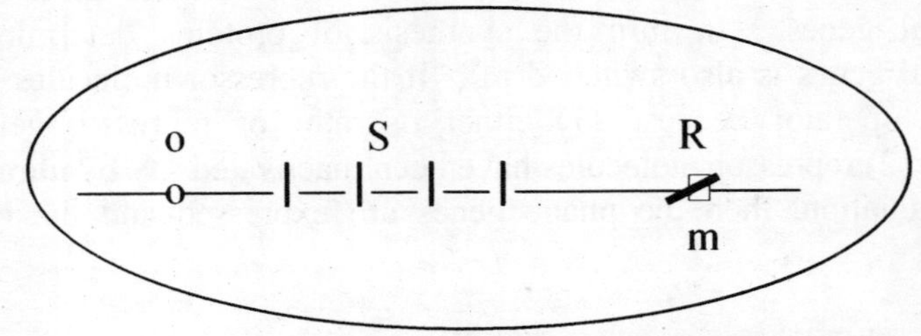

Mutation (m) in repressor gene, altered repressor or no repressor made

4. ***Mutation in operator region or operator constitutive***: Repressor though produced, yet cannot bind to mutated operator region, structural genes permanently active, lysis sets in.

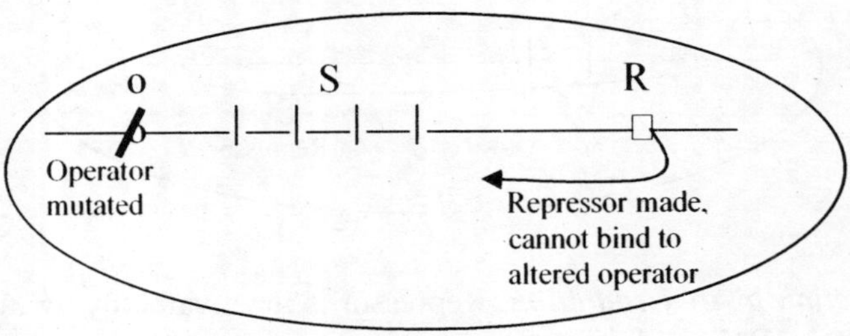

Jacob, Fuerst and Wollman investigated the function and regulation of the genes on λ chromosome. They classified the genes in to two classes.

1. **Early function genes** affecting DNA replication (genes *N, O, P*).
2. **Late function genes** influencing synthesis of phage proteins, maturation and lysis (genes *A* to *J* and *R*). The λ-genes performing 4 types of additional functions were characterized later:

(i) Regulation of sequential expression of genes.

(ii) Repression for the maintenance of lysogeny (gene *C* containing sub-set of genes *C1, C2, C3*).

(iii) Gene responsible for homology and attachment with bacterial chromosome (gene *b2*).

(iv) Formation of cohesive ends, so that phage can circularize for insertion or exit from the bacterial chromosome.

Further reading

Campbell, A. Episomes. *Advanc. Genetics*, *11*: 101 (1962).

Jacob, F., and Monod, J. Genetic regulatory mechanisms in the synthesis of proteins. *J. Mol. Biol. 3*:318 (1961).

Jacob, F., and Wollman, E.L. Lysogeny. *In* The Viruses, (eds. F.M. Burnet and W.M. Stanley) vol.*2*, p.319, Academic Press, New York, (1959).

CHAPTER 11

Transduction

Whether *Salmonella typhimurium* auxtrophs can have conjugation like *E. coli K-12,* was explored by Lederberg, Lederberg, Zinder and Lively. They did get a small number of recombinants when cultures of two auxotrophic mutants were mixed, or even when the culture of one auxotroph was treated with the cell-free extract of the other. They termed this phenomenon ***transduction*** (meaning leading across). Zinder and Lederberg characterized the transducing agent to be a phage called *P22,* which lysogenized one parent and was able to infect and lyse (rupture the cell) the other parent. *In lysogenized state (or lysogenic bacteria) the phage exists in a bacterium as an integral part of the bacterial chromosome. The phage integrated with the bacterial chromosome is called 'prophage' or in 'prophage state'.* The frequency of recombination observed by scoring wild-type recombinants was found to be pretty low – one recombinant for every 10^5 or 10^6 phage particles present. In control experiments when mutant bacteria were treated with the phage grown on the same strain, the wild type recombinants observed were no more than the spontaneous revertants i.e one revertant per 10^8 phage particles present

Subsequently, transduction was established to occur in several species of bacteria such as *E. coli*, *Shigella*, *Staphylococcus*, *Pseudomonas*, *Proteus* and *B. subtilis*. The following properties related to transduction were observed during experiments.

1. The ratio of transducing titre to plaque titre of lysate remains constant during the phage purification process, such as centrifugation, treatment with chloroform, iso-amylalcohol, deoxyribonuclease or ribonuclease.
2. This ratio is also unaffected by selective inactivation of phage adsorption by heat-treatment or application of phage antiserum.
3. The phage receptor sites on *Salmonella typhimurium LT22* strain becomes saturated, when the *P22* phage titre reaches 10 per bacterium. The number of transductants increases proportionally

with multiplicity of infection to reach a plateau at 10 phage particles per bacterium.

4. Phage *P22* specifically adsorbed to all those species of *Salmonella*, which have somatic antigen 12, can transduce them. This is inspite of the fact that many of these species are not lysed or lysogenized by phage 22. The phage *22* does not adsorb to species devoid of antigen 12 and hence cannot transduce them.

All these correlations establish that the phage is the vector for transduction. Similar to the events in conjugation experiments, when inducible prophages are transduced to sensitive bacteria at 37° C, zygotic induction sets in. The initial stages of transduction should be carried out at a lower temperature, say 20 °C.

Establishment of genetic linkage

Lederberg mentioned that the small portions of bacterial chromosome are carried as 'passengers' by the virus vector. Only one out of 10^5 to 10^7 phage particles transduce a gene of donor bacterial chromosome to the recipient bacteria. If on an average 10 phages infect each bacterium (multiplicity 10) the frequency of transduction for a gene would approximately be $10 \times 10^{-5} = 10^{-4}$. The frequency of two genes being transduced simultaneously, but by two different particles = $10^{-4} \times 10^{-4} = 10^{-8}$. This frequency almost equals the probability of spontaneous reversion for a gene. Therefore, a spurious linkage of genes cannot be shown in transduction experiment. Only closely linked genes will be transduced together at frequencies at least 1,000 times higher than frequency of spontaneous mutations.

Size of the donor chromosome portion carried by phage

Two prominent sets of experiments were done to estimate the maximum length of donor DNA, which can be transferred to recipient bacteria by a phage particle. For this, the knowledge of closely linked markers on bacterial chromosome was quite useful. Amongst the linked genes *thr-leu-azi* (threonine requiring, leucine requiring and azide resistant, respectively), the region *thr-leu* is the maximum length of donor chromosome which can be incorporated by phage *P1* and transduced. From conjugation experiments this region is estimated to be 1/50 of *E. coli* chromosome. The molecular weight of the *P1* phage DNA is approximately 6 x 10^7 Daltons and that of *E.coli* chromosome is about 2.8 x 10^9 Daltons.

In another experiment phage *363*, which is closely related to *P1* was used. This phage was made to carry two prophages *82* and *434* and the *gal*$^-$ gene. It was found that this phage can simultaneously transduce these two prophages and a portion of bacterial genome carrying *gal*$^-$ gene. *Indeed, some transducing phages may be able to pack more than the normal complement of DNA.*

Types of transduction

Phages like *P22* can transduce *any* small region of donor chromosome containing a cluster of genes. This type of transduction is known as ***unrestricted*** or ***generalized transduction***. Demerec and Hartman used unrestricted transduction of phage *P22* for mapping a cluster of 5 *genes cysB-tryA-tryB-tryC and tryD.* The latter 4 loci determine steps in tryptophan synthesis in *Salmonella typhimurium*. Ames and Hartman did biochemical and genetic analysis of genes involved in histidine synthesis in *S. typhimurium*. Over 900 independent mutants requiring histidine for their growth were isolated and 540 of them were mapped into 9 genes by transduction. Along with this study the enzymes involved were isolated and studied. This study being one of the most extensive one using unrestricted transduction for fine structure mapping of the genes.

Restricted or localized transduction or high frequency transduction

Morse discovered that the phage λ, which lysogenized *E. coli K12* can also transduce a cluster of gene called *gal* region (galactose loci). The frequency is about one transductant per 10^6 λ phages. This is known as ***restricted*** or ***localized transduction*** as the prophage can attach to the donor bacterial chromosome at a specific site adjacent to the genes, which it can transduce. The main difference between unrestricted and restricted transduction is that unlike phage *P22* only the phage λ particles obtained by *ultra violet* (uv) irradiation induced lysis, possess transducing properties.

When λ phage particles obtained by induction of a lysogenic *gal*$^-$ bacteria are used at high multiplicity to transduce *gal* mutant of *E. coli K12*, a small number of *gal*$^-$ transductants are formed. These transductants can be isolated as the darkly pigmented clones on eosine-methylene blue (EMB) agar, containing galactose. Pure cultures of *gal*$^-$

transductants are obtained by re-streaking on EMB + galactose plates and picking isolated colonies. A majority of such *gal*$^{+}$ transductants differ from original *gal*$^{-}$ donor bacteria in 2 prominent ways.

1. These transductants were found to be unstable for *gal*$^{+}$ character and keep giving rise to *gal*$^{-}$ progeny, with a frequency of 1 per 1,000 cells per generation. The transductants are therefore diploid for *gal* region, such as *gal*$^{-}$ / *gal*$^{+}$. In contrast to the unrestricted transduction, the donor marker does not replace the recipient allele, rather donor fragment synapses with the recipient chromosome. Such partial diploids were called ***heterogenotic diploids*** by Morse, Lederberg and Lederberg. *The immigrant piece of DNA is called* ***exogenote*** *and the recipient allele is known as* ***endogenote***.

2. When the lysogenic culture containing such heterogenotes *gal*$^{-}$ / *gal*$^{+}$ was irradiated with uv light, quite low yield of phage was obtained. The prophage in the process of uv-induction picks up the adjacent region of *gal* gene of the bacterial chromosome and incorporates it into its own structure. So that λ *gal*$^{+}$ phages are liberated instead of λ phages. Such λ-*gal*$^{+}$ phages, containing a piece of bacterial chromosome, find perfect homology with recipient chromosome. These phage particles transduce *gal*$^{-}$ character to *gal*$^{-}$ recipient at higher frequency 50%. Such transduction experiments are known as ***high frequency transduction*** (HFT).

Lambda defective-*gal* phage λ-*dg*

Arber, Kellenberger and Weigle as well as Campbell discovered independently that transduction is carried out by HFT preparations of phage at very low multiplicity of infection (1 phage per 100 bacteria). Practically most of the heterogenotes formed are defectively lysogenic. The transductants are immune to superinfection, lyse on induction, but no phages are released and the lysate is devoid of transducing activity. However, if similar experiment is carried out with simultaneous infection with normal phage at higher multiplicity 3, normal lysogenic heterogenotes are formed and on induction yield HFT lysates.

The incorporation of the bacterial *gal* region into λ genome causes the loss of one or more phage functions. Part of the phage chromosome was replaced by the bacterial *gal* region. Such defective transducing phages were termed as ***λ-dg*** (*lambda defective gal*) and have 1/3 or 1/4 of their chromosome missing. The missing region usually contained genes *A-H* responsible for the structural features of the phage.

It was found by density gradient centrifugation that the deleted region of the phage chromosome is not substituted by the same length of the bacterial chromosome, usually it is of different length.

The heterogenote

Consider positions 1 and 2 as alleles within *gal* gene that yield almost all possible types of recombinants for the *gal* region. The high frequency of haploid segregants show that *λ-dg* has less stable association with host chromosome than λ. In addition the high frequency of double lysogenization with *λdg* and λ suggest that *λdg* used homology of *gal* region for transduction, while λ-specific site is used by wild type phage λ.

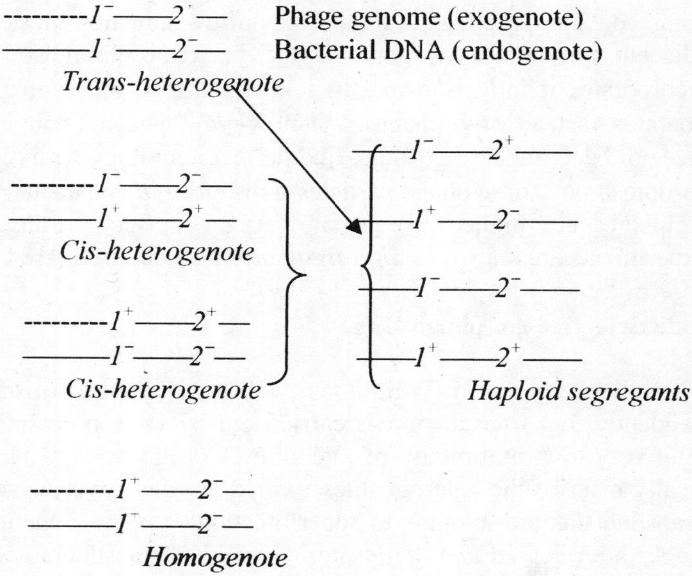

Fig.11.1. Diagrammatic representation of genotypes of possible recombinants from a heterogenote having two pairs of alleles in the galactose region.

All cis-heterogenotes ferment galactose. Trans-heterogenotes ferment galactose when mutations are in different functional loci (A crucial test for complementation). Homogenotes do not ferment galactose.

Mechanism of transducing-phage formation

Campbell's model very nicely explains, how a circular prophage can incorporate variable lengths of bacterial c[illegible]

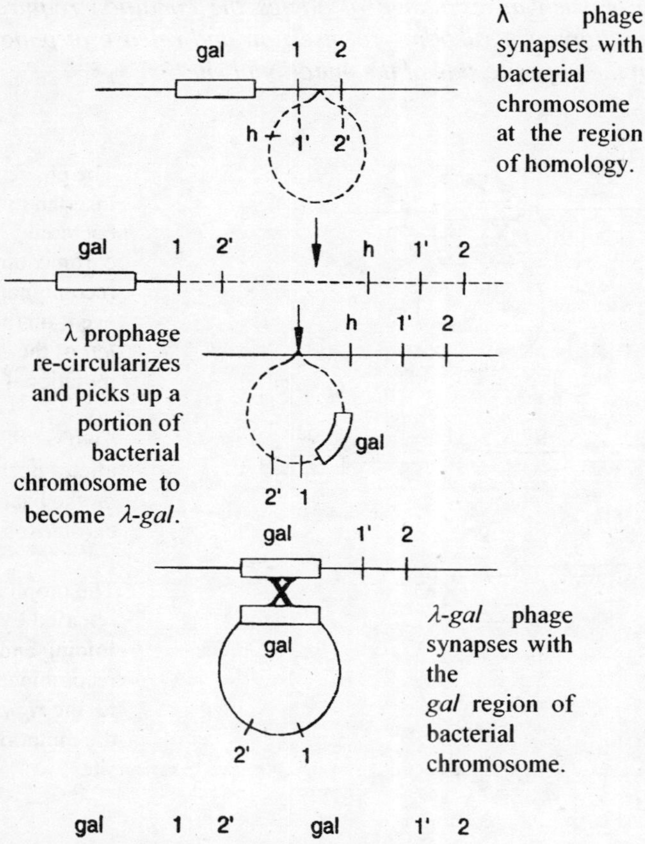

The integration of phage results in two *gal* sites on the bacterial chromosome.

1 and 2 represent normal attachment sites in gene cluster *C* of prophage on itself and bacterial chromosome; *h* = host range locus; *gal* = galactose utilizing gene-cluster.

Campbell's model also explains the mechanism of exchange of *gal* alleles between the transducing phage and bacterial chromosome. It explains as well the formations of *homogenotes* gal^{-} / λ-*gal* or gal^{+} / λ - gal^{+}

For such an exchange of alleles the condition required is the recombination events leading to insertion and release of phage should occur on the opposite side of the mutational site.

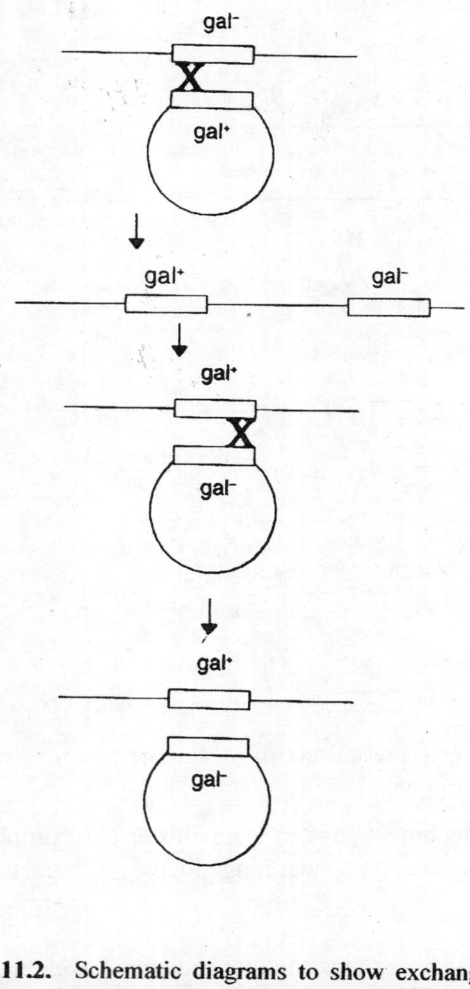

The phage is inserted in the bacterial chromosome by a recombination event on the *left* of the mutational site.

Two set of *gal* alleles occur on the bacterial chromosome.

The prophage is released by folding and recombination to the *right* of the mutation site.

The released phage carries the mutant allele, while the chromosome carries the wild type gene.

Fig.11.2. Schematic diagrams to show exchange of *gal* alleles between the phage and bacterial chromosome according to Campbell's model.

The mechanism of unrestricted or generalized transduction

In generalized or unrestricted transduction the frequency of transfer of a gene is around 10^{-5}, per phage particle. The prominent features of unrestricted transduction are:

1. Any bacterial gene can be transduced.
2. The vegetative phage picks up the bacterial DNA during lytic infection or lysis induction. Prophage does not seem to be involved.
3. The transferred piece of donor chromosome is usually integrated in recipient chromosome and does not exit as heterogenote.
4. As in the case of phage *P1*, most *Salmonella* transductants do not show any trace of residual phage.
5. Like restricted transduction, fragments of bacterial chromosome are incorporated in phage DNA to yield defective phages.
6. The phage genome is likely to have homology in many regions of bacterial chromosome. The phage recombines with homologous region during vegetative multiplication.

Abortive transduction

At times, the donor gene introduced by the phage vector in the bacteria, neither participates in recombination nor replicates, but is dominant and capable of synthesizing its own protein. When such a bacterial cell divides only one daughter cell inherits the donor gene. In subsequent cell divisions also, only one daughter cell gets the donor gene fragment. This process of *uni-linear inheritance of transferred gene* is known as ***abortive transduction***.

Two well established examples of abortive transduction are given here:

1. Motility is one of the traits transduceble by phage 22 in *Salmonella*. Stocker, Zinder and Lederberg grew phage *P22* on a motile *Salmonella* strain.The liberated phages are used to transduce a strain of non-motile, non-flagellated *Salmonella*. Transductants are plated on soft gelatin-agar. Non-motile cells form a colony, while the motile cells migrate out to form a trail of growth. Stocker, Zinder and Lederberg found a number of trails on such soft gelatin-agar plates. In each trail only one daughter cell inherits the motility gene and is able to move away from the parent colony. Similarly, at the next division only one daughter of this motile cell is motile and the others are non-motile. The non-motile cell remains there and forms a colony. The process continues likewise (Fig. 11.3 a).

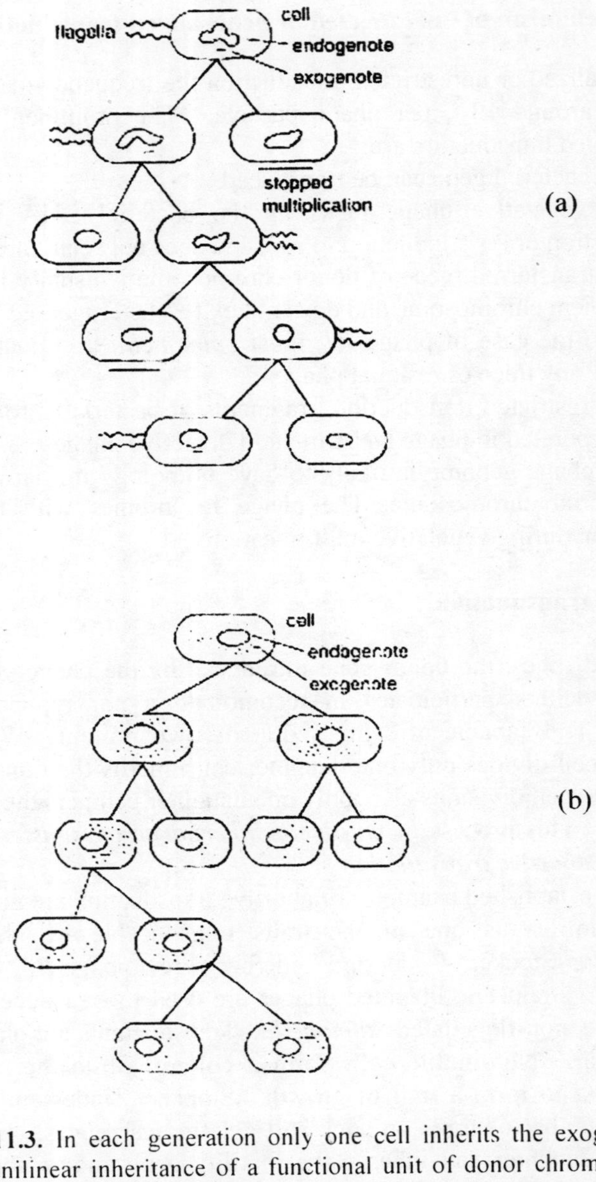

Fig. 11.3. In each generation only one cell inherits the exogenote. The unilinear inheritance of a functional unit of donor chromosome occurs in abortive transduction. (a) Abortive transduction for motility trait. (b) Abortive transduction for nutritional character.

2. Ozeki observed abortive transduction while transducing nutritional characters in *Salmonella*. He used phage preparation grown on wild type *Salmonella* to transduce an auxotrophic recipient with a single nutritional requirement. The transduced culture was plated on minimal medium agar. A large number of slowly growing colonies were formed, along with larger colonies of prototrophic recombinants arising out of transduction. If minute colony is re-suspended and the entire bacterial population plated on minimal agar, only one minute colony was formed, instead of a large number of minute colonies. The interpretation is that each minute colony contains only one cell, which can give rise to only a single minute colony (Fig. 11.3 b). In such experiment abortive transduction is 10-20 times more frequent than the normal transduction. Abortive transduction is quite useful for testing complementation of genes or rather their function. The numbers of abortive transductants for closely linked markers are approximately the same, even when the functions of genes are quite different.

Lysogenic conversion or phage conversion

Bacteriophages may play a role in altering the phenotype of bacteria, was realized even before the discovery of transduction. More than 100 years ago, even before genetics became an established science, Sam Felice reported that non-virulent strains of *Clostridium tetani*, which do not make tetanus toxin can acquire hereditary ability to do so by growing them in cell free culture filtrates of virulent *C. tetani*. Freeman found that non-virulent strains of *Corynebacterium diphtheriae* can be made to produce diphtheria toxin by treatment with phages grown on virulent toxigenic bacteria of the same species. This was <u>not</u> due to selection of bacteria by phage, rather due to the establishment of lysogeny by the phage. In addition, it was found that ability to produce toxin by the bacteria was lost when the bacterial cell lost the phage. This phenomenon since then was known as ***lysogenic conversion*** or in recent times as ***phage conversion***.

A few other exotoxins made by pathogenic bacteria have been found to be due to the carried phage.

1. Production of erythrogenic toxin by group A haemolytic *Streptococci*, causing skin-rash during scarlet fever.
2. Production of fibrinolysin by *Staphylococci*.
3. Production of somatic antigens by *Salmonella* group E bacteria.

Bacteria group	E1	E2	E3
Lysogenic phage	epsilon ε 15	ε34	
Antigens produced	3, 10	3, 15	3, 15, 34

It is quite likely that more and more such systems will be discovered, *where phages are really responsible for the apparent evils of bacterial virulence affecting the living beings.*

Further reading

Ames, B.N., Hartman, P.E., and Jacob, B.F. Chromosome alterartions affecting the regulation of histidine biosynthetic enzymes in *Salmonella. J. Mol. Biol. 7*: 23 (1963).

Campbell, A. Ordering of genetic sites in bacteriophage λ by the use of galactose-transducing defective phages. *Virology, 9*: 293 (1959).

Zinder,N.D., and Lederberg, J. Genetic exchange in *Salmonella. J. Bacteriol. 64*: 679 (1952).

CHAPTER 12

Plasmids: Sex Factors, Colicin Factors and Resistance Transfer Factors

Lederberg proposed the name ***plasmids*** for all extrachromosomal genetic structures which can replicate autonomously. Plasmids include *sex factors, colicin factors and drug-resistance transfer factors*.

Sex factor

It is a small piece of DNA, which imparts the ability to the bacterium to conjugate and transfer DNA to another recipient bacterium. Sex factor can exist in either of the two states in the host cell.

1. Sex factor exists in the cytoplasm and replicates independently of chromosome-division. Often it replicates a bit faster than the host chromosome and *there could be 2-3 copies of plasmid per cell.*
2. (a) Sex factor can get inserted in to the host chromosome at any one of the several possible sites. (b) Sex factor now replicates in unisen with host chromosome. (c) Promotes conjugation of the male host cell with female F^- bacterium. (d) Promotes the linear, oriented transfer of the donor host chromosome to the female bacterium in such a manner that sex factor is the last to be transferred at the chromosome tail-end. (e) The sex factor can also undergo infrequent genetic exchanges with adjacent region of the host chromosome. In this process it incorporates some bacterial genes in its own structure. The sex factor of *E coli K12* is one of the most thoroughly studied sex factors. It can promote conjugation (i) in many strains of *E. coli*, (ii) *E coli* and *Shigella*; *E. coli* and *Salmonella* as well as between *Salmonella* and *Salmonella.* The commonality of the sex factor substantiates that the genera *Escherichia*, *Shigella* and *Salmonella* are phylogenetically related <u>*Enterobacteriaceae*</u>. Some other bacteria which show sex factor mediated conjugation are: *Pseudomonas aeruginosa, Serratia marcescens* and *Vibrio cholerae.*

Colicins or bacteriocins

Some strains of *Enterobacteriaceae* are capable of producing bactericidal molecules, which can kill (but do not lyse), some other strains of the same family. These lethal molecules when produced by enterobactors are called ***colicins***, and when produced by any bacteria in general are called ***bacteriocins***. Colicins or bacteriocins are inactivated by the proteolytic enzymes, hence they are likely to be protein molecules. Colicin molecules adsorb to the specific receptors on the cell walls of sensitive bacteria and kill them. Colicin resistant mutants can be isolated, which lack such receptors or have defective receptors. Colicin producing bacteria (*col*) are called ***colicinogenic*** and carry one or more plasmids. *They are immune from the lethal action of their own colicins. In a culture of col*$^{+}$ *bacteria, at a time only a small proportion of them synthesize colicin and die in this process.*

Bhaskaran and Iyer found that a particular strain of *Vibrio cholerae* mixed with some other strains can give rise to a small number of recombinants (1 per 10^{6} cells). This *V. cholerae* strain also synthesizes a bacteriocin which lyses other strains. The plasmid P^{+} determining bacteriocin synthesis also seems to play the role of a sex factor. The crosses between P^{+} and P give highest recombination frequency. P^{+} x P crosses being less fertile, while P^{-} x P^{-} crosses are sterile.

Some *col*$^{+}$ plasmid-containing cells are able to promote chromosomal transfer by cell to cell contact. The different types of colicins are distinguished by their host specificity and diffusibility. They are designated by capital letters such as B, E, I, K or V, and if they have sub-classes they are given sub-fixes as E_1 or E_2 etc.

We owe a large part of our knowledge about colicins to Fredericq. The analysis of the bacteriocins of *colicin 1* and *E 1* in *E. coli K12* crosses throw some light on their nature.

F col I x *F col col*$_{I}{}^{r}$ when grown together, a proportion of *col* bacteria are converted to *col I*. The *col I* plasmid appears to promote conjugation and its own transfer. The *col E* is not transferred under similar conditions.

In F^{+} *col* E_1 x *F col* cross, *col* E_1 is transferred effectively, rapidly and is unassociated with any other marker except the sex factor itself. *Therefore col* E_1 *behaves like an autonomous cytoplasmic element, while col I seems to have some properties of a sex factor.*

Frédéricq found that *Salmonella typhimurium LT2* strain can be made colicinogenic for one or more *col*$^{+}$ factors by growing cultures together with *E. coli, Shigella* or other *Salmonella*, which harbour these factors.

High frequency transfer of colicinogeny (HFTC)

The *col* cells can be infected with *col I* donors in high proportion by overnight incubation. In the initial 5 hours the infection is quite low <0.5%. In the latter part of incubation *col I* spread rapidly, suggesting that newly infected bacterium can transfer *col I* factor more efficiently. Overnight culture of bacteria infected with *col I* factor can transfer *col I* to *col* bacteria at the rate of 50% in one hour. *Newly converted cells maintain the property of high frequency transfer of colicinogeny (HFTC), for 3-7 generations.* After that these cultures revert to a state where few are capable of *col I* factor transfer, though most of the cells remain colicinogenic. The cells of *F* *E. coli K12* on infection with *col I* factor behave in a similar manner.

Resistance transfer factors (RTF)

Beginning 1955 onwards, Watanabe and Fukasawa found that many isolates of *Shigella* from patients of bacillary dysentery are resistant to one or more, commonly used drugs such as chloramphenicol, ampicillin, streptomycin, tetracyclin and sulphonamide. About 10% of such isolates were resistant to all the four drugs. Later strains resistant to kanamycin, neomycin or penicillin were isolated by Anderson and Datta. A few years later Ochiai and Akiba found that this multiple drug-resistance can be transferred en bloc to *E. coli*, *Shigella* or *Salmonella* by cell to cell contact. Later Watanabe, as well as Meynell and Datta succeeded in transfer of drug resistance to phylogenetically remote species such as *Vibrio cholerae; Pasturella pestis, Proteus*, *Pneumococcus*, *Salmonella* and *Serratia*. ***Development of resistance to as many as 8 drugs have been found to be carried by a single factor.***

The phage *P1* can transduce multiple drug resistance in sensitive *E. coli K12* from quadruply resistant donors. In *Salmonella typhimurium* similar transfers can be achieved by phage *P22*. However results in both cases differ markedly. The quadruple drug resistance acquired by the *E. coli* transductants can be transferred to other sensitive *E. coli* strains by conjugation, where the RTF is transferred intact. In contrast, *Salmonella* transductants show segregation of drug resistance in 87% of population as streptomycin – chloramphenicol – sulphonamide resistance and in 13% as tetracycline resistance. In majority of transductants the ability of subsequent transfer of drug resistance by conjugation is lost. *This loss is due to some defect in the transfer factor.* The bacteria seem to be normal, as they are capable of normal transfer of the same RTF by conjugation.

Anderson studied the pattern of transfer of resistance for 3 drugs: ampicillin (A), streptomycin (S) and tetracyclin (T). The resistances to these drugs were transferred independently. The results suggested tence of a ***transfer factor***, which interacts with each resistance factor mediates their transfer to sensitive strain. If the strain A, has a transfer factor, which may be transferred to strain B by conjugation. In strain B the ***'transfer factor'*** picks up the ***'resistance factor'*** and transfers it to another strain C. The strain A and B alone could not transfer resistance factor to strain C. It can be summarized as:

$$A(t) + B(R) \rightarrow A + B(tR)$$

$$B(tR) + C \rightarrow B + C(tR)$$

Where t = transfer factor or sex factor
R = immobile resistance determinant.

Amongst two prominent groups of factors associated with resistance transfer, one can produce sex fimbriae (pili) on *E. coli* bacteria, which can adsorb RNA phages and in turn identifiable. Meynell and Datta by using this method found that, amongst 26 sensitive strains of *E.coli*, 6 were found to posses transfer factors.

Acquisition of drug resistance transfer factor

A plausible initial step could be the selection of resistant bacterial cells in intestines in the presence of the ingested drugs. Such bacteria on acquiring transfer factors can pass on drug resistance to co-existing sensitve bacteria, pretty rapidly. *The factors carrying resistance for single different drug can recombine to give multiple drug resistance transfer factors.* Similarly, reservoirs for the acquisition of drug resistance factors by *Salmonella* are cattles from farms doing intensive breeding with extensive use of antibiotics.

In *Staphylococcus aureus*, the genetic locations of the resistance to penicillin, erythromycin and metal ions such as mercury are on non-transmissible plasmids and are not on the chromosome. It is most likely that transmissible resistance to drugs is normally determined by plasmids, which get incorporated into transfer factors by recombination. This mechanism of attaining drug resistance works in addition to the usual chromosomal mutations, which can also be transferred to other cells by sexual process of recombination. Like F^- factor, the resistance transfer factors can be eliminated from the cell by treatment with acridine or more effectively with acriflavin.

A number of resistance transfer factors termed *fi* ***(fertility inhibition)*** can very much reduce the fertility of F^+ or F donor bacteria. But *fi*+ resistance transfer factors can promote the formation of ***sex fimbriae*** **(*sex pili*)** in male donor cells. Though the sex fimbriae formed under the influence of F^+ and fi^+ are morphologically and serologically different. F^+ type fimbriae are 20 μm long, while fi^+ type fimbriae are 1.5 μm long and thinner. Both fimbriae have a terminal knob of unknown function.

In summary sex factors are a group of cytoplasmic elements, which are capable of self replication, promote conjugation of cells and determine donor characters of the cell. Sex factors include colicin factors, drug resistance transfer factors and the sex factor F that is involved in the transfer of bacterial chromosome. The sex factor F also promotes the efficient transfer of colicin factors E 1 and E 2, which are otherwise non-transmissible. However, col I and col B factors can promote chromosome transfer. The col V factors promote chromosome transfer with efficiency almost equal to that of sex factor F. On the other hand F' (prime) factors transfer part of bacterial chromosome as their own structure. Several factors with as diverse functions as production of surface antigen, hemolysin and enterotoxin have been characterized.

E.coli sex factor *F*	= 10^5 base pairs long
Colicin factors	= 10^4 — 10^5 b.p.
Resistance transfer factors	= 5 x 10^4 b.p.

Superinfection

Bacteria harbouring a plasmid usually cannot be re-infected in a stable manner with a similar plasmid. This characteristic property is known as ***superinfection immunity***. However, different plasmids *F*, fi^- and various colicin factors can stably exist in the same cell. Such plasmids with reference to their co-existence property in a cell are referred as ***compatible***. Plasmids, which cannot coexist in a cell because they are similar, are referred as ***non-compatible***. *Recombination is known to occur amongst different plasmids and sex factors, giving rise to hybrid structures.*

Complementation test between plasmids

Complementation tests between compatible plasmids can be performed for the determination of dominance, while suitably marked incompatible plasmids allow the construction of linkage map. The bacteria infected with sex factor *F* and the resistance transfer factor fi^{-} produce fimbriae of *F* type. Defective *F* and *fi* RTF do not complement. The results indicate that the formation of fimbriae depends upon more than one gene and not on production of a single type protein molecule.

Plasmids found in *Staphylococcus aureus*

Staphylococcus aureus is one of the most prevalent causes of pus formation and wound infection in human beings. Emergence of multiple drug resistance amongst the population of *Staphylococcus* in hospitals is a serious problem. Resistance to penicillin has emerged in Staphylococci by their capacity to produce an *exo-enzyme* penicillinase, which inactivates the penicillin molecule by opening its β-lactum ring. ***It is interesting to note that penicillinase producing bacteria existed even before penicillin was used as a drug***. The sealed soil-samples collected with plant specimens as early as 1689 AD contained *B. leicheniformis* which produced penicillinase. Staphylococcal penicillinase is an inducible enzyme. In the presence of penicillin the rate of enzyme synthesis increases 30 fold.

Penicillinase producing plasmids isolated from different Staphylococcal strains may be distinguished from each other by:

1. Natural markers carried by them.
2. Production of immunologically different penicillins of different molecular structure.

The plasmid of one type could be transferred by transduction to another cell harbouring a different type of penicillinase producing plasmid.

Several types of penicillinase producing plasmids known as α, β, γ, ...were isolated from different Staphylococcal strains. Amongst the first three have been studied in detail. The plasmids α and β as well as β and γ are compatible. Recombination is rare between them. However, plasmids α and γ are incompatible and segregate 95% of the time in the very first division. Plasmids α and γ as well show frequent recombination. By using α and γ plasmids Richmond constructed the linkage map:

$$— i — p — Hg — em\ ,$$

where *i* gene produces repressor, *p* is the structural gene for penicillinase production, *Hg* is the gene for resistance to mercury, and *em* gene determines the resistance to erythromycin. All these genes are located on a single plasmid and can be transduced by a phage simultaneously. In most of the strains of *Staphylococcus* penicillinase production seems to be determined by a plasmid. However, in some strains the penicillinase gene behaves like a chromosomal gene in transduction.

Further reading

Bhaskaran, K., and Iyer, S.S. Genetic recombination in *Vibrio cholerae*. *Nature*, London, *189*: 1030 (1961).

Datta, N. Transmissible drug resistance in an epidemic strain of *Salmonella typhimurium*. *J. Hyg*., Cambridge, *60*: 301 (1962).

Frédéricq, P. Colicins. *Ann Rev. Microbiol. 11*: 7 (1957).

Watanabe, T. Infectious heredity of multiple drug resistance in bacteria. *Bact. Rev. 27*: 87 (1963).

CHAPTER 13

Control of Genetic Expression

Thousands of different types of molecules are in continued synthesis during cell growth and multiplication, which proceeds normally in an ordered manner. It is expected that cellular processes and biochemical reactions proceed in a controlled manner for orderly growth. In principle there are at least 4 ways of controlling genetic expression. The ***negative*** or ***positive control*** acting on ***inducible*** or ***repressible*** systems give 4 control systems.

1. Negative control of induction.
2. Positive control of induction.
3. Negative control of repression.
4. Positive control of repression.

The definitions of negative control, positive control, induction and repression are given as under.

1 Genes under *negative control* are not expressed so long repressor is capable of interacting with *operator gene* (control site on genome).

2. Genes under *positive control* are expressed only when an *active regulator protein* is present.

3. *Inducible gene* functions only in the presence of a small molecule (called *inducer*).

4. *Repressible gene* functions only in the absence of small molecules, called *repressors*.

In the negative control, the functioning of a synthetic pathway is switched off by the excess of the end-product, whereas in the positive control the enzyme synthesis is switched on when the substrate or its analogue is present in significant concentrations.

Feedback inhibition or end product inhibition (negative control)

In the cell, a majority of the biosynthetic pathway which form small molecules such as amino acids, nucleosides or essential metabolites are controlled by the end product of the pathway.

1. The end-product or its analogue inhibits the activity of the first enzyme on the pathway.
2. When branched pathways are involved, the end product inhibits the '***branch point***' enzyme. Metabolic pathways control their activity according to the rate of utilization of the end product. If the end product accumulates, the pathway is inhibited in its activity.
3. The action is immediate and independent of the presence of preformed enzymes.
4. The inhibitory end-product molecule usually has no steric resemblance to the normal substrate of inhibited enzyme.
5. The interaction of the end product and substrate with the enzyme is not of a competitive inhibitor type.
6. Mild treatments, such as application of heat which partially denature enzymes, may result in loss of interaction between enzyme and the end product, without affecting the enzyme-substrate interaction.
7. The enzymes, which are crucial in feedback control, usually have a structure with *two non-overlapping binding sites*, which were called by Monod and Jacob as ***allosteric sites***.
8. A mutation can alter the end product binding site on the enzyme and result in release of the inhibition of the pathway. In such a situation the end product would continue to be synthesized and probably excreted by the cell into medium, e.g. excretion of tryptophan by 5-methyltryptophan resistant mutant.
9. The feedback inhibition mechanism could operate in reverse. Some enzymes instead of being inhibited by end product may be activated by ***allosteric effectors***.

Enzymes which are inhibited by one metabolite and activated by other metabolite are known, e.g. threonine deaminase is inhibited by the end product isoleucine but valine increases the enzyme activity. In general the feedback or end-product inhibition mechanism not only applies to single cells but also to other phenomena, such as differentiation, hormonal action and carcinogenesis.

Coordinated repression of enzyme synthesis (negative control)

The end product inhibition is a very efficient mechanism to regulate the synthesis of small molecules. However, it is not effective in controlling the synthesis of enzyme and protein molecules. Cohen and Monod showed that by providing tryptophan to a bacterial culture, production of tryptophan synthetase was inhibited. Similarly, the presence of exogenous methionine repressed the enzyme, methionine synthetase. In case of arginine synthetic pathway too, the supply of exogenous arginine repressed the production of most of the enzymes, forming the pathway.

The switching off of most of the enzymes of a sequence by the end product is known as ***coordinated enzyme repression*** or ***repression***. This type of repression can be released by a single mutation in such a manner that the end product does not repress the production of enzymes of the pathway. *The mechanism of coordinated enzyme repression works as a coarse control for the economy of protein synthesis, whereas the feedback inhibition is used by the cell as a fine control for regulating the synthesis of small molecules.*

Induction of enzyme synthesis (negative control)

Some enzymes are synthesized in appropriate concentration only in the presence of their substrate. Monod and Cohn termed this mechanism of control as *induction of enzyme synthesis*.

1. Inducible enzymes in bacteria are mainly involved where interaction with exogenous substrate is required. Some well known example being β-galactosidase and penicillinase.
2. Inducer or its new degradable analogues are very specific for a particular enzyme e.g. lactose and its analogues, thiogalactosides work as inducers for β-galactosidase enzyme.
3. When several enzymes are responsible for the utilization of a substrate, all of them are coordinately induced by the inducer.
4. Mutants of inducible bacteria can be obtained which synthesize enzyme even in the absence of inducer substrate. Such mutants are called ***constitutive mutants***. The enzymes produced by constitutive strain are identical with those produced by wild type strain on induction with substrate molecules.

Most of our knowledge about the induction and repression of enzyme synthesis is based on the studies by Jacob and Monod about the control of lactose fermentation in *E. coli K 12*.

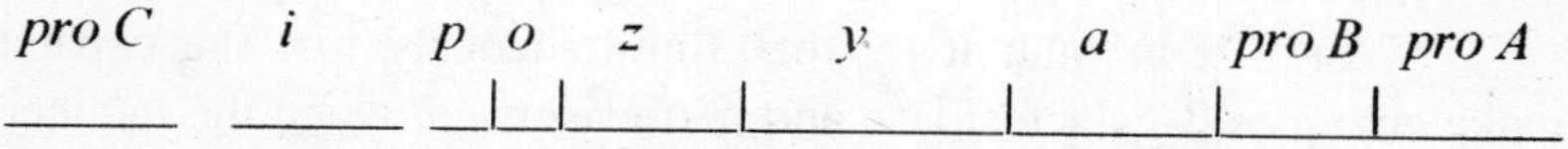

Fig. 13.1. A map of the *lac* region of *E. coli K 12* showing the relative positions of its genetic units: *z, y,* and *a* are genes adjacent to each other specifying the structures of β-galactosidase, permease and galactoside transacetylase respectively. The region *p* is known as ***promoter*** and *o* the ***operator*** region. A region *i* known as ***inducer gene*** separated from the structural gene *z* controls inducibility of lactose utilization.

The z^- mutants do not produce active β-galactosidase enzyme. However, *some* z^- mutants produce inactive, but serologically similar protein to the active enzyme. Such serologically similar inactive protein is called ***cross-reacting material*** or CRM (pronounced crim). All *y* mutants do not synthesize permease, so lactose cannot enter the cell. The β-galactosidase enzyme is known to consist of a number of polypeptides and hence denoted as a *multimeric enzyme*. Some alleles of *z* mutants are partially complementary. However, a srain with a deletion mutation in the transacetylase gene, where the transacetylase production is knocked off, are able to ferment lactose and grow.

Constitutive i^- mutants produce β-galactosidase and permease even in the absence of an inducer: a galactoside. The *i* gene is a separate gene linked to *z* gene.

Male / Female zygote	Production of β-galactosidase
$z^+ i^+ / z^- i^-$	+
$z^- i^- / z^+ i^+$	–

The *i* gene is responsible for the production of a *repressor* protein, which stops the z^- gene from functioning. There is a lag of 60 minutes in the synthesis of repressor, after the entry of *i* gene in the recipient cell in a conjugation experiment.

An *E. coli* mutant i^s that simultaneously lost the capacity to make enzymes β-galactosidase and permease even when the inducer was present, threw light on the mechanism of induction. The phenotype of this mutant i^s is: (i) not due to deletion in both genes *z* and *y*, since mutant yields recombinants with z^- and y^- mutants. (ii) i^s is dominant over i^+ in diploids as $i^s z^+ y^+ / i^+ z^+ y^+$ do not ferment exogenous lactose nor produce β-galactosidase nor permease.

Jacob and Monod explained the results by suggesting that i^s mutation causes synthesis of an *altered* repressor (***super-repressor***), which is not inactivated by lactose inducer molecules, resulting in repression becoming permanent.

A second mutation in i^s gene (not a back mutation) at a different site will produce double mutants $i^- i^s$ which should not produce active repressor and behave as a ***constitutive*** lactose fermentor. In fact this was found to be so experimentally.

This led to the classification of genes into two categories.

(1) **Structural gene** carrying the genetic information about the structure and function of the protein formed.

(2) **Regulatory gene** determines the production of a type of cytoplasmic molecules, which control the activity of a structural gene or a set of structural genes. Regulatory genes are found in inducible enzyme systems, as well as in systems having coordinated enzyme repression.

The concept of operon and the operator region

Jacob, Perrin, Sanchez and Monod proposed that the repressor molecule synthesized by the gene *i* interacts with an *operator* region on the chromosome and switch off the transcription of a set of contiguous genes. Some *additional properties of the* ***operator*** *are as follows:*

1. A single operator can switch on a set of contiguous genes.
2. Structural genes and the operator controlling it, together make an integrated unit of function called ***operon***.

To prove that there is indeed an '*operator*' region on the chromosome, Jacob *et al* used a novel method. They looked for permanently derepressed mutants among the heterogenotes, which were made homozygous for i^+ gene such as $z^+ i^+ / F^- z^+ i^+$. Permanent derepression can be obtained by ***operator constitutive*** o^c mutants or very rarely by two successive mutation of i^+ to i^-.

As expected from the Jacob *et al.* hypothesis:

1. o^c mutants are dominant over o^+. In o^+/o^c heterogenotes both enzymes β-galactosidase and permease are produced to constitutive levels.
2. o^c mutants are insensitive to super repressor, as in $i^s o^+ / F - i^+ o^c$ heterogenote.
3. All o^c mutations map in a small region between *i* and *z* genes, close to *z* gene.
4. o^c mutations function in *cis* configuration with other genes in a heterogenote.
5. In a heterogenote

$o^+ z^- / F - o^c z^+$	Produce galactosidase constitutively
$o^c z^- / F - o^+ z^+$	Enzyme not synthesized
$o^+ i^+ z^+ / F - z^-$ CRM, $o^+ i^+$	Produce both active β-galactosidase and CRM
$o^c i^+ z^+ / F - o^+ i^+ z^-$ CRM	only active enzyme
$o^+ i^+ z^+ / F - o^c i^+ z^-$ CRM	only inactive protein

There are now many known examples of such operator controlled cluster of genes, e.g. galactose (*gal*), tryptophan (*try*) and histidine (*his*), where in all these cases enzymes of the pathway are coordinately repressed or induced.

The hypothesis could be extended that all genes of an operon are transcribed together into a polygenic messenger RNA. In other words, *an* ***operon is a coordinated genetic unit of transcription*** *or one operon leads to a single type of polygenic messenger RNA. The synthesis of separate polypeptides occurs during translation of* ***polygenic mRNA***.

The promoter region

A large number of mutants displaying o^c (*operator constitutive*) phenotype for *lac* operon were isolated by plating bacteria on another sugar mellibiose. The bacteria initially were made to have heterogenotes $i^+ o^+ z^+ y^- / F^- i^s o^+ z^+ y+$. The i^s (super-repressor) switches off z^+ and y^+ genes. The use of mellibiose as a sole source of carbon selects cells that have *y* gene active and operator constitutive o^c. The *z* gene function is not essential in such a situation. All such mutations were found to be deletions involving *o* region. It was implied that there is an essential region close to *o* and *z* genes, which is needed for the expression of *lac* operon. Jacob *et al* called this region ***promoter*** *p* region. It was also observed that ***partial defects in the operator region do not affect the rate of mRNA transcription***. The rate of enzyme synthesis in turn depends upon mRNA synthesis. *The most likely role for the promoter p region seems to be the initiation of mRNA transcription by allowing the RNA polymerase to bind.*

Positive control

Positively controlled systems are known mediating the breakdown of arabinose and rhamnose; penicillinase production in *Staphylococcus*, alkaline phosphate synthesis in *E. coli* etc.

Catabolite repression (positive control)

As long as glucose is available in the growth medium *E. coli* does not use any other sugars such as lactose. In the presence of glucose the utilization of lactose is repressed by preventing the transcription of the genes of lactose operon. This effect is known as ***catabolite repression***. Similar effect is observed for galactose or arabinose operons.

Catabolite repression works *via* reduction in the level of c-AMP (cyclic AMP) in the cells by glucose. A catabolite activator protein (CAP) is found to be necessary for initiation of transcription of genes. CAP needs cAMP as a small molecule inducer. By decreasing the level of cAMP CAP is prevented from binding to the control region. This in turn prevents RNA polymerase from binding to DNA and no initiation of transcription occurs. In this way glucose levels positively control the transcription of quite a few genes.

A unified mechanism for the coordinated enzyme induction or repression

In coordinated enzyme induction hypothesis of Jacob and Monod, a group of contiguous genes contain a promoter, an operator region and a few structural genes. Such a cluster of genes that is switched *off* or *on* together, in a coordinated manner is known as an '***operon***. A regulator gene, situated a little away synthesizes a repressor protein, which interacts with the operator region so that the *RNA polymerase which initially binds to the promoter region can no longer transcribe mRNA*. If an inducer or its analogue is supplied to the cell, inducer molecules bind to the repressor molecules and inactivate them. The inactivated repressor can no more bind to the operator and as such the site is free. In such a situation the structural genes are usually transcribed in the form of a polygenic mRNA.

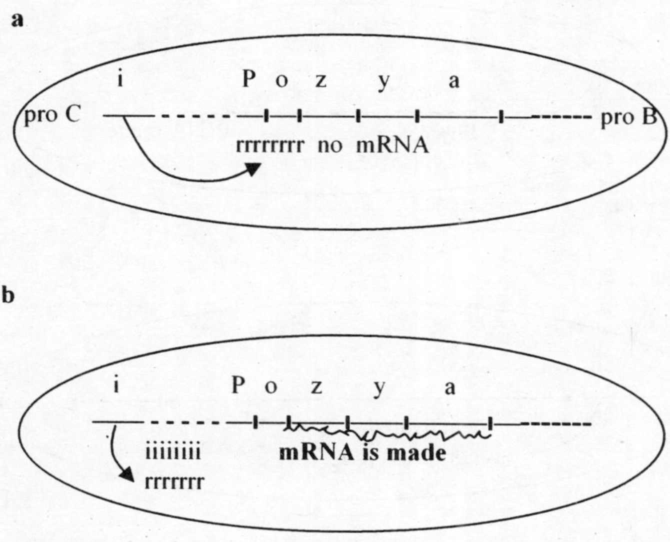

Fig. 13.2. Schematic diagrams showing the co-ordinated *induction* (regulation) of enzyme synthesis according to Jacob and Monod. (**a**) Repressor binds to operator, no mRNA made so no enzyme synthesis. (**b**) Low molecular weight inducer binds to the repressor, resulting in configurational change and inactivation of repressor molecules. The inactivated repressor cannot bind to operator, hence mRNA can be synthesized and the enzyme made.

Such coordinated enzyme induction is known to occur in pathways of (a) lactose break down, involving genes β- galactosidase and permease and (b) galactose utilization involving three enzymes kinase, transferase and epimerase. *However, many gene clusters responsible for the syntheses of amino acids are coordinately repressed by the end product of the synthesis pathway.*

The mechanism of gene regulation proposed by Jacob and Monod can also explain the mechanism of repression, after slight modification. The product of regulator gene is regarded as a ***co-repressor***, which on its own cannot interact with operator. ***Co-repressor** is activated by the **end product** of the pathway so that the (co-repressor + end product) complex acts as a repressor.* The small molecules could be the end product of a pathway, such as amino acids can activate or

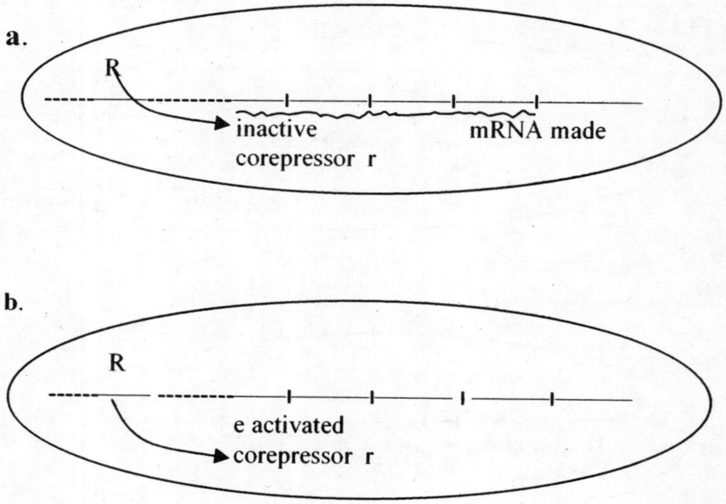

Fig. 13.3. Schematic diagrams showing repression of enzyme synthesis according to Jacob and Monod. **(a)** The co-repressor synthesized by the regulator gene on its own cannot interact with operator, keeping the enzyme synthesis ON. **(b)** The co-repressor on interaction with the end-product of the pathway get activated and can bind to the operator. This results in shutting OFF of enzyme synthesis.

inactivate the product (**r**) of the regulator gene *R. They are given a general name allosteric effectors (**e**), so that in enzyme induction **r** is the repressor, while in repression **re** is the repressor.*

These are the two simpler examples of positive and negative controls of enzyme synthesis, though a few more complicated examples are known. For example *the coordinated repression of tryptophan pathway in Salmonella typhemurium* contains 5 enzymes and the genes are located on the chromosome in the same sequence as enzyme pathway. The operator is located at one end. A large number of deletions on analysis showed that, deletion in the first gene inactivates second gene as well. However, genes 3, 4 and 5 continue to function at 50% level and no longer subject to tryptophan repression. The existence of a ***second promoter*** has been suggested for genes 3-5.

The strength of the operon hypothesis is its great flexibility. It can be applied to explain induction and repression as well as negative and positive systems of control of widely diverse nature such as the pathway of arginine synthesis. The synthesis of arginine is mediated by 8 enzymes in *E. coli* or *S. typhimurium*. For 4 enzymes, the genes 2, 3, 5, and 8 are clustered near *methionine B* and the remaining are located at different locations on the chromosome. All genes are repressed by arginine. Mutants resistant to canavanine (an arginine analogue) can synthesize all 8 enzymes in the presence of arginine. All de-repressed mutants map in a narrow region (*R arg*) near streptomycin resistance locus. A single co-repressor is made by *R arg* gene, which is activated by arginine. A logical conclusion is that arginine genes 1, 4, 6, 7 and (2, 3, 5, and 8 group) have individual operators and do not form a part of single operon.

The nature of repressor

The repressor of *lac* operon is shown to be partly protein, has approximate molecular weight 20,000 Daltons and approximately 10 molecules per i^+ gene are present in a cell. The phage repressor has also been isolated and shown to bind to its DNA. For histidine pathway in *S. typhimurium* the histidyl-t RNA may itself control synthesis by directly blocking a site on mRNA, where synthesis of polypeptide begins. Another possibility is that aminoacyl-t RNA synthetase; a protein is a co-repressor itself.

Mode of Control	Negative Control	Positive Control
Repression	Tryptophan operon **Inactive + effector = Active.** Repressor deletion gives recessive constitutive.	**Active + effector = Inactive.** Repressor deletion Uninducible.
Induction	*lac* operon **Active + effector = Inactive.** Deletion in *i* gene results in recessive constitutive.	Catabolite repression **Inactive + effector = Active.** Repressor deletions become uninducible.

Repressible or inducible operon (sets of genes) can be controlled in negative or positive manner by repressor protein and small molecules.
Active = active repressor; **effector** = small molecule; **Inactive** = inactive repressor.

Further reading

Jacob, F., and Monod, J. Genetic regulatory mechanisms in the synthesis of proteins. *J. Mol. Biol. 3*: 318 (1961).

Jacob, F., and Monod, J. On the regulation of the gene activity. *Cold Spr. Harb. Symp. Quant. Biol., 26*: 193 (1961).

CHAPTER 14

Ribonucleic Acids and their Role in Protein Synthesis

Ribonucleic acids have chemical composition similar to that of DNA. However, ribonucleic acid (RNA) differs from DNA in 4 important ways.

1. The pentose sugar, D-ribose forms the backbone of RNA instead of 2-deoxy-D-ribose.

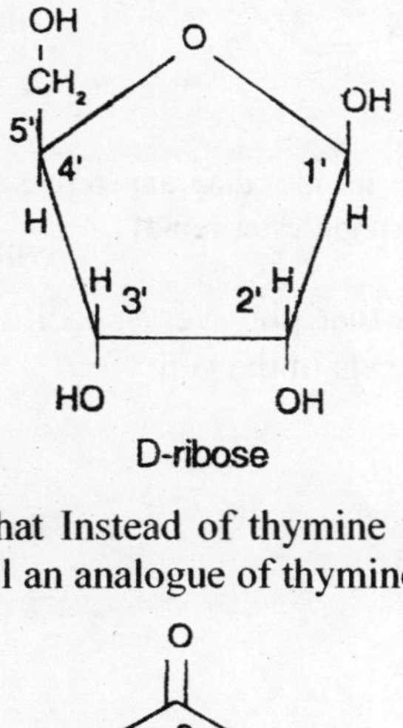

D-ribose

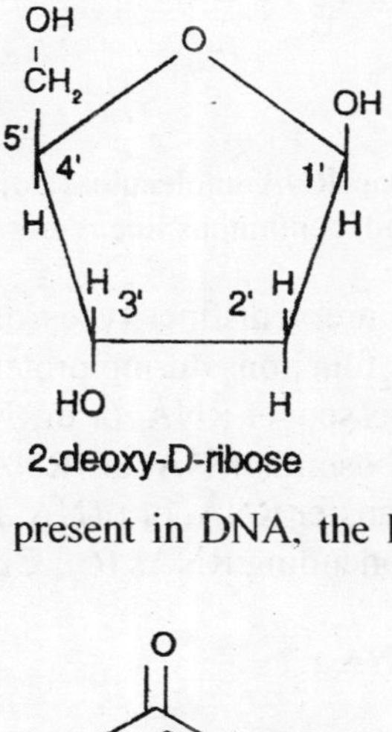

2-deoxy-D-ribose

2. that Instead of thymine usually present in DNA, the RNA contains uracil an analogue of thymine.

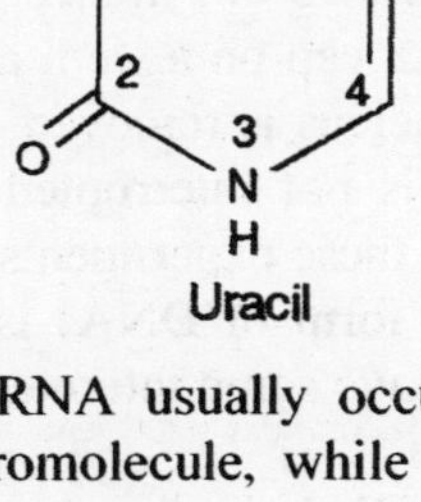

Uracil

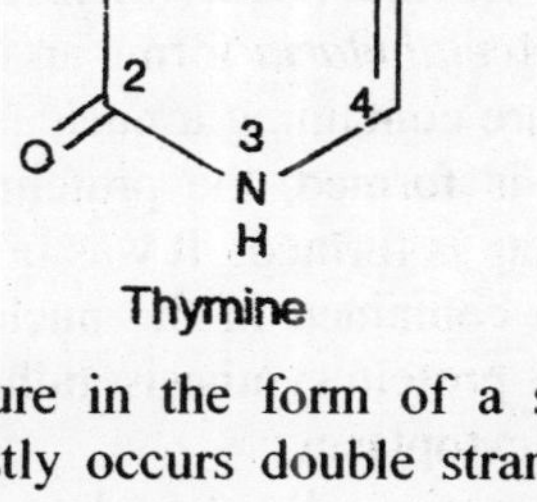

Thymine

3. RNA usually occurs in nature in the form of a single stranded macromolecule, while DNA mostly occurs double stranded, except in

some viruses such as ϕX 174, where it is present in single stranded form. The DNA can form triple stranded structures in some special conditions.
4. Unlike double stranded DNA, where the ratio of purines (Pu) to pyrimidines (Py) is 1, in RNA it is different. In *E.coli* RNA Pu/Py = 1.3.

X-ray diffraction and other physical methods show that regions of the RNA molecule are double stranded. This could be as high as 80%, where A pairs with U and G pairs with C located on the different regions of the same molecule. Unpaired bases tend to form a single stranded loop.

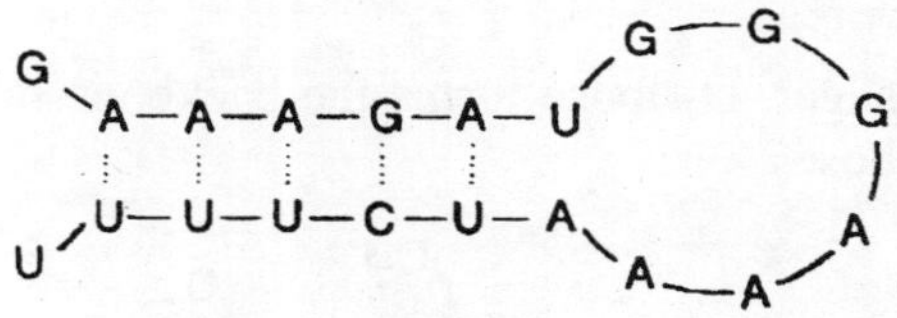

Fig. 14.1. An RNA molecule (Dotted line in the diagram represents hydrogen bond, continuous line represents phosphodiester bond)

There are 4 distinct types of RNAs that play very specific and quite different functions during protein synthesis in the cell:

(i) messenger RNA or mRNA,
(ii) ribosomal RNA or rRNA,
(iii) transfer RNA. or tRNA, and
(iv) noncoding RNAs (*Cf.* **Chapter 16**).

Messenger RNA

To find out that where in the cell protein is synthesized Bracket used a unicellular alga *Acetabularia*, which can grow up to 5 cm in size. On differentiation *Acetabularia* forms an umbrella like cap on a stem and a root like structure containing a nucleus. If the nucleus is removed even before the cap is formed, the protein synthesis is not interrupted and eventually the cap is formed. It was inferred from these experiments that the information contained in the nucleus (in the form of DNA) is not directly used for protein synthesis, rather it is used *via* some intermediate molecule in the cytoplasm.

In eucaryotic cells though most of the DNA in the form of chromosomes is located in the nucleus, yet proteins are synthesized only in the cytoplasm. An autoradiography of epoxy embedded sections of the eucaryotic cells fed with radioactive labelled amino acid, show that the radioactive label is confined to the cytoplasm. This indicates that there is a molecule that carries the information encoded in DNA, in the form of a message from the nucleus to the cytoplasm.

Hershey, Dixon and Chase found that when virulent phages T2 or T4 infect *E. coli* bacteria there is no significant increase in total RNA content of bacteria. However, a small quantity of RNA with higher turnover rate was made. Volkin and Astrachan further investigated this high-turnover- rate RNA by labelling it with P^{32}. Radioactivity measurement of such hydrolyzed RNA samples gave (Adenine + Uracil) / (Guanine + Cytosine) ratio in RNA fraction close to 1.7. It is similar to that of phage DNA (A+T)/(G+C) = 1.8. It is differing from bacterial DNA where ratio is 1.0 and the bulk RNA having ratio 0.85.

In another experiment the gene z^+ responsible for the production of enzyme β-galactosidase was introduced in *E. coli* z^- cells by conjugation. The enzyme synthesis in the zygote begins within a minute of entry of the z + gene. If the z^+ gene happens to be labelled with P^{32} it gets inactivated by P^{32} decay to S^{32}. In turn the rate of β-galactosidase production declines. Ribosomes are known to be comparatively stable and conserve their RNA for a minimum of 3 generations. These experiments suggest that information for β-galactosidase synthesis is transported from gene to ribosomes by means of rapidly produced but unstable '***messenger***' molecules.

Hall and Spiegelman performed an elegant *experiment to conclusively prove* ***mRNA*** *molecule is complimentary to DNA sequences.* P^{32} labelled mRNA was isolated from *E. coli* bacteria infected with phage T2. In addition, H^3 labelled T2 DNA was prepared and heat denatured so that both strands separate. H^3 labelled denatured DNA and P^{32} labelled mRNA were mixed and slowly cooled so that DNA-RNA hybrid molecules could form.

In CsCl density gradient, (single stranded DNA + single stranded mRNA) hybrids have buoyant density intermediate to those of RNA and double stranded DNA. RNA being heavier than DNA. In control experiment mRNA was annealed with DNA from *E.coli*, not infected with phage T2. No DNA-RNA hybrids were formed in the control experiment. Uninfected *E. coli* cultures also produce similar high turnover mRNA.

The messenger RNA constitutes about 2% of total RNA in the cell and contains molecules of varying sizes. The sedimentation coefficient of these mRNA molecules as determined by ultracentrifugation range between 8 and 30S, corresponding to 600 – 5000 nucleotide long molecules.

Rho factor

During *in vitro* RNA synthesis from certain stretches of DNA, a heterogeneous population of RNA with varying lengths and different 3'-ends is produced. The termination of each RNA molecule's synthesis by the enzyme RNA polymerase is not precise at a particular base sequence on the DNA template. Rather it occurs chance after the polymerase. encounters termination signal. The termination signal could be in the form of a base sequence either on DNA or RNA produced or in both. The base sequence on DNA template, which directs RNA polymerase to cease RNA synthesis, is called a terminator.

It was discovered that a protein called ***rho*** factor of the molecular weight 55,000 Daltons, when added to *in vitro* transcription system of *E. coli*; RNA molecules of uniform length with precise 3'-ends are produced. This showed that the terminator sequence with such DNA, can only be recognized precisely in the presence of *rho* factor. Such transcription is known as ***rho*** *factor dependent termination*. The effect of *rho* factor is best visualized at low ionic strength of in vitro transcription system. However, at higher ionic strength at times with some streches of DNA template the termination of RNA molecules is precise even in the absence of *rho*-factor. This is known as ***rho-independent termination***.

The sequence analysis of DNA showed that both types of terminations have palindromic sequence in the DNA just prior to termination-site, usually they are GC rich sequences

GGCCGGCC
CCGGCCGG

Such sequences on transcription give rise to hair-pin structure in the RNA, by complementary base pairing between G and C

The sequence analysis of RNA produced revealed the following features:

1. The *rho* factor independent termination occurs after a short sequence of U-residues in RNA.
2. The *rho*-factor dependent termination does *not* depend on any such sequence restriction.

RNA polymerase moves about 1,000 bases on DNA every minute. However, on encounter with a terminator, the polymerase pauses for about a minute. At *rho*-independent terminator, the polymerase dissociates from DNA template and releases the product RNA. The stretch of U-bases immediately following the hair-pin structure forms weakly bonded rU-dA (RNA-DNA) hybrid, which help in dissociation of RNA product from DNA template. A set of U bases on RNA corresponding to A-A bases on DNA, indicating that A-T rich regions on DNA are involved in termination of transcription. A-T rich regions are as well important in initiation of transcription.

Ribosomal RNA

Approximately 80% or more of total cellular RNA occurs in ribosomes in association with proteins, and have a sedimentation coefficient of 70S. In a suspension of ribosomes, if the Mg (II) ion concentration is brought down to 10^{-3} M, each 70S ribosome dissociates into two unequal particles of sedimentation coefficients 50S and 30S.

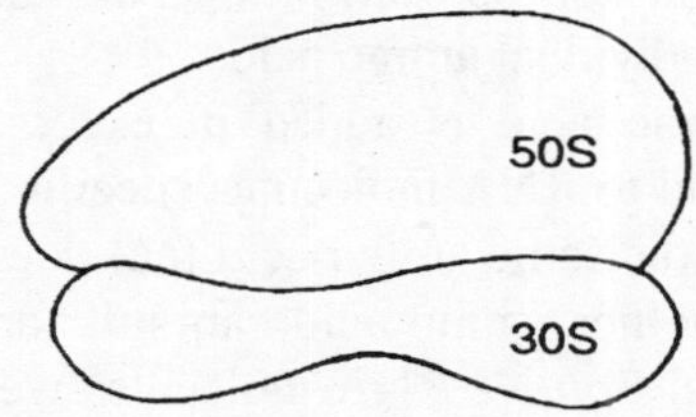

If RNAs are extracted separately from these particles the 50S particles yield 23S RNA (mol. wt. 1×10^6 Daltons) and 30S particles yield 16S RNAs (mol. wt 0.5×10^6 Daltons)

At 10^{-2} M Mg(II) concentration, 70S ribosome particles associate with mRNA. However, protein synthesis is usually associated with rapidly sedimenting trains of ribosomes (140 - 160S) held together by individual strings of mRNA molecules. Such trains of ribosomes formed with mRNA are also known as ***polyribosomes*** or ***polysomes***. Indeed, electron microscopy does show arrays of ribosomes connected with an approximately 10 Å diameter string-like molecule. Both subunits of the ribosome attach to the 5' end of the mRNA molecule to form intact ribosomes. These intact ribosomes slide towards the 3' end translating the bases on mRNA into the sequence of aminoacids in the newly formed (*nascent*) *polypeptide*. Sequence of three bases in mRNA code for each amino acid in the nascent polypeptide. The synthesis of nascent polypeptide is completed when a chain terminating codon on mRNA such as (*UAG* called Amber; *UAA* called ochre; or *UGA* known as Opal) is encountered by the ribosome. *At this point the ribosome detaches from mRNA by falling apart into two subunits.* The specificity of forming a particular polypeptide or protein lies in mRNA and not in ribosomes. According to Hurwitz and Furth, ***an mRNA molecule could 'hire' any one from the surrounding pool of ribosomes***. Initiation of the synthesis of the second polypeptide molecule could begin even before the first polypeptide is complete. As soon as 5' end of mRNA is free, it could be occupied by any other ribosome from the pool around. In this way, several ribosomes could be engaged by one mRNA molecule at a time, in synthesizing that many polypeptides.

Amino acid – transfer RNA

Hoagland and co-workers disrupted rat liver cells and the lysate was subjected to high-speed centrifugation to sediment ribosomes. The supernatant was found to contain a set of RNA molecules. These molecules were distinguished as ***'soluble'*** RNA and were capable of bonding selectively to individual amino acids.

If a single amino acid is added in excess to soluble RNAs preparation, it could bind to RNA molecules specific to that amino acid. Subsequent addition of the same amino acid (aa) does not form RNA.aa complex. However, another amino acid can still form complexes with RNA specific to it. Such *soluble* RNA molecules were re-designated as ***amino acid-transfer RNA*** or simply ***transfer RNA*** abbreviated as tRNA.

The tRNA molecules have a sedimentation coefficient close to 4 – 5 S. They are 70 – 80 nucleotides long with molecular weights in the range of 25,000 – 30,000 Daltons. Soon after, *Crick proposed that, amino acids could recognize with the help of an adapter molecule, their own corresponding sequence of bases* ***(codons)*** *on mRNA. This adapter could be an oligonucleotide, having a sequence of bases complementary to the coding sequence for each amino acid.*

Nucleotide sequences of many tRNA molecules have been determined. Some common features emerge. The acceptor 3'-end of all tRNA molecules e.g. yeast tRNA specific for alanine, serine, and tyrosine have identical trinucleotide sequence C.C.A or to be precise pC.pC.pA. While, the 5'-end of tRNA has a G or guanylic acid. In addition, the tRNA molecules have a few unusual bases, such as dihydrouridylic acid, inosinic acid, and some methylated bases. A few regions of the molecule fold back on themselves giving rise to some double stranded arms and some single stranded loops. Until recently the cloverleaf type of structure for tRNA was in vogue. It has three major loops and a minor loop (Fig. 14.2). *The 3 bases in the* ***anticodon loop*** *are able to specifically recognize three consecutive bases (a* ***codon****) in mRNA*. The pairing of bases of codon (mRNA) and anticodon (in tRNA) is ,antiparallel. as in the 2 strands of a DNA molecule.

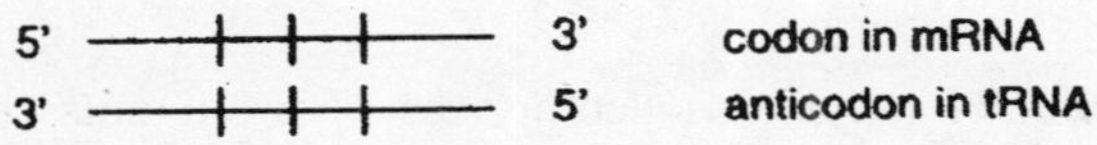

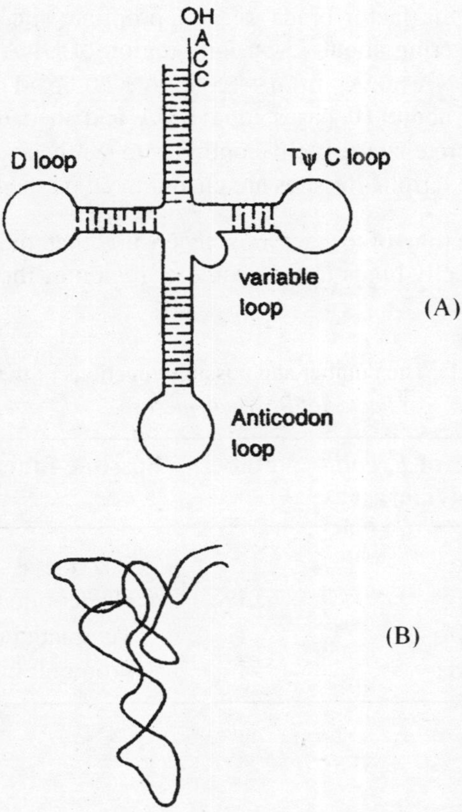

Fig.14. 2 . (A). Clover leaf model of tRNA molecule. (B) L-shaped molecular model of RNA.

RNA polymerases, accessory factors and the transcription of DNA

The first step in gene expression is the transcription of DNA to form RNA. Transcription is undertaken by *RNA polymerase*. Accessory factors like sigma (σ) factor in bacteria, are needed for the correct initiation of transcription. In *E. coli* and a few other prokaryotes, a single RNA polymerase is capable of transcribing all types of RNA in the cell

Bacterial RNA polymerase and the sigma (σ) factor

The *bacterial RNA polymerase* comprises of 5 subunits $\alpha_2\beta\beta'\sigma$. The $\alpha_2\beta\beta'$ form the enzyme core and are less variable. However, the ***σ factor*** varies widely amongst different species. Initially, RNA polymerase together with sigma factor binds to an appropriate site called *promoter* on the DNA, covering about 75 bp long region of DNA. The promoter binding site on DNA ranges from – 55 bp to + 20 bp. The $\alpha_2\beta\beta'\sigma$ (holo-enzyme), makes about 10 bases long RNA and then the sigma factor detaches. The core enzyme $\alpha_2\beta\beta'$ continues to synthesize RNA molecule until one or more terminator sites are encountered on the DNA.

The function of σ factor is to ensure that the bacterial RNA polymerase correctly binds to the promoter region of the DNA and at no other region.

Table 14.1. The number and possible functions of the subunits of *bacterial RNA polymerase.*

Subunits of *E. coli* RNA polymerase	Number	Possible function
α	2	Enzyme assembly
β	1	Nucleotide binding
β'	1	Template binding
σ	1	Promoter binding

Terminators

Two types of terminators have been characterized in *E. coli*.

Intrinsic terminators

The core enzyme polymerase can terminate *in vitro* RNA synthesis in the absence of any other factor. Intrinsic terminators have 2 structural characteristics.

(a) A hairpin in the secondary structure of RNA formed by inverted repeat sequences, which are usually G•C rich.
(b) A stretch of 6U bases at the end of synthesized RNA molecule.

Rho-factor dependent terminators

Addition of rho-factor during *in vitro* synthesis of RNA is required for the termination of RNA synthesis. Rho (ρ), is an essential protein in *E. coli*, though rho-dependent terminators are only a few in this organism. Most of the rho-dependent terminators are also found in the phage genomes. Sequences recognized by rho-factor have been identified, which are rich in C and poor in G.

Rho-factor protein has a molecular wt. of 46,000 Daltons and is probably active in a heaxameric form. In a *bacterial cell* as soon as RNA polymerase (holoenzyme) makes nascent RNA, the rho-factor and ribosomes compete with each other to climb over RNA molecule. Rho and ribosomes move along newly synthesized RNA molecule. However, the rho-factor trailing behind a ribosome cannot jump over the ribosome associated with RNA and get ahead of it. In the meanwhile RNA polymerase continues to synthesize RNA. It pauses on reaching a terminator site on the DNA. The ribosome gliding along RNA on reaching the terminator site, falls apart into 50S and 30S subunits, thus clearing the way for rho-factor to eventually reach terminator site. Rho-factor on reaching terminator site swelling, releases RNA polymerase, the synthesized RNA molecule and itself.

If termination of RNA synthesis is prevented at a termination site, the polymerase continues to read through the following genes on the DNA, till it meets another terminator.

Eukaryotic RNA polymerases

In eukaryotes, 3 types of RNA polymerases exist in the cell. The ***RNA polymerase I*** present in the nucleolus makes ribosomal RNA (rRNA). The ***RNA polymerases II*** and ***III*** are present in the nucleoplasm and synthesize pre-messenger RNA (or heterogeneous hnRNA, the precursor of mRNA), and tRNA respectively.

Table 14.2. Some inhibitors of transcription and the target RNA polymerase enzymes

Inhibitor	Target enzyme	Mode of action
Rifamycins	Bacterial holoenzyme	Binds to β subunit prevents initiation
Streptolydigin	Bacterial core enzyme	Binds to β subunit prevents initiation
Actinomycin D	Eukaryotic polymerase I	Binds to DNA Prevents elongation of RNA
α-Amanitin	Eukaryotic polymerase II	Binds to RNA polymerase II

Promoters of eukaryotic RNA polymerases

Each **promoter** contains a specific set of sequences on the DNA. These sequences are recognized by appropriate accessory factors and the RNA polymerases.

The promoters for RNA polymerase I and II are usually located upstream of the start point. Some promoters of RNA polymerase III are situated down stream of start point. In principle a ***generic promoter*** can be expressed in any cell and it is not influenced by sequences expressed under tissue specific control.

TATA box

Most promoters have a sequence known as TATA box. It is situated about 25 bp upstream of start point of RNA synthesis. It consists of 8 bp consensus sequence of A•T base pairs and is flanked by G•C rich region. TATA box sequences at –25 are identical with –10 sequences found in bacterial promoter. A TATA binding protein helps recognition of TATA box. Several other proteins are also involved in the interaction.

An ***enhancer*** can change the activity of a promoter by increasing initiation at the promoter. An enhancer is located away from promoter either up stream or down stream. It is likely enhancer and promoter come close to each other by coiling and folding of DNA.

1. Enhancer can change the structure of trmplate by modifying the supercoiling.
2. Enhancer can facilitate the location of template e.g. by attaching it to nuclear matrix.
3. Enhancer can create an 'entry site' for DNA polymerase or accessory proteins to attach with DNA.

Interaction between ribonucleic acids and the protein synthesis

The various major steps in protein synthesis are as follows:

1. A group of enzymes known as amino-acyl tRNA synthetases, each being specific for one of the 20 amino acids, activates the amino acid by reacting its carboxyl group with ATP to produce aminoacyl adenylate and pyrophosphate.
2. The activated amino acid remains anchored to aminoacyl tRNA synthetase.
3. The aminoacyl tRNA synthetase attaches the carboxyl group of anchored amino acid to the appropriate tRNA molecule. The carboxyl group of amino acid is transferred to the 3' terminal adenylic residue A of the sequence C-C-A in tRNA. Within the adenylic residue 2' or 3' OH group of ribose ring attach with the CO group of amino acid.
4. Aminoacyl-tRNA complex is formed; simultaneously AMP and the enzyme tRNA synthetase are released.
5. Aminoacyl-tRNA complex attaches to 50 S subunit of the ribosome.
6. The 30 S subunit of ribosome gets attached to mRNA.
7. The 50 and 30 S subunits join together to form 70 S ribosomes.
8. The choice of a particular amino acid for incorporation in the polypeptide chain must be dependant upon the specific interaction between codon on mRNA and anticodon on the tRNA, so that complementary bases can hydrogen bond. This interaction does not depend on the attached amino acid, e.g. a tRNA charged with cystein can be chemically altered to become alanine charged tRNA. Such chemically altered alanine charged tRNA can be used *in vitro* protein synthesizing system. Since the anticodon is still for cystein, this altered tRNA incorporates alanine, where cystein should have been incorporated.

9. Ribosomes contain two slots, where tRNA molecule charged with amino acid aa_1 fit in, so that the anticodon of correctly matched tRNA aligned and hydrogen bonded with the codon on mRNA
10. According to the next codon (sequence of 3 bases) on mRNA, the second slot on ribosome is occupied by tRNA charged with another aminoacid aa_2.
    The attachment of aminoacyl tRNA to ribosome requires (a) prior attachment of ribosome to mRNA, (b) activity of the enzyme transferase and (iii) GTP
    (guanosine triphosphate) as a source of energy.
11. The amino acid is joined to tRNA by its carboxyl group, so that amino group is free. In vitro protein synthesis shows that the peptide bond is formed between carboxyl group of aminoacyl $tRNA_1$ and amino group of aminoacyl $tRNA_2$. The di-peptide so formed is attached to the $tRNA_2$ in the second slot of the ribosome. For the synthesis of protein to proceed further, $tRNA_2$ attached with dipeptide moves to slot 1 of the ribosome, simultaneously displacing $tRNA_1$, from slot 1. At the same time the ribosome moves three bases forward on mRNA in 5'→ 3' direction, so that the third codon is in juxtaposition with second slot of ribosome.
12. Depending upon the sequence of bases in the third codon, appropriate tRNA loaded with aa_3 comes in the second slot. Peptide bond is formed between NH2 group of aa_3 with CO group of aa2. The polypeptide chain grows by the sequential attachment of different aminoacyl tRNA molecules to second slot of ribosome. *The second slot of ribosome is also known as **aminoacyl-tRNA slot**.*
13. In this manner peptides bonds keep forming until the end of mRNA is reached or a chain terminating codon (Amber, Ochre or Opal) is encountered by ribosome on mRNA. In the absence of a chain terminating codon on mRNA as in the case of synthetic messenger poly U (UUUU……), the synthesized polypeptide remains attached to the polysome.

In many bacteria including *E. coli,* the polypeptide chain initiation codon on mRNA is AUG, which normally codes the incorporation of methionine. However, these cells have two types of tRNA molecules for methionine – $tRNA_F$ carrying formyl methionine (HCO-NH) and $tRNA_M$ carrying methionine, *in vitro* as well as *in vivo* formyl methionine is the first aa_1 to be incorporated in the polypeptide

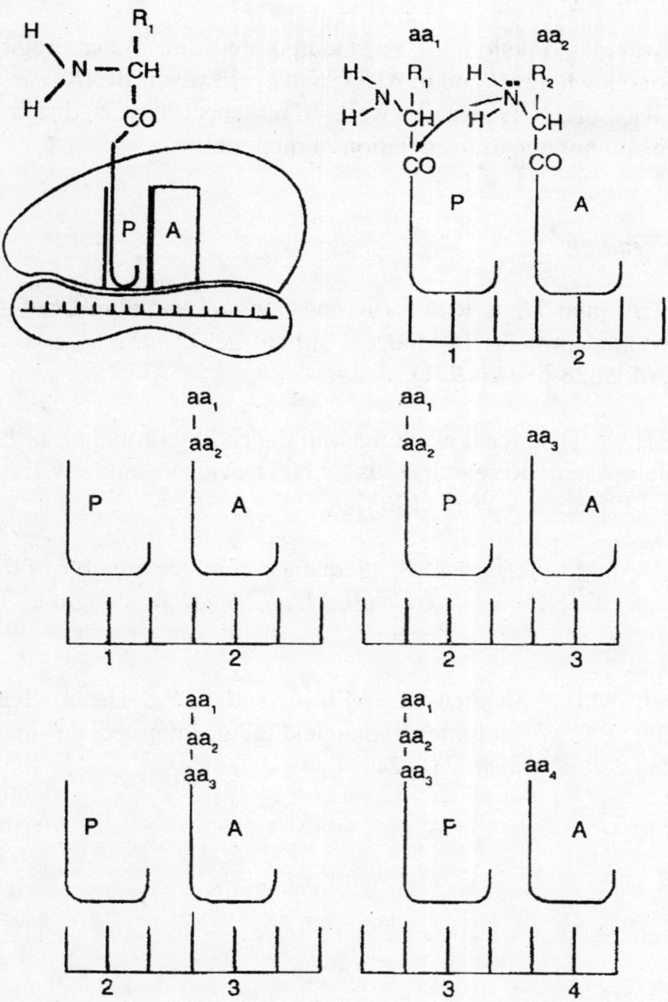

Fig.14.3. The translation of mRNA for the synthesis of polypeptides.

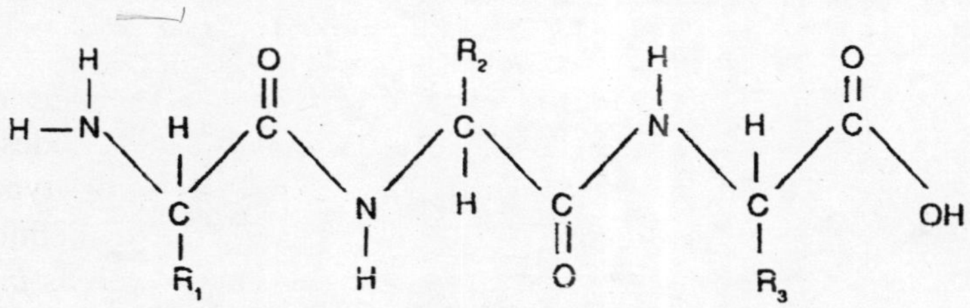

Fig.14.4. A schematic diagram of a polypeptide.

chain, whereas metionine is incorporated in other regions of polypeptide., wherever codon AUG exists. However, $tRNA_F$ can bind to AUG; GUG or UUG equally well. This specificity is due to tRNA molecule and not due to formylation of methionine.

Further reading

Bickle, T.A., and Traut, R.R. Differences in size and number of 80S and 70S ribosomal proteins by dodecyl sulfate gel electrophoresis. *J. Biol. Chem. 246*: 6828-6834 (1971).

Crick, F.H.C. The recent excitement in the coding problem. *In* Progress in Nucleic Acid Research (eds. J.N. Davidson and W.E. Cohn), Academic Press, New York (1963).

Hall, B.D., and Spiegelman, S. Sequence complementarity of T_2-DNA and T_2-specific RNA. *Proc. Natl. Acad. Sci.*, Washington, *47*: 137 (1961).

Hoagland, M.B., Stephenson, M.L., Scott, J.F., Hecht, R.J., and Zamecnik, P.C. A soluble ribonucleic acid intermediate in protein synthesis. *J. Biol. Chem. 231*: 241
(1958).

CHAPTER 15

Maturing and Splicing of RNA

With the exception of mRNAs in bacteria, which are put to use (translated) by the cell usually as soon as they are transcribed from DNA, most other ribonucleic acids (RNAs) need some processing before the RNA molecules could become functional. The RNA processing need to be highly specific to produce molecules with precise 5' and 3' ends. This processing is usually done by two sets of enzymes *RNA–endonucleases* and *RNA–exonucleases*.

RNA endonuclease cuts an individual covalent bond within the polyribonucleotide and usually separates functional polyribonucleotide from the flanking region. On the other hand, RNA exonuclease digests polyribonucleotide from one end removing one ribonucleotide at a time. The enzyme could attack polyribonucleotides randomly, removing one ribonucleotide each from different molecules or bind to one molecule and continue removing several ribonucleotides until functional RNA is created.

Most of the ribonucleases can be characterized by two parameters.

1. Biochemical properties of enzyme.
2. Obtaining a mutant when enzyme has altered properties. This can also show that an enzyme possesses two different activities in the same molecule.

   On these two criteria *E. coli* is estimated to have about 10 ribonucleases.

Polycistronic mRNAs of bacteriophages

The early genes of bacteriophages T3 and T7 are transcribed as polycistronic messages, which are cleaved by RNAse III to make mRNAs corresponding to individual genes. RNAse III acts at the bubble like structure formed by unpaired nucleotides in the duplex hairpin formed by polycistronic mRNA. RNAse III cleaves this polycistronic message into 5 mRNAs and a leader sequence at the 5'end.

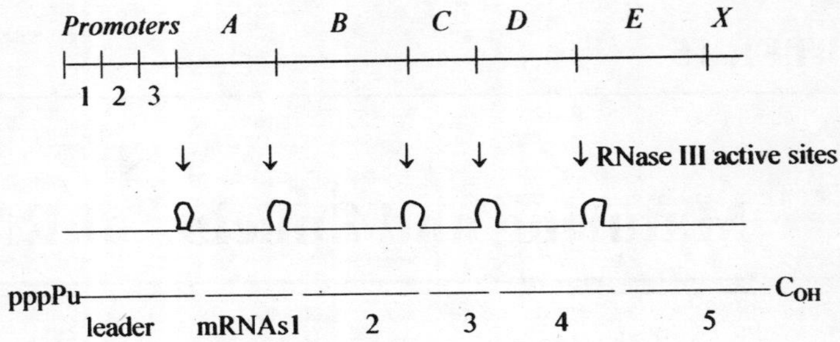

Heterogeneous nuclear RNA (hn RNA)

Non-ribosomal, non-tRNA nuclear RNA was analysed in sucrose gradient after radioactive labelling it with RNA precursors. It was found to contain very large molecules of heterogeneous size, called ***heterogenous nuclear RNA*** or *hn RNA*. The average size was 10 times the length of mRNA in cytoplasm and has a half-life around 3 minutes. Up to 200 nucleotide long tail of A-A residues was found at the 3' end of *hnRNA*. Subsequently ***5'caps*** on hnRNA were discovered. In a *cap*, GTP reacts with the triphosphate at the 5' terminus to make a 5'-5' bond by the addition of a guanine nucleotide, giving the structure ***3'-G-5'ppp5'-N-3'p-----***. This linkage is different from 3'-5' phosphodiester bond usually found in DNA and RNA molecules. *The number of caps and tails represent the number of functional mRNAs present in a hnRNA.*

The evidence that the well-separated regions on eucaryotic DNA can code contiguous regions of mRNA molecule came from the study of adenovirus mRNA produced late after infection in human cells. In addition the following facts emerged from similar studies:

1. The mRNA molecule has a ***3'-G-5'ppp5'-N-3'p*** cap structure at the 5' end.
2 Most mRNAs have identical 11nucleotide long region at 5' end. This region is not resistant to ribonuclease action in a RNA-DNA hybrid, showing that this region does not have complementary bases on DNA.
3 Many different mRNAs have common leader sequences of ~ 200 nucleotides at their 5' ends. These sequences are coded by 3 separate regions on DNA.

Similar results were obtained from the investigations with chicken ovalbumin genes. The experiments showed that 8 widely separated regions on the genomic DNA specify the mRNa of ovalbumin.

DNA-RNA hybridization and R-looping experiments

If an RNA and complementary DNA duplex are incubated, so as to form RNA-DNA hybrids, then the DNA strand complementary to RNA is displaced by RNA and it forms a loop. Such loops are called ***displacement R loops*** and can be seen by electron microscope. Their position on DNA can also be mapped with respect to restriction enzymes map of DNA (*cf.* **Chapter 21**).

Exons and introns in DNA

Segments of DNA that specifically code for mRNA and expressed are called ***exons***. An *exon* includes the untranslated leader and tail-end sequences, as well as the sequences prescribing polypeptide. The poly A tail of mRNa is not coded by any part of the genome, rather added as a post-transcription event. Regions of the genome not represented in the functional mRNA are known as ***intervening sequences*** or ***introns***.

Although the list of interrupted or split genes with intron-exon-intron-exon- structure is growing regularly, yet many genes, especially protein coding genes in lower organisms, and some genes in eucaryotes are contiguous and not interrupted. A few examples are:

1. Interferon proteins produced in vertebrates on viral infection are usually coded by un-split genes.
2. Genes for making histone proteins used for packaging eucaryotic DNA in nucleosomes are mostly contiguous.
3. Many viruses infecting mammals do not have introns.

The genes making a protein in a lower organism often do not have introns, whereas the same protein made in higher organisms is prescribed by genes having introns. Alcohol dehydrogenase gene in yeast is continuous, while the same gene in *Drosophila* has introns. In yeast cytochrome c gene has no introns, while rat and human cytochrome c genes are split. *It became clear that both in protein and RNA coding genes, the removal of introns occurs by RNA splicing.*

In bacteria the rRNA and tRNA are fairly stable and constitute 98% of total RNA of the cell. ***However, only 1% of DNA duplex is devoted for their transcription.*** Most of the DNA is assigned to make varieties of mRNA molecules, which have a short half-life of approximately 3 minutes.

Ribosomal RNAs

In *E. coli* the ribosomal RNAs of different sedimentation values ***16S***; ***23S*** and ***5S*** are transcribed together as a single polyribonucleotide. When this transcript is treated with ribonuclease III *in vitro*, produces molecules which have slightly extra ends than 16S, 23S and are called their precursors ***p16*** and ***p23*** respectively. It is not known, how these extra ends are specifically removed by the cell to form functional ribosomal RNA molecules.

Maturation of eucaryotic rRNA

The maturation process of rRNA in mammals could be followed more precisely as the intermediates form at a slower rate and can be isolated from different types of mammalian cells e.g. HeLa cells and L-mouse cells. As inferred from the intermediate RNA molecules, there are slightly varying pathways for maturation in different mammalian systems. Mature *18S*; *28S*; and *5.8S* rRNA are released from *45S* precursor by cleavages in the 3 spacer sequences *sp1 – sp3*. It is known that *45S* rRNA associates with protein soon after its synthesis. Therefore the processing steps involve ribonucleoprotein and not free RNA. Many steps are not known in detail. More than100 methyl groups are added to ribose moieties of *45S* rRNA, soon after transcription. A few are added in the cytoplasm. Methyl groups are conserved during the processing

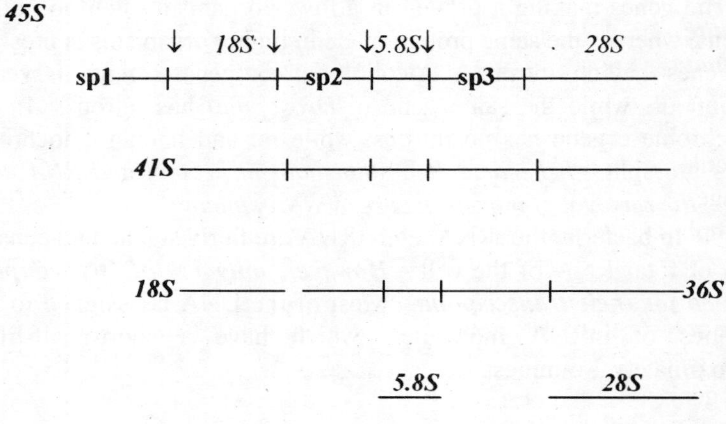

and possibly used for identifying mature RNA in primary transcript. There are about 75 methyl groups on *28S* and >40 methyl groups on *18S* mature rRNA.

Maturation of tRNA

The tRNA molecules are transcribed with additional intermediate and flanking sequences. From one to seven tRNAs specific for different amino acids are transcribed as a chain called *pre-tRNA*. These pre-tRNA molecules have variable stretches of extra sequences at 5' and 3' ends. These extra sequences are removed by an enzyme ***ribonuclease P*** or (*RNase P*).

Ribonuclease P

RNase P is an endonuclease cutting off 5'- flanking sequences with 3'OH end, leaving 5'-P group on tRNA. RNase P does not seem to recognize any specific sequence for cleaving the pre-tRNA, rather it is believed to recognize or sense the whole three dimensional structure of tRNA molecule and then make the appropriate cut. Unlike most other enzymes, which are proteins, ***RNase P*** *is a mixture of protein and RNA*. It contains 377 bases long RNA and a polypeptide of 20,000 daltons, held together as a ***non-covalent moiety***.

Interestingly, the RNA portion of RNase P alone is capable of cutting pre-tRNA molecule efficiently and precisely even *in vitro* in the presence of Mg^{++} ions or spermidine. ***The example of RNase P enzyme is quite unique in showing that RNA molecule too could have enzymatic activity like proteins.***

RNase D is another enzyme involved in trimming of *pre-tRNA* molecules. It is an exonuclease and releases 5'- monophosphates. It manages to cleave pre-tRNA until it reaches CCA end. How it accomplishes this feat is not clear.

Some tRNA molecules are transcribed together as pre-tRNA. While some tRNA are transcribed along with rRNA-transcripts, as these tRNA genes are embedded in several dispersed stretches of ribosomal RNA genes.

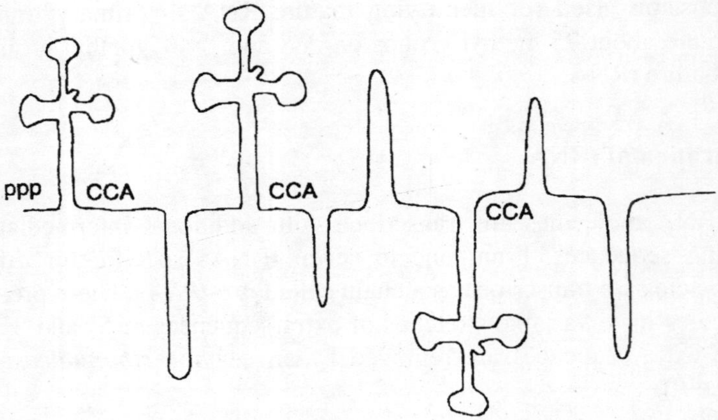

Fig.15.1. One to seven tRNA molecules specific for different amino acids are synthesized as a continuous long polynucleotide called pre-tRNA. Pre-tRNA has many hairpin-like loops, in addition to tRNA molecules. Enzymes like RNase P and RNase D cleave the pre-RNA to generate functional tRNA molecules.

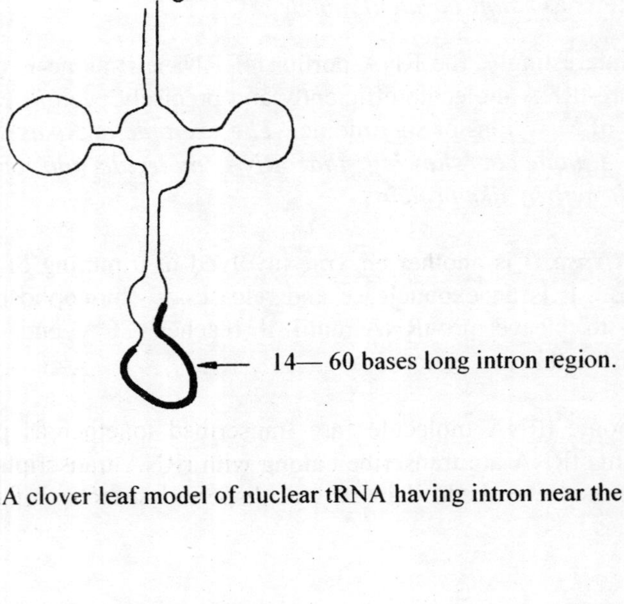

Fig. 15.2. A clover leaf model of nuclear tRNA having intron near the anticodon loop.

Introns in (nuclear) tRNA genes

The transfer RNA genes in eucaryotic cells have 14-60 bp long introns. They are located adjacent to 1st or 2nd nucleotide 3' to the anticodon.

Introns in mitochondria and splicing of RNA by proteins

In mammalian cells the mitochondrial DNA does not have introns, whereas in lower eucaryotes DNA has introns present. Splicing of mitochondrial transcripts is done in different ways:

1. By nuclear encoded proteins.
2. Through polypeptide coded by the same intron sequence or another intron.
3. By sequences within introns.

The role of proteins coded by introns is quite unique for the splicing in mitochondria. They modify their own mRNA.

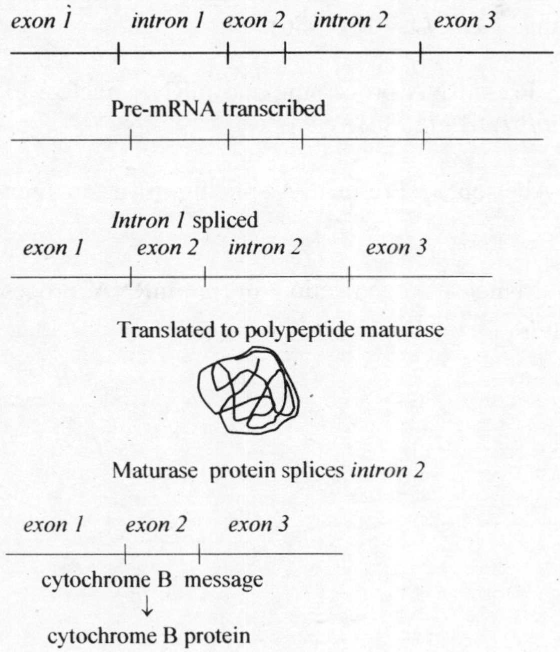

Fig.15.3. Splicing of mRNA in mitochondria by self transcribed protein.

The presence of introns in eucaryotic genes along with the ability to excise them at RNA level could be used with great advantage by these organisms.

1. As the distance between two genes increases because of intervening introns, so does the recombination frequency between the genes.
2. Lower probability that the crossover will occur in exon region so that any unequal crossover could alter the protein subsequently formed.
3. If the unequal crossover occurs in the intron region the chances are the errors in crossover will not be passed on to the protein structure. The error would be removed during the splicing of mRNA.
4. Introns permit a new protein to be tested by the organism, while the expression of original protein is retained.

Further reading

Cech, T.R. The generality of self-splicing RNA: relationship to nuclear mRNA splicing. *Cell*, *44*: 207 (1986).

Green, M.R. Pre-mRNA processing and mRNA nuclear export. *Curr. Opin. Cell Biol. 1*: 519 (1989).

Ruby, S.W., Abelson, J. Pre-mRNA splicing in yeast. *Trends Genet. 7*: 79 (1991).

Spector, D.L. Nuclear organization of pre-mRNA procesing. *Curr. Opin. Cell Biol. 5*: 442 (1993).

CHAPTER 16

Noncoding RNAs

During transcription many messenger RNAs of known functions are produced. In addition, a large number of ***transcripts of unknown functions*** (TUFs) are also produced which include:
(i) Alternative splice isoforms of many protein coding genes.
(ii) Frequent transcription of anti-sense RNAs and
(iii) Abundant non-coding RNAs (***ncRNAs***).

Noncoding RNAs

Over a period of 40 years several functional types of *ncRNAs* have been identified:

1. ribosomal (*rRNA*),
2. transfer (*tRNA*),
3. micro (*miRNA*),
4. small nucleolar (*snoRNA*),
5. small nuclear (*snRNA*),
6. *pi*-interacting (*piRNA*).
7. anti-sense (*asRNA*),
8. double stranded (*dsRNA*),
9. small interference (*siRNA)*,
10. interference (*RNAi*) and
11. small RNAs.

Besides rRNA and tRNA, which are two distinct functional classes, other ncRNAs have been assigned many different functions such as (i) transcriptional activation, (ii) gene silencing, (iii) imprinting, (iv) dosage compensation, (v) translational silencing, (vi) modulation of protein function and (vii) binding to regulatory metabolites as ribo-switches.

Noncoding microRNAs (miRNAs)

The *miRNAs* are one of the best-characterized classes of ncRNAs and were cloned in the nematode *C. elegans*. They comprise a family of approximately 22 nucleotide long regulatory RNAs, which are essential for different cellular processes.

The expression patterns of miRNAs determine:

a. cell fate and differentiation during development,
b. can control cellular proliferation,
c. can act as tumor suppressors,
d. supress initiation of protein synthesis,
e. promote mRNA degradation and turnover, as well
f. initiate transcriptional silence.

Hundreds of miRNAs are likely to be associated with the human genome and estimates are that 20-30% of human genes are regulated by miRNAs. However, the function of a majority of miRNAs is yet to be characterized.

Small nucleolar RNAs (snoRNAs)

The roles of snoRNAs are becoming evident in (a) the processing of rRNA, (b) post-transcriptional methylation and pseudouridylation of target rRNAs and snRNAs.

The *pi*-RNAs

They are 26-31 nucleotide long and are found to be associated with the *pi-proteins* in germ cell development.

Double stranded RNA (dsRNA) and RNAi

Double stranded RNA triggers the gene-silencing through RNAi (RNA interference). RNAi is operationally distinct from anti-sense RNA based inhibition of gene expression. RNAi is small RNA derived from longer *dsRNA precursors* that guide protein complexes to target genes or mRNAs to silence their expression or translation. In addition:

a. a few molecules of dsRNA can destroy larger amounts of corresponding mRNA.
b. RNAi may be transmitted across generations.
c. RNAi is present in almost all eukaryotes.

d. RNAi and DNA plus histone modification pathways are responsible for silencing of transposable elements in plants.
e. In mammals as in plants, RNAi has an early role in gene silencing which is later reinforced by DNA methylation. However, in *C. elegans* (nematode) transposable elements (TE) are highly active in somatic cells in spite of ample RNAi. Indications are that the germ line cells must have specific silencing factors needed for TE silencing.
f. Genetics of any organism whose gene sequence is known is feasible using RNAi.

Fire and Mello were awarded Nobel Prize in 2006 for the discovery of *RNAi*.

siRNA

This 25 nucleotide long RNA is involved in guiding DNA methylation in plants and animals, which includes *de novo* methylation of unmethylated DNA and maintenance methylation of hemi-methylated DNA. The RNA silencing proteins RDR2 and DCL3 are required for production of endogenous 24 nucleotide long si RNA.

The siRNA is bound to the chromosome *via* methylated histones. The enzyme Pol IVa has been implicated in the production of siRNA using dsRNA as a template. The siRNA directed DNA methylation and histone modifications have been reported in human cells.

small RNAs

Small RNAs are 21 nucleotide long and begin with base U. They originate from thousands of loci in many broad regions of chromosome IV of nematode. They guide modification of chromatin structure and formation of heterochromatin.

Meiotic silencing of unpaired DNA (MSUD)

In *Neurospora crassa* methylation of DNA is found in transposon elements and flanking repeats and depends on methyl-transferase H3K9, but does not depend on RNAi. Two RNA-silencing phenomena (i) *quelling* and (ii) *meiotic silencing of unpaired DNA (MSUD)* were identified.

Quelling is post-transcriptional gene silencing (PTGS) directed by siRNA that occurs during vegetative growth and prevents expression of transgenes occurring in more than one copy. Several quelling defective genes (~6-20) have been identified *in S. pombe, A. thaliana, C. elegans, Drosophila, H. Sapiens, Neurospora* and *Tetrahymena* all belonging to RNAi pathway.

In *Neurospora* two haploid nuclei of opposite mating type fuse and give a diploid nucleus, which soon undergoes meiosis followed by a mitotic division giving 8 linearly arranged *ascospores* in a sack called *ascus* (plural *asci*). ***MSUD detects and silences any un-paired gene during chromosome pairing as well as all homologous copies of that gene even if they are paired.*** *For MSUD it is critical that ' a region of un-paired gene is transcribed (or dares to get transcribed) during meiosis'* (Fig.16.1). Neither DNA methylation nor chromatin modifications are present during MSUD.

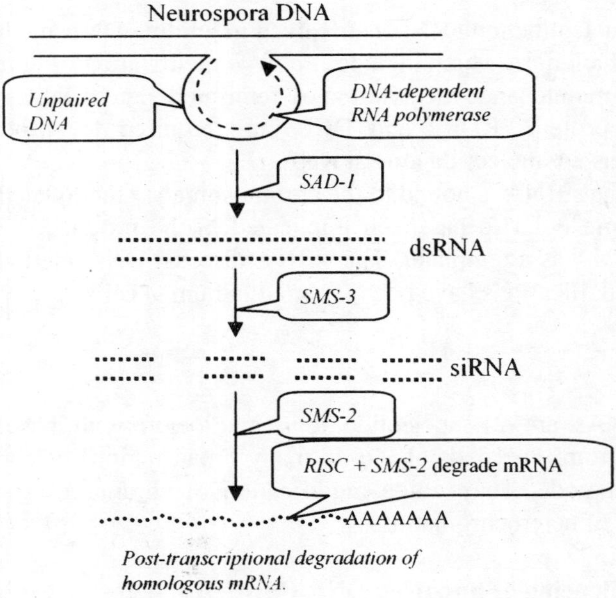

Fig.16.1. Transcriptional regulation by degradation of homologous mRNA

In this pathway DNA is transcribed by DNA-dependent RNA polymerase (DdRP) to generate a transcript that is processed into dsRNA by RNA dependent RNA polymerase (RdRP). Dicing by enzyme SMS-3 produced siRNAs from dsRNA. The siRNA is incorporated into RISC complex together with SMS-2. The RISC complex guided by siRNA degrades homologous mRNA. (Fig. 16.1).

In *C. elegans* during meiosis un-synapsed (un-paired) chromosomal regions are silenced by a mechanism parallel to MSUD. Upto production of dsRNA by germline specific RdRP, it is similar to *Neurospora*. It is not known further, if siRNA is produced from dsRNA or whether the long dsRNA transcripts themselves guide methylation of unpaired transcripts through methyl transferase H3K9 (Fig. 16.2)

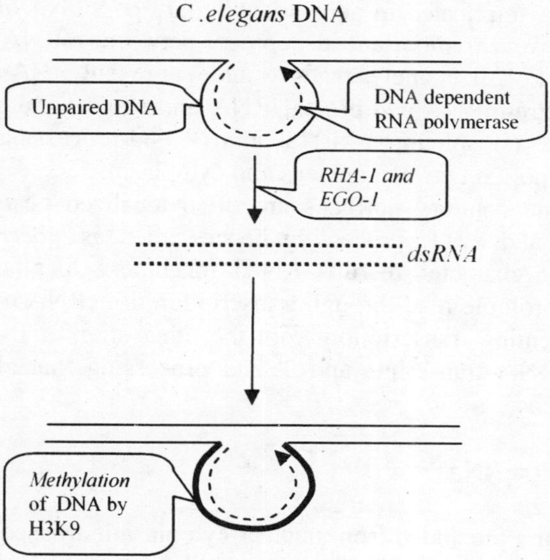

Fig.16.2. **Transcriptional regulation by methylation of DNA silences the genes.**

Elimination of DNA in Protozoa

As in all ciliates, the unicellular *Tetrahymena thermophila* contains two distinct nuclei. One nucleus is germline diploid micronucleus (Mic) and a somatic polyploid macronucleus (Mac). All transcription during vegetative growth occurs in Mac. Mic is transcriptionally inactive until conjugation. Both nuclei develop from a zygotic nucleus formed byn fusion of two haploid micronuclei during conjugation. A new Mac differentiates by extensive deletion of Mic-specific DNA sequences, called internally eliminated sequences (IESs), followed by flanking Mac-destined sequences. Approximately 6,000 IESs are removed, which is equivalent to ~15% of *T. thermophila* Mic genome.

Non-genic, heterogenous, bi-directional transcription of Mic genome occurs during the early stage of conjugation. Injection of dsRNAs to Mac sequences that are retained causes elimination of these sequences during conjugation. Conjugation specific small 26-31 nucleotide long RNAs known as scanRNAs (scnRNAs) appear prior to DNA elimination by dicing of dsRNA.

ncRNA mediated gene silencing

Most nc RNA implicated in gene silencing are possibly synthesized by Pol II. However important difference between mRNA and other products of Pol II namely mRNA and some snURNA is in their processing. Pre-mRNA and pre-snURNA undergo several co-ordinated modifications: (i) splicing , (ii) 5' and 3' end-processings, and (iii) actively transported between nucleus and cytoplasm.

On the contrary ncRNAs are often localized near the site of transcription and evade processing hence called as *'aberrant'* RNAs. This aberrant character recruits RNAi machinery for their disposal. RNAi may promote read-through transcription of ncRNA on one strand thereby preventing transcription from the other strand. By preventing splicing of RNA transcripts and 3' end processing that also prevents transcript release.

Biogenesis of ncRNA

As ncRNAs are precluded from nuclear-cytoplasmic transport this limits their scope of action. miRNAs are exported from nucleus a requirement for maturation. Similarly siRNA could be transported out of nucleus and act in *trans* (cytoplasmic stage of siRNA in *Tetrahymena*).

Co-transcription with ncRNA may cause gene silencing

The gene silencing caused by ncRNA can bring nearby genes under their influence. Transposable elements (TE) silence neighbouring genes. This relates with cotranscription from TE promoters. Also imprinted loci are often associated with ncRNA genes that overlap some some of the imprinted genes. Co-transcription may be a mechanism for spreading heterochromatin character.

It is suspected that ***ncRNAs*** probably play major role in more cellular processes that the protein coding mRNAs as well tRNAs and rRNAs. Involvement of ncRNAs has been shown in diseases such as autism, schizophrenia, lung and prostate cancers. For bioactivity the ncRNAs probably rely on their secondary structure and are more tolerant for mismatch. Hence ncRNAs are likely to have greater plasticity than mRNAs. *Usually many miRNAs need to be deleted to get a phenotype.*

It appears that > 90% of non-repeat portions of human genome is transcribed. Analysis of transposable elements (Transposable Elements are described in Chapter 22) occurring within *functional transcriptional units (FTUs)* shows that > 50% of the genome comprises of FTUs and one-third of these are ncRNAs. ***Hence approximately 15% of the human genome may be assigned for ncRNAs.*** The architecture of transcribed regions of the genome seems to be quite complex. *Most of the* ***transcriptomes*** *have overlapping transcriptions, where the same genomic sequences give rise to portions of separately regulated transcripts. This has made the boundaries and the concept of* ***gene*** *less defined than earlier notions.*

It is expected that the existence of such a transcriptional diversity of *ncRNAs* on one hand and the large number of protein coding genes occurring in different species such as *Drosophila* (~14,000), nematode (~21,000) and human (~23,300) would result in vast phenotypic distinctions in these as well as other species.

Further reading

Fire, A., Xu, S., Montgomery, M.K., Kostas, S.A., Driver, S.E., and Mello, C.C. The mechanisms underlying RNA interference. *Nature, 391*: 806-811 (1998).

Storz, Gisela, Altuvia, S., and Wasserman, K.M. An abundance of RNA regulators. *Annu. Rev. Biochem. 74*: 199-217 (2005).

Willingham, T.A. and Gingeras, T.R. TUF Love for 'Junk' DNA. *Cell, 125*: 1215-1220 (2006).

Zamore, P.D. RNA interference: Big applause for silencing in Stockholm. *Cell, 127*: 1083-1086 (2006).

Zaratiegni, M., Irvine, D.V., and Martienssen, R.A. Noncoding RNAs and gene silencing. *Cell, 128*: 763-776 (2007).

CHAPTER 17

Chromosome Structure and the Organization of DNA

The genomes of most living organisms consist of nucleic acids, usually DNA and rarely RNA (such as in tobacco mosaic virus and retroviruses). Exception to these are infectious protein-particles '*Prions*' (pronounced preeons), which are devoid of nucleic acid genome.

Bacteriophage-genome

From the point of view of the chemical constitution of various genomes, perhaps the bacteriophage genomes are the simplest. The bacteriophage genome mostly constitutes DNA, with traces of basic-proteins such as polyamines, spermidine, and putrescine, and an acid insoluble protein containing mainly aspartic acid, glutamic acid and lysine. These internal proteins are released along with the enormously long thread-like DNA from the phage tail, when bacteriophages are given osmotic shock (a phage suspension in 2M salt solution, dropped gently on distilled water surface). In the Hershey and Chase experiment the phages whose protein was radioactively labeled with S^{35}, injected their DNA into bacteria along with 1– 3% of proteins. These internal proteins probably neutralize the acidity of DNA and help in its compact packaging inside the phage head.

1. The genetic crosses show the existence of a single linkage group, meaning a single chromosome in the phage.
2. In T2 phage the DNA when extracted gently by phenol and subjected to ultracentrifugation gave a molecular weight 1.3×10^8 Daltons. Assuming an average molecular weight of each base as 357 Daltons and base pair are separated by 3.4 Å, the length of extended DNA molecule will be around 58 μm.
3. Cairns did autoradiography of T2 DNA labeled with tritiated (H^3), thymine. This DNA was gently extracted with phenol with minimal

shear and in the presence of an excess unlabelled DNA as a protection. The DNA solution was dialysed in a dialysis bag. The DNA sticking to dialysis bag was autoradiographed by placing in contact with photographic emulsion. The average length of extended DNA molecules was found to be 52 μm.

4. The DNA released by osmotic shock given to T2 phage, spreads like a rosette in a protein monolayer. Kleinschmidt examined this DNA in an electron microscope. The DNA appears as a single thread approximately 50 μm long with 2 free ends. A 50 μm long thread-like DNA needs to be folded about 500 times to stack into a 0.1 μm long hexagonal head of T2 phage or it could be wrapped around a few thousand times like ball of wool-thread.

Birefringence study of intact phage suggests that DNA is mostly arranged in bundles parallel to the long axis of the head or tail. It is likely that the organized cross-linking of DNA inside the head is helped by 'internal' proteins.

Genetic constitution of some prominent types of viruses

T2 or T4	Double stranded DNA Circularly permuted, Terminal redundancy. Longer than full genome.	Such as : 0123456789012 or 4567890123456.
T3	Double stranded DNA.	Non-permuted, identical terminally, redundant sequences, such as: 01234567890123 and 01234567890123.
T5	Double stranded DNA.	DNA with 4 gaps: three on one strand and one on the other.
λ	Linear double stranded DNA, with single stranded complementary ends. Not circularly permuted, but vegetative prophage stages circular permutations of each other.	
øX174	Single stranded DNA.	
RNA viruses.		
Retroviruses		

The terminal redundancy of base-sequences in phage T2 is elegantly demonstrated by partial digestion of 3'-hydroxyl ends of double stranded DNA by the enzyme exonuclease III. The enzyme treatment exposes single strands at the two ends having complementary redundant base sequences. On annealing, these complementary single stranded ends produce circular molecules. Depending upon the extent of digestion of 3'-OH ends of single strands of DNA duplex, essentially 3 types of circles could form.

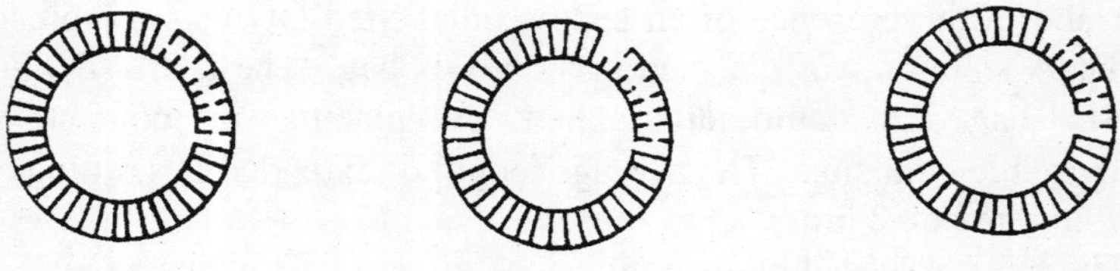

No gap One gap Two gaps

or else two or more molecules of DNA duplexes with sticky single stranded strands can form concatenate (linked together) molecules.

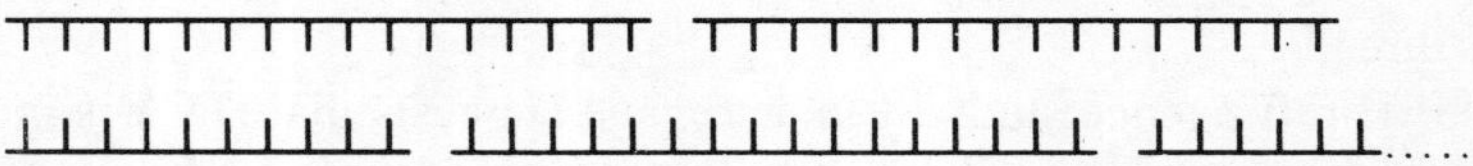

Biological assay for fragments of λ DNA molecules

The idea of *'helper phage'* put to use by Kaiser and Hogness evolved into a method for biological assay of fragments or pieces of λ DNA molecules. Initially the sensitive *E. coli* bacteria are infected with defective, mutant λ particles, which on their own cannot produce plaques. Then the wild type λ DNA or fragments of λ DNA to be assayed for biological activity are added to the same culture. The λ DNA alone is not infective and needs 'helper phage' to penetrate the bacterial cell. If a particular piece of DNA carries the normal gene for which the *'helper phage'* is defective, they can complement each other and produce plaques.

Replication of the phage DNA

To investigate, whether the phage DNA replicates in a semi-conservative manner like bacteria or in some other way, experiments similar to those of Meselson and Stahl were conducted. The DNA of phage T4 was made heavy by growing phages in bacteria grown in N^{15} (*non*-radioactive heavy isotope of nitrogen) containing medium. The N^{15} labelled heavy DNA phages were allowed to grow in ordinary nitrogen N^{14} (light isotope) containing medium. Since T4 undergoes more than 5 rounds of recombination during its growth cycle in the DNA pool, the existence of hybrid density DNA could be demonstrated only when DNA was fragmented into small pieces by sonication or mixer-blender. Normally one HH double strand DNA of phage, infects the bacterium. This is likely to form 2 HL molecules along with 50 other LL molecules. With 5 rounds of recombination among these molecules the label HL gets pretty much distributed among LL molecules. HL can be detected only by reduction in DNA fragment-size by sonication.

However, the temperate phage λ goes through on average only 0.5 rounds of recombination per growth cycle. Hence it is easier to show the existence of hybrid density DNA molecules and *establish the semi-conservative replication of λ chromosome.*

Organization of bacterial chromosome

Bacterial cytoplasm is rich in RNAs. As RNA and DNA have quite similar staining properties the RNAs need to be degraded to visualize the presence of DNA in the chromatin bodies of bacteria. The RNA in bacteria was degraded by treatment with 1 Normal hydrochloric acid solution or by the enzyme ribonuclease and subsequently stain bacteria with a dye, basic fuchsin. The chromatin bodies appear as pink blobs, arranged along the long axis of the bacterium. This staining was specific for DNA as was demonstrated by pre-treatment with enzyme DNAse, which degrades DNA and abolishes this staining. Cells of stationary cultures have predominantly 1 chromatin body each and those of rapidly growing cultures have several of them in each cell.

The chromatin bodies can also be visualized in unstained, living bacteria by phase contrast microscopy.

The genetic analysis of *E. coli* chromosome has shown that all its known genes are organized on a single circular likage map. Taking a cue from phage DNA, we might anticipate that bacterial DNA is a single molecule of considerable length, 1,000 μm or more, while an *E .coli* cell is usually 1 to 5 μm long. Autoradiography of tritiated (H^3) thymidine labeled DNA of *E. coli* by Cairn's method gave similar estimates of the length of DNA.

Protoplasts of the bacterium *Micrococcus lysodeikticus* were mixed with basic protein cytochrome C and lysed on water surface. The DNA emerging from lysed bacteria gets embedded in a monolayer of the basic protein. Following Kleinschmidt's method, the DNA was visualized in electron microscope after shadowing with noble metal such as platinum-palladium alloy or gold, or staining with saturated solution of uranyl acetate. The bacterial chromosome was found to be very long enormously tangled thread of thickness similar to *double stranded DNA with no observable free ends.*

Further information about the organization in the chromatin bodies was revealed from the ultrathin section of 60 to 80 nm thickness, from fixed, dehydrated and resin embedded *E. coli* bacteria and protoplasts of *B. subtilis*:

1. Chromatin bodies in prokaryotes do not have nuclear membrane unlike eukaryotic cells, which have a well defined nuclear envelope.
2. DNA of the chromatin body is rather in contact with bacterial membrane. Such association of DNA with membrane forms structures called *mesosomes*, which possibly make sure that the chromatin body has completed duplication before cell division. No spindle-like structures are formed during bacterial cell division.

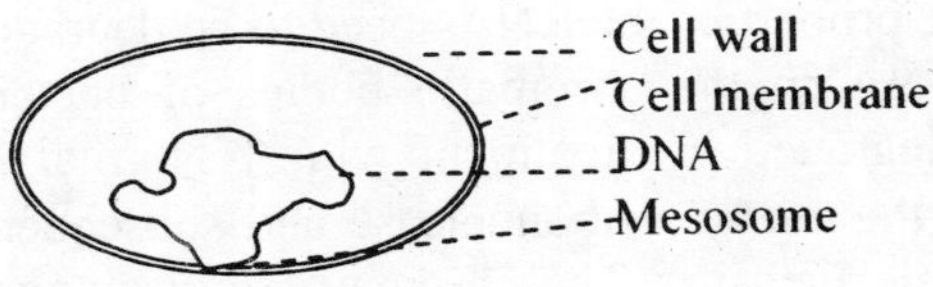

Fig. 17.1. Attachment of DNA with cell membrane forms *mesosomal* structure, which establishes link between DNA replication and cell division.

3. The chromatin body is filled with 2–6 nm thick fibres. These fibres are organized into bundles, each containing about 500 parallel fibres of DNA. The manner of DNA folding suggests some kind of flexible tertiary structure within chromatin bodies, as they occur in various shapes.
4. The DNA contained in the chromatin bodies is in hydrated form, similar to the phage DNA while replicating in the bacterial cytoplasm. But the DNA packed inside the phage head exists in compact form.
5. Several DNA binding proteins have been isolated in *E. coli*. The protein HU possibly condenses DNA into beaded structure and stimulates DNA replication. Protein H1 probably affects the local topology of DNA in relation to gene-expression.

About 80% of the DNA of the chromatin bodies can be isolated as rapidly sedimenting complex (*mesosomes*). Treatment of this DNA with ethidium bromide shows that the DNA molecules are in the form of closed circular or looped duplex structures. The molecules of ethidium bromide *intercalate* (sandwich) between base pairs of DNA, to produce positive superhelical turns in covalently linked closed loop of circular molecules. An 'open' loop or circular molecule that has a nick in one strand of DNA can rotate freely when ethidium bromide intercalates between the bases. In response to intercalation, free rotation of the molecule relieves tension in the molecule. Intercalation would produce no tension in a linear DNA molecule as it is free to rotate on its axis.

If a natural closed DNA is negatively supercoiled, ethidium bromide initially removes negative supercoils, then introduces positive supercoils by intercalation. The negative supercoiling can be estimated by titration with ethidium bromide so as to get zero supercoiling.

During the isolation of rapidly sedimenting complex (*mesosomes*) some nicks do occur in DNA. However, this does not abolish the formation of positive supercoils by ethidium bromide, indicating that the large DNA molecule has several independent 'loops' or domains. *The supercoiling of any loop is not affected by a nick in another loop. Rotational events from one loop are not transferred to the adjacent loop.* There are approximately 100 such 'loops' per chromatin body and each loop is about 40 kb of DNA (or 13.5 μm long).

Supercoiling of *E. coli* DNA was established *in vivo* by cross-linking with *psoralen*, which binds to DNA having torsional tension. *E. coli DNA was found to have one negative superhelical turn per 200 base pairs.*

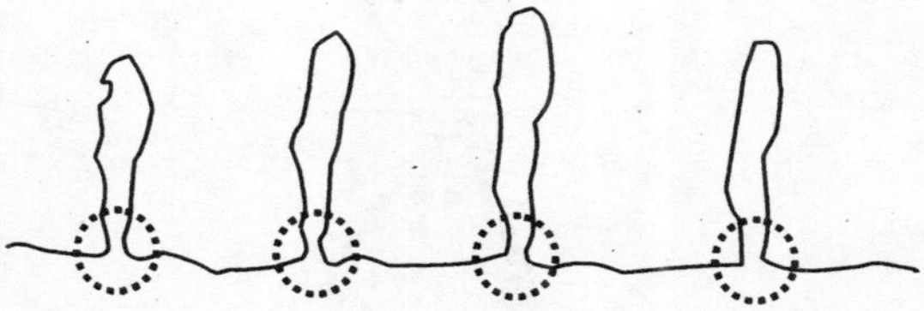

Fig. 17.2. Diagram showing the looped structure of a chromatin body.

Chromosomes of eukaryotic cells

In eukaryotic cells, chromosomes assume different appearances during the cell division cycle. Interphase chromatin occupies most of the nucleus and appears like a jumbled mass having some regions known as *heterochromatin*, which is more compact or dense than the rest of the chromatin appearing more dispersed and known as *euchromatin*. In contrast, the metaphase chromosomes appear highly organized and have characteristic shapes. The DNA is 5 to 10 times more condensed in metaphase chromosomes than in interphase. Carefully made preparations of metaphase chromosomes, when examined through electron microscope show that each sister chromatid is fibrillar and consists of 30 nm diameter beaded fibre. The fibre seems to be more densely packed near the centromere, possibly giving rise to heterochromatic characteristic appearance on staining. Condensation of genetic material is possibly related to its *inactivity*. However, the converse may not be true.

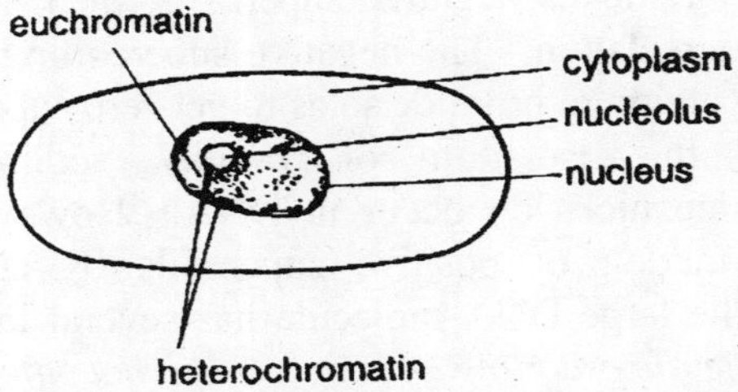

Fig. 17.3. Nucleus of an eukaryotic cell.

Most of the active genes are located within *euchromatin*, but at any time only a small number of genes are transcribed. *For expression of a gene, its location within euchromatin is necessary, but not sufficient.*

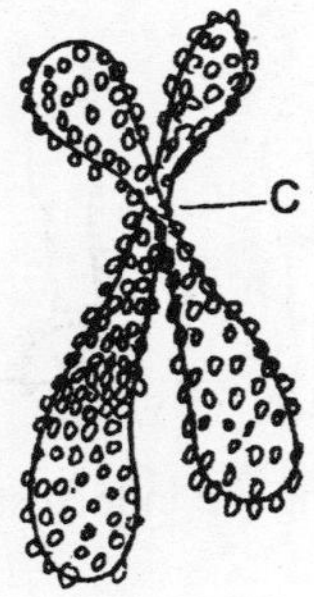

Fig.17.4. A metaphase chromosome, where two sister chromatids or daughter chromosomes formed by division are still joined together near centromere C. Specks denote 30 nm diameter beaded fibre.

Heterochromatin

Heterochromatin has two subtypes:

1. *Constitutive heterochromatin* comprising regions of chromosome that

are not expressed such as regions near the centromere. They usually have short repeated sequences of bases in DNA.

2. *Facultative heterochromatin* exists where the entire chromosome is inactive in one cell lineage. An excellent example of facultative heterochromatin is mammalian *X* chromosome in female. Amongst the two copies of *X* chromosome present in female cells, only one is active and the inactive *X* chromosome (also known as *Barr body* due to its specific staining character and named after its discoverer) exists in heterochromatic state. ***Though identical DNA sequences are present in both types of X chromosomes, yet their structural organization and transcriptional activities differ***. Inactive X chromosome (Barr body) is shown to be associated with lot of non-coding RNAs, indeed is coated by Xist ncRNAs.

Heterochromatin is present in centromeres, telomeres and nuclear organizers and can temporarily silence some neighbouring genes. Heterochromatin has highly repetitive DNA sequences with no or little coding capacity. This distinguishes it from euchromatin. Heterochromatin DNA is highly methylated. Histones are also methylated and hypo-acetylated.

Heterochromatin in cetromeres is present in distantly related organisms such as fission yeast, plants, insects and mammals. The budding yeast *Saccharomyces pombe* is an exception where centromere is highly reduced and has no histone H3K9, methyl-transferases as well as all RNAi making machinery. However, the three centromeres present in fission yeast *Saccharomyces cerevisiae* have a common similar structure. Heterochromatic transcriptional silencing is maintained due to coordinated action of DNA-binding proteins and RNAi processing. Small RNA duplexes of 22-24 nucleotides are unwound and associated with RNA-induced transcriptional silencing complex (RITS). The peri-centromeric transcripts are processed to siRNA by methyl-transferase H3K9.

The function of heterochromatin in many eukaryotes depends upon the non-protein coding and transposon derived transcripts, which are processed by RNAi. Dynamically silenced and condensed heterochromatin serves as the structural need of centromere formation and function. According to Zaratiegui and colleagues centromeres can as well be considered as, *"Transposon farms, recruiting and domesticating retroposons that reside within them."*

Morphological landmarks on a chromosome

Many physico-chemical methods, including various types of staining reveal several features of a chromosome.

Kinetochore: The formation of a spindle or a spindle-fibre system, comprising of microtubules is a major feature of dividing cell (*Cf.* **Chapter 29**). Some spindle fibres connect the poles (also called *centrosomes*) of the cell, while other spindle fibres connect a pole to a darkly staining fibrous body called *kinetochore,* which is located in the constricted region – *centromere* of the chromosome. Kinetochore is around 400 nm in diameter. Removal of tubulin subunits from the ends of the spindle fibre shortens the fibre and is responsible for the movement of chromosomes during mitosis as well as meiosis. About 120 bp stretch of DNA is essential for centromeric function to attach the chromosome to the spindle. *Centromeres are interchangeable and are not involved in distinguishing one chromosome from another.*

G – bands

Usually untreated chromosomes stain uniformly. But by subjecting chromosomes to a series of chemical treatments and then staining with Giemsa stain, several stained bands appear across the chromosome. Each chromosome can be identified by its typical banding pattern. Even translocations from one chromosome to another can be identified by the study of the *G – bands*. Human chromosomes have been divided into distinct regions according to their *G-banding* pattern.

Fig.17.5. G–bands of human *X*-chromosome.

The existence of G–bands in chromosomes implies the existence of certain long range structure. Most probably, it has to do with the packaging of a long single DNA molecule, which can become cyclically less or more compact as well as transcribe, replicate and recombine.

C – bands

By subjecting chromosomes to another set of chemical treatments and staining, the centromeres of all chromosomes can be intensely stained selectively.

Telomere

The broken-off ends of chromosomes are sticky and they tend to attach to other chromosomes. Intact ends are somehow sealed and non-sticky. It is suggested that, the ends of chromosomes have *telomeric* sequences. Telomeric sequences of many organisms are known and all can be denoted in the general form C_n (A or T)$_m$, where n>1 and m ranges between 1– 4.

Chromosome	Repeating bp at the 5'–3' end Telomere to centromere direction.
Yeast	C-C-C-A(CA)1-3.
Peanut	C-C-C-T-A-A-A.
Human	C-C-C-T-A-A.

The length of telomere is likely to be under genetic control. Telomeres are essential for the survival of the chromosomes and centromere is needed to support segregation of chromosome during cell division.

Chromosomes approximately contain 65% protein; 32% DNA and 3% RNA by weight. Most of the RNA molecules are nascent ones, associated with DNA template. Chromosomal proteins may be classified into 2 types: histones and non-histones. On the basis of the proportions of lysine and arginine, 5 types of histones H1; H2A; H2B; H3 and H4 were found in chromosomes of the most of the eukaryotes.

If interphase nuclei are suspended in water they swell and lyse, releasing from some regions of chromosomes, disc or cylinder-like nucleosome particles of uniform size (diameter 11 nm). A continuous strand of DNA was found to run through nucleosome particles by electron microscopy.

Individual nucleosomes may also be obtained by treating chromosomes with an enzyme micrococcal nuclease. This enzyme being an endonuclease, cleaves DNA at the junction between nucleosomes. An individual nucleosome contains approximately 200 bp of DNA and an octameric protein comprising 2 peptides each of H2A; H2B, H3 and H4 histones. The molecular weight of these histones varies between 11,000

– 15,000 Daltons. In addition a histone molecule called H1 of molecular weight 24,000 is peripherally associated with each nucleosome.

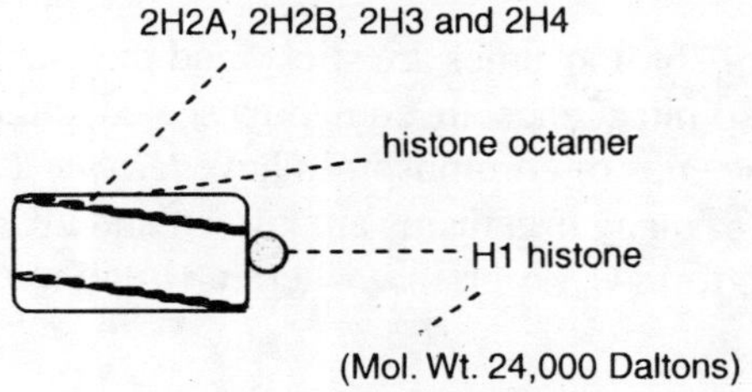

Fig. 17.6. A diagrammatic composition of nucleosome 6 nm high and 11 nm wide with approximate molecular weight 262,000 Daltons.

Indeed the action of micrococcal nuclease on chromosomes usually generates groups of nucleosomes having 1, 2, 3, 4, 5, ...nucleosomes. This preparation on sucrose gradient centrifugation and fractionation shows several peaks corresponding to monomer and multimers of nucleosomes.

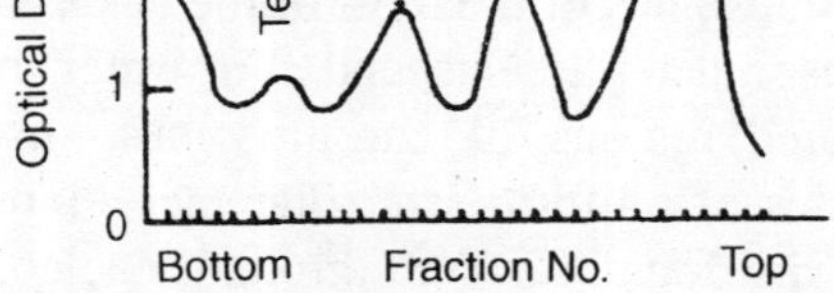

Fig. 17.7. Profile of a sucrose gradient fractionation, of a preparation of nucleosome obtained after the treatment of chromososme by micrococcal nuclease.

If the DNA extracted after the micrococcal nuclease digestion of chromosomes is subjected to gel electrophoresis, several bands like a *ladder of DNA* are formed. These DNA-bands correspond to molecular weight 200; 400; 600; 800; 1,000 base pairs (bp) and so on.

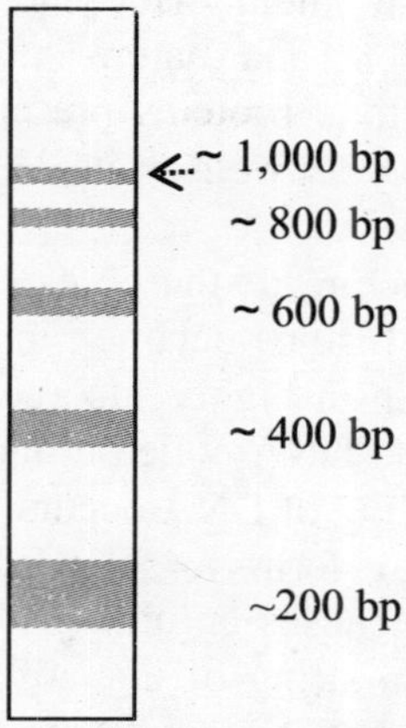

Fig. 17.8. DNA fragments formed by treatment with micrococcal nuclease digestion of chromosomes. A ladder-like pattern is formed on gel electrophoresis

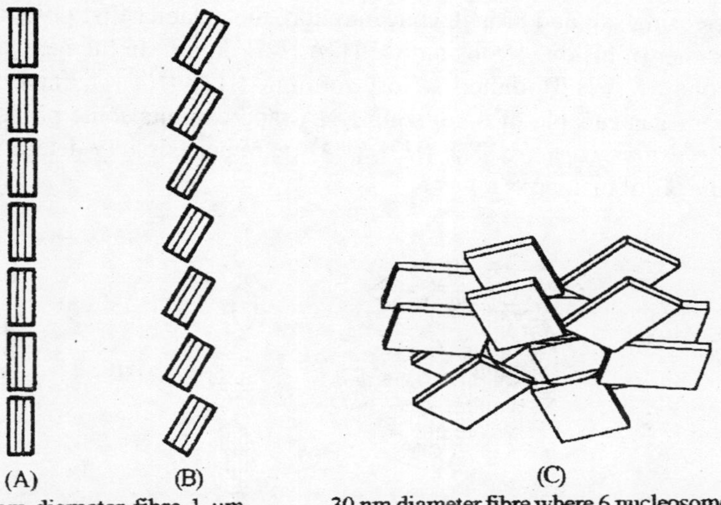

10 nm diameter fibre 1 μm length of fibre contains 6μm long DNA duplex. Packing ratio = 6.

30 nm diameter fibre where 6 nucleosomes are organized per turn of helical fibre, 1 μm long fibre contains 40 μm long DNA. Packing ratio 40 is close to that of whole chromosome.

Fig. 17.9. The arrangement of nucleosomes in 10 and 30 nm diameter fibres.

The H2A, H2B, H3 and H4 histones can *in vitro* reconstitute to give rise to the core particle of nucleosome. These core particles can as well organize DNA in them. But the supercoiling of DNA in reconstituted core particle and natural nucleosome differ. Possibly histone H1 and non-histone proteins present in chromosome influence the supercoiling of DNA as well as its length associated with histone octamer core.

The crystal structure of the core particle suggests that DNA is wound 1.8 turns around histone octamer, in the form of a flat helix. The DNA exists in chromatin in highly supercoiled form. The first type of supercoiling is due to the DNA coiled around in each nucleosome. The second type of supercoiling of DNA occurs due to coiling of nucleosome particles themselves, to form a solenoid-like 30 nm thick thread. Removal of H1 histone causes unfolding of 30 nm diameter fibre to 10 nm fibre that contains a string of nucleosomes held together by DNA duplex. In the absence of the second type of supercoiling, nucleosomes form an array, appearing as a fibre where nucleosomes are stacked with 0-20° tilt along the fibre.

The histone octamer can be extracted from the chromatin. Under decreasing salt and protein concentration, the octamer first gives rise to a hexamer of histone by losing one H2A.H2B dimer. In the next stage the second H2A.H2B dimer is lost forming $(H3)_2.(H4)_2$ tetramer. This tetramer is capable of organizing DNA, and exhibits some properties of *core histone particle*. The $(H3)_2.(H4)_2$ tetramer possibly determines the diameter of histone octamer.

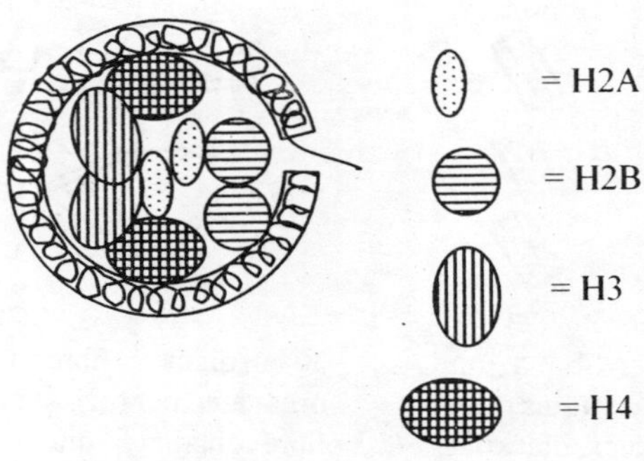

Fig. 17.10. The organization of histones in the octamer of a nucleosome.

With some difficulty, the histone octamer can also be formed by the association of individual H2A, H2B, H3 and H4 histones under high salt and protein concentrations.

The examples of lampbrush chromosomes of amphibian oocyte and polytene chromosome of *Drosophila* indicate that the transcription of genes involves the unwinding of DNA. This requires DNA duplex to unfold in the restricted region of the chromosome.

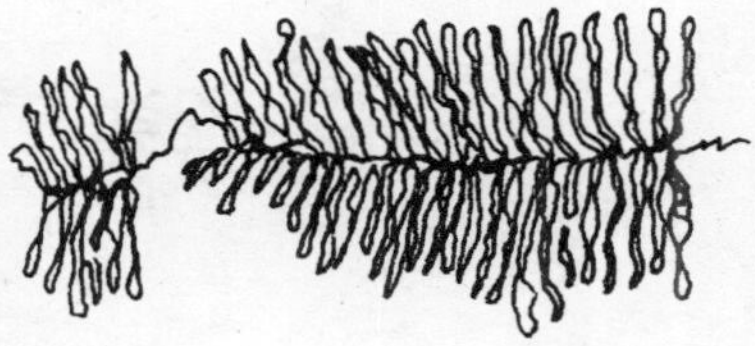

Fig.17.11. A portion of a lampbrush chromosome, where a large loop of chromatin emanate from the chromosomal axis.

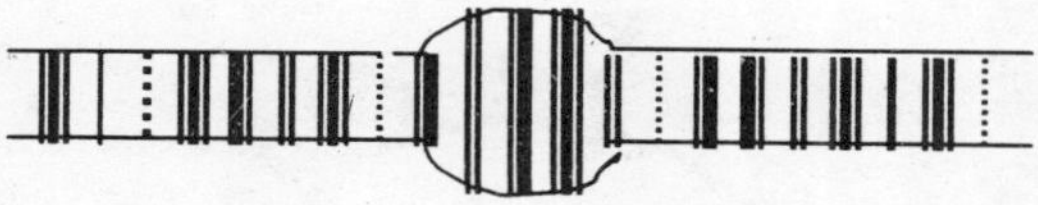

Fig.17.12. A part of *Drosophila* salivary gland polytene chromosome showing a puffed region of active transcription.

Eukaryotic enzymes including RNA polymerase are usually large proteins, with molecular weight > 500,000 Daltons, while nucleosome has molecular weight 260,000 Daltons. It is known that during transcription RNA polymerase binds tightly to ~ 50 bp region of DNA and locally unwinds 12 bp region. This need to unwind the DNA makes it unlikely to keep it attached to a nucleosome during transcription period.

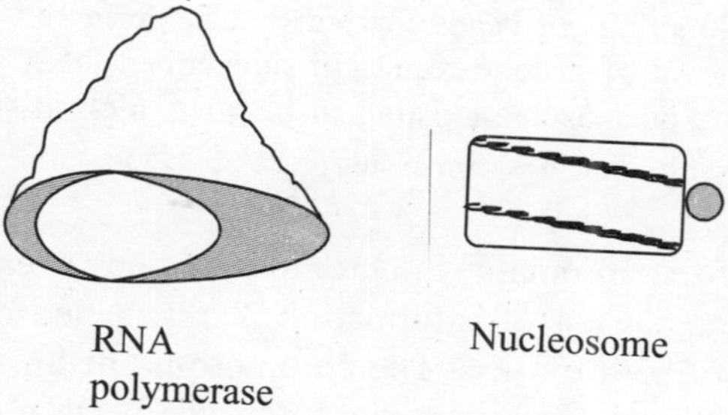

Fig. 17.13. RNA polymerase, Mol. Wt. 500,000 Daltons and nucleosome, dimension 6 nm x 11 nm, Mol. Wt. 250,000 Daltons.

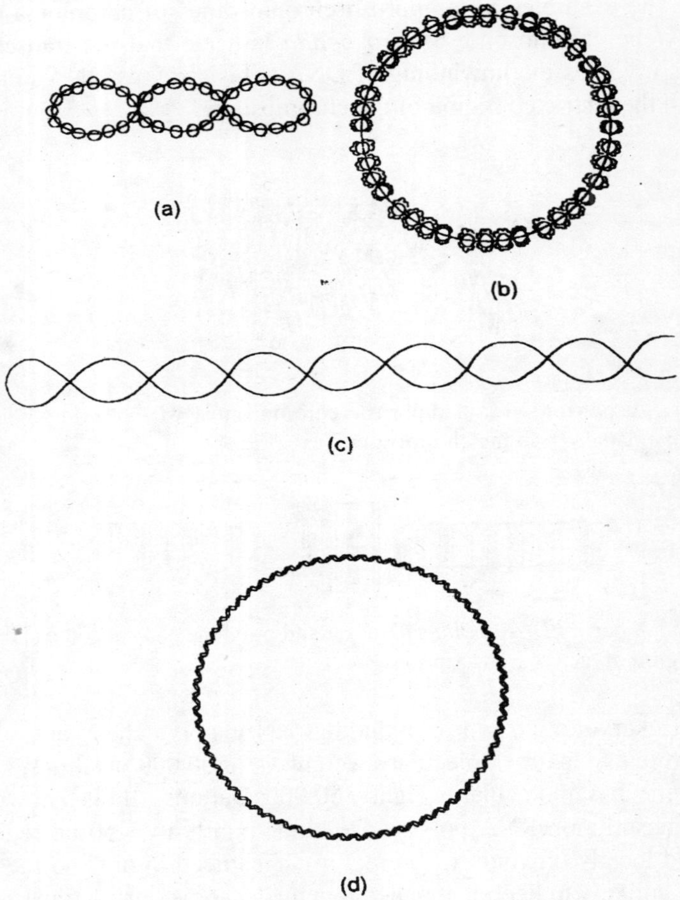

Fig.17.14. Minichromosome of SV40 virus. (a) A supercoiled chromosome of SV40. (b) Flexible strings of beads formed by change in salt concentration of solution. (c) Removal of histone results in supercoiled DNA. Each supercoil corresponds to one nucleosome existing in b. (d) A nick in supercoiled DNA produces a relaxed circular DNA molecule.

Most of the chromatin in chromosomes however, have DNA in supercoiled form. A lot of information about nucleosomes has come from the study of SV40 virus. The chromosome of SV40 virus is only 5,200 bp (or 1,500 nm) long, circular molecule of DNA. It is packaged in a number of nucleosomes in the virion, as well as inside the infected cell nucleus. The contour length of minichromosome of SV40 is 210 nm, resulting in a packing ratio 1,500 / 210 ≈ 7, which is close to that of nucleosome that is usually 6. By changing the salt concentration, the supercoiled structure can be converted to a flexible circular string of beads. If then histones of the octamer are extracted, the DNA is released to take a free path. Every supercoil which was restrained by nucleosome will appear as −1 turn in deprotenized DNA.

Methylation of bases

Methylation of certain bases, especially CG goublets occurs at specific sites. In eukaryotes 2-7 % of cytosine residues in DNA are methylated and methyl groups are concentrated in the *constitutive heterochromatin*, which is not expressed or transcribed. Demethylation also controls the transcription of genes in euchromatin. Often cytosine residue of the short palindromic sequence:

$$5'C_pG^m3'$$
$$3'G_pC^m5'$$

is methylated on both strands. If the methylation occurs only on one strand the site is called *hemi-methylated*. Identification of such sites can be done by restriction enzymes Hpa II and Msp I. Both restriction enzymes cleave the sequence CCGG. However, if the second site is methylated C^mCGG, the enzyme Hpa II cannot recognize it, unless Msp I can still cleave the site.

It is observed that of the methylated gene is inactive and the non-methylated gene is active. Demethylation seems to be a pre-requisite for the gene to be transcribed.

Further reading

Kornberg, R.D., King, A. The nucleosome. *Sci. Am. 244(2)*: 52 (1981).

McGhee, J.D., and Felsenfeld, G. Nucleosome structure. *Annu. Rev. Biochem. 49*: 1115 (1980).

Price, C.M. Centromeres and telomeres. *Curr. Opin. Cell Biol. 4*: 379 (1992).

Stewart, A. The functional organization of chromosomes and the nucleus — a special issue. *Trends Genet. 6*: 377 (1990).

Zaratiegui, M., Irvine, D.V., and Martienssen, R.A. Noncoding RNAs and gene silencing. *Cell, 128*: 763-776 (2007).

CHAPTER 18

The Genetic Code

The *sequence hypothesis* proposed by Crick and his colleagues stated that:
1. The sequence of 4 nucleotides along the polynucleotide chain specifies the sequence of amino acids' residues in the derivative polypeptide.
2. Genetic and physico-chemical measurements indicate that, each amino acid is coded by the sequence of a small number of nucleic acid bases. This number being termed as *coding ratio*.
3. *The genetic code is that inscribed in messenger RNA (mRNA)*.

The genetic code was deciphered essentially by following three approaches,

(a) *theoretical reasoning*, (b) *genetic approach* and (c) *biochemical experiments*.

Theoretical aspects of coding

According to the sequence hypothesis a linear array of 4 types of nucleotides codes for a linear sequence of 20 amino acids. In other words, an alphabet of 4 letters such as A, B, C, and D should form a language of 20 words.

The single-letter words will be 4 words.

Two letter words could be 4 x 4 = 16 words.

Both these possibilities individually or taken together are insufficient to meet the requirement of 20 amino acids. In a continuous sequence of bases with no punctuation marks, a single letter word cannot be distinguished from the word formed by two letters. The number of possible 3 letter words will be 4 x 4x 4 = 64 words, which seem to be quite sufficient to code for 20 amino acids.
The number of bases present in a gene divided by the number of amino acid residues present in the derivative protein gave the coding ratio close to 3 in many instances. The genetic data obtained by Benzer during the

recombination experiments with phage T4 also indicated that coding ratio is close to 3.

If the code is read as a triplet code, in what manner it is read? Could the genetic code be read as an overlapping code?

Overlapping code

In an overlapping code six bases in a sequence

ABCABC

of mRNA will code for 4 amino acids e.g. ABC; BCA; CAB and ABC. If one base is mutated, it should affect three amino acid residues. However, a single point mutation or base substitution results in change of a single amino acid in the polypeptide.

By now amino acid sequences of several proteins such as insulin, ribonuclease, haemoglobin, tobacco mosaic virus protein, and tryptophan synthetase enzyme are known. If the genetic code was read in an overlapping manner, then there should be significant associations of amino acids occurring as neighbours in the polypeptide. As amino acid coded by ABC is bound to be followed by amino acid coded by BCX. No such neighbour association has been found in any of the known protein sequences. Therefore the mechanism of *overlapping code* reading is ruled out.

Non-overlapping triplet code

If we are dealing with a non-overlapping triplet code, how is it read? There must be some way of distinguishing the meaningful triplets from others in the polynucleotide. Could it be a punctuated code, where every fourth base is represented by a comma?

ABC,ABC,ABC.......

However, homogeneous poly-U messenger RNA is found to yield poly phenylalanine in the *in-vitro* protein synthesizing system. This indicates that there are no punctuation marks as comma observed during the reading of the code.

Un-punctuated triplet code

An un-punctuated triplet code could be '*deciphered*' if 2/3 of the possible combinations of 3 letters were meaningless, so that in a sequence

ABCABCABCABC

the BCA and CAB triplets are meaningless. If such a scheme was operative, all triplets with the same letters AAA; BBB; CCC; or DDD must be regarded as meaningless, since adjacent triplets AAAAAA or BBBBBB would give overlapping sense and would be read as 4 identical words instead of 2 words. In order to read the code correctly, we should first eliminate 4 same-letter triplets and then 2/3 of the remaining 60 as being '***nonsense***' triplets i.e. 64 – 4 = 60; then 60 x 2/3 = 40. Therefore 4 + 40 = 44 triplets should be subtracted from possible 64 triplets, i.e. 64 – 44 = 20. Thus 20 exactly corresponds to the number of amino acids need to be coded by the genetic code.

Despite the elegance of reasoning and the excellence of fit, this mechanism is not acceptable for 2 good reasons.

1. The genetic code is *degenerate* – more than one sequence of bases (*triplet* or *codon*) can specify a single amino acid.
2. If 2/3 triplets are *'non-sense'* and do not specify any amino acid, a substitution in a meaningful triplet is likely to give nonsense triplet with 2/3 probability. This does not seem to be true from a large number of lysozyme mutants of phage T4 and tryptophan synthetase mutants of *E. coli*. A great majority of base analogue induced mutations result in the substitution of one amino acid by another. Most alterations of a single letter in code lead to ***'mis-sense'*** and not *'non-sense'*.

Illiterate way of reading the genetic code

In this mechanism, the reading of the code begins at *a prescribed position* and proceeds in steps of three bases in a single direction.

DNA	O ABC ABC ABC ABC ABC
mRNA	*ABC ABC ABC ABC ABC*
tRNA	⊥⊥⊥ ⊥⊥⊥ ⊥⊥⊥ ⊥⊥⊥ ⊥⊥⊥
amino acids	$a.a_1$ — $a.a_2$ — $a.a_3$ — $a.a_4$ — $a.a_5$

Direction of reading the code-message and the protein synthesis →.

The synthesis of mammalian haemoglobin studied by giving a radioactive pulse label shows that, the polypeptide is made by sequential addition of amino acids.

Genetic analysis of the code

Yanofsky isolated a large number of tryptophan synthetase mutations of *E. coli* and located their positions on the genome by recombination mapping. Changes corresponding to these mutations were identified in the enzyme protein. It was found that the order of various mutations on the genome tallies with the corresponding alteration in the protein molecule This experiment strengthened the view that there exists *a colinearity between the gene and its protein.*

The *colinearity* between the gene and its protein was further proved by an elegant experiment done by Sarabhai and coworkers. They studied a number of *amber* mutations for the head protein of phage T4. *The amber mutation on the mRNA is read as end of polypeptide synthesis*. Depending upon the distance of amber mutations from the initiation point, polypeptides of different lengths are produced by different amber mutants of the phage. It was found that the distance of different amber mutations from the initiation point on the genome tallies well with the lengths of polypeptides they produce.

The role of acridine-induced mutations and their suppressors in deciphering the genetic code

Crick, Barnet, Brenner and Watts-Tobin induced mutations in the r_{II} (pronounced as *r* two) region of phage T4. Acridine (Proflavin) dye intercalates between the bases in DNA helix and causes addition or deletion of a single base pair during subsequent replication. Addition or deletion of a base pair is in essence a mutation in the genome and called ***frame shift mutation***. Such frame shift mutations *derail* the protein synthesis down stream of the mutation.

O ABC ABC ABC ABC ABC ABC ABC

Original genome

O ABC AXB CAB CAB CAB CAB CAB

The sense of message changes downstream of **X**.

Crick *et al.*, isolated spontaneous reversions of proflavin induced r_{II} mutations. The r_{II} system was found to be suitable for such studies because of its inherent enormous power of selection as is evident from the Table 18.1 given below.

Table 18.1. Appearance of plaques formed by mutant r and the wild type T phages

Phage T4	*E.coli B*	*E. coli S*	*E.coli K*
wild	*wild*	*wild*	*wild*
r_I	*r*	*r*	*r*
r_{II}	*r*	*wild*	—
r_{III}	*r*	*wild*	*wild*

wild = small and fuzzy plaque; *r* = large and clear boundary plaque; *K* = *E. coli K12* lysogenic for λ phage; *S* = non-lysogenic sensitive strain of *E. coli K 12*.

If 10^8 phage particles of r_{II} are plated on *E. coli K12* strain, only *r+* wild type particles, which have reverent phenotype only grow. These are purified by plating on *E. coli B*. The wild type and the revertant are crossed. It was found that these revertants are not true revertants at the site of original mutation. Rather *if the original mutation had one additional base 'X' added to the genome this revertant had a base subtracted* (a base B at the arrow) *down stream nearby.*

O ABC ABC ABC ABC ABC ABC ABC

wild type

↓deletion of **B**

O ABC AXB CA**B** CAB CAB CAB CAB

mutant

O ABC AXB CAC ABC ABC ABC ABC

revertant phenotype

The original reading frame is restored after the deletion of a base near by the original mutation. Amongst 20 revertants, 18 were found to form a different type of colony on *E. coli B* strain and hence were called *pseudowild type* revertant. They are *suppressors* of the first mutation of r_{II}. If we designate the first mutation as a plus (+) mutation, then the supressor of the first mutation will logically be a negative (–) mutation.

Each *pseudowild type* phage isolate was crossed with wild type phage. If these so called pseudowilds were true revertants the progeny from such a cross would have been all wild type. Contrary to this, progeny also consisted of r_{II} phenotype phages. As is evident from the diagram given below that the pseudowild type revertants were formed by a suppressor mutation at a different but closely linked site. A recombination event between wild type $r+$ and pseudowild strain containing r_{II} and *su* (*suppressor*) mutation would result in r_{II} and *su* progenies.

— r_{II} ——— *su* —
X →
——+———+—
Original

— r_{II} ———+—
and
——+———*su*—
Both recombinants have r_{II} phenotype.

If both recombinant progenies r_{II} + and + *su* are back crossed to r_{II} + mutant:

— r_{II} ———+—
X →
— r_{II} ———+—

No wild type recombinant phages.

——+———*su*—
X →
— r_{II} ———+—

Wild type phage.
——+———+—
— r_{II} ——— *su* —
Pseudowild type phage.

These suppressor mutations showed the following properties:

1. They formed *pseudowild* type colonies on *E. coli S* strain. These colonies looked different from the wild type colonies of phage T4 carrying r^+ gene.
2. All form non-leaky r_{II} phenotype colonies.
3. It is different from complementation, as suppressor mutation acts only in *cis* position on the same chromosome, whereas complementation can work in *trans*, position on different chromosome.

These suppressors were called *first generation suppressors*, and displayed r_{II} phenotype. They were again allowed to revert and form pseudo-wilds by another suppressor mutation. The *suppressor of suppressor* or *second generation suppressors* were isolated by recombination with wild type. Carrying out similar step once more, the *suppressor of suppressor of suppressor* or *third generation suppressors* were obtained

If we assume that the original r_{II} mutation induced by proflavin was by addition of a base pair, then pseudo-wild revertants were due to a deletion of the base pair near by. We can designate the original r_{II} mutant as + mutation, the first generation suppressor will be –; the second generation suppressors will be + and the third generation suppressors will again be – mutations. Amongst the 80 suppressors isolated some were + and some were – mutations.

If the genetic code is a triplet code then two pluses ++ or two minuses – –, would still show a r_{II} phenotype. This was found so in all 14 such alleles.

Five triple mutants +++ and one triple mutant – – –, all displayed pseudo-wild phenotype on *E. coli B*.

These experiments conclusively showed that coding ratio is most probably 3, if a single base is added or deleted by proflavin at one site from the DNA. If it is more than one base at a time, the coding ratio could be a multiple of 3.

Biochemical analysis of the genetic code

In vitro protein synthesizing systems can be prepared from cell free extracts of *E. coli* cell-lysate. The cell-lysate is centrifuged at low speed to remove fragments of cell wall and membrane. High speed centrifugation yields a pellet containing ribosomes. Bacterial DNA is destroyed by treating the supernate by the enzyme DNAse, whereas mRNA in *E. coli* is labile and decays within a few minutes on its own. The supernatant already contains tRNA and enzymes required for protein synthesis. The supernatant is active in synthesizing polypeptide on providing RNA, energy source of ATP, ribosomes and amino acids (preferably radioactive labelled to monitor the polypeptide synthesis reaction). Nirenberg and Matthaei in 1961 used synthetic *polyuridylic acid* or *poly U* as messenger RNA in the *in-vitro* protein synthesizing system. They found that polyphenylalanine is formed in this *in vitro* experiment, establishing that UUU in mRNA, equivalent to AAA in DNA must be the codon for phenylalanine.

In a similar *in vitro* set up homopolymers poly A, poly C or poly G, directed syntheses of poly lysine and poly proline or poly glycine respectively.

Therefore AAA codes for lysine,
CCC codes for proline, whereas
GGG codes for glycine.

Ochoa and Heppel synthesized heteropolymers by using the enzyme polynucleotide phosphorylase to link together ribonucleoside phosphates. The nucleotide bases are incorporated randomly in the polynucleotide chain. The frequency of occurrence of bases is proportional to their initial concentration in the mixture e.g., if uracil and cytosine are present in proportion 3 : 1, then the most frequent triplet will be UUU, whereas UUC, UCU or CUU will be less frequent. Triplets having 2C+1U or 3C will be rarer. If such a messenger RNA is provided for protein synthesis, after phenylalanine, serine is the most frequent amino acid in the synthesized polypeptide. This indicates that any of the codons having 2U + 1C codes for serine. But whether triplet UUC, UCU or CUU codes for serine cannot be inferred.

A more precise method was developed by Khorana, where polynucleotides of known sequences could be synthesized such as:

GUG UGU GUG UGU GUG UGU GUG
yields val — cys — val — cys— val — cys — val —

Similarly polynucleotide of 3 bases such as :
AUC AUC AUC AUC AUC AUC AUC
yields ileu — ileu —ileu — ileu —ileu —ileu — ileu —

UCA UCA UCA UCA UCA UCA UCA
yields ser — ser — ser — ser — ser — ser — ser —

and CAU CAU CAU CAU CAU CAU CAU
yields his — his — his — his — his — his — his—

i.e three types of homopolymers, polyisoleucine, polyserine and polyhistidine respectively, depending upon the reading frame selected for making protein. These experiments not only deciphered many codons of the genetic code, as well firmly established that genetic code is a triplet code with coding ratio 3. Such techniques permitted decoding of about half of the total 64 codons.

The tRNA — ribosome binding assay

Nirenberg and Leder in 1964 developed another technique for codon assignment. They found that a trinucleotide of known sequence can make corresponding aminoacyl-tRNA to bind to a ribosome in the *in vitro* protein synthesizing system. This process essentially mimics codon–anticodon recognition between mRNA and tRNA inside ribosome. The triple complex so formed has trinucleotide + aminoacyl tRNA + ribosome, which can be filtered out on a nitrocellulose filter as ribosomes bind to the filter. The tRNA alone does not bind to the filter. The *in vitro* protein synthesizing system is set up in small quantities in 20 test tubes, each containing a different radioactive labelled amino acid in addition to usual components of protein synthesizing mixture. A triplet to be decoded is added to each tube and contents of individual tube filtered through nitrocellulose filters. Wherever tRNA ribosome binding has occurred, the filter shows enhanced radioactivity than rest of the 19 tubes, e.g. UUG or to be precise 5'UpUpG binds leucine or UGU or to be precise 5'UpGpU binds cytosine.

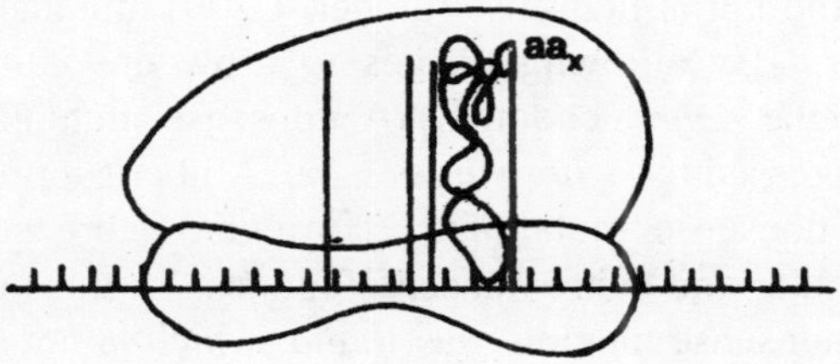

Fig. 18.1. The tRNA and ribosome binding assay in the presence of synthetic triplets.

Both the techniques together could assign meaning to 61 codons, representing incorporation of 20 amino acids. These experiments showed that ***the genetic code is highly degenerate, meaning that a single amino acid could be specified by more than one codon.***

Signal for termination of protein synthesis

Benzer and Champ while studying r_{II} region of phage T4, found that in normal phage, r_{II} genome is divided in two regions A and B. These regions direct synthesis of two proteins A and B. In a mutant of phage

T4, a deletion joined the region r_{IIA} and r_{IIB} so that a single joint polypeptide is formed. This polypeptide has protein B activity in addition to protein A activity. If another mutation is created by the side of the deletion, such that proteins A and B continue to be synthesized then the second mutation is a *mis-sense* mutation. If because of second mutation no protein is formed for B region then the mutation is a *nonsense* mutation. These nonsense mutants in phage displayed an unusual property. The behaviour depended on the *E. coli* strain used as a host for the phage. This formed a *conditional lethal* system. In a *non-permissive* strain of bacteria, phage mutants cannot grow because nonsense mutation in phage terminates prematurely the protein synthesis. However, the same phage can grow in a *permissive* strain, because permissive strain has suppressor mutation that overcomes the nonsense mutation of phage. *The suppressor mutation causes the formation of an altered mutant aminoacyl tRNA, which is able to introduce an amino acid in place of termination codon, so that protein synthesis proceeds un-interrupted beyond the site of the nonsense mutation.*

The suppressor mutations define 3 classes of nonsense mutations. All the initial nonsense (amber, UAG) mutants responded to same suppressor. By allowing phages to grow on *amber-suppressor* strain of *E.coli*, the *ochre*, codon UAA nonsense mutants were found, which were suppressed by *ochre suppressor*. Amber suppressor does not suppress ochre nonsense mutations. However, ochre suppressor can suppress both amber and ochre nonsense codons. A third category opal, codon UGA of nonsense mutants was found, which is not suppressed by amber or ochre suppressors, nor its suppressor act on amber or ochre. These results are summarized in the next Table 18.2.

Table 18.2. Some characteristics of amber, ochre and opal suppressors

Nonsense codon	Amber suppressor suppresses	Ochre suppressor suppresses	Opal suppressor suppresses
Amber UAG	+	+	–
Ochre UAA	–	+	–
Opal UGA	–	–	+

It is known that in all sequenced genes, one or more of these nonsense codons lie immediately after the codon for C-terminal amino acid of the protein. So these nonsense codons are indeed *natural termination signals* for protein synthesis.

In addition,

1. None of the termination codons has its tRNA.
2. There are protein factors that react with ribosomes, when termination codon is reached.
3. Nonsense codons act as termination signals or punctuation signals for protein or polypeptide synthesis.

Overlapping reading frame

Overlapping code was ruled out initially on theoretical grounds. But it was found in phage φX 174 that two open reading frames exist in different overlapping regions for a considerable length. On one strand of mRNA 3 reading frames are theoretically possible in a triplet code. Only one frame is usually read efficiently the other two frames are blocked by frequent termination codons e.g.

AUG ABC ABC ABU AAC ABC **UAG**

UGA B C A B C A B U A A C A B C U A G

GAB CAB CAB **UAA** C A B C U A G

Looking at some of the secrets of genetic code, one wonders at the elegance and economy of information content of the code. In addition, genetic code seems to be universal in the known living systems studied, as messages from one organism can be translated *in vitro* with cell components of the other systems.

Further reading

Champe, S.P., and Benzer, S. Reversal of mutant phenotypes by 5-fluorouracil : an approach to nucleotide sequences in messenger RNA. *Proc. Natl. Acad. Sci.* Washington, *48*: 532 (1962).

Crick, F.H.C., Barnett, L., Brenner, S. and Watts-Tobin, R.J. General nature of the genetic code for proteins. *Nature*, London, *192*: 1227 (1961).

Khorana, H.G. Nucleic acid synthesis in the study of the genetic code. In Nobel Lectures in Molecular Biology, 1933-1975; Elsevier, pp. 303-331 (1977).

Nirenberg, M.W.; and Matthaei, J.H. The dependence of cell-free protein synthesis in Escherichia coli upon naturally occurring or synthetic polyribonucleotides. *Proc. Natl. Acad. Sci.* Washington, *47*: 1588 (1961).

Ochoa, S., and Heppel, L.A. Polynucleotide synthesis. In The Chemical Basis of Heredity (eds. W.D. McElroy and B. Glass). John Hopkins Press, Baltimore, p. 615 (1957).

Woese, C.R. Nature of the biological code. *Nature*, London, *194*: 1114 (1962).

CHAPTER 19

Replication of DNA

The entire genome of a cell must replicate precisely once in every generation, to have viable progenies. The process of DNA replication should logically be linked with cell division.

Connection between DNA replication and cell division

The bacterial DNA and membrane are attached at a site called *mesosome*. This could provide a mechanism for precise replication of DNA in unison with cell division.

In a cell the DNA replication is usually controlled at the stage of initiation. Once the DNA replication is initiated, it continues until completed for a certain part of chromosome. This region of the chromosome in which the cell controls each replication cycle of DNA is called a *replicon*. Usually a bacterial chromosome is a single replicon. However, the chromosomes of eucaryotes may each have many replicons.

The chromosome of *E.coli* replicates from an origin *ori C* and proceeds in both directions. The origin of replication from DNA has been isolated in *E.coli and S. typhimurium*. Their size is around 300-400 bp long. The *ori C* has many single stranded loops like a typical cloverleaf structure in the DNA duplex.

This large secondary structure is formed by the presence of many *palindromic* sequences (*which read the same in forward and backword directions, such as the word MALAYALAM*). In addition this structure is made stable by the pressure from supercoiling and is stabilized by attached proteins. This secondary structure most probably interacts with enzymes such as DNA polymerase.

Bacteria may harbour plasmids, in addition to their own chromosomes. Plasmids may be present in a single copy or multiple copies. If they are not integrated to the bacterial chromosome, they exist as *separate replicons* and control their own rate of replication.

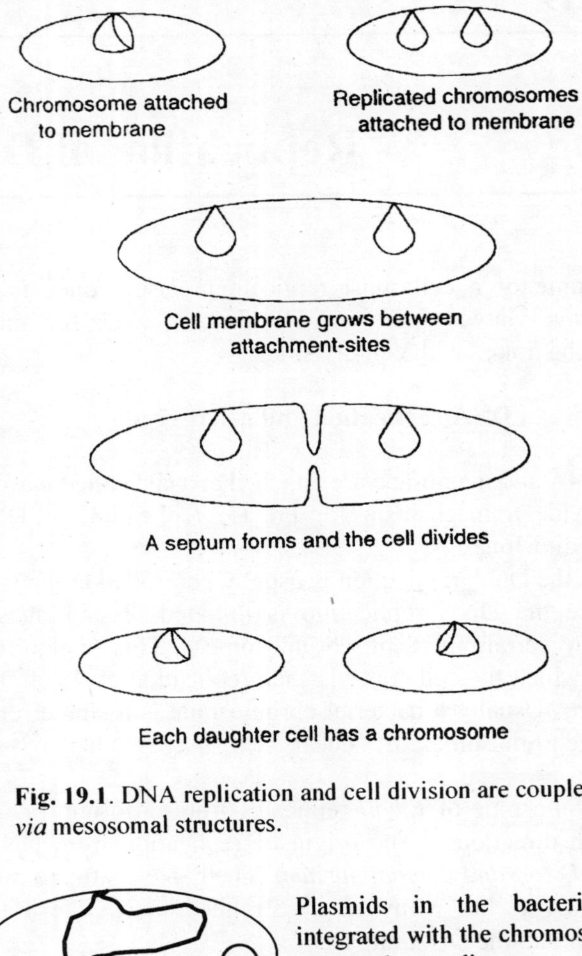

Fig. 19.1. DNA replication and cell division are coupled *via* mesosomal structures.

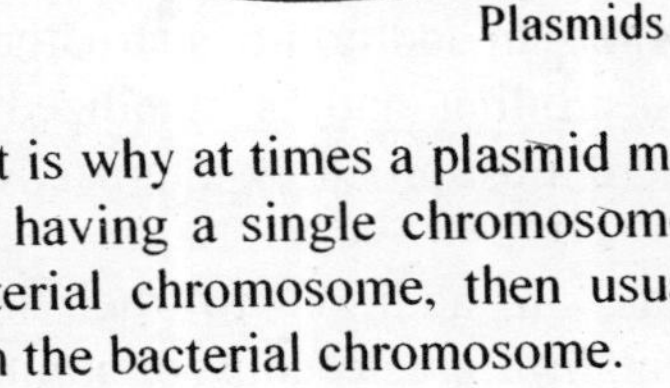

Plasmids in the bacterial cell if not integrated with the chromosome, function as independent replicons.

That is why at times a plasmid may be present in 20 copies in a bacterial cell having a single chromosome. If any plasmid is integrated to the bacterial chromosome, then usually its replication proceeds in unison with the bacterial chromosome.

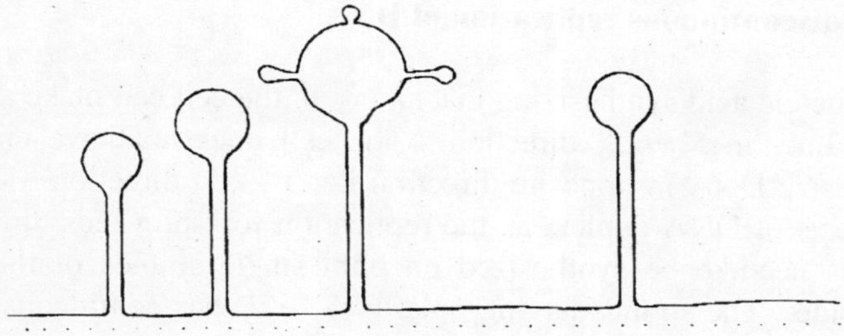

Fig.19.2. A complex secondary structure at the origin of replication in *E. coli* DNA at the locus *ori C*. A mirror image secondary structure existing on the complementary DNA strand (dotted line) is not shown here.

The replication of bacterial chromosome can be followed by giving two successive pulses of higher and lower concentrations of radioactivity, (e.g. tritium labelled thymidine) and subsequent autoradiography of the DNA. It was found that the bacterial DNA is replicated bi-directionally from a single origin. Usually a replication eye in the shape of a *theta (θ)* like structure is formed in a circular DNA during replication.

The bacterial transformation experiments showed that the number of copies of genes near the origin is more than the genes in the terminal region of the chromosome, in a rapidly dividing population of bacteria. It is known as *dichotomous replication.*

A non-dividing chromosome of *B. subtilis.*

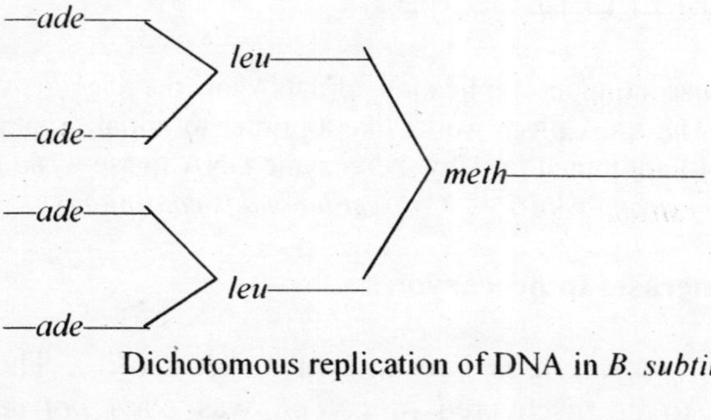

Dichotomous replication of DNA in *B. subtilis.*

The rate of replication in a bacterium is approximately 50,000 bp/min, whereas in mammals it is around 1,000 – 3,000 bp/min.

Semi-discontinuous replication of DNA

The nucleic acid synthesizing machinery in the cell can make a strand of DNA only in 5'→ 3' direction. The cell does not have enzymes to synthesize DNA in opposite direction i.e. 3'→ 5' direction. During the synthesis of DNA duplex, as the replication fork proceeds, the daughter strands need to be synthesized on both single strands of the parental molecule. The strands having polarity 5'→ 3' has continuous synthesis of daughter DNA strand on it. However, on the opposite parental strand, where the polarity is 3'→ 5' (is called *lagging* strand or *trailing strand*), the synthesis of daughter strand is still maintained in 5'→ 3' direction but in a ***discontinuous manner***, synthesizing 1,000 to 2,000 nucleotide long pieces at a time and then joining them by enzyme DNA *ligase*. These pieces of DNA are known as *Okazaki fragments* after their discoverer. They can be identified by a short pulse of radioactivity, and have a sedimentation constant 7-11 S on centrifugation. *For the initiation of synthesis of each Okajaki fragment, an approximately 10 nucleotide long RNA primer is needed.*

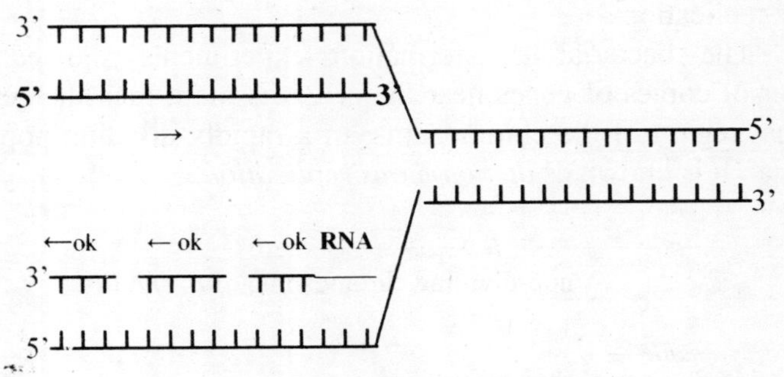

Fig. 19.3. Discontinuous replication of DNA on the lagging strand by nick translation. The RNA piece works like a primer to initiate synthesis. Okazaki fragments (ok) are joined later by the enzyme DNA ligase. *The DNA synthesis on the leading strand is in **5'→ 3'** direction and is **continuous**.*

DNA polymerases in procaryotes

Three *DNA polymerases* are known in *E. coli*. The first DNA polymerase to be discovered in *E. coli* was *DNA polymerase I*, also known as *Kornberg enzyme* or *Kornberg polymerase*. It was found to be responsible for the repair of damaged DNA and is coded by gene *pol A*. If part of the pre-existing strand of DNA molecule is replaced by newly synthesized sequence of DNA, made by *DNA polymerase I*, it is called *nick translation*. As the new segment of DNA is synthesized by DNA polymerase I, *the existing damaged strand in DNA duplex is displaced during nick translation*.

The *DNA polymerase II* is coded by gene *pol B*, but its function in the cell is not clear.

The *DNA polymerase III* is a large multimeric protein. One sub-unit of polymerase III is coded by locus *pol C* or *dna E*. ***The DNA polymerase III is indeed a replicase and responsible for the synthesis of new strands of DNA***. Each of these polymerases extends a DNA strand by adding a nucleotide at a time to *3'OH end*. However, none can initiate a strand on its own and need an *RNA primer* to begin the synthesis. Different combinations of various sub-units such as α (alpha), β (beta), γ (gamma), δ (delta), ε (epsilon), θ (theta) and τ (tau) *constitute varied forms of DNA polymerase III*.

Table 19.1. Some properties of the three DNA polymerases in *E.coli*.

Properties	**Polymerase I**	**PolymeraseII**	**Polymerase III**
Mol. Weight Daltons	109,000	120,000	>250,000
Sub-units	1	—	Heteromeric
Number in a cell	~ 400	—	10 – 20
Enzyme activities	5'-3'chain elong. 3'-5'exonuclease 5'-3'exonuclease	3'-5'exonuclease	3'-5'exonuclease 5'-3'exonuclease
Mutants	*pol A*	*pol B*	*pol C*, *dna A* *Dna X*, *dna Z*

B. Subtilis is also known to have 3 similar DNA polymerases to those of *E. coli*. There are some minor differences in their properties. DNA polymerase II is associated with the physiological status of the bacterium. It is absent in spores which are dormant, and appears after 30 minutes of germination to the vegetative state. The phages T4, T5 and T7 are also known to code for DNA polymerases.

DNA polymerases in eucaryotes

Similar to procaryotic cells, the eucaryotes also have 3 DNA polymerases α, β and γ. Unlike bacterial polymerases, *eucaryotic DNA polymerases α, β or γ do not have exonuclease activity or proofreading ability*. Indeed, they have only synthesizing activity. The level *of DNA polymerase* α rises during S phase of cell division, indicating that it *may be responsible for DNA synthesis during S phase of cell division cycle.* DNA polymerase β seems to be involved in the *damage repair function* in DNA. While *DNA polymerase γ replicates mitochondrial DNA* and its role in the nucleus is not clear.

Table 19.2. Properties of three mammalian DNA polymerases.

Properties	**Polymerase α**	**Polymerase β**	**Polymerase γ**
Occurrence	Nuclear	Nuclear	Nuclear and mitochondrial
Activity proportion	80%	10- 15%	2-15%
Sub-units	Many	1	Unknown
Molecular Wt. Daltons	110—220,000	45,000	6,0000

DNA replication in eucaryotic cells

Each eucaryotic chromosome has many replicons. Cells undergoing divisions in the early embryonic development have much smaller replicons than those do in the somatic cells. The replication of DNA can be explained in terms of (1) θ or *eye structure model*, (2) *Rolling circle model*, or (3) *D-loop model*.

θ or eye structure model

The replication fork generates an eye or θ like structure while it progresses in one or both directions in a linear DNA molecule.

Rolling circle model of DNA replication

A nick is generated in the DNA molecule and the 3' OH end generated by the nick is extended by DNA polymerase. The growing point can be visualized to roll around the circular template strand. In principle such a replication can continue indefinitely until the nutrients are exhausted or the temperature is unfavourable. As the replication fork moves on the template, it extends the outer strand and displaces the previous complementary strand.

In rolling circle model of DNA replication, initially a multimeric single stranded tail is generated. This single stranded tail is converted to double stranded form by synthesis of a complimentary strand. Such a mechanism of DNA replication can also explain chromosome replication in φX 174, concatameric DNA formation in phage λ, and amplified γ-DNA of *Xenopus* frog oocytes.

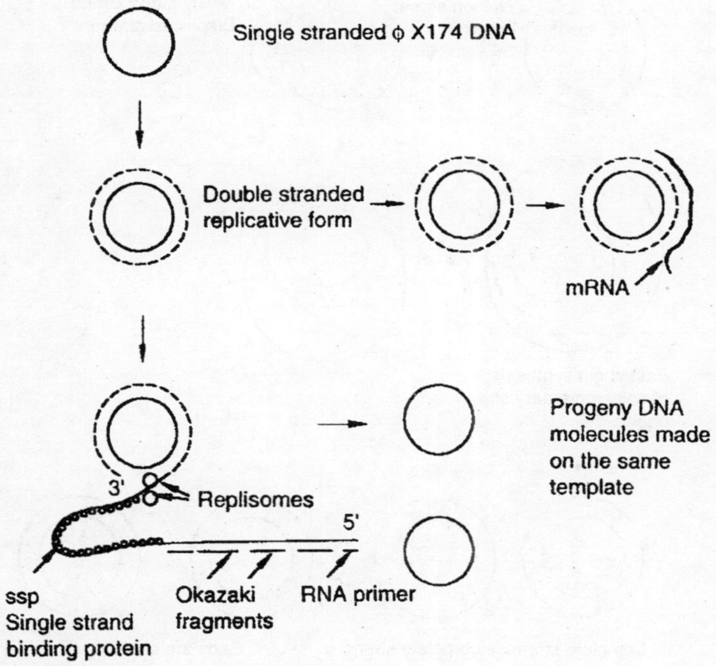

The displacement or D-loop model of DNA replication

In the D-loop model, synthesis of a single strand of DNA begins at the origin and displaces the former pre-existing strand as a D-loop. As the replication proceeds along the circular DNA, the outer D-loop expands. When the displaced strand extends beyond the origin, the synthesis of complementary strands starts. On completion of the circles the gaps are sealed by the enzyme DNA ligase.

DNA replication in the chromosomes of mitochondria, in the ciliate *Tetrahymena* and in chloroplasts of higher plants is known to follow the D-loop model of replication.

There could be more than one D-loop formed at a time in various organisms, e.g. the DNA in chloroplasts of higher plants has 2 D-loops and that of *Tetrahymena* has as many as 6 D-loops during replication.

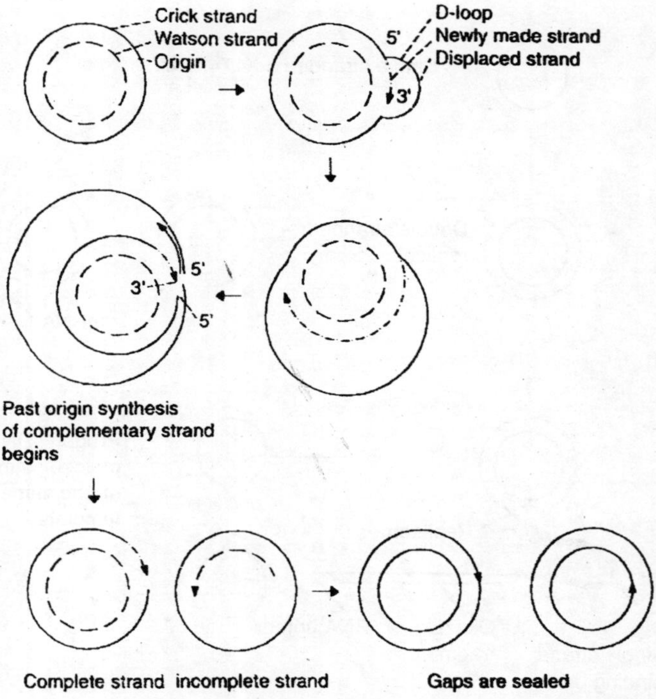

The replication of DNA in eucaryotic cells is limited to the part of the cell division cycle. The cell division cycle of an eucaryotic cell may be divided into 4 stages *G1, S, G2* and *M.* The *G1* and *G2* denote gaps 1 and 2; *S* stands for synthesis of DNA and *M* represents mitosis.

In a typical mammalian cell culture, the cell is in diploid state during *G1* phase, which is the longest for a cell (~ 12 hours) and most variable amongst different cells. The synthesis of DNA occurs during *S* phase, which lasts for a few hours (6-8 h) in eucaryotic cells. At the end of *S* phase, the cell becomes a *tetraploid.* The cell remains in this tetraploid state throughout the *G2* gap phase for a few hours (4 h), and then undergoes mitosis lasting 1 hour. *Mitosis produces two diploid daughter cells from a tetraploid cell.*

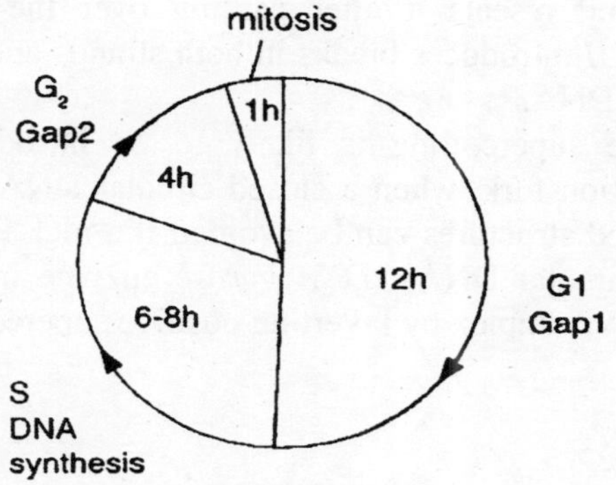

The eucaryotic chromosome arranges DNA replication into thousands of replicons, which are *not* active simultaneously. During the *S* phase at any point of time, only a few replicons are engaged in DNA replication. Probably there is a definite sequence in the activation of different replicons of chromosomes.

The average length of a replication in higher eucaryotes is around 100 – 200 kb. In a diploid genome a mammalian cell may have 40,000 – 60,000 replicons. In Drosophila and yeast the size of replicon is less around 40 kb, while the number of replicons being 7,000 and 1,000 respectively as a diploid cell complement.

Topological features of DNA replication

A revolution about its own axis by DNA double helix produces super coiling in its structure. If the revolution is in the same direction in which the double helix is wound, it is denoted as *positive supercoiling*, and it *overwinds* the double helix. If the revolution is in opposite direction it is called *negative supercoiling* and it *unwinds* some coils in the DNA molecule. The *extent of supercoiling of DNA* is measured in terms of *linking number. The total number of times the two strands of double helix of a closed DNA molecule cross each other denotes its linking number.* The linking number could be altered by enzymatic events, where a strand is broken and rejoined after increasing or decreasing the coiling by one step. The DNA molecules identical in all aspects except supercoiling or linking number are called ***topological isomers***. The enzymes *DNA topoisomerases* can interconvert topological isomers by increasing or decreasing the supercoiling. Topoisomerases have been grouped into 2 classes. The *topoisomerase I* introduces a transient single strand break and reseals it after passing over the unbroken strand. *Topoisomerase II* introduces breaks in both strands and then changes the supercoiling of DNA.

Positive supercoiling is likely to be introduced ahead of a moving replication fork, when a closed circular DNA is replicated. But these supercoiled structures can be avoided if a nick is generated in one strand of the circular DNA. *DNA gyrase* enzyme introduces negative supercoils in DNA duplex by inverting positive supercoils.

Further reading

Baker, T.A., and Wickner, S.H. Genetics and enzymology of DNA replication in *Escherichia coli*. *Annu. Rev. Genet. 26*: 447 (1992).

Kornberg, A., and Baker, T.A. DNA replication, 2nd ed. W.H. Freeman, New York (1992).

Ogawa, T., and Okazaki, T. Discontinuous DNA replication. *Annu. Rev. Biochem. 49*: 421 (1980).

CHAPTER 20

Genetic Recombination

The shuffling of hereditary information amongst chromosomes is known as *recombination*. This exchange of information when occurs in the germ line cells, it is likely to be passed on to the next generation of the organism and is known as *genetic recombination*. If the exchange of information has occurred in the chromosomes of a cell other than germ line cell, i.e. in the body cell, it is known as *somatic recombination* and its effects are usually limited to the lifetime of an organism.

The information content of an individual chromosome can change in two main ways:

A. *Mutation*.

B. *Recombination*.

Mutation produces change within a chromosome, usually without the direct involvement of other chromosomes. In the process of *recombination* at least two chromosomes are involved in information sharing.

1. In the absence of recombination deleterious mutations would accumulate and ultimately eliminate the chromosome. Even favourable mutations would be lost with deleterious mutations.
2. Recombination allows the separation of favourable and unfavourable mutations and testing them in new combinations.
3. Recombination promotes survival and spread of favourable mutations and elimination of deleterious mutations, through the process of natural selection.
4. Partial information loss in a chromosome by way of deletion or damage can at times be retrieved from the homologous chromosome by recombination and repair mechanisms of the cell.
5. Site specific recombination can regulate gene expression.
6. Errors or mismatch in homologous recombination can create mutations, deletions and duplications in genes.

7. The study of genetics would not have been possible, without involving mutation and recombination. But even to date recombination is one of the least understood phenomena.

Some models of recombination

1. *Copying choice model of recombination*

Belling correlated recombination to the process of chromosome duplication as early as in 1931. Currently modified, Belling's model proposes that, in paired chromosomes during replication the new structure forming on one chromosome (e.g. paternal) switches to another chromosome (i.e. maternal). When the new structure being formed on another (i.e. maternal) chromosome reaches the former switch point, it has no choice except copying the paternal chromosome thereafter. In this manner two reciprocal recombinant chromosomes are formed. Lederberg later called this mechanism as *copying choice*.

The *copying choice model* restricts the recombination process to the duration of chromosome replication. This model does not tie up recombination to any morphological stage such as meiosis. In copying choice model the recombinant chromosomes are synthesized *de novo* (*from the new material*) and inherit only the information from the paternal chromosomes. No physical material is exchanged in the copying choice mechanism of recombination, only information is exchanged.

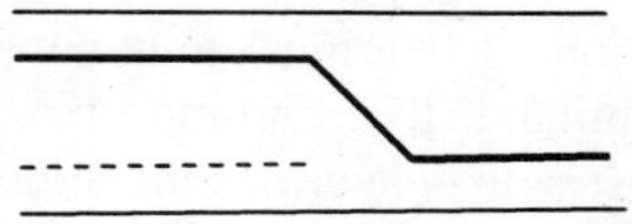

Synthesis switches to copy other chromosome.

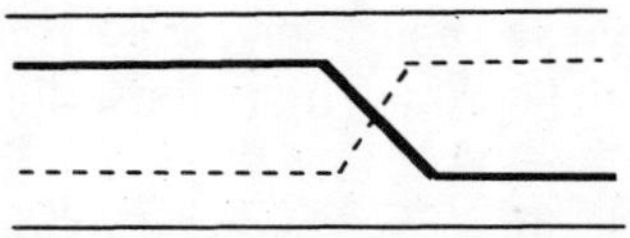

Copies of reciprocal recombinants.

The copy choice model does explain quite well the non-reciprocal recombination for very closely linked intracistronic sites. Initially the non-reciprocal recombination was found in pyridoxineless mutants of *Neurospora*. Since then it has been known to occur in

Aspergillus, yeast and *Drosophila*. The characteristic feature of non-reciprocal recombination is that for *intracistronic sites*, the tetrad contains ***3 parental*** and one recombinant chromosomes. However, for less closely linked, out side markers, reciprocal recombination occurs in the same system.

If in the copy choice mechanism, non-synchronous replication of paired strands is assumed then the ***replication of one strand is more advanced than the other.***

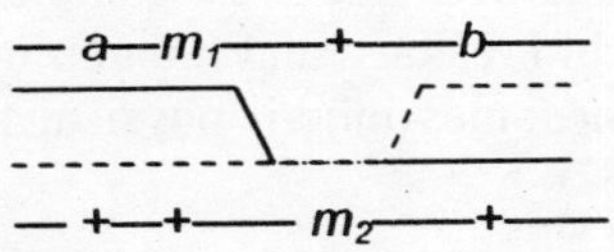

Paternal chromosome

Paternal chromosome

Products of tetrad

— a—m_1——+——b—— Parental for m_1 —+.

— +—+—— m_2——+—— Parental for +— m_2.

—a— m_1— m_2——+—— Recombinant for m_1— m_2.

— +—+—— m_2——b—— Parental for +— m_2.

(Three copies of $\mathbf{m_2}$ *locus have been formed by non-reciprocal recombination, instead of the usual two copies formed in reciprocal recombination).*

The leading replication point switches over to the other strand between the markers m_1 and m_2. By the time the trailing replication point reaches the switch over point, the leading replication point has moved further. There is ***no*** compulsion for the trailing replication point to switch over at the same place between mutations m_1 and m_2 and it can continue further on the same strand and part of it is copied twice — by the leading, as well as by the trailing replication points. If the trailing replication point switches over between m_2 and b sites, non-reciprocal recombinants are produced. Copying choice model beautifully explains the occurrence of non-reciprocal recombinants.

Breakage and reunion model of recombination

Based on the behaviour of chrosomes during meiosis, Darlington in 1935 developed the theory of gene exchange. During first meiotic division the homologous chromosomes pair and start coiling. This creates tension in the strands, which is relieved by breakage of two non-sister chromatids. The broken ends of the sheared chromatids may join across to produce two recombinant and two parental chromatids. The time of recombination in this model is when the chromosomes have paired and formed tetrads. Probably the recombination event is complete after chromosome duplication is complete. In breakage and reunion model of recombination, the recombinant chromosomes inherit physical material from the parental chromosomes.

Chromosomes coil against each other and break at homologous points.

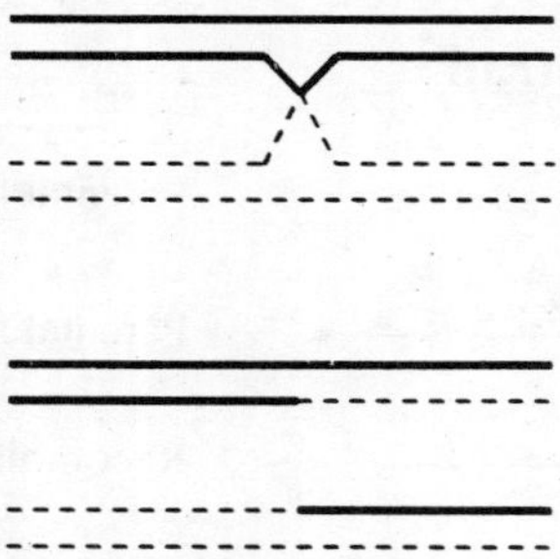

Chromosomes join cross-wise and form recombinants.

Fig. 20.1. Diagram showing the salient features of the breakage and re-union model of genetic recombination.

Pairing of chromosomes

The pairing of homologous regions of the two chromosomes is the *first* essential step in recombination. The *second* step is the exchange of genetic information (or material) which leads to the formation of recombinants. Theoretically, the pairing should occur between precisely the corresponding (homologous) sequences, so that not a single base pair is added or lost during this exchange, otherwise the genes involved may get mutated. In bacteria and bacteriophages, usually the DNA molecule itself is involved in recombination and topologically it should not be difficult for two DNA molecules to synapse (align) for recombination.

However, the mechanism of precise alignment of base pairs of homologous DNA duplexes for recombination in chromosomes is still not clear.

In eucaryotes however, the DNA is tightly packaged into nucleosomes. The electron microscopy of synapsed chromosomes (synaptonemal complex) shows that the homologous DNAs are not in contact at all. The distance between both 2 nm thick DNA duplexes located in two chromosomes is more than 200 nm.

Theoretically, the frequency of recombination is likely to be the product of the frequencies of pairing and genetic exchange. There are two alternative ways in which a particular recombination-frequency (say10%) is achievable.

1. The pairing of genomic segments is complete but the genetic exchange with in the segment occurs randomly with low probability (say 0.1). Final recombination frequency, 1 x 0.1 = 0.1.
2. The pairing of genomic segments is discontinuous with low probability, while genetic exchange occurs with probability 1. Final recombination frequency 0.1 x 1 = 0.1.

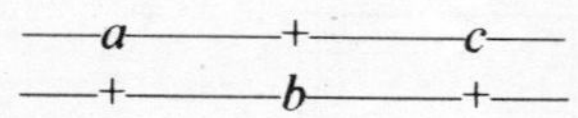

Complete pairing, but **low probability** of genetic exchange.

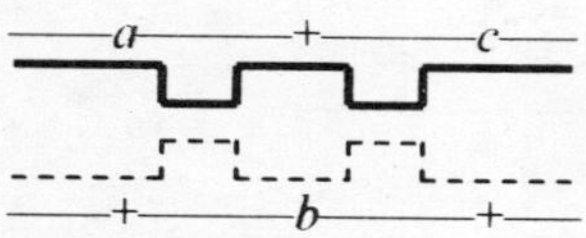

Discontinuous pairing, but **high probability** of genetic exchange.

Experimental evidence for discontinuous pairing

If the pairing of two chromosomes is complete, then it cannot be further increased by the presence of a third homologous chromosome. However, if the pairing occurs discontinuously at a few points in homologous and random regions, then it could be increased up to 3 fold by the presence of a third homologous chromosome within the cell. Pritchard found that *chiasma frequencies* are often higher in *triploid* (*for all chromosomes*) and *trisomics* (*for a particular chromosome*) than in diploids. Group mating is known to occur in the crosses of bacteria and phages, where more than 2 genomes participate in one single mating event. This also raises the possibility of discontinuous and incomplete pairing of chromosomes.

Double-strand-break **repair model of DNA recombination**

Szostak and colleagues including the famous Stahl proposed double-strand-break repair model **(A)** of DNA recombination. According to it the recombination is initiated by double-strand breaks in the DNA. Nucleolytic digestion of the 5' end on single strands gives 3' single stranded unequal protruding ends of DNA. One 3' end invades the D-loop formed by a single strand of the (crossing partner) homologous DNA.

(A)

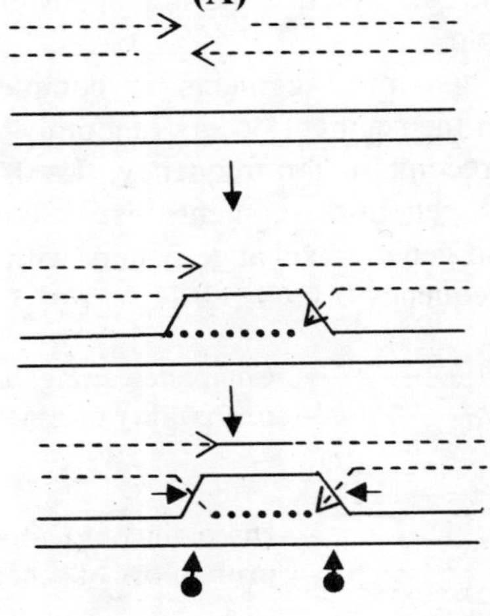

Extension of the 3' invading end occurs by fresh DNA synthesis and copying the juxtaposed homologous strand sequences. In the next step this extended strand joins with the other original fragment of the same DNA strand. Strand discontinuities and gaps are filled by DNA synthesis and ligation.

Any mismatch correction may lead to *gene conversion*. Each Holliday junction is resolved by cleavage of strand at either of the two locations. *In this model the two single strands of the homologous chromosome remain unbroken until the final step of Holliday junction cleavage.*

In addition to double-strand-break repair mechanism 2 additional modes of recombination are envisaged:

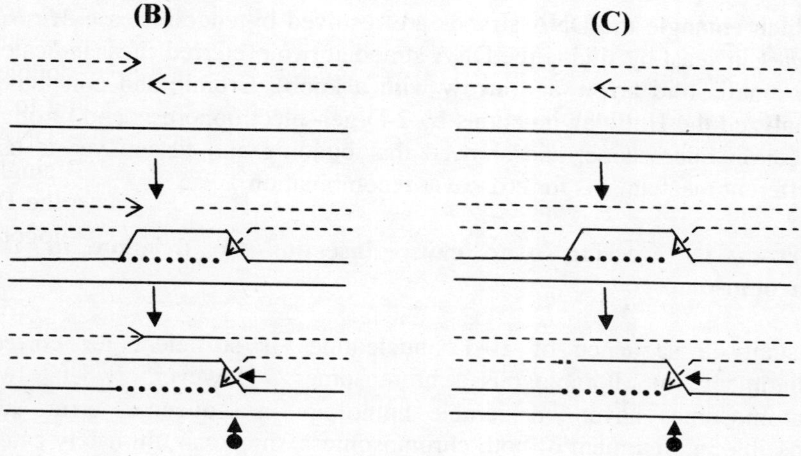

(B) Copy choice or synthesis dependent *D-loop nicking* type of recombination

The extended D-loop is nicked in one place, thereby releasing the loop forming strand, which joins to the juxtaposed strand of the other chromosome. Whereas the extended 3' freshly synthesized strand anneals with the strand that it was copying. Annealing, repair synthesis and ligation form a single Holliday junction.

(C) Copy choice or synthesis dependent *non-crossover* type recombination

In this type of *single strand breakage* and recombination the extended 3' end of DNA strand is *displaced from the D-loop* and joins the second end of the recipient. Repair synthesis and ligation completes a non-crossover recombination.

The crossing over between homologous chromosomes is believed to take place during the first division of meiosis. The topology of DNA strands requires that during crossing over of strands *'cross-strand structures'* called ***Holliday junctions*** form. The budding yeast (*Sacccharomyces cerevisiae*) predominantly shows such double Holliday junctions between homologous chromosomes during meiosis. However, the fission yeast (*S. pombe*) shows single Holliday junctions preferentially between sister chromatids. These Holliday junctions which entangle the DNA strands are resolved by endonuclease *Mus81-Eme*1 in yeast by slicing the DNA strand at two preferred sites (indicated by small solid arrow and arrow with a knob). Cromie and colleagues analyzed the Holliday junctions by 2-D gel- electrophoresis and through electron microscope, and showed that budding and fission yeasts use different mechanisms for crossover recombination.

Errors in crossing over cause insertion or deletion in the chromosome

Usually a sequence of 10-12 nucleotides is sufficient for correct alignment of homologous chromosomes. However, when two chromosomes have considerable homology in sequences, errors are possible in alignment of both chromosomes, which can ultimately cause large portions of DNA to be deleted or duplicated.

A recombination event may cause gene conversion and / or crossovers. Gene conversion results in the non-reciprocal transfer of sequence information from one homologue to the other. In crossing over, reciprocal exchange of both DNA strands occurs between two homologous duplexes. Although not common yet gene conversion and crossing over may occur together in a recombination event.

Retrieval of the damaged or missing region of chromosome by recombination

Double strand breakage in DNA can occur by irradiation with X-rays or by the formation of thymine dimers. If the broken piece of DNA is lost, the sequence lost can be retrieved by recombination. Rec BC protein unwinds the broken ends of DNA. Rec A protein combines with single stranded ends so created and aligns them with the intact, complementary strands of homologous chromosome. Information on the intact complementary, single homologous strand is copied by extending the broken strands of DNA by a DNA polymerase.

Gene expression regulated by site specific recombination

The recombination between two sites located on a single chromosome, either cause deletion or inversion of the intervening segment. This depends on the orientation of the interacting sites.

Interference in recombination

The effect of a recombination event on the probability of occurrence of a second recombination event nearby is called *interference*.

—*a*———+———*c*—
I II
—+———*b*———+—

1. The frequency of recombination f_I in interval **I** = the percentage of ++*c* and *ab*+.
2. The frequency of recombination f_{II} in interval **II** = the percentage of *a*++ and +*bc*.
3. The frequency of recombination $f_{I,\ II}$ in intervals **I** and **II** = percentage of +++ and *abc*.

When $f_I \times f_{II} = f_{I,\ II}$ No interference present.
$f_I \times f_{II} > f_{I,\ II}$ *Positive interference.*

That is the occurrence of recombination in one interval suppresses recombination in adjacent interval.

When $f_I \times f_{II} < f_{I,\ II}$ *Negative interference.*

Meaning, the recombination in one interval favours recombination in the adjacent interval. This is usually by means of effective pairing of chromosomes leading to recombination. If the genes are quite close together, then both genes can undergo recombination in a single paired region. The probability of two recombinations occurring together is *not* independent in such a situation. Such recombinations occur together with high probability.

Proteins known to participate and help recombination

It seems that breaks in DNA greatly stimulate crossing over. The irradiation with ultra violet rays, X-rays and treatment with chemicals or enzymes that create double stranded breaks in DNA enhance crossing over.

Rec A protein specifically recognizes single stranded DNA and on an average one molecule of Rec A binds to 5 nucleotides in the DNA, forming a *DNA – protein filament*. Rec A protein in the filament unwinds and probes different regions of the DNA duplex, until a complimentary sequence is found and in this region the pairing is firmly established. In the presence of energy giving molecule ATP, the pairing reaction is taken to completion in 5'→ 3' direction of single strand. The Rec A protein is displaced as new hybrid DNA is formed. Breaks in DNA molecules encourage nucleases to create single strands and allow interaction with Rec A, which facilitates recombination. Probably in simpler organisms like phages T4 or λ, nucleases alone are sufficient to create breaks and single strand regions in the DNA molecules to promote recombination. However, in more complex organisms, proteins like Rec A and Rec BC are needed for successful recombination. The Rec A protein is specified by a gene *rec A* in *E. coli*, while Rec BC protein is a large protein specified by two genes *rec B* and *rec C*. Rec BC has a nuclease activity, DNA unwinding as well as rewinding activities. The unwinding activity of Rec BC is faster than rewinding activity, creating single stranded regions where Rec A protein can interact with DNA. Quite a few proteins such as DNA ligase, are expected to be involved in the process of DNA recombination.

Further reading

Bishop, D.K. Multiple mechanisms of meiotic recombination. *Cell, 127*: 1095-1097 (2006).

Cromie, G.A., Hyppa, R.W., Taylor, A.F., Zakharyevich, K., Hunter, N., and Smith, G.R. Single Holliday junctions are intermediates of meiotic recombination. *Cell, 127*: 1167-1178 (2006).

Kobayashi, I. Mechanisms for gene conversion and homologous recombination: the double-strand break repair model and successive half crossing-over model. *Adv. Biophys. 28*: 81 (1992).

Kourilsky, P. Molecular mechanisms of gene conversion in higher cells. *Trends. Genet. 2*: 60 (1986).

Messelsohn, M.S., and Radding, C.M. A general model for genetic recombination. *Proc. Natl. Acad. Sci.*, Washington, *72*: 358 (1975).

Radding, C.M. Homologous pairing and strand exchange in genetic recombination. *Annu. Rev. Genet. 16*: 405-437 (1982).

Szostak, J.W., Orr-Weaver, T.L., Rothstein, R.J., and Stahl, F.W. The double-strand-break repair model for recombination. *Cell, 33*:.25-35 (1983).

CHAPTER 21

Recombinant DNA and Genetic Engineering

In the last 25 years, the progress of Molecular Biology has made it possible, to isolate selected regions of DNA from an organism and recombine it with a smaller genome of a plasmid, virus or a bacterium. This *recombinant DNA* can be amplified and analyzed with confidence. This process is also called '*cloning*' of the gene. Recombinant DNA molecules can be constructed by joining any two non-homologous DNA molecules even from widely different species or genera. The genome into which the foreign or *exogenous* DNA piece has been incorporated is known as a '*vector*'. The organism that allows maintaining, multiplying and re-harvesting of the *vector* is known as '**host**'. Bacteria, yeast and cultured cell-lines are popular hosts for various vectors.

Vectors

Vectors are usually well-characterized small molecules of DNA with their own origin of replication. The multiplication (or cloning) of the vector with recombinant DNA should be easy and reliable, without any loss of recombinant DNA. Plasmids, bacteriophages, cosmids and single stranded phages are some favourable vectors in vogue.

Plasmids

Plasmids are quite suited as vectors being mini-chromosomes with circular DNA and can replicate in a host cell autonomously. Plasmids can carry drug resistance markers allowing the selection of cells harbouring recombinant DNA-plasmids. During cell growth and multiplication 20-50 copies of a plasmid could be present per cell. On stopping the protein synthesis, on an average up to 1,000 copies of PBR 322 plasmid, which harbours genes for the resistance to ampicillin and tetracyclin could be harvested per cell.

Bacteriophage λ

Bacteriophages usually package a *head-full* of DNA, irrespective of the source of DNA. Bacteriophage λ can package 45 kb long DNA in to its head. Fifteen to 20 kb long pieces of recombinant DNA piece can be reliably carried and cloned (multiplied or amplified) by λ. Larger pieces if incorporated tend to be lost during cloning. The DNA inserts usually replace the central region of λ-chromosome and the ends are kept intact, as they are needed for circularization of λ-DNA and its replication in the host bacterium *E. coli*.

Cosmids

Cosmids are made by adding cohesive (*cos* ends) ends of λ to a plasmid. They utilize the discovery that fewer genes are needed for *in vitro* packaging of DNA into phage head. So some λ genes can be dispensed with and the size of insert (DNA) could be increased. *Cosmids can have DNA inserts upto 45 kb.* Cosmids are maintained by *in vivo* replication but harboured for recombinant DNA by *in vitro* packaging.

Single stranded phages

Single stranded phages like *M13* get converted to double stranded replicative form in *E. coli.* On re-infection of a suitable host, single stranded phages are generated, whose DNA can be sequenced directly. For making the vectors more useful from the point of view of transcription and translation of inserted genes (or cloned genes); *expression vectors* have been constructed. The DNA-insert is spliced close to *lac*-operon promotor putting its expression under the control of *lac* repressor. A *bi-functional expression vector* can be expressed in two different hosts. A composite plasmid called *shuttle vector* contains origin of replication from plasmid *PBR 322* as well as from virus *SV 40*. This allows the shuttle vector to grow in *E. coli* as well as in mammalian cell culture.

Restriction enzymes

The discovery of restriction enzyme *Hind II* from *Haemophilus influenzae* by Smith in 1970, was an important landmark in the development of *recombinant DNA technology*, popularly known as *genetic engineering*.

The enzyme *Hind II* cleaved phage DNA in to 40 fragments. The cleavage by Hind II was always in the middle of the following sequence (arrow marked):

$$\begin{array}{c} \downarrow \\ -5'\text{–G–T–Py–Pu–A–C–}3'- \\ -3'\text{–C–A–Pu–Py–T–G–}5'- \\ \uparrow \end{array}$$

(Where the arrows indicate the site of cleavage by the restriction enzyme and Pu = Purine A or G; Py = Pyrimidine C or T). The cleavage by *Hind II* was always in the middle of above sequence, wherever they occurred on ϕ T7 DNA. Such a sequence of *base pairs* that reads the same in 5'→ 3' direction *on complementary strands*; or tandem inverted repeats and are known as *palindromic* sequences. For example the word *MALAYALAM* reads the same in forward and back word directions

Smith also showed that host induced methylation of base **A**. close to the cleavage site protects DNA from *Hind II* action

$$\begin{array}{c} \mathbf{X} \\ \downarrow \quad \mathbf{m} \\ -5'\text{–G–T–Py–Pu–A–C–}3'- \\ -3'\text{–C–A–Pu–Py–T–G–}5'- \\ \mathbf{m} \quad \uparrow \\ \mathbf{X} \end{array}$$

*(Methylation = m, of the base A, prevents (**X**), Hind II from cleaving at the modified site).*

It became clear that *restriction enzymes produce sequence-specific cuts in DNA to generate a heterogenous population of pieces with identical ends*. More than 100 restriction enzymes have been characterized. Restriction enzyme can also cleave a stretch of palindromic sequence by introducing a staggered cut on both strands between non-complementary bases, thereby producing single stranded ends. The *site of cleavage* by restriction enzyme is also known as *target site*.

Hpa II restriction enzyme from *Haemophilus parainfluenzae* cleaves

↓
–5'–C–C–G–G–3'–
–3'–G–G–C–C–5'–
↑

palindromic sequence between C-C bases in a staggered manner giving rise to cohesive ends. Some commonly used restriction enzymes are *Eco I; Eco II; Hind II; Hind III; Bam I ; Bgl II, Hpa II* etc.

Restriction maps of DNA

Like genetic mutations have been used for mapping chromosomes, *the restriction enzyme target sites* can also be used to produce maps of stretches of DNA from different organisms. The strategy to make restriction map of a circular DNA is as follows:
By partial digestion with a restriction enzyme A (for example), the circular DNA is cleaved to produce a linear DNA molecule with cohesive or blunt ends.

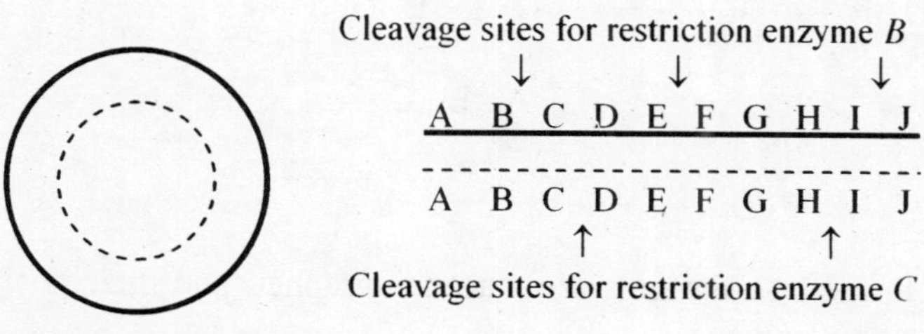

Circular DNA

The linear molecule so formed is labelled by P^{32} on its 5' ends.
It is partially digested with restriction enzyme B to produce fragments of varying lengths.

A B and C D E F G H I J

A B C D E and F G H I J

A B C D E F G H I and J

These fragments are labelled at 5'- end by P^{32} and separated by gel electrophoresis. The bands on the gel will be in the order of the fragment size.

A B C D E F G H I
C D E F G H I J
A B C D E
F G H I J
A B
J

The longest fragment is selected from the gel and its two aliquots are taken. One aliquot is again partially digested with restriction enzyme B and the second aliquot is partially digested with restriction enzyme C. The fragments so obtained by partial digestions are run separately on gels after labelling the 5'- ends with P^{32} label. The bands formed will be as under:

From restriction enzyme B.	From restriction enzyme C.
C D E F G H I	A B C D E F G H
A B C D E	D E F G H
F G H I	A B C
A B	I

The bands formed on the gels are autoradiographed and their positions determined on the gels.

By comparing the gel patterns of the partial digests of DNA by 2 or 3 restriction enzymes followed by some jigsaw puzzle like fitting of bands, it is often possible to make *a restriction map* of a stretch of DNA or genome.

Construction of recombinant DNA molecules

There are quite a few methods of constructing recombinant DNA molecules, which mostly depend upon the set of restriction enzymes used.

1. Formation of cohesive ends.
2. Tailing or extension by terminal transferase.
3. Blunt end ligation.

Formation of cohesive ends

The DNA to be cloned and the vector (e.g. Plasmid *SC101*) are treated with a suitable restriction enzyme say *EcoR I*. The plasmid *SC 101* has only one *EcoR I* restriction site. Digestion with this restriction enzyme converts the circular *SC 101* to a linear molecule with cohesive ends. The DNA to be cloned is also cleaved into pieces depending upon the occurrence of *EcoR I* sites in its sequences.

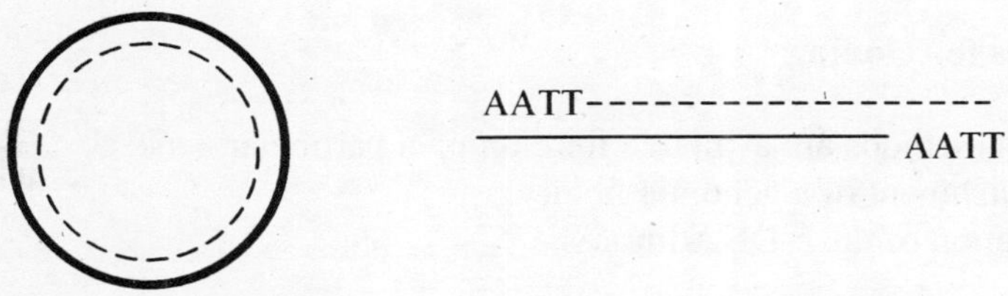

On annealing the sticky ends of plasmid and exogenous DNA fragment form hydrogen bonds. All four single stranded gaps are sealed by treatment with DNA ligase.

Extension by terminal transferase

The enzyme *terminal transferase* can create sticky ends on blunt DNA fragments by adding nucleotides to 3' ends of the two strands of DNA duplex. To one set of DNA fragments if d*A* (deoxyadenine) residues are added together with terminal transferase, an *AAAA* tail will be generated at 3' end.

5'——————————*AAAA*3

3'*AAAA*——————————5'

If to the other pieces of DNA to be joined, (d*T*) residues are added together with the enzyme terminal transferase, then a tail of *TTTT* is produced on 3' ends of both strands of DNA duplex.

5'——————————*TTTT*3'

3' *TTTT*——————————5'

These two complementary sticky ends can join and DNA ligase is used to join the gaps and establish covalent bonds. Similarly poly G and poly C tails can be constructed by using dG and dC respectively.

Ligation of blunt ends

Blunt ended DNA fragments can be joined by T4 DNA ligase. In this way even synthetically made double stranded DNA molecules containing restriction sites can be joined to blunt ended DNA fragments. Synthetic DNA linkers are quite useful as the treatment with appropriate restriction enzyme generates cohesive ends. In this manner by the use of sythetic DNA linkers and the DNA ligase, the cloning of DNA fragments initially having blunt ends is facilitated

Strategies for cloning

Two main methods are available for cloning a particular gene:
1. Establishment of a genomic library.
2. Formation of the c-DNA library.

Establishment of a genomic library

All fragments of DNA generated by a restriction enzyme digestion are cloned and then screened for the desired sequence. The cloning of random DNA fragments of higher organisms is called *shotgunning*. The entire collection of such clones is called *gene library* or *gene bank*.

A *genomic library* may be established by cloning all fragments of the genes in λ bacteriophages. The collection of λ phages is plated with sensitive bacteria to form plaques in the bacterial lawn. *Each plaque has a different fragment of DNA*. To identify a particular fragment of DNA the following procedure is adopted.

1. The plaque pattern on the bacterial lawn is replica plated on a nitrocellulose filter.
2. Phage-proteins are removed by enzymatic digestion.
3. The exposed recombinant DNA is denatured so it can adhere well to the filter.
4. The filter is treated with radioactively labelled probe, a DNA copy of the mRNA of the needed gene.
5. The probe hybridizes with any recombinant DNA having homologous sequence of DNA.
6. The position of the clone on the bacterial lawn is located by autoradiography.
7. The desired clone can be selected from the plaque formed on the bacterial lawn.

8. The gene carried by the bacteriophage can be amplified by growing the culture of phage in sensitive bacteria.

Identification of a cloned gene

Edwin Southern developed in 1975, a valuable technique known as *Southern blotting* for the detection of cloned gene amongst a collection of other genes. The following steps are carried out for Southern blotting. The piece of DNA expected to contain the desired gene is treated with a suitable restriction enzyme.
Restriction fragments generated from such treatment are subjected to gel or agarose electrophoresis, where they are separated as bands according to their size.
After electrophoresis, the gel is kept on a synthetic sponge sheet placed in a glass dish containing buffer solution. The gel is covered with a nitrocellulose filter-sheet and several layers of absorbent dry paper towels.

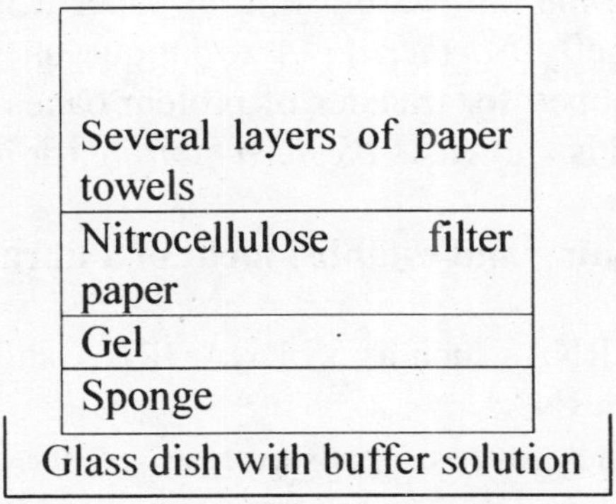

1. The buffer solution rises through the gel → nitrocellulose filter paper → absorbent paper towels, slowly by capillary action of fluid buffer. This vertical up-flow of buffer solution partly transfers double stranded DNA bands on the gel to nitrocellulose filter paper (similar to making an impression by a rubber stamp on a paper).
2. The DNA bands so formed on nitrocellulose filter paper are denatured to become single stranded. Single stranded DNA

sticks well to filter paper and is immobilized in a pattern similar to that formed in the gel-electrophoresis.

3. A known piece of P^{32} labelled DNA or RNA is used as a probe for hybridization with the affixed denatured DNA bands on nitrocellulose filter.
4. The labelled probes are also annealed with single stranded restriction fragments on the gel.
5. To prevent non-specific binding of probe to nitrocellulose filter, it is flooded with unlabelled single stranded DNA from unrelated origin.
6. The DNA bands that anneal to radioactive labelled probe are localized by autoradiography.
7. The DNA band of interest after localization may be cut out from the gel and eluted.

This technique is known as *Southern blotting* after its inventor Southern. If in an experiment, RNA fragments are transferred from the gel to the nitrocellulose filter paper it is called *Northern blotting* (or briefly *Northern*). A technique on similar principles has been developed for transfer of protein bands from SDS gel to filter paper and is known as *Western blotting* (or briefly *Western*).

The cDNA cloning and establishment of a library of cDNAs

Some types of RNAs such as 5S RNA, tRNA and rRNA are easier to purify than mRNA.

1. The enzyme reverse transcriptase is used for making a *complementary DNA strand* from a purified RNA or even from a partially purified mRNA molecule.
2. The single stranded complementary DNA is converted to DNA-duplex by the enzyme DNA polymerase I.
3. The *double stranded complementary DNA* is known as *cDNA* and can be easily purified.
4. The total population of cDNA of interest is incorporated in plasmids, so that each plasmid molecule integrated only one fragment of cDNA.

5. The bacterial cells are so transformed with these plasmid-molecules, so that each bacterium receives only one plasmid.
6. Clones formed from such single cells are tested for the unique cDNA of interest and identified.
7. The DNA from such identified clone is multiplied and can be put to several uses.
8. Make complementary mRNA.
9. Make corresponding protein.
10. Purified cDNA can be used as a probe to screen colonies from a gene-bank

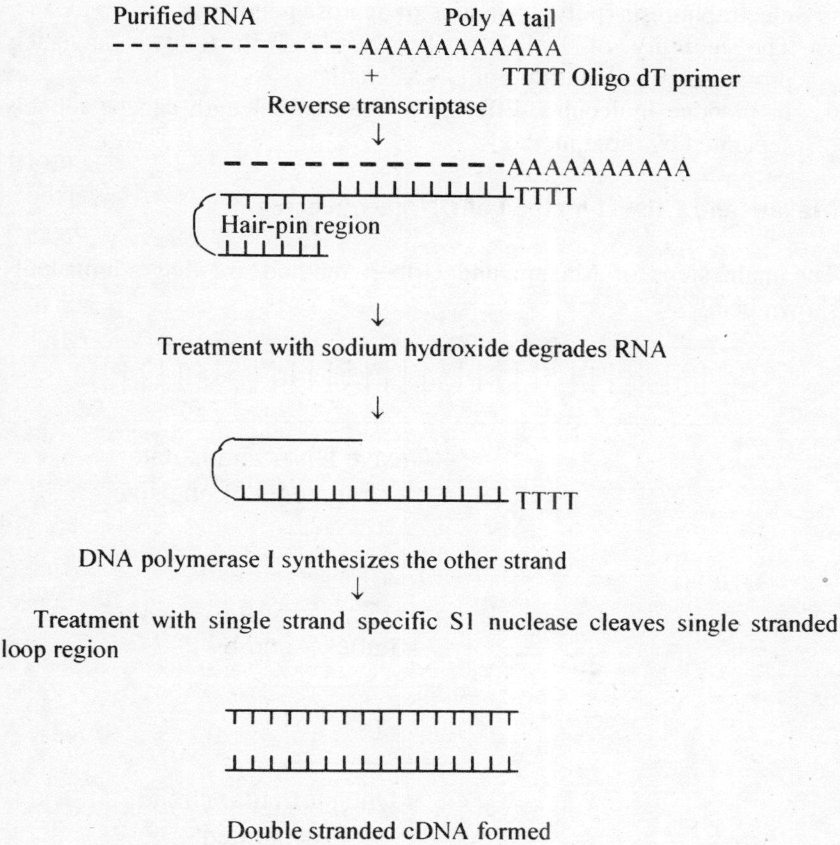

Fig. 21.1. A schematic diagram illustrating the methodology of cDNA cloning

Sequence determination of DNA or sequencing of DNA

Around 1977 two methods of *sequencing DNA* were developed independently: one by Maxam and Gilbert and the other by Sanger.

1. The principal requirement for DNA sequencing is to start with a defined fragment of DNA.
2. Label the DNA molecule at one end by P^{32}.
3. Generate from these homogeneous molecules of DNA a population of molecules of decreasing length. Each molecule differing by one base.
4. Separate the single stranded molecules of different sizes by gel electrophoresis (polyacrylamide or agarose gels).
5. The mobility of DNA-strand under electric field is inversely proportional to logarithm of DNA-length.
6. In practice molecules differing by one base length can be reliably separated by these methods.

Maxam and Gilbert method of DNA sequencing

The main steps of Maxam and Gilbert method are diagrammatically shown below:

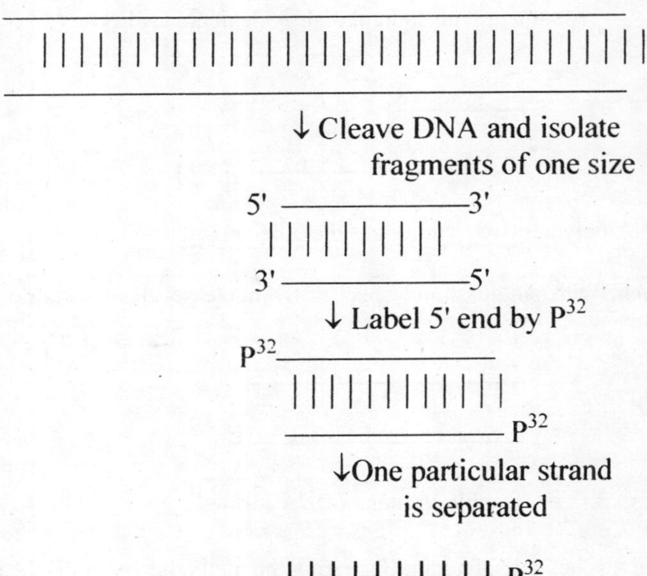

Four aliquots are taken from this sample and separately treated in individual test tubes by different reagents such that **

Electrophorese the contents of each tube separately, in parallel on a gel:

Test tube #	1	2	3	4
Destroyed base	**G**	**A, G**	**T, C**	**C**
A		—		
C			—	—
C			—	—
T			—	
G	—			
A	—	—		
C			—	—
G	—			
G	—	—		

** When this sample of single stranded DNA is treated with dimethylsulphate, the N7 position in Guanine and N3 position in adenine molecules are methylated. On heating, the methylated base is lost from DNA strand generating a break in the polynucleotide chain.

The cleavage at G is more frequent (forming a darker band in the gel) than adenine (forms a lighter band in the gel). The pattern of dark and light bands is reversed if DNA treatment is carried out in acidic conditions.

Pyrimidines are analysed by treatment with hydrazine, where cytosine and thymine are cleaved off from DNA, causing a break in the DNA strand. Hydrazine in presence of higher salt concentration cleaves at only cytosine.

Conditions of reaction mixtures are maintained in such a way that only 1 molecule in 50 molecules is cleaved, so that no molecule of DNA has been cleaved twice. Either there is no cleavage or only one cleavage in any molecule of DNA in the reaction mixture. Products of the reaction mixtures are analyzed in parallel by electrophoresis on the gel. The shortest fragments migrate faster and form band at the bottom of the gel and the DNA sequence is read upward from bottom of the electrophoretic lane.

Sanger's 2'-3' dideoxynucleotide (ddNTP) method of DNA sequencing

In *in vitro* DNA synthesizing systems, if a small amount of any di-deoxynucleotides ddATP; ddAGP; ddCTP or ddTTP (commonly called ddNTP) is present together with 4 normal 2'-deoxynucleotide triphosphates (dNTP), and by chance a ddNTP is incorporated in to the nascent polynucleotide chain, then it can no longer form bond with the next incoming dNTP and the growing DNA chain terminates there itself. Sanger, Nicklen and Coulson utilized this idea to sequence DNA of a single stranded phage *ϕX 174*, which has 5,400 nucleotides in its DNA. In Sanger's method a single stranded stretch of DNA whose sequence is to be determined is added as a primer to 4 *in vitro* DNA synthesizing test tubes. To each individual test tube 1; 2; 3; and 4 amongst the four tubes, a small amount of one of these ddATP; ddGTP; ddCTP or ddTTP is added respectively.

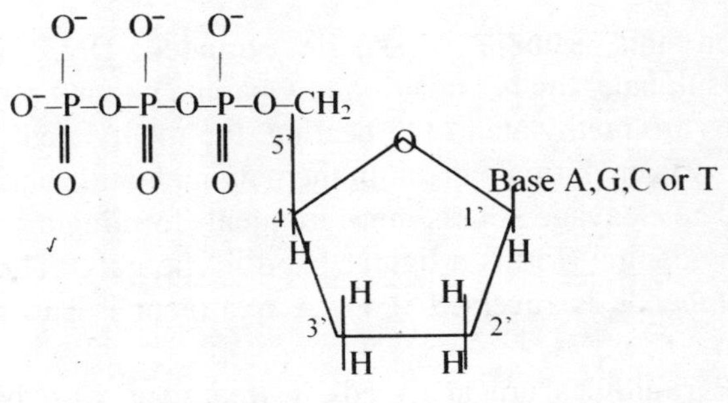

Dideoxynucleotide (ddNTP), where A = adenine; C = cytosine; G = guanine; P = phosphate group; T =thymine.

The contents of each test tube containing the DNA pieces so synthesized are electrophoresed in parallel on the same gel. The electrophoresis pattern obtained is similar to Maxam and Gilbert method and is read in similar fashion to deduce the sequence of DNA.

M-13 variation of the dideoxyribose method of DNA sequencing

1. The DNA fragment to be sequenced is inserted in the single stranded virus M13 at a precise location.
2. A DNA primer of 15-17 bases complementary to a region in M13 is annealed in immediate neighbourhood of inserted foreign DNA to be sequenced.
3. The same primer is used for all reactions in dideoxyribose method. The sequencing of DNA has become quite rapid and easy by this method.

Pulsed field gel electrophoresis (PFGE)

Pulsed field gel electrophoresis (PFGE) can separate larger DNA fragments by application of pulses of two electric fields across the gel at 90°. Fragments larger than 100 kb will move according to their size. The intact chromosomes of yeast or fungi can be separated by PFGE.

Mammalian chromosomes that are quite large for direct electrophoresis are cleaved by rare cleavers - restriction enzymes such as *Not I*; *Pvu I* and *Mlu I* to yield 100 - 2,000 kb long DNA fragments. These fragments can be separated by PFGE.

Polymerase chain reaction (PCR)

Polymerase chain reaction (PCR) developed by Mullis and coworkers in 1985, allows us to synthesize sufficient quantity of a particular DNA from its single molecule. The main steps are listed here.

1. A double stranded DNA containing the gene or sequence of interest is selected.
2. Strands of the DNA are separated by heating.
3. Two single stranded polynucleotides 10-12 bases long and complementary to each 3' end of DNA are made or obtained. These are called Primers say 1 and 2.
4. The primers are annealed to the single strand of DNA at 3' ends.
5. A high temperature-resistant polymerase known as *Taq polymerase* isolated from *Thermus aquaticus* is used. Taq polymerase synthesizes complementary DNA daughter strands, extending these primers annealed to original DNA molecule.
6. Since the original DNA strand may not have chain terminating codons, the polynucleotide synthesis may be of variable lengths.

7. The two DNA duplexes obtained after the first round of replication are heated again to yield 4 single strands of DNA.
8. Primer molecules are attached to two new daughter single strands at 3' ends.
9. *Taq* polymerase synthesizes new complementary DNA strands on all these 4 single stranded DNA molecules.
10. At the end of second round of DNA synthesis all strands of DNA have primer sequences at 3' ends and comlementary sequence for primers at 5' ends.
11. The process of DNA synthesis can be repeated many times by lowering and raising the temperature of the reaction mixture. At lower temperature *Taq polymerase* synthesizes DNA and at higher temperature DNA duplexes become single stranded.
12. The amount of DNA synthesized increases in geometric progression 2; 4; 8; 16; 32; 64; 128; 256; 512; 1024; 2048 and so on. Now a days automated PCR machines are available to provide temperature changes for required duration and synthesize sufficient DNA from a single molecule to begin with.

Chromosome walking

Individual vectors can clone a limited stretch of DNA. However, at times large stretches of DNA or chromosome need to be analyzed and as such sequence determination at times is needed. This is usually achieved by a method called *chromosome walking*. The method consists of the following main steps.

1. A decision is made to select a particular large region of DNA existing in a gene to be analyzed by *chromosome walking.*
2. A fragment called *probe* is selected from the gene bank.
3. The probe is used for screening the gene bank to obtain 2 clones, which have the *'probe sequence'* in common. Therefore these clones are likely to have *contiguous sections* (called *dyad*) on the chromosome.
4. A new probe is selected for the outer flanking regions of the dyad.
5. The gene bank is screened by individual probes to find two more clones that have contiguous region of chromosome.
6. Likewise the process is repeated several times to walk through a large region of chromosome.

It need to be pointed out that many fragments so identified will have uncleaved restriction enzyme sites, since the digestion was not taken to completion at the start of the gene-bank.

Some regions of chromosome will be present in fragments of different sizes.

Chromosome walking is still a time consuming effort and presence of repeat sequences on the chromosome can pose difficulties at times.

DNA Footprinting

Some proteins bind to regulatory DNA sequences that are usually located outside the coding region of the gene. To understand the function of the protein it is often desirable to determine the sequence of DNA to which the protein binds. These DNA binding proteins usually protect the DNA in the binding region from a specific chemical or enzymatic degradation.

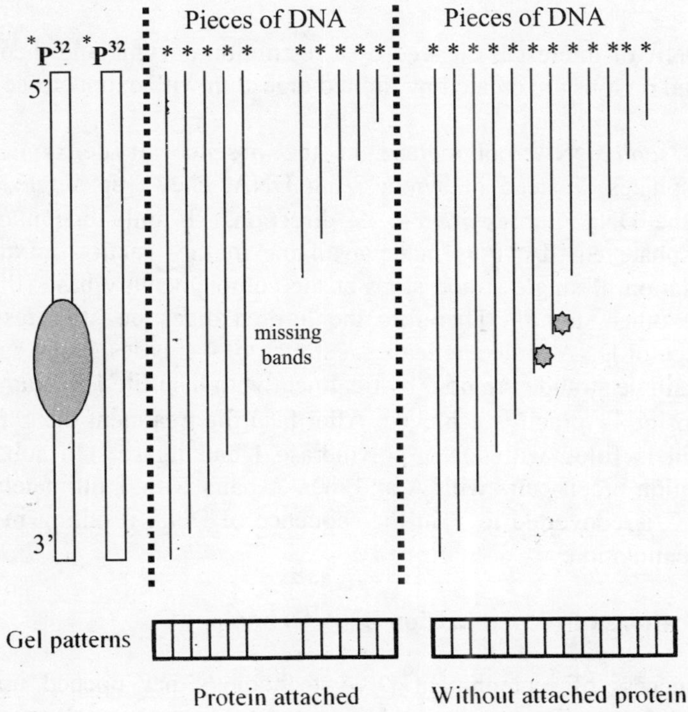

Fig.21.2. A schematic diagram showing the method of DNA footprinting.

To begin with, a pure and homogeneous preparation of DNA to which the protein is likely to bind is isolated. The 5'-end of the DNA is labelled with radioactive P^{32}. Two aliquots of this DNA solution are made. In one aliquot the protein is allowed to bind with DNA. Both samples are treated with a suitable nuclease usually DNaseI or a chemical at such a dilution that each DNA molecule gets randomly cut ***only once***. The DNA is denatured in both samples and the fragments separated on gel in two separate lanes. The DNA fragments of different lengths form discrete bands in the gel. The bands so formed are detected by autoradiography. Regions of DNA that are bound by DNA binding proteins are protected from digestion. Bands corresponding to those regions are missing, leading to footprints on the gel. These footprints define the precise location of binding of transcription factors and other DNA binding proteins to DNA.

Site specific *in vitro* mutagenesis

The DNA of interest is cleaved by a restriction enzyme and then single stranded regions are created by limited digestion with exonuclease III

OR

E. coli DNA polymerase in the absence of deoxynucleotide triphosphates instead of synthesizing DNA, chews up single strands from the DNA duplex in 3'→ 5' direction. If only one nucleotide triphosphate e.g dATP is made available in the reaction mixture the degradation of single strand stops at the complementary base (thymine) on the other strand. Therefore the limited digestion after restriction cleavage of DNA molecule leaves a stretch of 4-5 bases single stranded. In the single stranded region, by treatment with bisulfite *ion* deamination of cytosine → uracil is achieved. After bisulfite treatment the gap in the plasmid is filled with DNA polymerase I and ligase. In subsequent replication uracil pairs with A and then A pairs with T ultimately. As a result C is converted to T in the sequence of DNA resulting in a base change mutation.

Applications of recombination DNA technology

The success of recombinant DNA technology has opened up many possibilities in diverse areas of Biology, Medicine, Agriculture, Animal Husbandry and Chemistry. Some of its applications are listed below:

1. Genes can be altered at a desired site by in vitro mutagenesis.

2. Recombinant DNA technology is used for making transgenic plants and animals.
3. Human proteins or proteins from higher organisms can be synthesized by bacteria.
4. Genetic diseases can be diagnosed at an early stage.
5. Quality of crop or animals can be improved.
6. Shelf life of fruits may be extended, seedless fruits, high yielding milch cattle and plants can be produced.
7. In sexually reproducing organisms the progeny may be reproduced from mother only, dispensing the role of father. Normally an ovum from mother and a sperm from father, which have haploid number of chromosomes, pool together their chromosomes to become a diploid cell (egg) on fertilization of ovum with a sperm. Given the right conditions this egg can become a fully developed embryo.

In an experiment, a sheep ovum was *anucleated* and the nucleus of an *udder cell* from the same animal was put in its place. The egg was triggered to divide by parthenogenesis (*i.e* by pricking). The somatic cell of sheep-udder has a diploid number of chromosomes. By nuclear transplantation the diploid number of chromosomes in the egg was attained without fertilization by a sperm. Such an egg was replanted in the uterus of the same sheep. Under proper hormonal treatment of the sheep, the famous young Dolly sheep was born as a fit healthy sheep. But subsequent studies on enzyme patterns of Dolly sheep showed that she was aging probably faster than normal adult sheep. This is not unexpected, as the nucleus of the udder cell used was surely older than the freshly generated ovum and sperm involved in a normal fertilization.

Sequencing of the human genome

The human genome comprises of two sets of 23 chromosomes, where one set is inherited from each parent. The human genome is at least 3 billion chemical letters long message, where only a few percent (~3%) of its active genes. The rest is non-genes, and viral genes. Better understanding of human genome may vastly improve the fields of healthcare and medicine. However, the same knowledge for example, may be miused for denying a job and life insurance cover to certain people.

A consortium named Human Genome Project lead by Francis S. Collins and a private company Celera Genomics headed by J.C. Venter used two different methodologies to sequence the human Genome.

Consortium Method: The genome was broken down to 150,000 bp long pieces named BAC. Since the sequencing machine can analyze 500 bases long pieces, each BAC was analyzed from thousands of 500 bp long pieces. These pieces were arranged in a sequence by a computer by comparing the overlapping sequences near the ends. However, BACs do not always assemble correctly because repeat sequences in the human genome confuse the computer program. Chromosome nos. 21 and 22 were sequenced completely by this method. For other chromosomes about 85% of the sequences were deciphered.

Celera's Method: Human genome was broken down in a set of pieces 2,000; 10,000 and 50,000 bp long, which were analyzed separately. A single mammoth computer programme was used to arrange these sequences by using some clever tricks to overcome repetitive sequences in the chromosomes. Approximately 905 of the sequences are known by Celera" method.

In addition to the human genome, the sequences of the genomes of *Arabidopsis* and rice plants have also been more or less worked out.

From the studies related to human genome project, data for millions of *single-nucleotide polymorphism* (SNPs) became available for genome-wide association with common diseases and complex traits. By taking the advantage of the available information on SNPs, the high experimental genotyping ability, the access to DNA specimen banks and clinical data bases a genome-wide scan of candidate genes is feasible for known diseases.

DNA sequencing of the extinct species

It has become possible to extract the genetic information from the remains of the species that no longer are living on earth. The Remains of a close cousin of present day human beings were found in Neander Valley in Germany about 150 years ago. This species was shorter and heavier built than humans and were called Neanderthal man.

Svante Pääbo and his colleagues at Max Planck Institute, Leipzig, Germany have sequenced about 1 million letters of Neanderthal DNA extracted from a piece of bone. The technique used is known as '***pyro-sequencing***' is about 100 times faster than earlier techniques. The DNA is broken up in to short chunks, then shaken up in a mix of silicone-based oil, water, a large number of tiny plastic beads and DNA duplicating chemicals. This mix is applied to a tiny chip with 1 million wells in it. Under the right conditions of DNA replication each well contains one type of short DNA chunks. The sequence of bases in these chunks is analysed by fluorescence of different bases. It is fast as many batches can be analysed at the same time and the process is automated. Stretches of Neanderthal DNA were compared with the known human equivalent DNA sequences.

Edward Rubin and his team at the Lawrence Berkeley National Laboratory, California used '***metagenomic approach***'. In this approach specific areas of interest in DNA can be targeted. Individual DNA fragments are propagated in traditionl way in bacteria to create a gene library. They also developed a method of choosing specific sequences from the library to study any gene of interest.They found 29 streteches of Neanderthal DNA that are similar to humans. These findings suggest that genetically Neanderthals and humans are at least 99.5% identical.

However, there is hardly any resemblance between the mitochondrial DNA extracted from the bones of Neanderthals with any known modern humans. This led to the conclusion that there was no detectable interbreeding between the two species. *'No interbreeding' is also an important criterion that separates one species from another.*

Recombinase-mediated genomic replacement (RMGR)

Replacement of a large segment (> 100 kb) of mouse genome DNA with the orthologous sequences of other species, including humans cloned in BAC libraries has become possible by RMGR.

For genomic segment in mouse ES cell chromosome to be replaced by orthologous human BAC, both the recipient and donor segments are initially modified by flanking them with heterotypic *lox* sites. The segments are exchanged by using *Cre* recombinase.

Using this technique Wallace and colleagues replaced the α– globulin regulatory domain with human syntenic region and generated homozygous mice that produced only human α– globulin chains.

Microarrays or DNA-chips

Until late 1980s Biology was still a lobour intensive and time consuming science. Scientists had to toil for months in laboratory to collect data about a few genes. The key to rapid success lay in automation and miniaturization of analytical tools. In 1988 Dr. Edwin Southern (Southern Blotting of DNA fame) from Oxford University, UK, came up with the idea of microarrays. However, Dr. Stephen Fodor and colleagues at Affymax Research Institute, California initiated the commercial utilization of high-density microarrays in 1989. They used photolithography, which had been used in semi-conductor technology to direct light to synthesize and deposit biological compounds in a tiny 20 µm square space. Special masks were used to prevent light from letting the reaction to occur in adjacent squares. Around the same time Brown and Shalon developed low cost method to print thousands of long gene fragments on an ordinary glass microscope slide. Pre-synthesized DNA probes were spotted on the slide by a robot.

DNA microarrays or DNA-chips consist of small silicon / glass chip dotted with more than 1 million tiny squares each about 20 µm wide. Several copies of a particular sequence of single-stranded DNA related to a particular gene are anchored to an individual square by photochemical reactions. All squares are anchored with single-stranded identical fragments of different genes. RNA fragments that are to be analyzed are extracted from a cell, are labeled with different fluorescent dyes. The micro array slide is flooded with the dye-labeled RNA suspension. The fluorescence by a particular subset of RNA molecules bound to single stranded DNA in a square shows that particular gene was actively transcribing in the cell from which RNA was isolated.

A similar process can detect genetic variations if a sample of DNA (or RNA from virus) is poured over a suitable microarray. Such chips can provide important information about pre-disposition to diseases and effectiveness of therapy. Similarly the microarrays of proteins are constructed. In the last five years microarrays of proteins or nucleic acids have come in vogue in reputed laboratories of the world. At present these microarrays are prohibitively expensive. In future with the advancement of technology and increase in production and usage the cost of microarrays are likely to be affordable for general use.

Microarrays can be used to measure the activity of the genes and identify the variations in genetic makeup of individuals. The entire human genome of 3 million bases can be analyzed in one go. In addition micrarrays are used in DNA sequencing, pathogen detection, gene expression, detection of mutations in HIV. Microarrays are useful in toxicology, virology, diagnostics and other fields of Biology. Indeed microarrays have revolutionized biological research and are likely to make the practice of medicine far more precise than present time.

For the benefit of scientific community Dr. DeRisi has posted on Internet instructions for making self-composed microarrays.

Further reading

Cohen, S.N. The manipulation of genes. *Sci. Am. 233*: 24 (1975).

Hirschhorn, J.N., and Daly, M.J. Genome-wide association studies for common diseases and complex traits. *Nat. Rev. Genet. 6*: 95-108 (2005).

Maniatis, T. *et al.* The isolation of structural genes from libraries of eucaryotic DNA. *Cell, 15*: 687 (1978).

Maxam, A.M., and Gilbert, W. A new method of sequencing DNA. *Proc. Natl. Acad. Sci.*, Washington, *74*: 560 (1977).

Saiki, R.K., Gelfand, D.H., and Stoffel, S. Primer-directed enzymatic amplification of DNA with thermostable DNA polymerase. *Science, 239*: 487-491(1988).

Sanger, F., Nicklen, S., and Coulson, A.R. DNA sequencing with chain terminating inhibitors. *Proc. Natl. Acad. Sci.*, Washington, *74*: 5463(1977).

Southern, E.M. Dectection of specific sequences among Dna fragments separated by get electrophoresis. *J. Mol. Biol. 98*: 503 (1975).

The Economist Technology Quarterly: New chips on the block. December 2, 2006, pp.24-26.

Wallace, H.A.C., Marques-Kranc, F., Richardson, M., Luna-Crespo, F., Sharpe, J.A., Hughes, J., Wood, W.G., Higgs, D.R., and Smith, A.J.H. Manipulating the mouse genome to engineer precise functional syntenic replacements with human sequence. *Cell, 128*: 197-209 (2007).

CHAPTER 22

Transposons and Transposable Elements

The primary cause of variation in the genome is mutations, which could be either spontaneous or induced. These mutations could involve a single base pair or even a region of the genome. This region of the genome could be lost (deletion), inverted (inversion), rearranged or duplicated. Phenomena such as combining of gametes during sexual reproduction or recombination of genomes during meiosis do accelerate the dissemination of variations in the genome.

Transposons or *transposable elements* provide another major cause of variation. *Transposons* are discrete sequences in the genome that can mobilise themselves to other locations within the genome. Transposable element does not require additional vector phage or plasmid DNA. Transposons may be major source of mutations in the genome. Genomes modify by acquiring new sequences as well as by rearranging pre-existing sequences.

Transposons may be classified into two broad categories:

1. Transposable sequences of DNA that code for proteins, which can directly affect DNA, so that a transposon can propagate within the genome.
2. Retroviruses make DNA-copies of their RNA transcripts and these DNA copies integrate at new sites in the genome.

Two copies of a transposon located either on the same or different chromosome can promote reciprocal recombination, deletion, insertion, inversion or transduction. Each transposable element can move to another location on the genome. Some transposable elements do not provide any selective advantage or disadvantage to the host genome and as such often referred as '*selfish DNA*', interested only in their own propagation.

Transposons were first characterized as spontaneous insertions in bacterial genome, preventing transcription / translation of the interrupted gene. By now many types of transposons have been characterized: 1. Insertion sequences, 2. Composite elements, 3. Replicative transposons and 4. Non-replicative transposons etc.

Insertion elements

The insertion elements are found in bacterial chromosomes and their plasmids. They are usually denoted as IS followed by a number e.g. IS1; IS4; IS10; IS50 etc. An *E. coli* cell may contain up to 10 copies of an IS element. Insertion at a particular site is denoted as name of the site :: element e.g. λ :: IS1. *Insertion elements are usually 700-1,500 bp long and have inverted repeat base sequence at either end and produce short repeat sequences at the site of insertion.*

For a particular insertion element target repeat sequences may vary, but their length is constant and is usually 9 bp. The region between two inverted repeats, codes for transposase, an enzyme responsible for transposition of IS element. The frequency of transposition of IS elements ranges between 10^{-3}—10^{-4} per element per generation. However, insertion at a particular site is close to spontaneous mutation rate 10^{-5}—10^{-7} per generation. The deletion of an IS element is 1,000 times less frequent i.e. rate of deletion of IS element is 10^{-6} to 10^{-10} per generation.

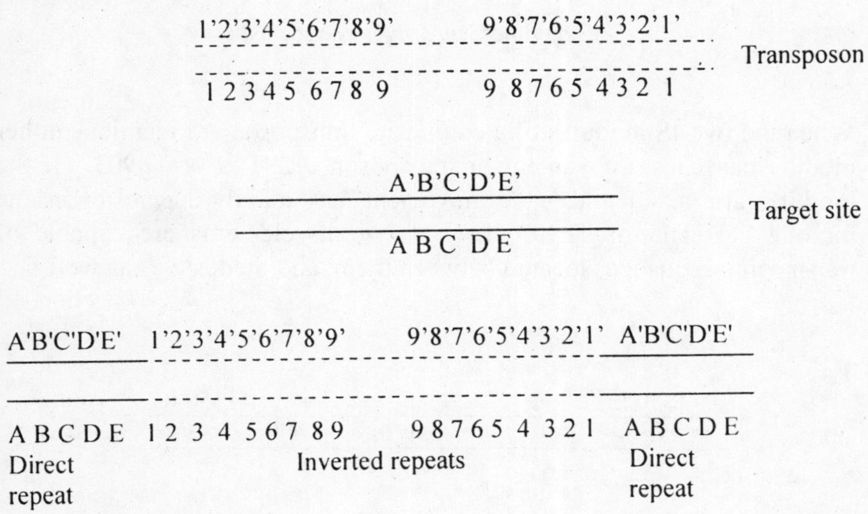

Sequences at the genome-site after incorporation of a transposon.

Fig. 22.1. Scheme explaining the incorporation of an insertion element.

Composite transposons

In addition to the transposase gene, some transposons carry genes for drug resistance or other traits and two IS modules on either end. Such transposons are called composite transposons and are denoted by Tn– followed by a number e.g. Tn5; Tn9; Tn10; Tn903. In composite transposons the sequences on either end are called arms that are indeed IS elements. Diagrammatically they could be shown as:

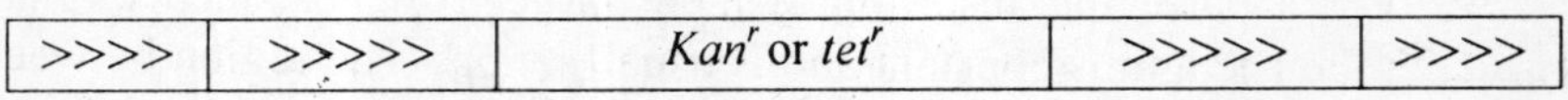

OR

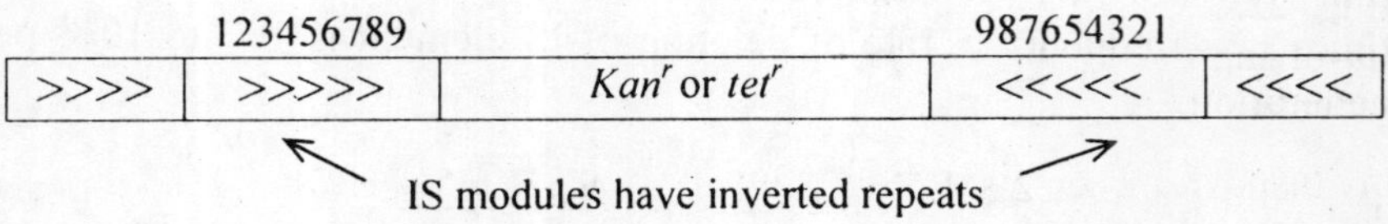

When the two IS modules of a composite transposon are identical, either module can cause movement of transposon e.g. Tn9 or Tn903. If the modules are not identical, the movement may mainly depend upon one module e.g. Tn5 or Tn10. In fact two IS elements are capable of transposing sequences located between them, and themselves as well.

Tn5

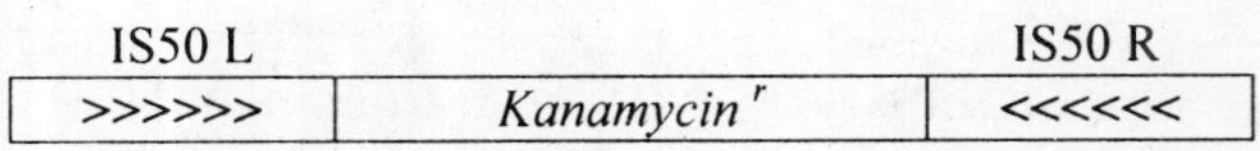

Composite transposon Tn5 contains two insertion sequences IS50 on either end, left arm (IS50L) and right arm (IS50R) have inverted sequences. In between these two IS modules, the gene for resistance to Kanamycin is carried. This transposon may migrate to a circular DNA.

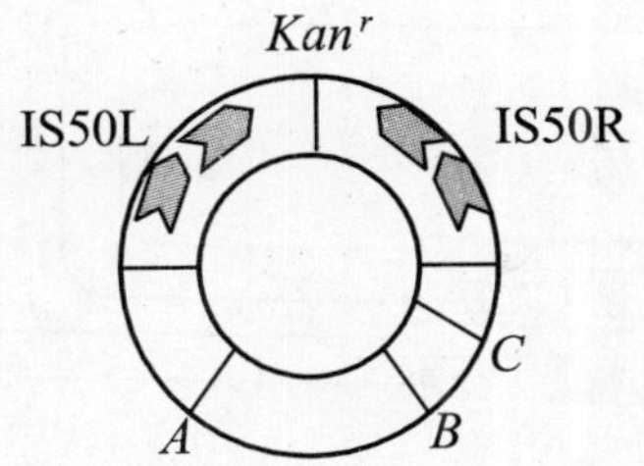

The circular structure may de-circularize and become linear

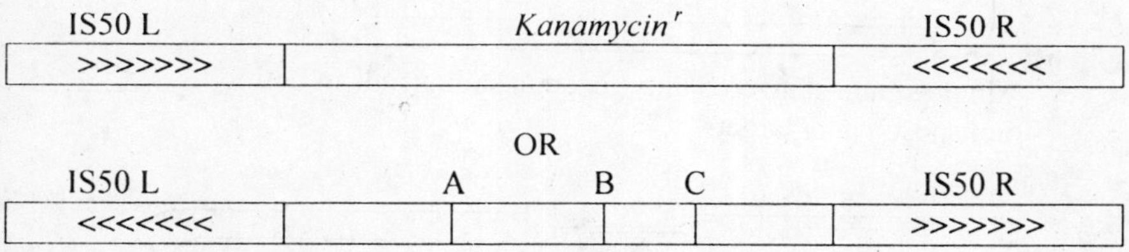

Fig. 22.2. IS50 L and IS50 R repeats can transpose either side of the circle involving either *Kan* ^{r} or *A,B*, and *C* markers. New transposon has opposite orientation of bases than original, in IS modules.

Transposition can occur either by non-replicative or replicative mechanisms. In either case two staggered breaks are made in the DNA duplex at the target site. The transposon joins to the protruding single strands at target site. Finally gaps are filled by the enzyme DNA ligase.

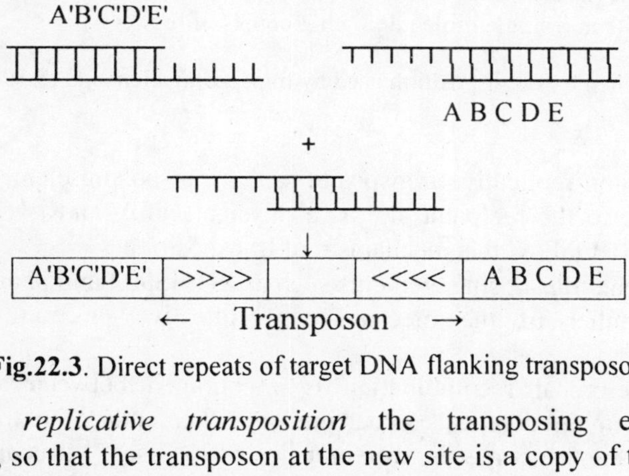

Fig.22.3. Direct repeats of target DNA flanking transposon.

In *replicative transposition* the transposing element is duplicated, so that the transposon at the new site is a copy of the original site, *where the original transposing element is still present*.

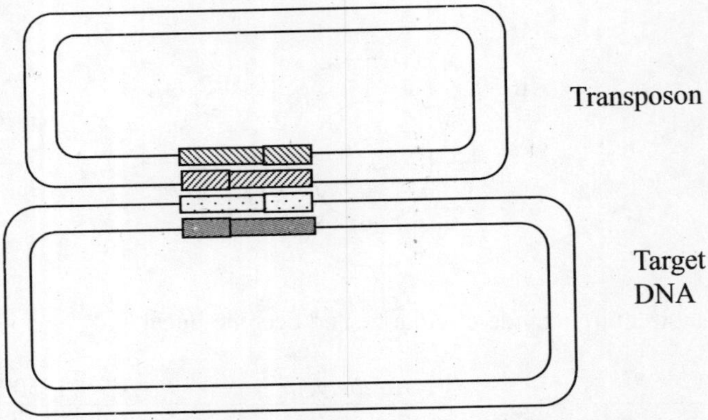

Single strand staggered cuts generate sticky ends in both: transposon and target.

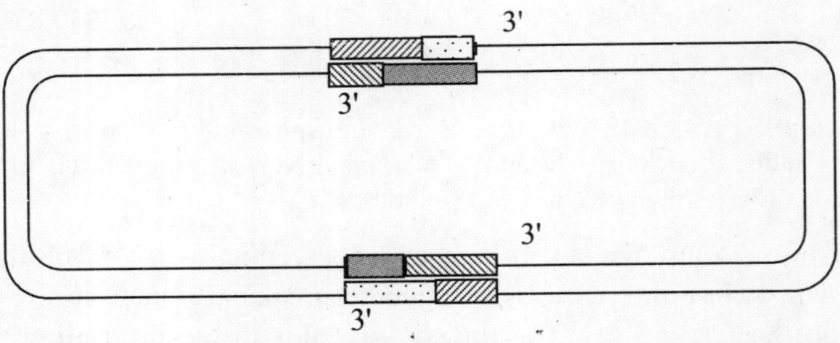

Two single strand-ends of transposon join to two single-strand ends of the target. Gaps are fille d by replication from 3' ends. This results in a single molecule with 2 copies of replicon.

Fig.22.4. Scheme of transposition used by transposing elements IS 1; IS 903 and phage μ.

In non-replicative transposition, the transposing element moves from donor to the recipient site as a physical entity and is conserved. Tn5 and Tn10 follow this mechanism of transposition.

Some transposing elements such as IS1, IS903 and phage μ (Mu) can use either of the mechanisms: replicative or non-replicative transposition.

Reciprocal recombination is encouraged between the direct repeats or inverted repeats occurring on either ends of a transposon. However, the outcome is different in both cases. Recombination between direct repeats, excises the stretch of DNA between them as a circular molecule. The host DNA as well as the product circular DNA, both have one copy of the direct repeat sequences.

Direct repeats

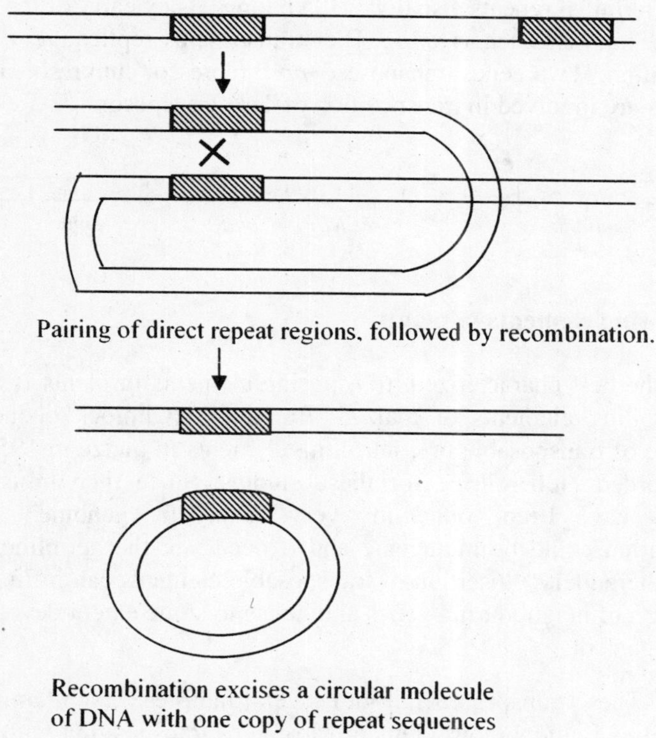

Inverted repeats

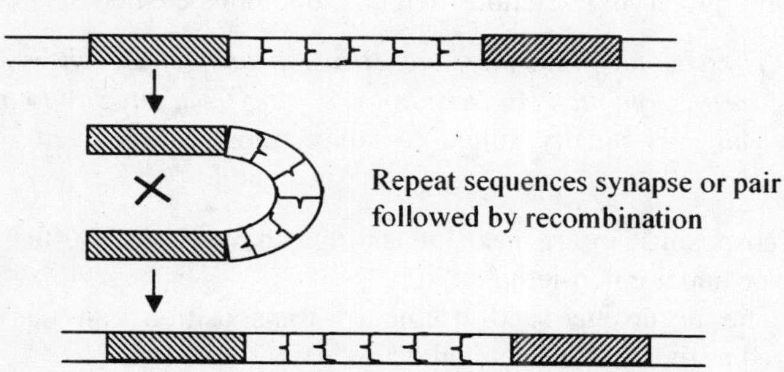

Larger transposons: transposons of TnA family

Transposing elements of the TnA family such as Tn3 and Tn1,000 (rδ) comprise of larger transposons, 5 kb long. They have quite similar inverted terminal repeats, usually ~ 38 kb long. They carry drug resistance markers such as *amp*^{r}. They transpose by replicative transposition. Two genes transposase *tnpA*, repressor cum resolvase *tnp R* and *res* are involved in transposition of TnA transposon.

Transposing elements in plants

One of the best characterized, transposing elements in plants is a group of controlling elements of maize. Barbara McClintock deduced the existence of transposable or controlling elements in maize in 1951. She was awarded Nobel Prize for these studies. Since then transposable elements have been found in every eukaryotic genome. Active transposition could be mutagenic and if occurs in the germline, which become hereditary. Insertion of transposable elements can influence the expression of neighbouring genes and hence to some extent development of the organism.

These transposons fall into several families. Each family has a single type of autonomous element capable of transposition with several non-autonomous elements lacking the ability to transpose without autonomous element. Non-autonomous elements are usually formed by incorporating varying deletions in the autonomous element.

These controlling elements (transposons) cause changes in the genome during somatic cell division by moving from one site to another.

Maize is ideally suited to study transposition events for two reasons:

1. Transposons insert near genes that have visible effect on the phenotype and are non-lethal.
2. The occurrence and timing of transposition can be precisely visualized as maize shows clonal development.

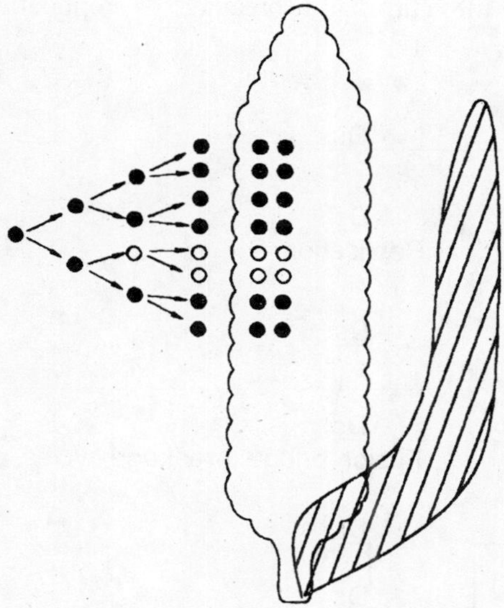

Fig.22.5. Maize kernel with a clone of transposed phenotype showing variegation — patch or patches of one colour appear within another colour.

In clonal analysis progeny of an ancestor cell of maize can be identified from the change in phenotype caused by transposition event. The tissue specificity of the transposition is characterized by the location of the clone and the timing of transposition by the size of the clone

Autonomous elements

Autonomous element Ac is ~4,500 bp long. It is transcribed into a single RNA molecule, which is spliced to produce mRNA of 3,500 bp. It contains a gene with 5 exons; its ends have inverted repeat sequences of 11 bp and at the site of insertion a target sequence of 8 bp is duplicated.

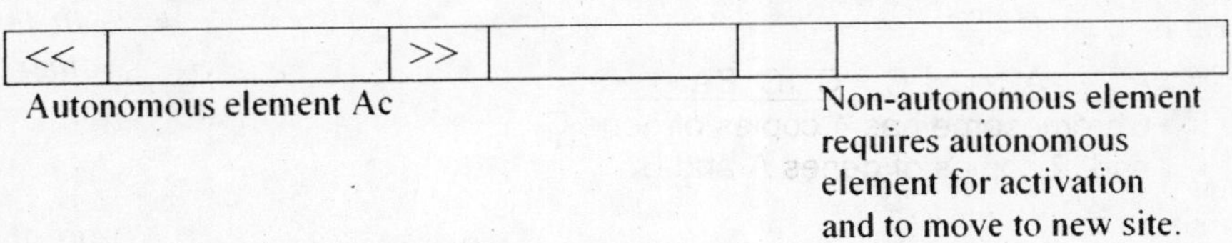

Ds elements are shorter but related to Ac. They carry deletions of varying lengths. Upon activation by Ac, at times Ds element provides a

site to initiate the chromatid breakage – replication–fusion–bridge–breakage cycle.

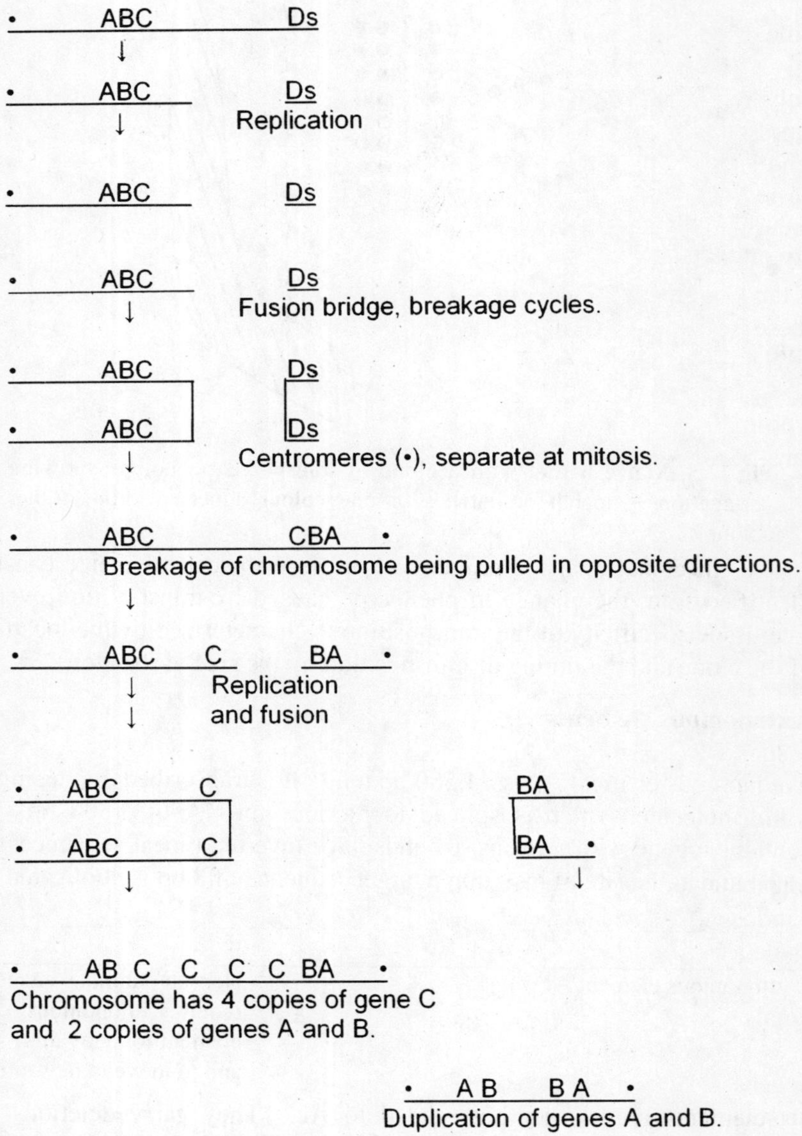

Since both chromosomes have two centromeres each, they will be pulled in opposite directions during cell division, resulting in breakage again. This process carries on likewise.

Role of transposons and tandem repeats in imprinting

Only one allele of *imprinted genes* in higher plants and mammals is expressed. For instance the homeobox gene *FWA* and the polycomb gene *MEDEA* in *Arabidopsis* seeds is expressed from *maternal chromosome only*. The expression of gene depends on *de-methylation* of promoter region by DNA glycosylase in the maternal gametophyte. The *FWA* promoter region contains a transposing element *SINE* and two sets of tandem repeats generated by the insertion of the transposing element. These repeat sequences are targets of methylation and correspond to siRNA.

It was found that transgenic tandem repeats can partly silence hypo-methylated mutant *fwa* in *trans*; resembling a ***paramutation***— a trans-acting silencing mechanism, which also depends on tandem repeats and RNA dependent RNA polymerase (RdRP). This evokes the possibility that RNAi might be involved in silencing the imprinted genes.

Transposons causing hybrid dysgenesis in *Drosophila*

Difficulties arise during interbreeding of some strains of *Drosophila*. The progeny shows a number of defects, such as mutations, chromosomal aberrations, defective meiosis and sterility. co- occurrence of such related defects is known as *hybrid dysgenesis*. Two systems have been identified:

1. Inducer-reactive, (I-R) systems and
2 P-factor system, or P+M (Paternal contributing and maternal contributing) system.

In inducer – reactive (I-R) systems it was observed that:
I male x R female, show reduced fertility and *hybrid dysgenesis*.
F1 progeny has normal somatic cells, but gonads do not develop.
R male x I female, gives normal progeny..

In PM systems, any chromosome of P male can induce hybrid dysgenesis when crossed with M female. Many regions of each chromosome are able to cause dysgenesis indicating that P males have 30-50 sequences of P factor in their chromosomes. The P element of *Drosophila* forms a typical transposable 3 kb system. Different P elements vary in length up to 3 kb, but all have inverted repeats of 31 bp, and create on transposition the direct repeats of 8 bp in the target DNA.

On an average one transposition of P–element to M chromosome occurs per generation. Though P elements are transcribed in somatic tissue and the germ line both, *yet its activation carrying transposition occurs only in the germ line*. Tissue specificity is provided by the difference in splicing pattern.

The P element of *Drosophila* has 4 exons separated by 3 introns. In somatic tissue RNA from only first 3 exons is spliced. In the germ line tissue, RNA from all 4 exons are spliced together and expressed.

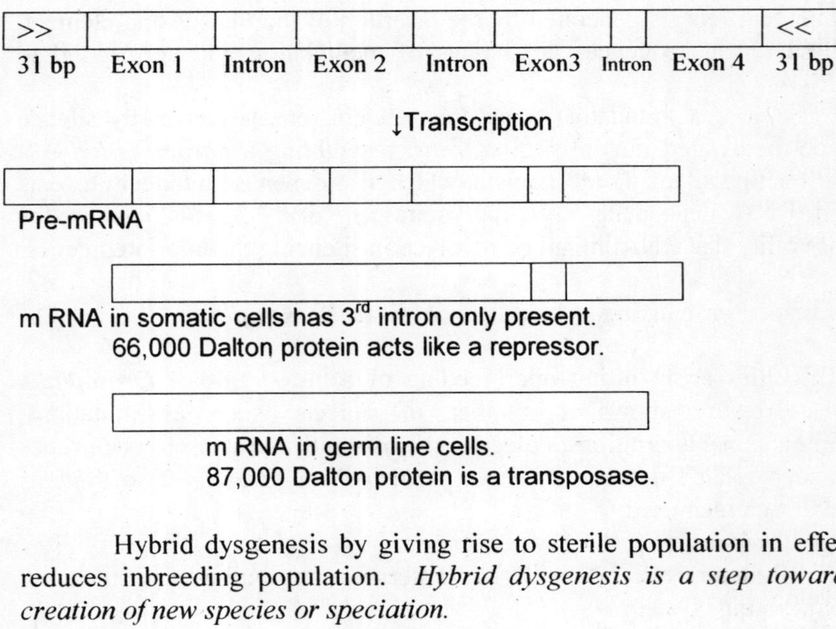

Hybrid dysgenesis by giving rise to sterile population in effect reduces inbreeding population. *Hybrid dysgenesis is a step towards creation of new species or speciation.*

Further reading

Gierl, A., and Frey, M. Eukaryotic transposable elements with short terminal inverted repeats. *Curr. Opin. Genet. Dev. 1(4)*: 494 (191).

Haniford, D.B., and Chaconas, G. Mechanistic aspects of DNA transposition. *Curr. Opin. Genet. Dev. 2(5)*: 698 (1992).

CHAPTER 23

Retroviruses and Retrotransposons

The '*central dogma*' of molecular biology, applicable to most of living systems, proposes information flow from DNA→RNA→Proteins. However, some RNA containing viruses are an exception to the central dogma. Temin and Mizutani as well as Baltimore in 1970, independently discovered the presence of a novel enzyme '*reverse transcriptase*', in RNA containing viruses, also known as '*retroviruses*'. They are also called '*plus strand viruses*' as the viral RNA itself codes for proteins. The plus strand RNA of the virus is copied by the enzyme reverse transcriptase into a complimentary DNA. Reverse transcriptase enzyme has a DNA polymerase activity, which it utilizes to synthesize double stranded DNA from single stranded DNA, *a reverse transcript of RNA genome*. Reverse transcriptase also has another enzyme activity RNAse H activity, which can degrade a portion of RNA–DNA hybrid. Similar to other DNA polymerases, *reverse transcriptase (RT)* needs tRNA as a primer, which is connected near the 5' end of viral RNA molecule.

Retroviruses are classified into seven groups α, β, γ, δ, ε retroviruses, plus lentiviruses and spumaviruses.

Life cycle of retroviruses

A retroviral particle usually contains two RNA molecules 8,000—10,000 nucleotide long, surrounded by 1,500 — 2,000 copies of Gag proteins, which in turn are enveloped by a lipid membrane containing the envelope glycoproteins. These envelope glycoproteins mediate binding of the virus to the receptors on the cell surface, and allow fusion of the viral membrane with the host cell membrane Fusion allows entry of retroviral RNA into host cell cytoplasm. The retroviral RNA is reverse transcribed into double-stranded DNA (dsDNA) by viral reverse transcriptase (RT). The newly synthesized viral dsDNA flanked by *long terminal repeats* (LTR) at both ends enters the host cell nucleus, where it gets integrated into the host chromosome in a more or less random location. The integrated virus is known as a *provirus* and an infected cell may have 1— 10 copies of the provirus.

The LTRs flanking the provirus permit cellular RNA polymerase II (Pol II) to make viral genomic RNA. Similar to a cellular pre-mRNA, viral genomic RNA is spliced and exported from the nucleus to cytoplasm and translated by the host cell protein synthesizing machinery. Splicing of viral RNA does leave many viral RNA molecules un-spliced and equivalent to full genomic length of retrovirus. These molecules are used in packaging viral genomic RNA and assembly of new virions.

Retroviral protein synthesis

Retroviral mRNa is synthesized by cellular RNA polymerase II and possesses properties similar to eukaryotic mRNA such as a 5'-cap structure, 5'-untranscribed region (UTR), 3'-UTR and 3'-polyA tail. From nucleus it is exported to cell cytoplasm where free ribosomes synthesize structural proteins and enzymes from unspliced mRNA. Membrane bound ribosomes synthesize precursors of viral envelope proteins from spliced or partially spliced mRNA.

A polycistronic RNA is transcribed from the host integrated retroviral DNA. This polycistronic mRNA contains transcript of *gag*, *pol*, and *env* genes *the three essential genes for all retroviruses*. The transcript is spliced into 2 fragments, one having *gag* and *pol* genes, the other has *env* gene. Each fragment is translated as a polyprotein. The polyproteins are processed to give individual protein such as:

Gag polyprotein → virion core;

Pol polyprotein → reverse transcriptase-RNase H, integrase and protease;

Env polyprotein → components of virus envelope.

Soon after synthesis the structural proteins of retrovirus are transported to plasma membrane, where many types of retroviruses acquire envelope during the budding process. The proteolytic maturation of virus takes place after budding from the host cell.

Integration of retroviral DNA with host DNA is usually necessary for the production of further copies of viral RNA.

Transforming viruses and transformants

Integration of retrovirus DNA into a cell genome can cause *cell transformation* to a *tumourigenic* state, usually by undesirably activating some cellular genes Retroviruses can acquire sequences from the cellular genome and become *transducing viruses*. Transducing virus carries *oncogenesis gene onc*, which is responsible for producing tumours.

Usually it is a defective virus that carries *v-onc* gene in place of *pol* and *env* genes. *Such retroviruses need an intact helper retroviral genome for their perpetuation.*

Cellular *c-onc* genes are usually interrupted by introns and expressed at low levels in cells. While *v-onc* genes are uninterrupted and expressed at high levels. It is suggested that *v-onc* genes are formed by splicing of the *c-onc* RNA. Some diploid virus particles may contain defective transducing *onc* gene virus and intact helper virus.

The presence of such proviruses in the host genome leaves telltale signs:

1. Direct terminal repeats of the provirus.
2. Flanking short repeats at the target site.

Such endogenous provirus sequences have been found in mammalian and avian (bird) genomes. Similar transposing elements have been found as *Ty* elements in yeast and as *Copia* elements in *D. melanogaster*.

Internal ribosome entry segment (IRES)

The 5'-end in many retroviral genomic RNAs has an elaborate secondary structure comprising of several loops of varying shapes. This is usually untranslated region and called 5'-UTR.

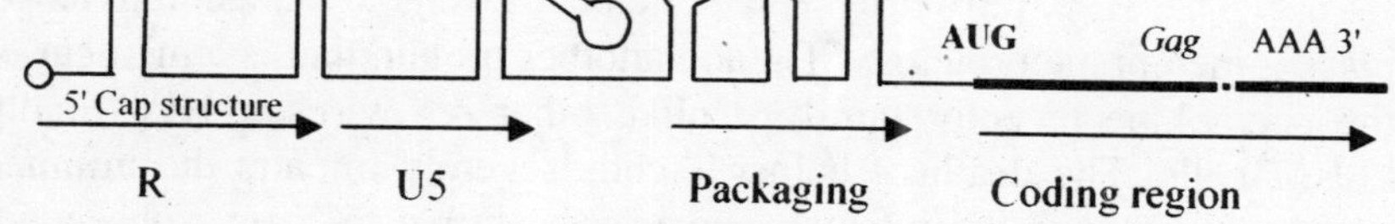

Fig. 23.1. A schematic diagram of 5'-UTR (leader region) of Simian immunodeficiency virus (SIV) genomic RNA (Balvay *et al*. 2007). DIS = dimerization initiation site; PBS = primer-binding site; Psi = packaging signal for core; R = the site of capping and (+1) site of transcription; TAR = stem loop. O = 5 '-cap of methylated guanosine (methylated at position 7).

Specific internal ribosomes entry segments (IRES) were characterized within genomic RNA of many viruses. Around 60 viral and more than 70 cellular IRES identified so far are quite diverse in sequence, structure and size. However, all IRES can bind ribosomes independent of cap-region. It is done in either of the two ways:

1. Small subunit of ribosome directly attaches to IRES.
2. Interaction between RNA-protein-ribosome-initiation factors.

After making contact with IRES the ribosomes have two options:
(i) to initiate translation from the site of contact *or*
(ii) scan the 5'-UTR in 5'—3' direction until an initiation codon AUG is encountered on the retroviral RNA molecule.

The IRES is found in all simple retroviruses of insects, birds and mammals. The presence of IRES in many species and their localization near viral packaging genes indicates towards their involvement in regulation of viral replication. IRES initiation can bypass the regular translation process and it is known to occur during stressful conditions faced by the cell, such as amino acid starvation, hypoxia, continuous heat shock and ìrradiation etc.

Human Immunodeficiency Virus (HIV)

Around 1982, people suffering from a new sexually transmitted disease were diagnosed with severe deficiency in their immune system. These people had a severe depletion of T-cells, multiple infections and were often afflicted with Kaposi's sarcoma, a cancer of the connective tissue. The disease was called '***acquired immune deficiency syndrome***' (AIDS). Culturing lymphocytes from patients at the early stage of the disease isolated a retrovirus known to be causative agent of AIDS. This retrovirus was named the '***human immunedeficiency virus***' (HIV) that has become one of the major killers of human population.

The HIV retrovirus enters helper T-cells by attaching to its plasma membrane proteins, CD4 and another protein that is a member of the chemokine receptor family. Unlike other retroviruses, HIV finally kills T-cells. The death of helper T-cells severely impairs the immune system and makes the infected person susceptible to many subsequent infections. As a *provirus* HIV can remain in latent phase in the host genome of the infected cell until some unclear event or stimulus activates the virus.

The genome of HIV consists of 9 genes spanning about 9,000 nucleotides. Three genes *gag*, *pol* and *env* are common with other retroviruses. Out of the other six smaller genes (*vif*, *vpr*, *tat*, *rev*, *vpu*, and *nef*), two require RNA splicing to produce corresponding Rev and Tat proteins.

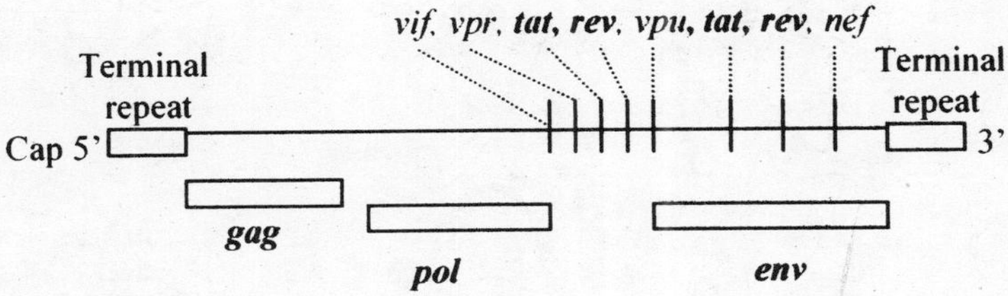

Fig. 23. 2. Arrangement of genes in the HIV genome. The three main genes ***gag***, ***pol*** and ***env*** are present like other retroviruses. Out of the six smaller genes two genes ***rev*** and ***tat***, each has two locations and requires RNA splicing.

Genetic footprinting in retroviruses

Conventional analysis of viral mutations involves individual isolation, upkeep and characterisation of mutants, which is labour intensive and time-consuming. In addition, the interesting mutants often are deficient in replication and cannot be subjected to positive selection.

Whereas, *genetic footprinting* of a sequence can generate a number of precisely defined mutations and then analyse them *en masse* for characterisation of the essential regions of the gene. Genetic footprinting can be applied to retroviruses, where a large number of mutations in the viral genome are generated and subjected to selection for function such as transcription, translation, assembly of virus or the release of virions. This technique has been used to analyse the 5'- end of HIV or sequences in Moloney murine leukemia virus (MoMLV) *env* and *gag* genes.

For example a portion of the *gag* gene was subjected to mutagenesis by MoMLV *integrase* enzyme, which causes an insertion of 36 nucleotide-sequence in the *provirus gag* region. Each mutation contains a random insertion of 36 nt sequence in the *gag* gene. The library was sub-cloned in a Momlv plasmid *pNCA*. For selection of *gag* functions cells were transfected with library. Virus obtained from these cells was used to infect Rat2 cells at low multiplicity of infection so that one cell is not infected by more than one virion. Low molecular weight DNA isolated from these Rat2 cells constituted *selected DNA*.

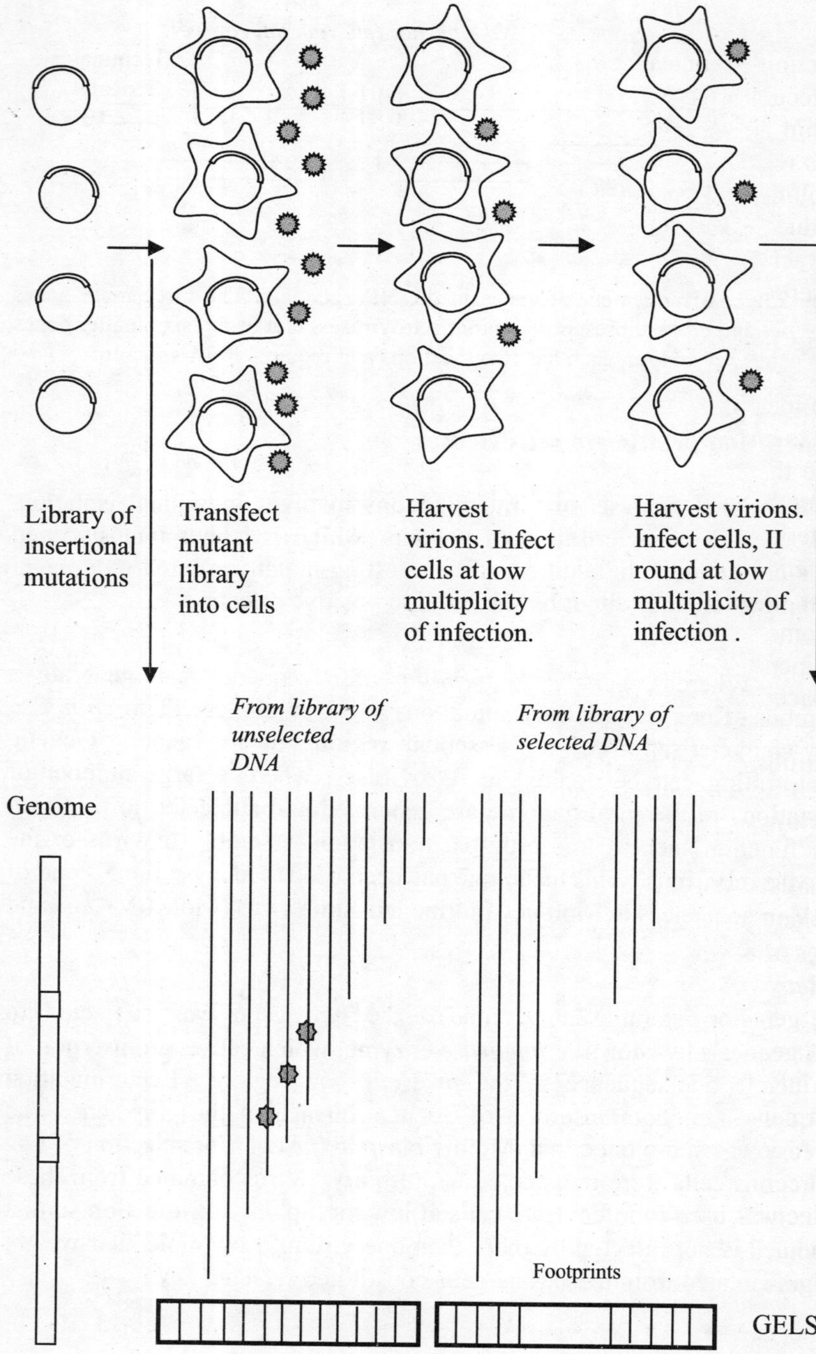
Library of insertional mutations
Transfect mutant library into cells
Harvest virions. Infect cells at low multiplicity of infection.
Harvest virions. Infect cells, II round at low multiplicity of infection .
From library of unselected DNA
From library of selected DNA
Genome
Footprints
GELS

The library of mutations, prior to selection of mutations for functions, served as control. PCR was done on *control* and *selected* low molecular weight DNA samples. A primer complementary to a site within *gag* and the other complementary to insertion were used in PCR. This resulted in products of different lengths in PCR and at single base resolution on polyacrylamide gels. Mutants that failed selection did not produce product in PCR and the missing bands ***'footprints'*** on polyacrylamide gel correspond to the essential regions of the *gag* gene (Auerbach *et al.*, 2003).

Gene Therapy

The idea that one could modify the nucleic acid content of the diseased cell to cure it from the disease gave birth to *gene therapy.* A precursor of gene therapy for example was production of *human insulin* in bacteria, where human genes were incorporated in bacterial DNA. The modified bacteria make insulin which is harvested and injected in people who are diabetic and cannot produce enough insulin of their own. However, in most gene therapies a gene with normal function is introduced into a genome having 'abnormal' disease causing gene. The normal gene could get incorporated in the neighbourhood of abnormal gene or ideally could replace it. It has the potential of being done is somatic cells or germ line cells. But usually it is attempted in somatic cells of the body as modifications in germ line cells are controversial.

Vectors used in gene therapy

Usually a carrier of the therapeutic gene called a *vector* is needed to implant it in the target cells. At present the following most common types of vectors are used in gene therapy.

1. ***Retroviruses***

The genetic material of retroviruses is composed of RNA, whereas the host genome contains DNA. On infection with a retrovirus, the RNA of the infecting virus and some proteins / enzymes are internalized in the host cell. The enzyme *reverse transcriptase* of the retrovirus makes a DNA copy of the retroviral RNA. The DNA copy so produced in the host cell is free in the nucleus and needs to be incorporated in the DNA molecules contained in the chromosomes. This is carried out by an enzyme called *integrase* also carried by the incoming retrovirus. Integrase enzyme however, incorporates the incoming gene at any random place and not at a specific place on the chromosome. If the incorporation of incoming gene happens in the middle of a host gene, then the host gene will be disrupted and mutagenized. Similarly if the incorporation happens at the controlling region of cell division, then the cell may become cancerous. By including some sequences, efforts are on to direct the site of integration at a particular chromosomal site.

Gene therapy has been tried to treat severe combined immunodeficiency (SCID) in some patients with success.

2. ***Adenoviruses***

These viruses have double stranded DNA as their genetic material. In humans they cause common cold, eye and intestinal infections. Although the DNA of adenovirus enters the host cell on infection, yet it does not get incorporated in the host genome. Hence the descendants of the cell may not inherit a copy of the adenovirus genes. This necessitates the re-administration of adenovirus therapy in a growing cell population. This vector system has shown promise in treating cancerous cells.

3. ***Parvoviruses or adeno-associated viruses (AAV)***

They are single stranded DNA viruses and can infect non-dividing cells such as neurons. They are non-pathogenic and are being tried to treat eye and muscle disorders.

4. ***Chimeric vectors or pseudotyped viruses***

For the purpose of gene therapy one may want to limit or extend the range of host cells susceptible to transduction by the vector. For this purpose *chimeric vectors* have been constructed, which are a mixture of those parts of viral proteins necessary for carrying the therapeutic gene as well as proteins meant to interact with specific host cell. Currently one of the popular retroviral vectors for gene therapy trials is a lentivirus Simian Immunodeficiency virus having its envelope proteins and G-protein from Vesicular Stomatitus virus. This vector is called VSV G-pseudotyped lentivirus and can infect almost all types of cells. Vectors with chimeric envelope proteins incorporating antibody fragments have the potential of *magic bullet* gene therapy.

5. ***Non-viral methods***

Injections of purified DNA or oligonucleotides to inactivate diseased gene or siRNA to cleve mRNA transcript or doublestranded oligodeoxynucleotides as a decoy for transcription machinery have been used with limited success.

A lipid micelle or liposome carrying DNA could be cationic, anionic or neutral depending upon the charge carried by the lipid used.

Cationic micelles have been most effective. Because of their positive charge they protect negatively charged DNA, facilitate endocytosis and release of DNA in cytoplasm and protect DNA from degradation by the cell machinary.

Tiny gold balls coated with DNA have been injected directly into cells by high pressure micro air gun.

The concept of gene therapy has been present for the last 30 years, but the progress has been very slow because of many difficulties.

1. Problems with viral vectors. An ideal target specific vector is yet to be devised.
2. Short-lived nature of gene therapy. Usually the desired genes are introduced in somatic cells that have a limited life span in the body.
3. Immune response, against viral proteins, making subsequent rounds of treatment ineffective or filled with complications because of secondary immune response.
4. Multigenic disorders are difficult to tackle at present as the methodology for curing monogenic disorders has yet to be perfected.
5. Chance of inducing a tumour. In the absence of a target specific vector the virus has a chance of becoming mutagenic and tumourigenic.

It is expected that with the construction of newer vectors and discoveries of newer methodologies gene therapy will ultimately become a reliable discipline in treating genetic disorders.

Retrotransposons

Approximately half of the human genome consists of retrovirus-derived DNA.

Transposable elements, numbering $3x10^6$, form 45% of human genome.	=	Transposons numbering $0.3x10^6$, form 3% of human genome.	+	Retrotransposons number $2.7x10^6$, form 42% of human genome. Where 8% are LTR and 34% are non-LTR.

Ty elements of yeast are typical *retrotransposons*, transposing through intermediate RNA molecule. Yeast cells infected with *Ty* elements, show the presence of virus-like *pseudovirus particles*, which are not infectious. *Although virus-like particles contain full length RNA,*

DNA duplex, reverse transcriptase and integrase activity. The *Ty* elements in essence are like a retrovirus, which has lost the *env* gene and therefore cannot package itself properly to make it an infectious virion.

Three prominent types of transposable elements are known in *D.melanogaster*: *Copia*, *FB* (Fold back) and *P*. In *Drosophila* cell culture, the rate of transposition temporarily increases to 10^{-3} – 10^{-4} event per generation. Usually in flies it is in the range of 10^{-6} event per generation.

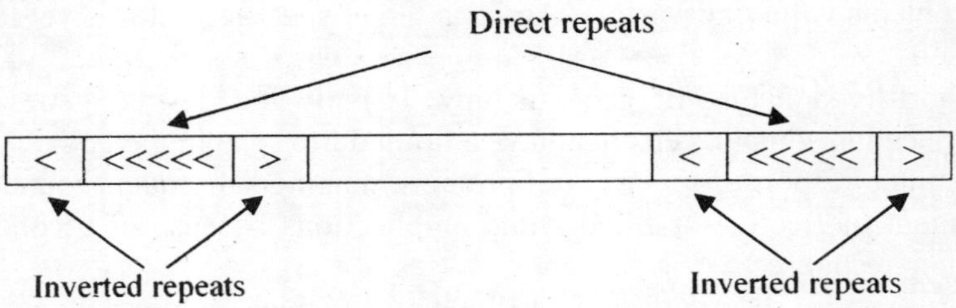

Fig. 23. 3. *Copia* element of *Drosophila* approximately 5,000 bp long. Twenty to 60 copies of *Copia* element per genome are known to occur.

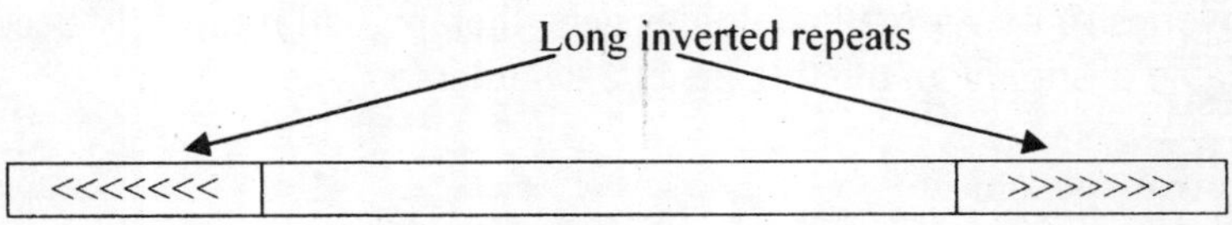

Fig. 23. 4. *Fold back (FB) element*, approximately 500 to 5,000 bp long with long inverted repeat sequences at both ends.

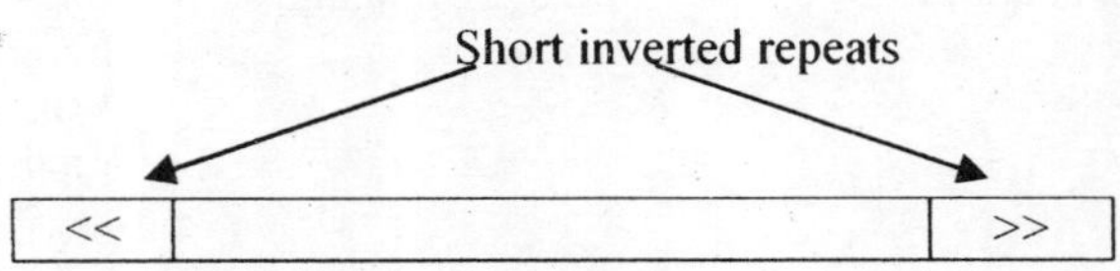

Fig. 23. 5. *P element* is 500 to 3,000 bp long with short inverted repeats at the ends.

Two *FB* elements can co-operate to transpose an intermediate segment of DNA, similar to the *composite transposons* of bacteria.

The transposition events presently observable in the genomes of these systems could be *footprints* of ancient systems. For these transpositions to survive and perpetuated, it is necessary that they occur in the germ line. Possibly similar transpositions occur in somatic cells but last only one generation.

Retrieval of extinct viruses

During infection retroviruses usually insert a copy of their genes in the genome of the host cell. Around 100,000 segments in human DNA have close similarity to the sequences of retroviruses. According to a rough estimate 8% of human genome consists of viral DNA, known as *human endogenous retroviruses* or ***HERVs***. Many HERVs occurring in human genome have counterparts in other species and were transmitted from generation to generation. It may be assumed that these disabled HERVs descended from virulent ancestors. Over the passage of time HERVs were inactivated by subsequent mutations. Heidmann and his colleagues compared the DNA of HERVs from a family. By comparing the differences in DNA, the genetic makeup of an ancestral retrovirus was deduced. A homologous piece of DNA of similar sequence was synthesized and was used to infect human cells. Some of the cells made new HERVs that could infect other cells. The reconstructed virus was named '*Phoenix*'.

Earlier new copies of the influenza virus that caused the epidemic in 1918 were reconstructed using recombinant DNA technology.

Further reading

Auerbach, M.R., Shu, C., Kaplan, A., and Singh, I. Functional characterization of a portion of the Moloney murine leukemia virus *gag* gene by genetic footprinting. *Proc. Natl. Acad. Sci.*, Washington. *100*: 11678-11683 (2003).

Baltimore, D. Viral RNA-dependent DNA polymerase. *Nature, 226*: 1209 (1970).

Balvay, L., Lastra, M.L., Sargueil, B., Darlix, J.-L., and Ohlmann, T. Translational control of retroviruses. *Nature/reviews/micro/ 5*: 128-140 (2007).

Bannert, N., and Kurth, R. Retroelements and the human genome: new perspectives on an old relation. *Proc.Natl.Acad.Sci. U.S., 101*: 14572-14579 (2004).

Porteus, M.H., Connelly, J.P., and Pruett, S.M. A look to future directions in gene therapy research for monogenic diseases. *Plos Genetics, 2*: 1285-1292 (2006).

Ribet, D., Pierron, G, and Heidmann, Thierry. *Genome Research, 16*: 1557-1565 (2006).

Singh, Ila; Crowley, R., and Brown, *P. Proc. Natl. Acad. Sci.*, Washington. *94*, 1304-1309 (1997).

Varmus, H. Retroviruses. *Science, 240*: 1427 (1988).

Whitcomb, J.M., and Hughes, S.H. Retroviral reverse transcription and integration : progress and problems. *Annu. Rev. Cell Biol. 8*: 275 (1992).

CHAPTER 24

Immune Response and the Reorganization of Genes

Except for the occurrence of a rare spontaneous mutation or a somatic recombination event, the genetic constitution of all somatic cells is usually considered similar in a multicellular organism. However, as more and more knowledge about the genes is accumulating, we find exceptions to this condition. A few examples of such exceptions are:

1. In the immune system of vertebrates the content of genome changes, when recombination produces active genes in lymphocytes.
2. Change in mating type of yeast.
3. Formation of the new surface antigens by trypanosomes.

The *immune response* is a protective system of the body of a multicellular organism (animal), which distinguishes foreign macromolecules from organism's own macromolecules. Any *foreign material* capable of eliciting immune response is known as '***antigen***'. The *antigen* is usually a protein or protein-attached moiety, in the form of a toxin, a virus, bacteria or pollen etc., which has gained entry into the circulatory system of the animal.

The region of a macromolecule provoking the immune response is known as ***antigenic determinant*** or ***epitope***. A macromolecule may have more than one epitope, one more effective than the other may in evoking immune response. Small molecules may have epitopes, but usually they are not effective in eliciting immune response. These small molecules, when coupled with a large molecule (usually a protein) can provoke immune response better. Such small molecules used for provoking immune response are known as ***hapten***.

Exposure to an *antigen*, evokes immune response by the body. The body tries to produce specific proteins, known as ***antibodies***, which have the potential of recognizing and destroying the antigen. Indeed, a small region of 5-6 amino acids on the surface of a macromolecular-antigen interacts with the specific antibody as a *binding site*. An antigen may have more than one binding site.

Immune response is principally elicited by white blood cells: the B and T lymphocytes and macrophages.

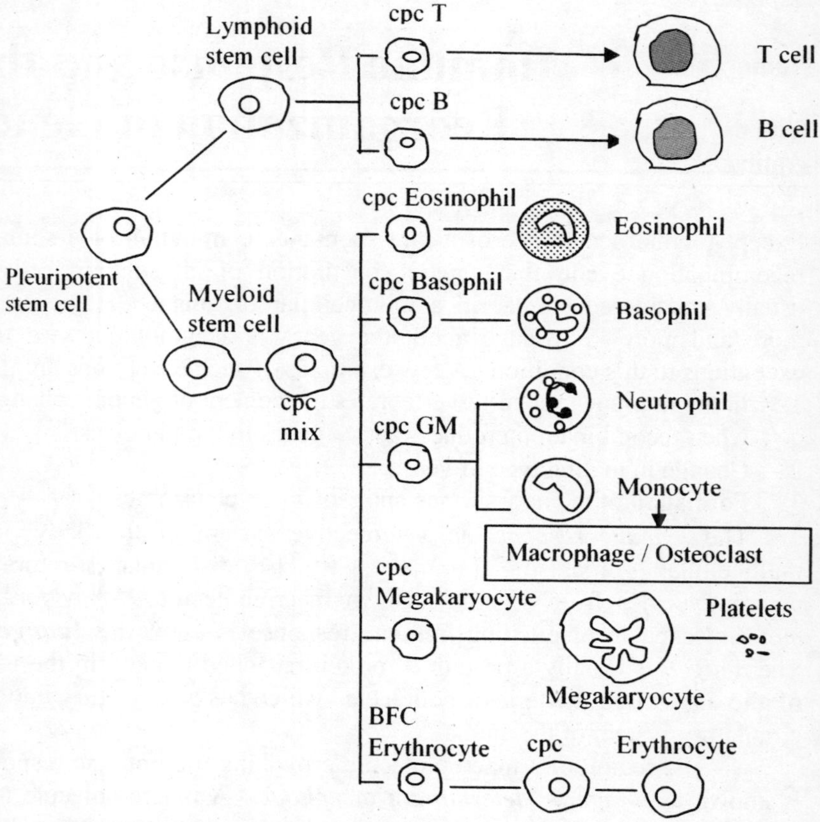

Fig. 24.1. A probable scheme of hemopoiesis. cpc— Committed progenitor cells. In adult mammals, all hemopoietic cells except T-lymphocytes develop in the bone marrow. T-lymphocytes develop in thymus. Macrophages and osteoclasts develop from blood monocytes. ***Pleuripotent stem cells*** also produce other tissue cells, such as natural killer cells, mast cells, antigen presenting cells etc.

The *B lymphocytes* mature in the bone marrow, while *T cells* mature in the thymus. Extensive rearrangement of DNA occurs in lymphocytes for producing a very large variety of protein molecules, known as *immunoglobulins*, where one type of *immunoglobin protein* molecule is best suited to interact with the antigen and nullify it.

Immune response could mainly be of two types, depending upon whether it is chiefly executed by B cells, then known as *humoral response*; or by T cells causing *cell mediated response*.

Humoral response

With the help of helper T cells, the B cells secrete antobodies. Antibodies bind specifically to the antigen.

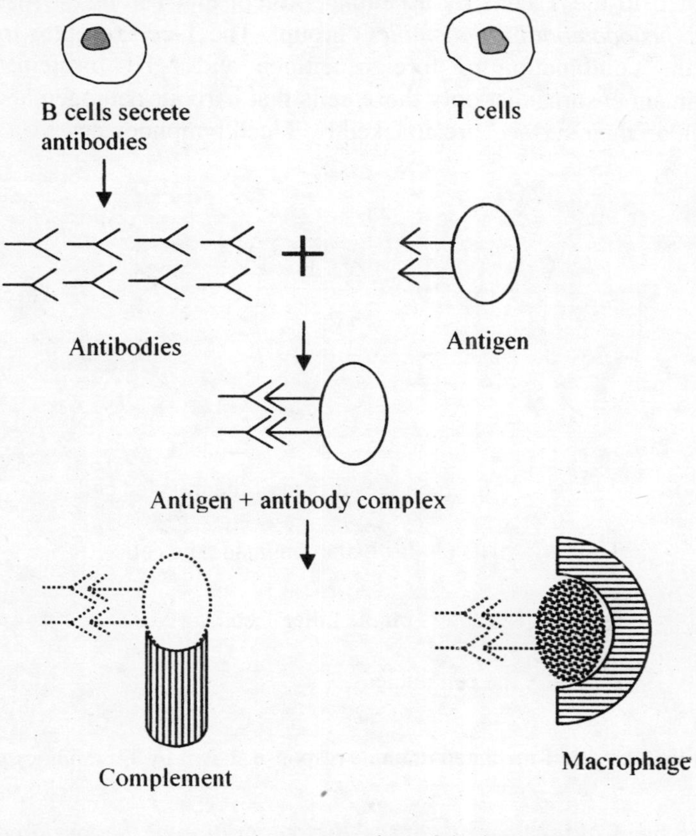

Fig. 24.2. A schematic representation of the humoral response.

Complements comprising of a group of 20 proteins, that have proteolytic activities, bind to the antigen-antibody complex. They lyse infecting target cell, attract macrophages which scavenge the target cells and their products. In addition, antigen-antibody complex once formed is scavenged by macrophages.

Cell-mediated response

Lymphocyte T cells, called cytotoxic (killer) T cells execute the cell-mediated response. A cell-mediated response is normally elicited, when a pathogen (e.g. virus or bacteria) is present inside the cell of the body. Because of the viral infection some viral antigens are displayed on the cell surface. These antigens are recognized by T-cell receptors. The important condition of this recognition is that, the antigen must be presented to the T cells by a cellular protein that belongs to the *MHC* (*major histocompatibility complex*) group. The T-cell receptor interacts with the combination of foreign antigen and MHC protein. This mechanism ensures that only those cells that harbour pathogen and show antigen on their surface, are attacked by T-cell lymphocytes.

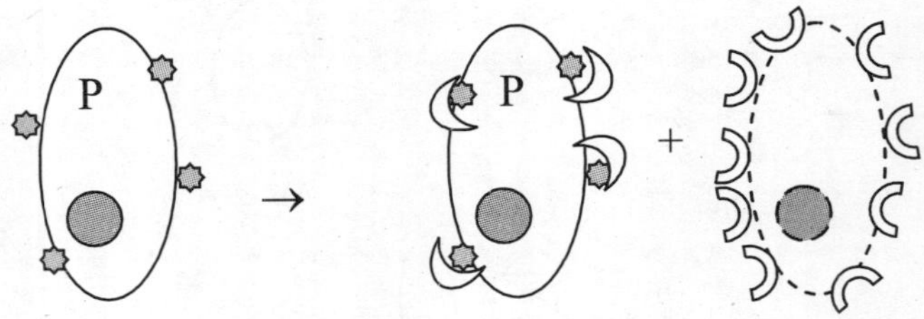

= Antigen on the surface of the infected cell.

= MHC. P= Pathogen inside the cell.

= Receptors on the killer T cell surface.

= The cell nucleus.

Fig. 24.3. Cell-mediated immune response shown by T-lymphocytes.

In both types of immune responses, the recognition of the foreign antigen is the responsibility of B cell immunoglobins or T cell receptors. These cells are normally able to distinguish between '*self* ' and '*non-self* ' or '*alien*'. This property of lymphocyte cells not to attack 'self ' is known as '*tolerance*'. Absence of this property causes *auto-immune* response (a disease), where the immune system attacks, its own body. The '*tolerance*' shown by B and T cells, probably is imprinted early in lymphocytic development. The B and T cells that recognize 'self' and are hostile are destroyed early in the development. This is known as '*clonal deletion*', which in essence is a ***negative selection***. In addition, T cells bearing certain receptors are *positively selected.*

Infected target cell degrades pathogen P to antigen

If an organism survives an onslaught of a pathogen, it usually develops immunity to subsequent attacks of similar pathogen. Attainment of '*immunity*' can be nicely explained by '*clonal selection theory*'.

Clonal selection theory

The body contains a large pool of immature B lymphocytes, as well as immature T lymphocyte cells. *Each immature lymphocyte produces a single unique type of immunoglobulin and each immature T lymphocyte produces a single unique type of receptor.* So to begin with, there is an immense variety of immunoglobulins and T-receptors. Immature B cells as well as T cells are morphologically indistinguishable amongst their own classes. However, on exposure to an antigen, any B cell whose immunoglobulin (antibody) is capable of binding to the antigen, or T cell whose receptor can recognize the antigen is stimulated to undergo cell divisions.

The immature B or T cell on stimulation with antigen, matures and increases in size. All the descendants from such a single B or T cell represent a clone of the originally responding B or T cell. The multiplication of B or T cell of a clone in response to the first exposure to an antigen is known as '*primary immune response*'. ***B cells secrete large quantities of antibodies.***

The organism retains some B cells and T cells as '*memory cells*', after a successful primary immune response. Developmentally, '*memory cells*' are at intermediate stage between immature cells and mature cells. They are long lived and can rapidly change to mature cells, if challenged with the same antigen again. This is called '*secondary immune response*'.

A mammal may contain ~10^6—10^8 immature lymphocytes with antibodies or receptors representing different potential-antigens. The total umber of mature lymphocytes is around 10^{12}. Amongst these about 10^6 cells are formed by clonal selection and multiplication in response to an antigen. The remaining large number of lymphocyte cells (10^{12} – 10

^{6}) = 9.99 x 10^{11} have still new specificities as the organism has not seen corresponding antigen as yet.

Lymphocytes originate from immature '*stem*' cells located in bone marrow of the mammal. Immature lymphocytes migrate to the peripheral lymphoid-tissues: spleen and lymph nodes *via* blood stream to become B cells and *via* thymus where they become T cells. The lymphocytes of all possible specificities circulate in blood and lymph. When a particular lymphocyte very specifically binds to the antigen, the clonal multiplication of this lymphocyte initiates the immune response in the body.

Assembly of immunoglobulin genes in lymphocytes

Usually, an animal cannot anticipate the structure of attacking foreign antigen. Still the animal is capable of defense by building specific antibodies. Normally an individual mammal can produce 10^6—10^8 different specific antibodies. The generation of this vast amount of diversity can be better understood by examining the structure of the antibody molecule.

Two heavy and two light chains of proteins combine to form a double lined Y-shaped immunoglobulin molecule with several unique domains indicated in the Fig.24.4. The top end of the Y shaped immunoglobulin molecule has N-terminal of 4 protein chains. The upper half of Y-arms, has variable region of the molecule. The variable region imparts ability to immunoglobulin for recognition of antigen. The constant region of the light chain C_L is associated through S–S bond to C_H, the constant region part of the heavy chain. Each arm of the Y-shaped molecule has a variable light, variable heavy, constant light and constant heavy domains denoted as V_L, V_H, C_L and C_H respectively. Four disulphide bonds and the interaction between heavy chains stabilize the structure of the molecule. The effector function of immunogloulin molecule is determined by the heavy chain constant regions (C_{H1}, C_{H2} and C_{H3}). Approximately 10 types of heavy chains are known. During the formation of immunoglobulins, assuming that any light chain can associate with any heavy chain, to have a capacity to produce 10^6 —10^8 potential distinct antibodies, the animal requires 10^3—10^4 light chains and equal number of heavy chains. However, there are many stretches of DNA coding for V- (variable) regions, but a few stretches of DNA code for C-(constant) regions. In this system two stretches of DNA (two genes) code for one polypeptide.

The somatic recombination occurs in B-lymphocytes, so that one of the many V genes is joined to one of the few C genes. But all the diversity exhibited by immunoglobulins is not coded in the genome alone. Some diversity is generated during re-structuring of a functional gene. Similar echanism for the formation of functional genes exist in T cells, one having α and β chains and the other having γ and δ chains. They include V and C regions, which are brought together in active T cells. *The important fact emerges from immune response is that the arrangement of V and C genes in B and T lymphocytes producing immunoglobulins, is different from all other somatic or germ line cells.*

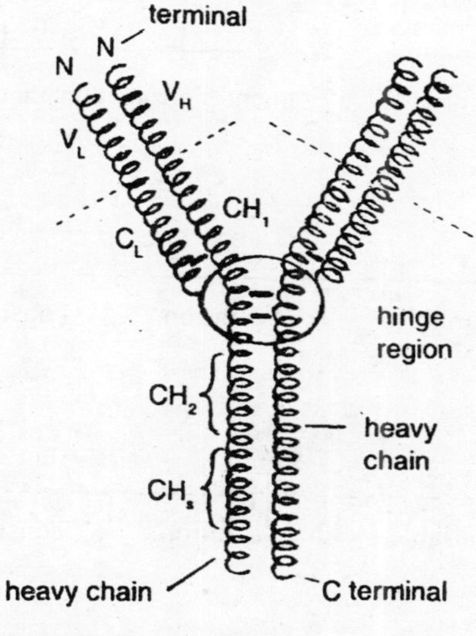

Fig.24.4. Basic structure of an antibody molecule. C= C terminal of polypeptides; C_{H1-3} = constant region of the heavy chains; C_L= constant region of the light chains; V_H= variable region of the heavy chains; V_L= variable region of the light chains; N= N terminal of the polypeptides; — = S—S bond.

Light chain immunoglobulins belong to 2 families κ (kappa) and λ (lambda) and heavy chain immunoglobulins belong to one family. The genes for each family are located on different chromosomes with own set of V and C genes. In germ line or somatic cells of any animal, V and C genes are quite apart. But in an antibody producing cell, an intact single gene codes for one κ or λ chain along with one heavy chain. Somatic recombination brings V and C genes together. The introns are removed by RNA splicing.

Assembly of λ-light chain immunoglobulin genes

In germ line cells V and C genes are quite apart. The J segment forms part of the C gene. However, in the lymphocyte DNA, the J segment finally becomes part of the variable region and codes for 13 amino acids.

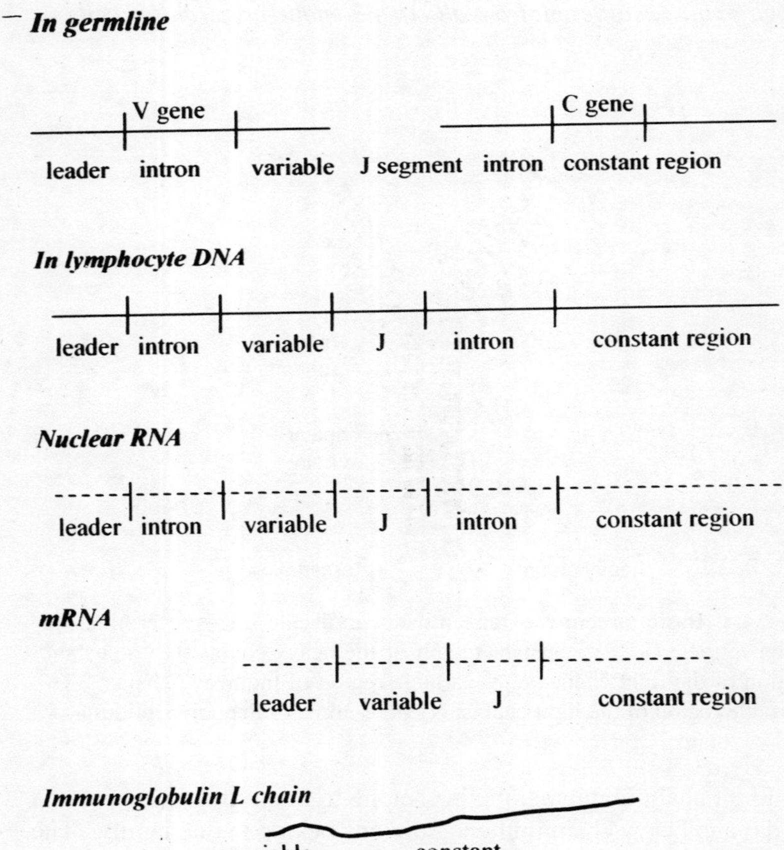

Fig. 24.5. Rearrangement of genes during the assembly of λ-light chain immunoglobulin genes.

Assembly of κ-light chain immunoglobulin genes

The κ-light chain is also assembled from the genes located in two places. A 500-700 bp long stretch of DNA contains five J_1 —J_5 segments that are joined to a constant region gene Cκ through a 2-3 kb long intron. A Vκ gene may join with any J segment. Any J segments upstream to recombination point are lost, while those downstream have signal for splicing to C exon.

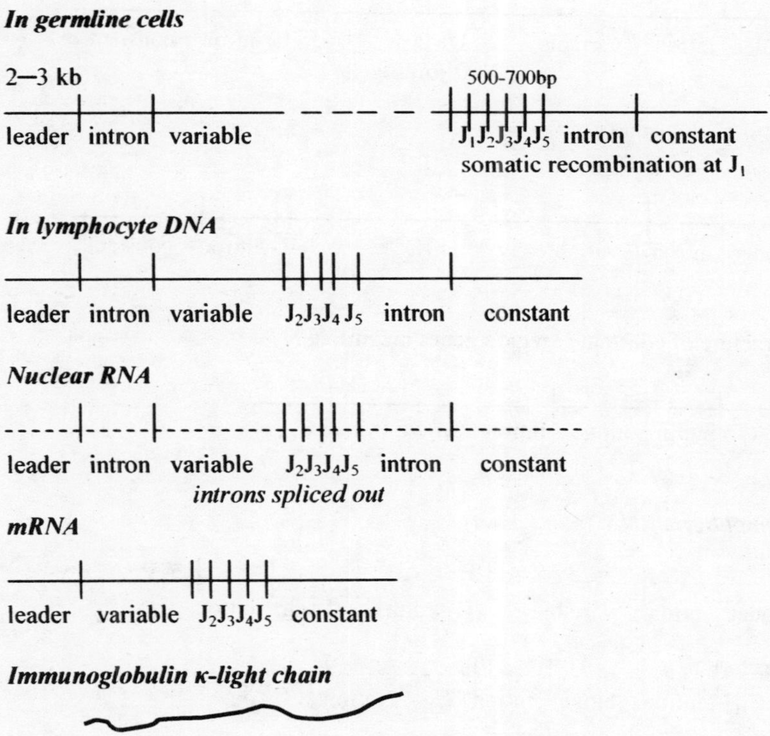

Fig. 24.6. Rearrangement of genes during assembly of κ-light chain immunoglobulin genes.

Assembly of heavy chain immunoglobulin genes

The heavy chain immunoglobulin genes have arrangement similar to that of light chain genes, except that an additional segment containing an array of more than ten D segmcnts (denoting diversity) is located between V and J segments.

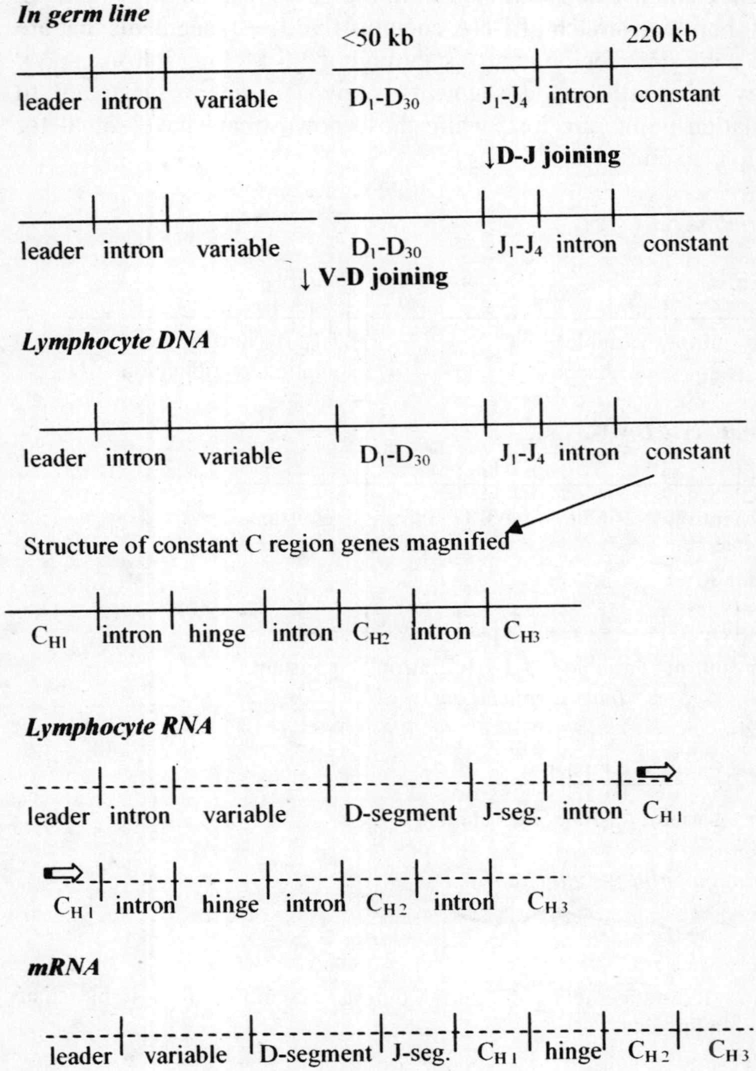

leader sequence is responsible for interaction with membrane

Fig.24.7. Rearrangement of immunoglobulin heavy chain genes.

The V genes of all 3 immunoglobulin polypeptides Vκ, Vλ or V_H have similar organization. The first exon codes for signal sequence, responsible for membrane attachment. The second exon about 100 codon long forms variable region followed by D_1– D_{30} segment only in heavy chains. The constant region for κ and λ light chains is coded by a single exon each. For the heavy chains, the constant region is coded by C_{H1}, hinge, C_{H2} and C_{H3} genes each about 300 bases long, separated by ~300 bases long intervening introns.

Approximately 300 germ lines are expected in each of the categories of Vκ, Vλ and V_H polypeptides. There are at least 6 J segment genes in all categories and 30 D (diversity) genes for heavy chain immunoglobulins. There are 9 functional C_H genes and 2 pseudogenes.

When considering the diversity of the variable region or 300 Vκ genes or 300 Vλ genes combined with one of the five J segments can produce ~3,000 different types of chains. For the heavy chains 300 V_H genes, 30 D segments and 4 J segments in different combinations can give ~36,000 variable regions corresponding to any C_H gene. ***V genes and C_H gene taken together generate a diversity 3,000 x 36,000 = 1 x 10^8 combinations.*** *Additional diversity may be generated by somatic recombination.*

The expression of V gene is controlled by an upstream located *promotor*. An *enhancer* located amongst C genes or downstream, activates the promotor at V gene. The enhancer is tissue specific and is active only in B cells. *Every B cell expresses only one type of light chain and a single type of heavy chain.* The alleles on the other chromosome are not expressed in the same cell by the phenomenon known as *allelic exclusion.*

Table 24.1. Various types of immunoglobulins and their important properties

Type of Ig	IgA	IgG	IgD	IgE	IgM
Heavy Chain	α	γ	δ	ε	μ
Composition	2 L2	γ 2, L2	δ 2, L2	ε 2, L2	$(\mu 2, L2)_5$ J
Proportion	14%	80%	1%	1%	5%
Function	Found in secretion such as saliva.	Activates complement. Lead to destruction of invading cells.	Development of tolerance. (?)	(Allergic response and defense against parasites.	Activates complement)

The productive life of all immature lymphocytes begins by synthesizing IgM. The IgM producing lymphocytes have C_H gene-cluster.

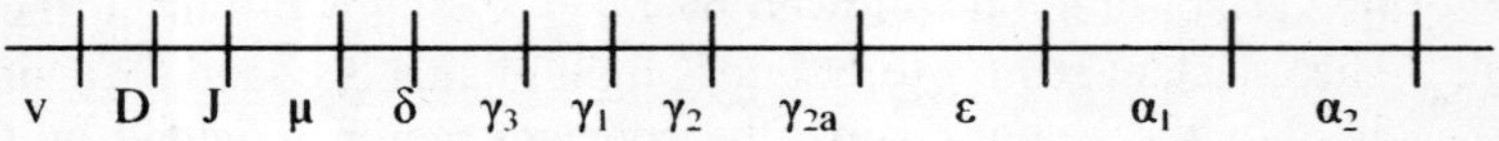

Fig.24.8. C_H gene cluster.

Classes and class switching

The class and function of immunoglobins is determined by the C_H region of the molecule. Five prominent types of immunoglobulins (Ig) are known: IgM, IgA, IgG, IgD, and IgE. *All Ig types are tetrameric, except IgM, which has an additional joining protein J.*

The joining of V—D—J genes initiates the expression of $C\mu$ gene and the production of IgM. During the cell lineage the lymphocyte may change to produce a different type of Ig. A change in expression of lymphocyte is called *class switching*. Switching involves only C_H gene, while V_H gene expression does not change. *Class switching* can be triggered by environmental factors such as the presence of growth factors. The *linear deletion model* suggests that recombination occurs between two sites $S\mu$ and $S\alpha_1$ and the intermediate region is removed as a circle. The α genes are brought closer to VDJ region and the expression of lymphocyte changes to $C\alpha$.

As a rule the linear deletion model puts a restriction on the expression of lymphocytes. Once a lymphocyte undergoes a *class swictch*, it is impossible for this cell to express any genes that have been deleted.

Somatic mutations can generate more diversity in the antibodies as well as in the memory of secondary response. These somatic mutations occur due to epigenetic reasons and are induced by stimulation from antigen. Somatic mutations occur during clonal proliferation of lymphocytes at the rate $\sim 10^{-3}$ per bp per cell-generation. *In a clone about half the population has at least one mutation.*

Primary and secondary responses occur in a mammal on exposure to an antigen. Amongst a large population of existing B cells, a unique B cell respondes to the antigen. The clonal expansion of this B cell generates a large number of plasma cells, specific for the antigen. A large population of cells causing primary response do not survive after the primary response is over. The protection against secondary infection

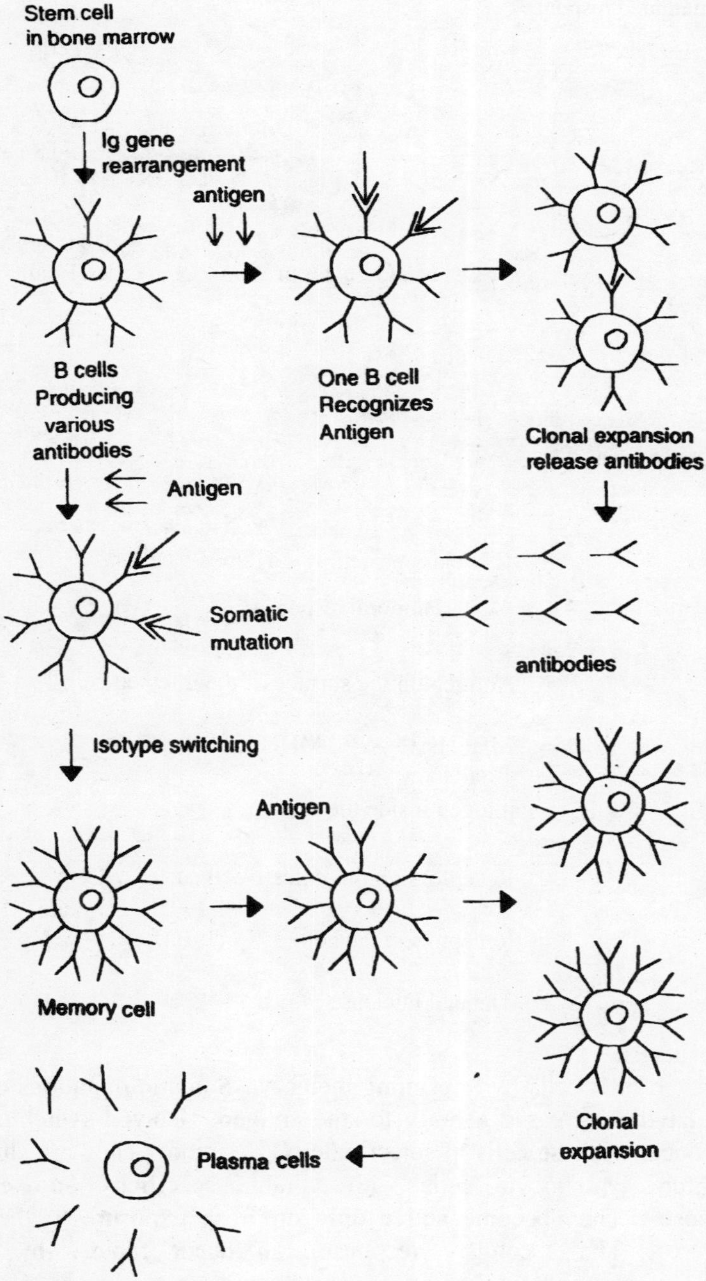

Fig.24.9. Diagram showing generation of primary and secondary immune-responses.

Cell mediated response

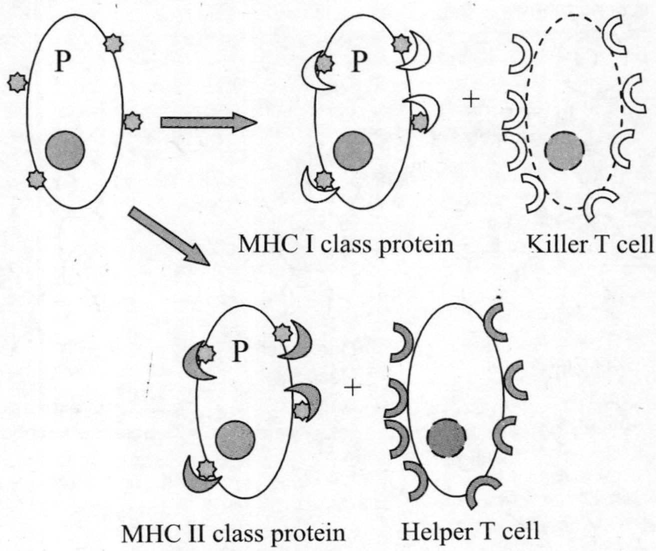

Humoral response

= Antigen on the surface of the infected cell.

= MHC I. = MHC II.

P = Pathogen inside the cell.

= Receptors on the killer T cell surface.

= Receptor on the helper T cell surface.

= The cell nucleus.

is created in B cells by imprinting memory. Somatic mutations creat B cells having increased affinity for the antigen. Isotype switching also may occur in these cells to select other C_H region. They are stored as immature lymphocyte cells with suitable specificity and effector response. They become active only on fresh exposure to the same antigen. The secondary response can occur rapidly by clonal multiplication. Additional somatic mutations or isotype switching are needed for secondary response. Acquired immunity is attained by B cell differentiation. Premature B cells propagate in bone marrow.

T-cell receptors

Similar to B lymphocyte cells, the T cells make proteins having variable and constant region. Variable region of the molecule provides diversity and the constant region serves a few effector functions. Five percent of cell population produces 2 receptors γ and δ in early development. The 95% of cell population makes other receptors α, and β later in development. The T cell receptor (TcR) α β are involved in the cell mediated immunity, where antigen and host histocompatibility antigen are recognized simultaneously. T cells making TcRαβ may be divided into subtypes according to their functions:

1. *Cytotoxic (killer) T cells* can lyse infected target cell.

2. *Helper T cells*, help T-cell mediated target cell killing or B-cell mediated antibody-antigen reaction.

Helper T cells and killer T cells, both recognize simultaneously the foreign antigen and MHC protein on the presenting cell. However, they use different MHC proteins. Foreign antigen needs to be presented by MHC class I protein to killer T cells and MHC class

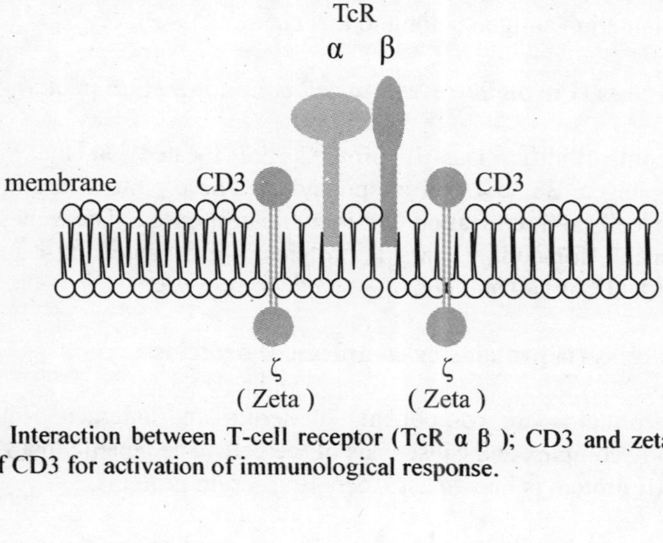

Fig.24.10. Interaction between T-cell receptor (TcR α β); CD3 and zeta (ζ) sub-unit of CD3 for activation of immunological response.

II protein to helper T cells. Killer T cells involved in *cell mediated immunity* and helper T cells involved in *humoral immunity*, both use T-cell receptor Tcα β.

A complex transmembrane protein CD3 is associated with TcR When an antigen binds to the variable region of TcR, the CD3 protein transmits the signal from the outside surface of the cell to the inside to a ζ (zeta) sub-unit of CD3 protein , which in turn activates the T cell for immunological response.

The major histocompatibility locus

The H2 locus in mice and HLA locus in humans, contain many genes responsible for functions of immune response. The products of many individual genes have been identified. Many alleles of a gene differing in base sequences have been found in the population. For this reason the locus is described as *polymorphic*. Genes determining some other functions are located in HLA region. Histocompatible antigens may be classified into 3 categories according to their immunological properties: class I, II and III.

MHC class I proteins or transplantation antigens

These proteins are responsible for the rejection of foreign tissue or protein by the mammalian body. The human HLA – A,B,C transplantation antigen belong to this class.

MHC class II proteins or cell to cell communication protein

Histocompatibility class II proteins are located on the surface of macrophages, B and T cell lymphocytes. These proteins are involved in cell to cell communication for immune response. The genes HLA–D responsible for coding class II proteins, are arranged in 4 sub-regions DR,DQ, DZ or DO and DP.

MHC class III proteins or complement proteins

These proteins are components of serum and interact with antigen-antibody complex and cause lysis of the cell. The genetic locus for MHC class III protein is known as S, denoting serum proteins.

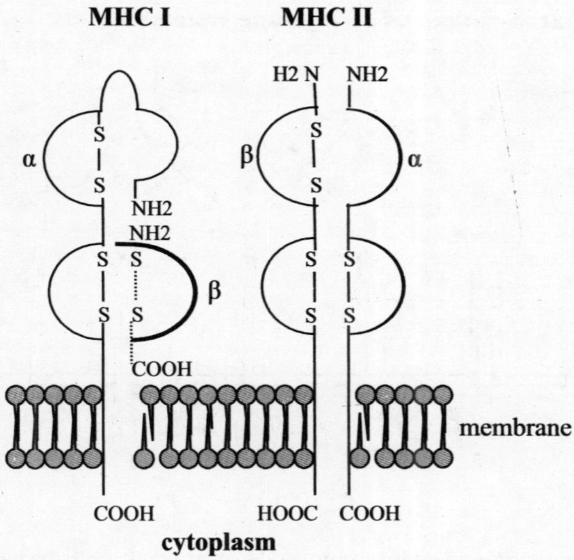

Fig.24.11. Schematic diagram of MHC class I and II proteins, where the letters α and β denote the α and β chains.

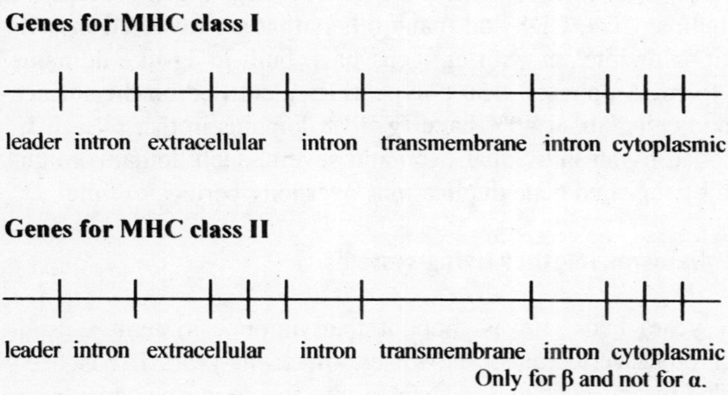

Fig. 24.12. Diagram showing the arrangement of MHC class I and II genes.

MHC class I-III genes are interrupted by interons. *All MHC proteins are transmembrane dimers, with major portion of protein protruding outside.*

Family of macro-molecules of immune systems.

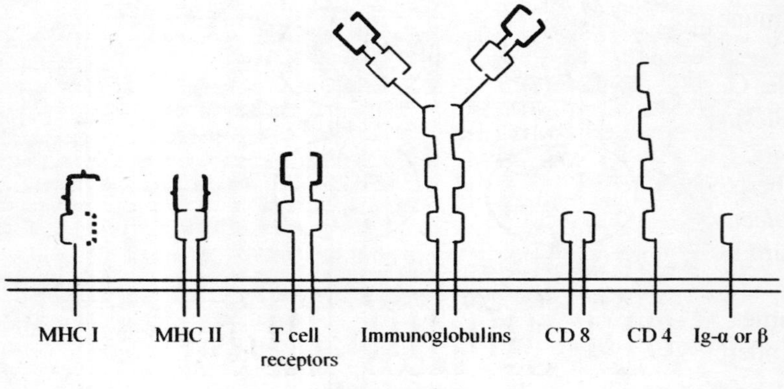

Fig. 24.13. Some prominent macromolecules of immune systems having built-in **Ig**-like domains. [= Ig polypeptide with disulphide bond; [= antigen binding polypeptide with disulphide bond; { = antigen binding polypeptide with *no* sulphide bond.

Many polypeptides such as MHC I, MHC II, T-cell receptors, immunoglobulins, CD4, CD8 and many others that are involved in cell-cell interactions or interact with antigens have built-in **Ig**-like domains common in them. Amongst ~ 150 polypeptides identified on the surface of white blood cells, about 40% have **Ig**- like domains in them. Each **Ig** domain is coded by an individual exon and several such domains might have formed by repeated gene duplications over long periods of time.

Defence mechanisms in other living systems

Until a few years back it was thought that immune systems exit in mammals or other vertebrates. However, in recent years it has been discovered that insects such as *Drosophila* havs innate immune response. Anderson and her colleagues have found about 40 genetic loci devoted to immune response in *Drosophila*. But this immune response does not have memory cells to elicit secondary immune response. Probably, *Drosophila* with a life span of a few months at best, does not need a long term memory of immune response

Further reading

Abbas, A.K., Lichtman, A.H., and Pober, J.S. Cellular and Molecular Immunology, Saunders. Philadelphila (1991).

Ada, G.L., and Nossal, G. The clonal selection theory. *Sci. Am. 257*: 62 (1987).

Alberts, B., Bray, D., Lewis, J., Raff, M., Roberts, K., and Watson, J.D. *Molecular Biology of the Cell*. Garland Publishing Inc., New York, Third Edition, p.1294 (1994).

Burnet, F.M. The clonal selection theory of acquired immunity. Venderbilt Univ. Press, Nashville (TN), (1959).

Janeway, C., and Travers, P. *Immunobiology*. Current Science and Garland, London (1994).

Kuby, J. *Immunology*. W.H. Freeman, New York (1992).

CHAPTER 25

Genes in Development

The role of genes in conception, birth, development, maintenance, reproduction and death has been recognized for the last several centuries or rather millennia.

1. Marriages in Northern regions of India are banned amongst the same *'Gotra'* (the descendants of the same *Sage* from ancient times), as well as between relatives of either parent for the last 7 known generations.
2. Humans have been breeding pet animals and plants for improvement in certain qualities for a long time.

In unicellular organisms such as bacteria, which multiply by binary fission, the parent and progeny cells are usually alike, barring the occurrence of rare spontaneous mutants. There the genes are concerned with metabolism, growth and cell multiplication by fission or budding. However, in multi-cellular organisms different cells have different specific roles. Usually animals reproduce sexually, whereas plants can reproduce sexually and vegetatively. In animals and plants reproducing sexually the egg (ovum) is fertilized by a sperm / pollen, remains *totipotent* for the first few cell divisions, which means that every cell or rather all cells in the early life of embryo can form in principle any part or organ of the adult body. Such a cell is said to be in *undifferentiated state* or is an *undifferentiated cell.*

Often the success of an experiment in biology depends upon:

1. The question asked.
2. The biological system chosen to answer than question.

From the stand point of suitability of experiments in embryology or developmental biology hydra, nematode *C. elegans*, sea urchin eggs, newts, frogs, mice, humans or *Drosophila* etc., have been quite popular. In addition fertilized chicken eggs, chick-embryo eye chamber have been used for cell and organ culture in the past. Sea urchin (Echinoderm) eggs were favourable for such studies because they are

1. Available in large numbers,
2. Easy to handle and fertilize,

3. They are transparent, so that one can observe them through a microscope and follow the development of individual cell as embryo develops.

The sea urchin egg has a distinct polarity, the place of attachment to the ovary is *animal pole* and the opposite end is *vegetal pole*. One hour after fertilization the egg divides in two cells, and then cells divide almost every half an hour interval. The second cleavage plane is perpendicular to the first and the third is perpendicular to second. For a few early divisions, each cleavage plane is perpendicular to the previous cleavage plane.

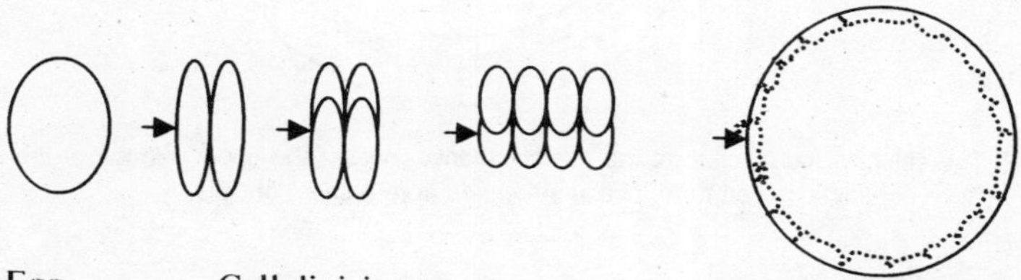

Egg Cell divisions Blastula

Repeated cell divisions cleave egg many times, resulting in a multicellular structure. Since growth is not essential during the early cleavage, repeated divisions of cells turn the egg into a hollow ball with cells arranged as a spherical sheet. This structure is called *blastula.* The next stage of development is called *gastrulation*, when the form of animal starts to appear. The cells of blastula move and rearrange so that they approach the form (*gastrula*) from which the animal develops. During the *gastrula* formation the front and back and the top and bottom become visible and the body plan is laid down. For example, during gastrulation the cells that are going to form gut move inside from the surface of the embryo. About 40 cells move away from the wall and extend thin *filopodia*, which can adhere to the cell wall, contract and pull the cell to get attached to the cell wall.

Folding of cell-sheets

The folding of cell sheets is the basis of early development of many organs such as heart, brain, eye and lung etc. The early development of brain, known as *neurulation* causes a major change in the shape of embryo. A flat sheet of cells on the upper surface folds up to form a tube, which will develop into brain and spinal cord. Formation of a tube from the flat sheet of cells during neurulation is caused by actively contracting cells on the upper surface of the sheet, with the help of microfilaments. The different rates and different extent of cell-contractions can give rise to the varied forms.

A flat sheet of cells with microfilaments near the upper surface of the cells.

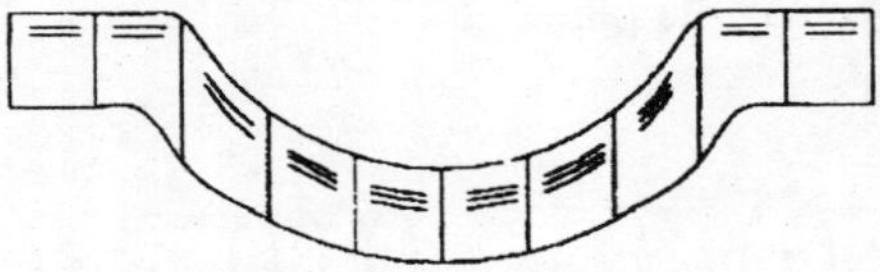

The selective contraction of the microfilaments contract the upper surface of the sheet. Such contractions can form tubular structures from a sheet of cells.

Crick, the famous molecular biologist said that *the embryo seemed to be very fond of stripes.* Embryos seemed to develop by repeating segments or patterns or similar segments. In vertebrates, shortly after gastrulation the brain is formed at the anterior end. Posterior to brain a pair of lines of somite exist that will form muscle and vertebrae. The first few anterior somites do not persist and merge into the head. Differences in cell adhesion guide the cells.

Cell migration

At the time cell sheets are folded, cells maintain contact with their neighbours. The cells of a sheet behave as a coherent group. However, individual cells do move over long distances such as:

1. Skeleton forming cells in sea urchin.
2. Neural crest cells and nerve cells in vertebrates.

The pathways taken by the migrating cells may be decided by the extracellular matrix, and the contact they make with other cells during migration. One may speculate that gradients formed by some chemicals may be guiding a cell to reach the target. However, only non-embryonic cells in a few systems show *chemotaxis*.

1. White blood-cells migrate to an infecting agent.
2. Slime mould cells aggregate in response to chemicals.

But for developing systems hardly there is any evidence of any chemical gradient involved in cell migration.

Growth

For generating changes in the form, growth is an important factor. Indeed growth is a process of moulding and occurs at a later stage of development, by that time the body plan is already laid down. For example the human face develops from several bumps like cell masses. Two bumps give rise to lower jaw, two bumps form the upper jaw and lips and one central bump gives rise to nose. One can imagine that one person could be handsome, the other ordinary and the third fearsome because of small differences in growth programmes of each region. In the words of famous developmental biologist, Wolpert: "*Beauty can be just one cell multiplication away*".

Pattern formation

In humans the development of identical twins or even multiplets shows the absence of a fixed pattern in the early egg. Identical twins in humans, rarely arise from the separation of cells at two cell stage, rather the separation occurs when the embryo contains many hundreds of celis. This indicates that in human embryo the fate of cells is not fixed even when there are several hundred cells in embryo. If these groups of cells separated into 2 groups, still 2 normal embryos would develop from them. However, the cells at later stages of development have assigned roles and get committed to become a certain part of the body.

The French flag model of development

The cells in an embryo know to make a right pattern. For making the reasoning simpler, imagine that the cells are arranged along a line. Each cell can turn say blue, white or red (the colours of French flag), in other words can become muscle, neuron or cartilage cell. If the cells know their position with respect to the ends, they can know which third they are located in – blue, white or red and develop accordingly. We can visualize how the system will regulate to normal if some cells are removed. This model envisages that:

1. Cells have to acquire positional information.
2. Use this information properly to form a pattern.

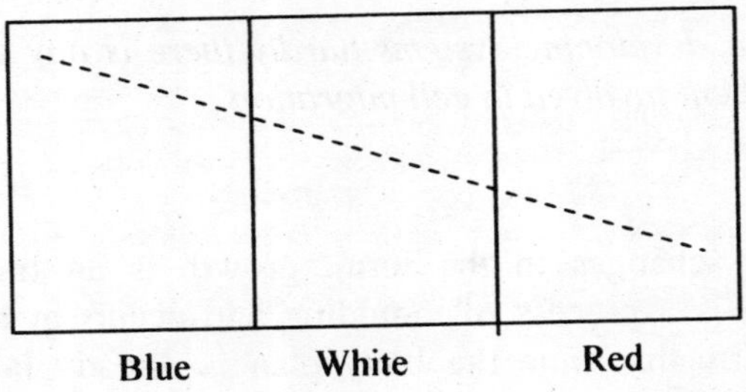

The concept of gradients of *morphogens* was introduced by Morgan, at the end of 19th Century. The dotted line in the diagram of the French flag indicates the probable gradient of a *morphogen* (*a chemical responsible for the differentiation of cell/s*). The slope of the gradient could vary for different morphogens or it could be just reverse slope too.

The communication between cells may take place in the following ways:

1. a message in the form of a chemical leaves one cell and diffuses to another cell, could form a method of communication. This can provide *positional information* to the cells. Such positional information will be limited by diffusion and can reach about 20 cells across i.e approximately 1/3 of a mm.
2. The other means of communication could be cell to cell contact through gap junctions. Only small molecules can pass through such water filled channels. The range of communication can be 3-4 cell wide.

If patterns are indeed laid down in such small fields, less than 1/3 mm across, then their later development is likely to be according to set program.

Regeneration

It is quite natural that organisms would meet accidents in their life span and part of their body would get damaged or even amputated. Some lower organisms such as hydra, newt, cockroach etc., have the capacity to regenerate complete limbs. Limb regeneration involves similar cellular activities to those happening during embryonic development. But in embryonic development limbs are formed from limb bud cells, while in regeneration the new limb is formed from the adult cells near cut or damaged surface. Regeneration in some aspects is similar to embryonic development. It may be said that in regeneration the lost potential-values of cells are being restored, so that they can multiply orderly.

Hydra

Hydra is one of the few organisms, which can survive decapitation (cutting-off of the head). A piece as small as 1/20 of a normal animal, will regenerate into a tiny complete hydra with tentacles, mouth and foot. Trembley had discovered the enormous regeneration capacity of hydra as early as the middle of 18th century.

For the convenience of interpretation hydra may be considered to have three body-regions head, body and foot, akin to French flag model blue, white and red regions. The fact was that no matter which region of hydra was removed, the complete animal can regenerate from the piece. Since the regeneration in hydra does not involve cell growth or cell multiplication, the cells need not change form from one state to another (like colour of a flag) and re-modelling the tissue by cell movement. *Growth occurs only when complete animal starts feeding again.*

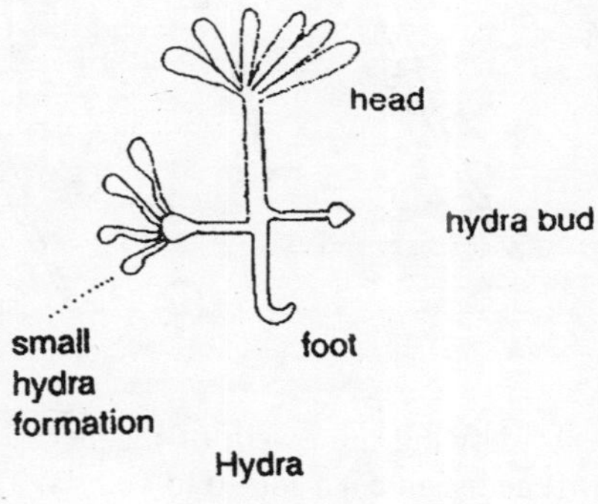

Hydra

Diagram of a typical Hydra with head, body and foot regions, developing a baby Hydra on the left and forming a Hydra-bud on the right.

It was proposed that head of hydra produces a diffusible inhibitor, which prevents formation of another head nearby. When the head is removed, the concentration of inhibitor drops and a head can form on the body. Once the head has regenerated the gradient is re-established. Hydra reproduces by budding out another small hydra around the mid-length of the body. The regeneration in hydra mainly involves two processes,

1. To eastablish boundary regions for head end and foot end.
2. To specify cell positions with respect to these two boundaries. In this perspective hydra regeneration is an excellent example of French flag model of development.

Regeneration of the cockroach leg

The leg of a cockroach is very good at regenerating. We can mark positions say 1 to 10 on the tibia of cockroach leg taking cue from bristle locations. Remove positions 2-9 and join positions 1 and 10. The missing 2-9 segments regenerate and give a normal tibia.

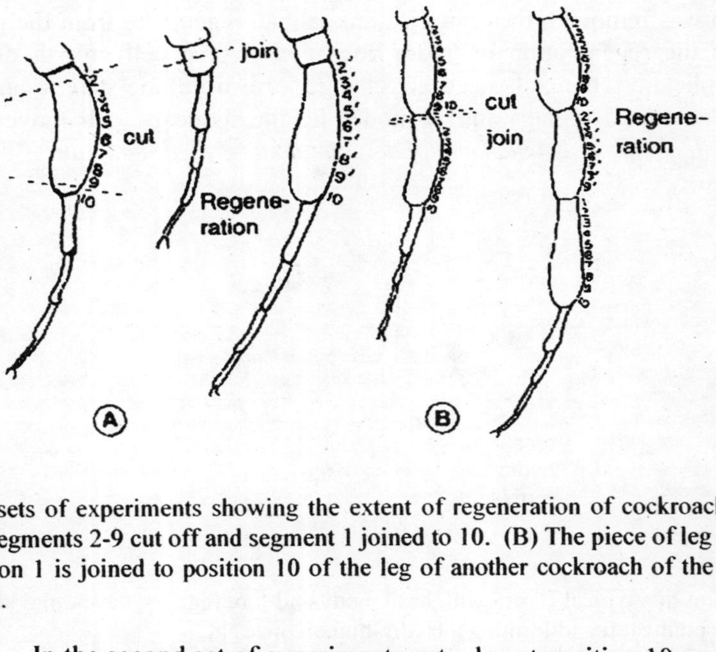

Two sets of experiments showing the extent of regeneration of cockroach leg. (A) Segments 2-9 cut off and segment 1 joined to 10. (B) The piece of leg cut at position 1 is joined to position 10 of the leg of another cockroach of the same brood.

In the second set of experiments cut a leg at position 10 and join the stub, to tibia from another cockroach (of the same brood) which has been cut out at position 1. In this case we have an excessively long tibia. To restore normal length tibia should have become shorter. However, tibia becomes still large by restoring segments 2-9 in between. It is evident from these results that the cells are not responding to global cells with respect to total length, rather they are concerned with local cells in that region alone.

Fate mapping

A cell in any region of embryo can be marked by a micro-injection of a fluorescent dye and its development followed. Using globe map of the world as a convenient system, one can denote the location of a cell on a spherical embryo. It was shown in 'newt' (a small amphibious creature with long slender body, a tail and short legs) embryo that the gut forms from the cells positioned near the South polar-region. The skin, eye and nervous system form from the distinct cell groups located in the Northern hemisphere. The skeleton, muscles and soft tissue originate from the cell-masses in the Southern hemisphere, near the equator.

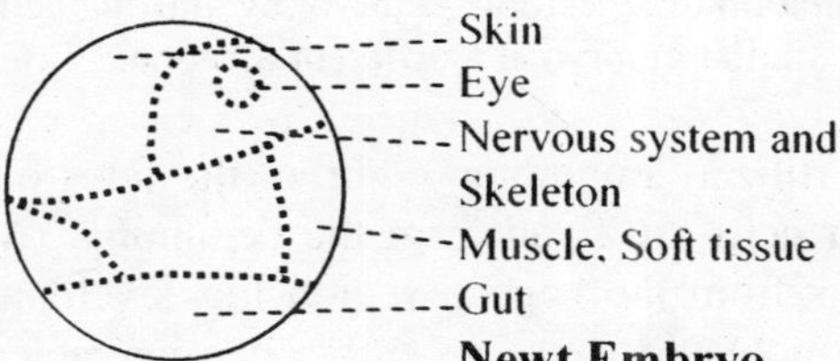

Newt Embryo

Similar *fate maps* have been determined in other organisms. Wolpert has compared *'fate maps' to train time tables*, which indicate what programme normally, would happen. But in abnormal conditions other solutions are possible. *The fate map of Drosophila melanogaster was constructed on the principle that farther apart the two regions of the body; greater are the chances of their being separated by a cleavage line during embryogenesis.* If cells in early embryo are moved from one region to another, they develop according to their new position and not from the place they were taken. *In early embryo the fate of cells depends on their new address.* However, this pliability of cell fate usually lasts until gastrulation stage. Thereafter the cells are more or less 'committed' or 'determined ' to form a part or an organ. The eye cells will form eye irrespective of their location in the embryo; even if transplanted in other region of embryo.

Induction

Speman and Mangold as early as 1924, took out a piece of tissue from the region where the cells had just begun to move in the embryo, and grafted the piece to another embryo on the opposite side. A whole additional embryo like a 'Siamese twin' formed from the grafted embryo. The grafted cells had induced the host cells, adjacent to the graft, to change their fate of development and form an *ectopic* embryo. The grafted cells in such a case are called *organizer*. Embryonic induction encouraged people to look for the nature of the signal from organizer that resulted in the development of a second ectopic embryo.

Fig. 25.1. The formation of an ectopic embryo, by grafting cells of an amphibian embryo in another similar embryo at a different location.

In the fertilized amphibian embryo, the fates of all cells except muscle precursor cells are fixed from the beginning. Muscle precursor cells need signals from the vegetal region for development to muscles. These signaling molecules have recently been characterized. They are proteins and are similar to growth factors. One of them known as activin is also involved in hormonal control of reproduction. It seems that the same signaling molecules could be used for different purposes in embryo at different times.

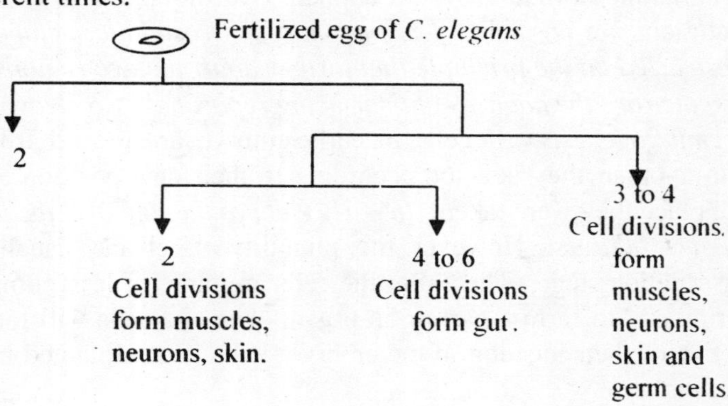

Fig. 25. 2. A summary diagram showing the cell-lineage during development, in the nematode *Caenorhabditis elegans*.

Brenner and his colleagues Sulston, White and Thomson have done extensive genetic, developmental and morphological studies on a small nematode *C. elegans*, which is only about 1 mm long and has approximately 1,000 somatic cells. Complete lineage of cells in the body, and structure of the entire nervous system has been worked out by Brenner and his colleagues. The cell division pattern from worm to worm was found to be invariant. Programmed cell death was observed in some cells. Do muscle-, skin-, gut- or nerve-cells form from an individual stem cell? It was found that muscles could form from cells widely apart in lineage. On the other hand muscle and neurons could be formed by sister cells. We still do not know why sister cells can develop autonomously on different developmental pathways.

Near the beginning of the 19th century, Morgan put forward the idea of *gradients controlling the development of embryo*. Morgan started working with the genetics of fruit fly *Drosophila*. Combination of embryological and genetic studies in *Drosophila* has identified genes regulating the patterning in early embryo. Studies with *Drosophila* have led to the discovery of a part of gene known as ***homeobox***, which has helped in identifying regulatory genes responsible for the formation of patterns in other animals, including humans.

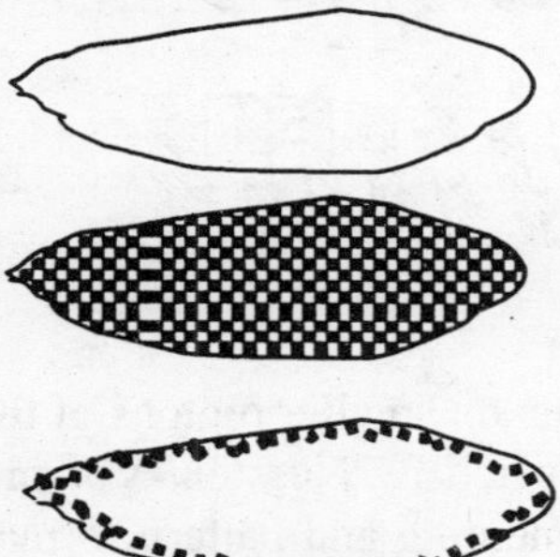

Fig. 25.3. Initial stages of development in *Drosophila* embryo.

The egg of *Drosophila* is almost ellipsoidal and the sperm enters from one end. The nucleus of sperm and the egg nucleus fuse to give a single nucleus. Unlike many other eggs, it does not undergo proper cleavage rather the nuclei keep dividing about every eight minutes. In about 2 to 3 hours about 5,000 nuclei float in the common cytoplasm. The nuclei migrate close to the surface and cell walls form around them. Thus the egg is lined with a sheet of cells from inside, and it becomes a multi-cellular embryo. This is followed by gastrulation and the larva emerges after 24 hours. A normal larva of *Drosophila* has a head segment followed by three thoracic segments and 8 abdominal segments. The larva eats voraciously, undergoes two successive moultings and develops to a pupa. After a few days the adult fly emerges from the pupa. The adult fly may also be considered to have repeated structures or segments: one head capsule, 3 thoracic and around 6 abdominal segments. In essence *Drosophila has two animals in one* the larva and the imago (adult).

Genes involved in segment and pattern formation in embryo

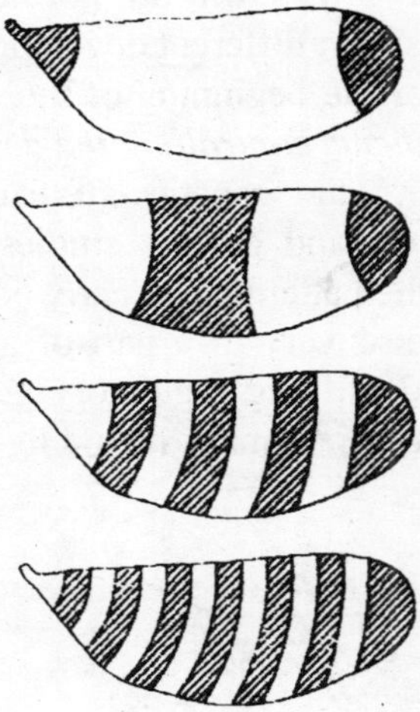

Maternal genes establish gradients from anterior to posterior poles.

Gap genes demarcate four broad zones in the egg.

Pair rule genes define seven stripes.

Segment polarity genes lay down 14 stripes.

Maternal and segmentation genes act on smaller regions of the embryo. About 50 genes have been identified by Nusslein-Volhard in *Drosophila*, which are responsible for segmenting and pattern formation in the embryo.

It was found that the segments are already laid down in the Drosophila embryo, before the cell boundaries are formed around the nuclei. ***In other words the segmentation exists in a single cell embryo.***

Considering the larval stage, mutations in the genes *hairy* and *fushi terazu* result in loss of every alternate segment of the larva. These genes are expressed well before the cell boundaries are laid down around nuclei and the embryo is still a single cell. *These genes are expressed in lines of nuclei perpendicular to the long axis of the embryo.* This results in the formation of stripe like pattern, giving segment boundaries.

Initially there are seven stripes formed, which later become 14 and these give rise to that many segments in the embryo.

It was also found that each stripe is formed separately and independently by the activity of genes which express earlier than pair-rule genes. This results in formation of pattern along the long axis of embryo.

Some important segmenting and pattern formation genes are listed here:

Gene	Type	Resulting Phenotype
hairy	Pair-rule gene	Every second segment missing.
fushi terazu	Pair-rule gene	Every second segment missing.
bicoid		Patterning of the anterior end of the embryo.
dorsal		Patterning of the ventral region of the embryo.

Another gene important in pattern formation is *bicoid* gene. The polarity of *Drosophila* egg for head and tail ends is decided when it is developing in the mother. A special molecule is included in the future anterior end of embryo. On egg being laid this molecule activates the synthesis of *bicoid* gene product, so that the *bicoid* gene product diffuses toward the posterior end of embryo. ***It is perhaps the first unequivocal demonstration in a developing system that gradient set up by a gene product establishes patterning***. The eggs lacking normal *bicoid* gene will as a consequence not have normal *bicoid* protein at the anterior end. These larvae develop lacking head as well as thorax. The mutant eggs can be rescued by a micro-injection of the cytoplasm from the anterior region of another, wild type egg.

The *bicoid* gene seems to be one of the first genes for pattern formation in the egg. The *bicoid* gene product activates other genes such as *pair-rule genes* at specific locations. This results in stripe-pattern. *Each stripe has its own address, having its own set of genes*. However, the things are not as simple as they sound.

Homeotic genes

Segment identity is specified by a set of regulatory genes called *homeotic genes*. There are a number of mutations in such genes, which result in replacement of one structure by another. Like, leg growing in place of antenna or a pair of wings growing in place of a pair of halteres, resulting in a 4 winged fly instead of the normal having 2 wings. The normal function of *homeotic gene* is to regulate structures grow at the correct place on the body. Mutations in these genes result in structures growing in wrong (*ectopic*) places. Some properties of *homeotic genes* are:

1. Unlike providing positional information, the *homeotic* genes provide each body segment with unique identity.

2. In early development, *homeotic* gene expression is mostly at the end of complex chain of gene interactions.

3. The order of genes on the chromosome corresponds well with the order in which they are activated in the body along the long axis.

4. A few facts emerge from the study of early development in *Drosophila*. Polarity in embryo must be established early to set up axis of symmetry for development. *This occurs in mother where the egg is made.*

5. The egg cytoplasm is provided with the positioning information at the anterior and posterior ends.

6. A separate gradient is set up along the *dorso-ventral axis of the organism.*

7. The gradient along the body axis activates or deactivates the genes, which control specific protein synthesis.

8. There is both spatial (with respect to space and structure) and temporal (with respect to time) hierarchy in gene activities resulting in segment formation.

9. *Homeotic* genes are at the bottom of hierarchy amongst the early genes for development. Whereas, they are at the top of hierarchy, when genes for development within a segment are concerned.

10. Nearly all *homeotic* mutations are in genes that normally act during the larval period of development.

Mutants belonging to the *bithorax* complex and *jab* loci are some examples of *homeotic* mutants.

Some *bithorax* loci	Phenotype
abx	Transforms T_2p to T_3a; T_3a to T_2.
bithorax (bx)	Transforms T_3a to T_2a.
Contrabithorax (Cbx)	Transforms T_2a to T_3a; T_2p to T_3p.
Ultrabithorax (Ubx)	Posterior segments acquire more anterior phenotype.
bithoraxoid (bxd)	Transforms A_1a to T_3a

Some *jab* loci	Phenotype
jab 2	Transforms A_2a to A_1.
jab 3	Transforms $A_{3\text{-}6}$ to A_2.
jab 4	Transforms A_4 to A_3.
jab 5	Transforms A_5 to A_4.
jab 6	Transforms A_6 to A_5.

(Where A— abdominal segment; T— thoracic segment; a — anterior segment; p— posterior segment; the numerals in suffix represent the segment number).

Transdetermination

In holometabolous insect such as *Drosophila*, the larva has tiny discs or drop-shaped cellular structures called *imaginal discs* that form eyes, antenna, wings, halteres, legs and gonads of the adult fly. Each of these adult organ is formed by a specific imaginal discpresent in developing larva.

In addition to homeosis, another phenomenon known as '*transdetermination*' can lead to changes in the determined state of cells in *imaginal discs*. The mechanism of transdetermination is not well understood, but it points to the existence of a mechanism, for switching between alternative states of determinations. Transdetermination from leg to antenna or leg to wing was known for the past many years. Transdetermination occurs when imaginal disc cells are cultured *in vivo* in the abdomen of the adult females or *in vitro* tissue culture. Transdetermination is assayed by re-injecting the cultured disc into a metamorphosing larva following terminal differentiation.

Homeobox

When sequences of some of the genes controlling early development in *Drosophila* were compared, a common feature emerged. A number of genes contained a similar stretch of 180 bp long sequence, while sequences of the rest of genes widely differ. This common 180 bp long sequence present in several genes concerned with early development is known as ***homeobox***. Studies with homeobox regions have shown that *homeobox codes for that part of the protein, which interacts with DNA and thus controls the activities of genes.*

Homeobox sequences are highly conserved across other species of animals such as: sea urchin, worms, chicken, mice and humans. There are indications that the genes expressed at different positions in *Drosophila* embryo are expressed in similar positions in mouse embryo. Anterior end genes in fly and mouse have some features common.

Homeobox genes are good example how studies with organisms apparently remote from humans can provide important information relevant to higher organisms including humans.

Further reading

Browder, L. W., Erickson, C.A., and Jeffery, W.R. Developmental Biology, 3rd edition., Saunders, Philadelphia (1991).

Gilbert, S.F. Developmental Biology, 3rd edition, Sinauer, Sunderland (MA) (1991).

Gurdon, J.B. The Control of Gene Expression in Animal Development. Harvard Univ. Press, Cambridge (1974).

Wilkins, A.S. Genetic Analysis of Animal Development, 2nd edition, Wiley-Liss, New York (1993).

Wolpert, L. Positional information and pattern formation. *Curr. Top. Dev. Biol. 6*: 183 (1971).

Wolpert, L. The Triumph of the Embryo. Oxford Univ. Press. Oxford (1991).

CHAPTER 26

Signal Transduction and Excitable Cells

Cells of the unicellular as well as multicellular organisms communicate with each other, so that they can coordinate their behaviour for mutual benefit. In unicellular organism yeast, one cell influencing the behaviour of another is known to exist. Yeast cell can communicate and influence another cell's proliferation, in preparation for mating. When a cell is ready to mate it secretes a peptide that signals cells of opposite mating type to stop dividing and prepare for mating. Yeast mutants deficient in mating show that a number of proteins forming a signalling circuit exist. The signalling circuitry includes:

1. Cell surface receptors
2. GTP binding proteins
3. Protein kinases

Signalling system in multicellular organism is more elaborate than unicellular yeast. Cells of multicellular organisms depending upon their complexity secrete hundreds of different types of signalling molecules such as:

1. Amino acids
2. Derivatives of fatty acids
3. Small peptides
4. Proteins
5. Nucleotides
6. Steroids
7. Retinoids
8. Dissolved gases nitrous oxide (NO) and carbon mon-oxide (CO).

Signalling cells secrete these molecules usually by

(A) packaging them in vesicles and then release in the surrounding medium by exocytosis.

(B) By diffusion through plasma membrane.

(C) Remain bound to the cell surface and influence those cells coming in contact with the signalling cell.

Irrespective of the nature of signalling molecule, the *respondent cell* or *target cell* interacts through a specific protein called *receptor protein.* Very often the receptors are transmembrane proteins on the target cell. Very low concentrations (10^{-8}M) of the signalling molecule or *ligand* could interact with the receptor tightly. Binding of the *ligand* to the receptor generates a cascade of intracellular signals to change the behaviour of target cells. For some categories of ligands , which are small hydrophobic molecules and can diffuse through the plasma membrane, the receptor could be located inside the cell membrane.

Types of signalling

1. **Paracrine signalling.** Signalling molecules act only on the target cells situated in the immediate neighbourhood of signalling cell. In such a situation the signalling molecule is not allowed to move too far. It is quickly taken up by target cells or destroyed by extracellular enzymes or tightly immobilized by cell surface structures.

2. **Endocrine signalling.** Endocrine cells control the behaviour of the entire organism by secreting molecules called hormones. These hormones reach the target cells in the body of the animal *via* blood and in plants they reach target cells through plant sap.

3. **Synaptic signalling.** In the larger multicellular organisms, specialized cells called *neurons* establish communication between cells as well as organs by sending electrical and chemical signals through *axon*, a specialized extension of the signalling cell, *neuron*.

When a neuron is activated by stimuli from the environment or other nerve cells, it may send an *electric impulse* down the axon. This *electrical impulse* is called ***action potential***, which can travel at the rate of ~ 100 m/ sec and reaches terminals called ***synaptic knobs*** or ***synaptic boutons***. ***The axon potential (signal) travels down the axon unattenuated and reaches synaptic knob.*** A synaptic knob may have several regions of contact called *synapses*, with other cells or neurons. A synapse could be *excitatory* or *inhibitory* depending on the *neurotransmitter* released by the signalling cell and behaviour of the target cell receiving those neurotransmitters.

The neurotransmitter is packaged in vesicles, which fuse in the membrane of the synapse and release signalling molecules called neurotransmitters in the ***synaptic cleft***. The target cell (also known in this case as ***post synaptic cell***) through the receptors in the synaptic cleft interacts with the neurotransmitters and appropriately responds. The neurotransmitter molecules are recycled by synaptic knob through adsorption and endocytosis.

Comparison between endocrine and synaptic signalling

In the body of higher animals endocrine cells and neurons work in co-ordination, to establish communication and control between millions or billions of cells. Different types of endocrine cells release different signalling molecules or hormones in the blood stream. Target cells having different kinds of receptors on their plasma membrane, selectively pick up these hormones from the blood stream flowing around them. Different hormones elicit different responses from different target cells. *In endocrine system a common vehicle — blood is used to transport all signalling molecules.*

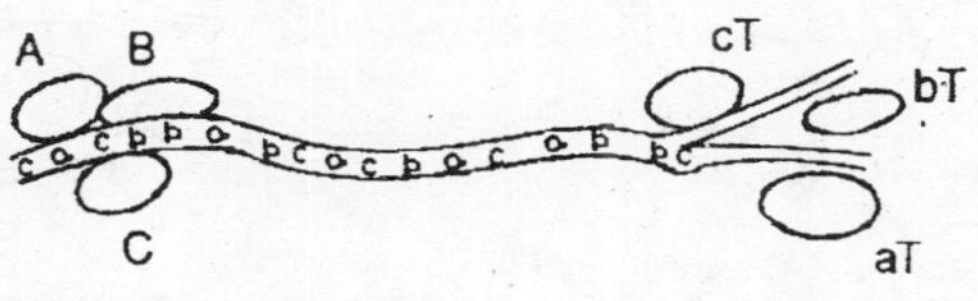

Fig. 26.1. A simplified diagram of the endocrine system. A, B, C endocrine cells release hormone molecules a, b, c respectively. The hormone molecules a, b, c reach the target cells aT, bT, cT respectively via blood stream and elicit different responses.

In comparison a neuron will have specific connection *via* an axon and a large number of synaptic knobs with several target cells which could be other neurons or muscles. In synaptic system of signalling each neuron makes a specific synapse with another neuron or target cell. Of course, the synapses are made and destroyed, depending upon their use or disuse during the lifetime of the animal.

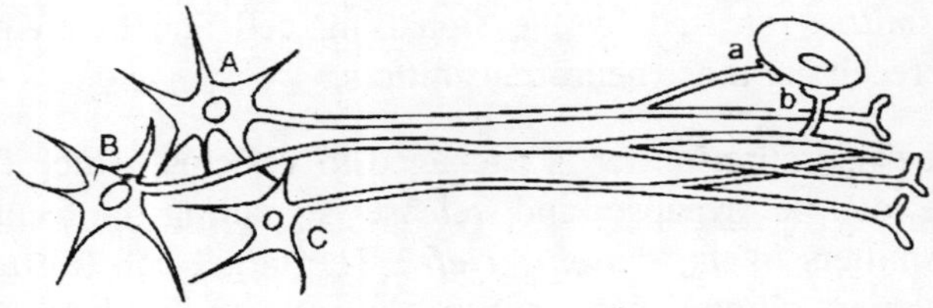

Fig. 26.2. A, B, C neurons forming synaptic knobs a and b on the target cells.

Autocrine signalling

A variation of the theme of the paracrine signalling is autocrine signalling. A group of cells can send signals to themselves. When a cell secretes signalling molecules, which can bind to its own receptors or receptors of a group of similar cells, it is called *autocrine signaling* (A). Autocrine signalling can reinforce development and differentiation by mutual synergistic action of secretion of signal molecules (B).

Fig. 26.3. A diagram of the synergistic action of autocrine signalling cells.

Signalling through gap junctions

Gap junctions are intercellular channels that connect the cytoplasms of adjoining cells. Often cells are connected with their neighbour through *tiny water filled channels* embedded in closely apposed plasma membranes. These channels allow exchange of small molecules, intracellular mediators like Ca (II) ions or cyclic AMP. But these channels are impervious to macromolecules like proteins or nucleic acids. From electron microscopy studies, these water filled tiny channels were named as ***gap junctions***. The presence of *gap junction* between any two cells can be either established by impaling electrodes in a pair of cells and recording electrical signals or more easily by observing the diffusion of an injected dye to the other cells. Gap junctions allow signalling molecules to reach up to 200 μm range by passive diffusion.

Preferential tethering of microtubules' plus ends at the *adherens junction* (cell-cell junction) facilitates delivery of *connexin hemichannels* to the plasma membrane, forming the common border of adjacent cells. Gap junctions are formed by lateral diffusion of *hemichannels* in the *plasma membrane*. The delivery of hemichannels to cell-cell junction is dependent on (i) microtubules, (ii) adherens-junction proteins N-cadherin and β-catenin, (iii) microtubule plus-end tracking protein (+TIP)EB1 and' (iv) interacting protein p150 (Glued). This is a specific mechanism of protein delivery to the point of cell-cell contact.

Responses of target cells to signalling molecules

Depending upon the type of receptors present on the cell, different cells respond differently to the similar signalling molecules. Some cells proliferate, some maintain and survive and others die, under similar populations of signalling molecules (say A, B,. C, D, E etc.).

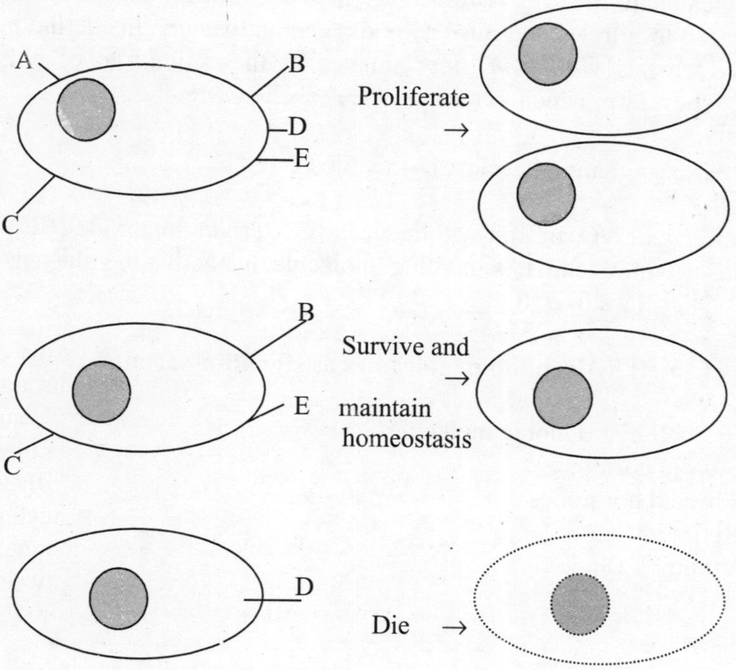

In addition, each cell may have more than one type of receptors and could specifically respond to a group of signalling molecules differently. Even to a single signalling molecule acetyl choline, the skeletal muscle responds by contraction, the heart muscle responds by relaxation and secretary cells release vesicles.

Theoretical reasoning would show that a group of cells capable of quick response to a signal need a signalling molecule with *a short biological half life*.

Small molecules as signalling agents

Nitric oxide (NO), carbon monoxide (CO), and small hydrophobic molecules can on their own pass through the plasma membrane of target cells. The role of NO and CO as a signalling molecule has been recognized recently. Endothelial cells of vertebrates synthesize and release NO under the influence of acetyl choline. NO signals smooth muscles to relax, thereby dilating the blood vessels. This in turn increases the blood flow through heart. NO released by autonomic nerves cause dilation of blood vessels in penis and result in its erection. NO is made in the body by an enzyme NO-synthetase from amino acid arginine by its deamination. NO acts only locally as it has a short biological half life of 5-10 seconds in the extracellular space, and is converted to nitrates and nitrites by oxygen and water. Inside the target cell NO reacts with *iron atom* situated at the active site of enzyme guanylyl cyclase, which in turn produces cyclic GMP

$$\text{NO} + (\text{Fe} — \text{guanylyl cyclase}) \rightarrow \text{cyclic GMP}$$

The effects of NO are felt within seconds. Carbon monoxide (CO) also acts as an intercellular signalling molecule by activating the enzyme guanylyl cyclase like NO.

Role of small hydrophobic molecules as signalling agents

Being small hydrophobic molecules

1. Steroid hormones
2. Thyroid hormones
3. Retinoids
4. Vitamin D and

5. Ecdysone the moulting hormone in insects
can diffuse directly through the plasma membrane of target cell and bind to intracellular receptor-proteins. In turn receptors are activated and, switches ON transcription of certain genes. These receptors as a class belong to *intracellular receptor superfamily* also commonly known as *steroid hormone receptor super family.* They all bind to DNA as *homodimers* or *heterodimers.*

Receptor binding domain □ on DNA blocked by inhibitory protein comprising of ***heat shock protein Hsp*** and some other proteins, results in no transcription of DNA, so there is no formation of mRNA transcript.

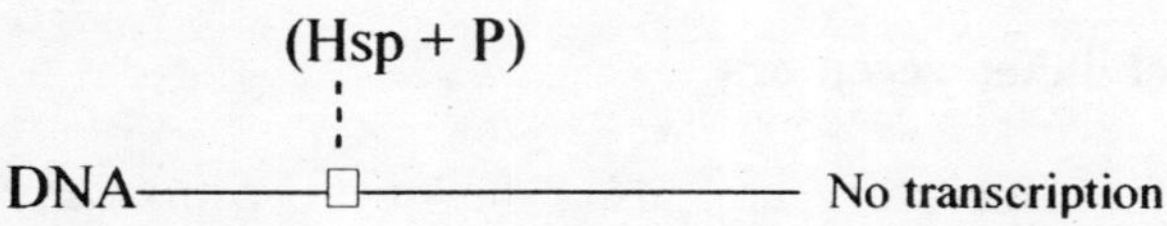

When a signalling molecule ***S*** (say steroid hormone) binds to the (Hsp + P) receptor , there is believed to be a conformational change in (Hsp + P) complex and the inhibitory action on DNA transcription is released so that transcription of gene starts and the mRNA transcript is formed.

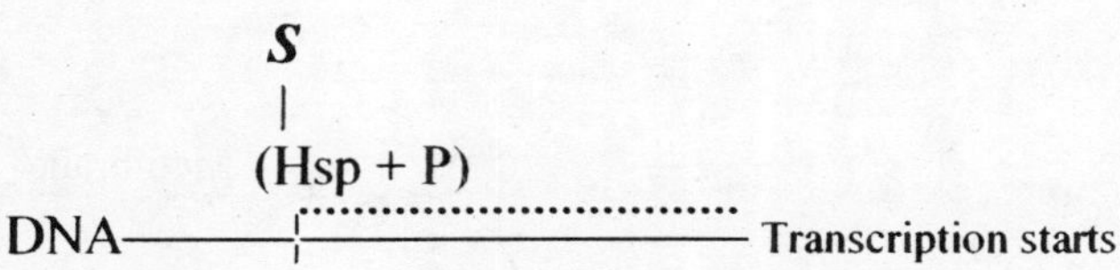

Most water-soluble signalling molecules, which flow through blood stream or tissue fluids are degraded within minutes. Neurotransmitters are scavenged within milliseconds to seconds. While steroid hormones and thyroid hormones remain in blood for hours and days respectively. Steroid hormones elicit two types of responses:

1. Early response within 30 minutes and
2. Delayed response.

Both responses involve sequential switching ON and OFF of genes. Though some models have been proposed for the mechanism of action, yet none seems to explain mechanism satisfactorily.

Types of cell-surface receptor proteins

Cell surface signalling receptor proteins are present only up to 0.01% of the total cell-protein. Cloning of DNA sequence that code for these proteins has accelerated the pace of research in this domain.

All water-soluble signalling molecules, such as neurotransmitters, protein-hormones, and growth-factor proteins bind to specific receptors on the surface of target cell. Then extracellular binding generates one to several intra-cellular signals altering the behaviour of the target cell. There are three broad classes of cell-surface receptors.

1. Ion channel linked receptors.
2. G-protein linked receptors
3. Enzyme linked receptors.

Ion channel linked receptors

These surface receptors are also known as ***transmitter-gated ion channels***. *Ion channels are formed by proteins.* A small number of neurotransmitters bind to the channel protein and operate the channel by briefly changing the ion-permeability of plasma membrane and the excitability of the post-synaptic cell. Ion channels operate between electrically excitable cells for quick synaptic signalling.

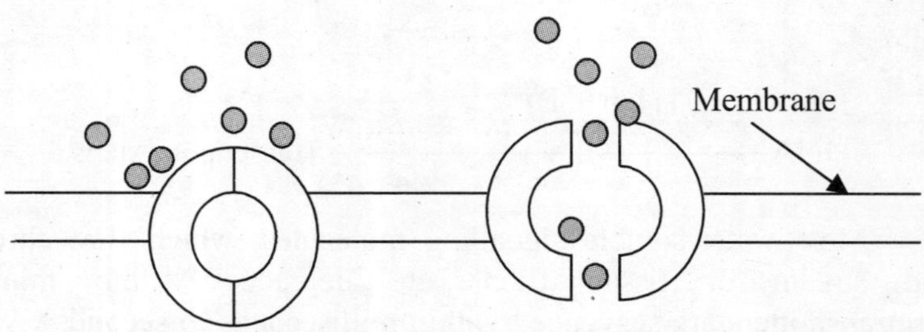

Ion channel closed

Ion channel open. By interaction between Neurotransmitter and channel proteins. Ions like ◉ Na^+, K^+ or Ca^{++} are allowed to pass. through channel.

G-protein linked receptors (GPLR)

These receptors control the activity of separate target-protein bound to plasma membrane. The target protein could be an ion channel or an enzyme. The link between receptor and target protein is established by a ***trimeric GTP binding regulatory protein*** (or briefly called ***G-protein***). The word trimeric means a molecule formed by 3 sub-units, similar to words monomeric (single unit) or dimeric (two subunits).

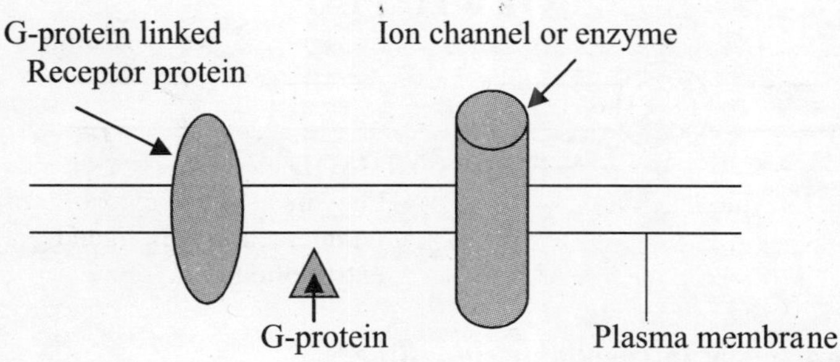

If the target protein is an ion channel, its activation changes ion permeability. If it is an enzyme, it changes concentration of one or more signal-cascade molecules or intracellular mediators. Most of the G-protein receptors have been identified by gene cloning and have > 100 types characterized in mammals alone. They form the largest group of cell surface receptors.

The sequence of interactions are as follows:

GPLR + G-P → G-P*

G-P* + Enzyme→ Enzyme * (active)

G-P* + Ion channel→ Ion channel* opens

All G-protein linked receptors come in the category of 'seven-pass' transmembrane proteins.

Enzyme linked receptors

These receptors are usually single-pass transmembrane proteins. The ligend binds to the outer region of protein and the catalytic side is inside the cell in cytosol. These receptors function directly as enzyme. The enzyme linked receptors are usually heteromers. They are either themselves protein kinases or associate with protein kinases, which phosphorylate group of proteins in the target cell.

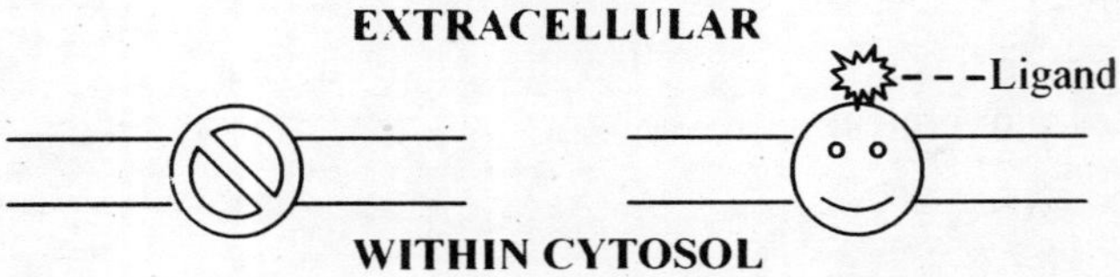

Enzyme inactive

Enzyme active in cytosol on interaction with ligand extracellularly.

Mechanisms of intracellular signalling

There are two main intracellular signalling processes.

1. Signalling by phosphorylation

Sp + ATP → Sp* + ADP

Signalling protein inactive (Sp); Signalling protein active (Sp*)

Sp* → Sp + Pi

Active signalling protein (Sp*); Inactive signalling protein (Sp); Phosphate (Pi)

2. Signalling by G-protein

Sp—GDP → Sp*—GTP

Inactive (Sp—GDP); Active (Sp*—GTP)

Sp*—GTP → Sp—GDP + Pi

Active (Sp*—GTP); Inactive (Sp—GDP); Phosphate (Pi)

In both processes addition of a phosphate group activates the signalling protein and removal of phosphate de-activates the signal protein.

The G-protein linked cell surface receptors generate small molecules as *intracellular mediators* by two main pathways

Cyclic AMP (or cAMP) and cyclic GMP (or cGMP)

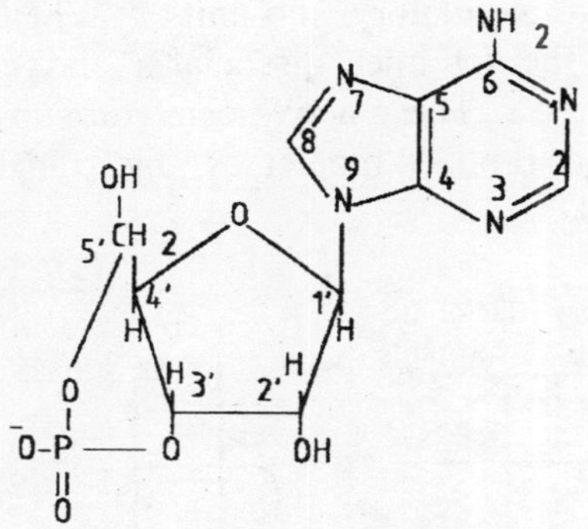

c-AMP

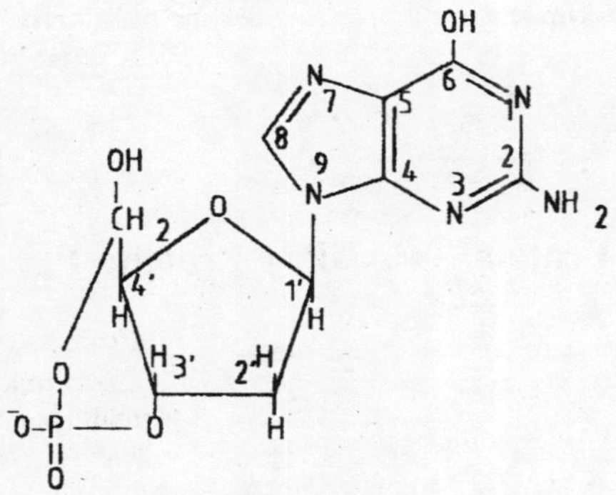

c-GMP

1. Ca^{++} ion pathway

Both cAMP and Ca^{++} act as allosteric effectors in relaying the signal. They bind to a specific protein and change its activity by allosteric modifications in protein structure.

A-Kinase propagating the effects of c-AMP in signalling

Cyclic AMP dependent protein kinase (known as *A-kinase*) is found in almost all animal cells and is responsible to mediate all the affects of c AMP in the cell. Cyclic AMP dependent phosphorylation of protein was first observed in glycogen metabolism studies with skeletal muscle cells. The cAMP also regulates ion-channels in olfactory (smell sensing) neurons. The substrates for *A-Kinase* differ for different cells.

A-kinase is a tetrameric protein, where 2 sub-units are catalytic and the other two are regulatory sub-units. When cAMP binds to regulatory sub-units, the tetramer dissociates and catalytic sub-units become active, and free. These active catalytic sub-units of A-kinase phosphorylate specific protein molecules, by transferring terminal phosphate group of ATP.

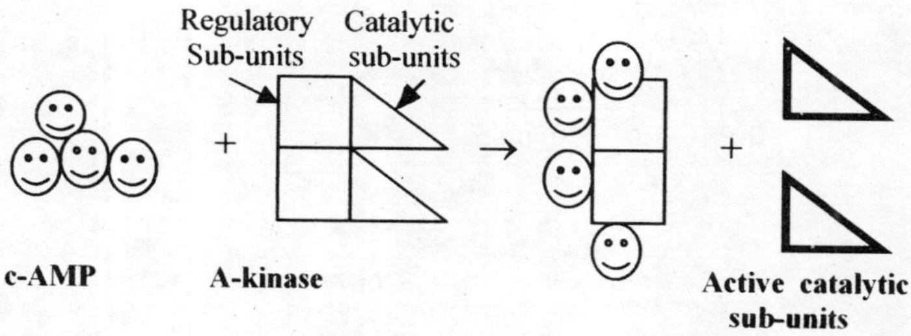

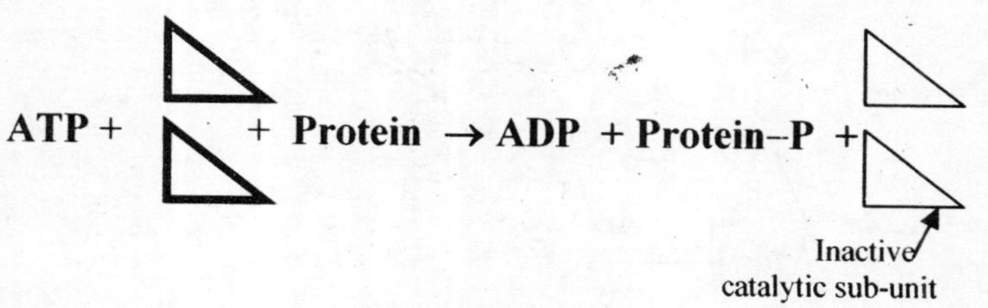

In Protein-P usually serine and threonine near amino-terminal are covalently phosphorylated

By the *law of mass action* of chemistry, if there is increase in concentration of chemicals on the right side of the equation, then the reaction will be tilted in favour of leftside. Therefore protein-P, with serine and threonine phosphorylated, reverse the effect of *A-kinase*.

Ca^{++} as intracellular signalling ion and maintenance of low Ca^{++} concentration in the cell cytosol.

The concentration of Ca^{++} in *endoplasmic reticulum (ER)* and outside the cell are high in the range of 10^{-3} M. While in cytosol, the concentration of Ca^{++} is low 10^{-7} M. This causes a large 1,000 fold concentration gradient with a tendency to drive Ca^{++} into the cytosol from outside as well as from ER. If a signalling molecule transiently opens Ca^{++} channels in the plasma membrane or on ER, the Ca^{++} rushes in cytosol, increasing the concentration 50 fold to 5×10^{-6} M, activating Ca^{++} responsive protein in cytosol. If the concentration of Ca^{++} increases beyond 1×10^{-5} M, the cell may get damaged. As a safety mechanism mitochondrial inner membrane comes into action as a low affinity, high capacity pump and takes up the excess Ca^{++} of the cytosol inside mitochondrion.

There are 2 mechanisms for export of Ca^{++} out of cytosol.

1. Na^{+} ion driven-in, and Ca^{++} ion exit channel.
2. ATP coupled Ca^{++} ion export by plasma membrane.

   There are 3 mechanisms to control intracellular (inside cytosol) levels of Ca^{++}

   1. Proteins binding Ca^{++}.
   2. Ca^{++} ATPase in endoplasmic reticulum, ATP is converted to ADP and Ca^{++} is taken in.
   3. Electrochemical gradient across mitochondrial membrane during oxidative phosphorylation takes up Ca^{++} in mitochondrion.

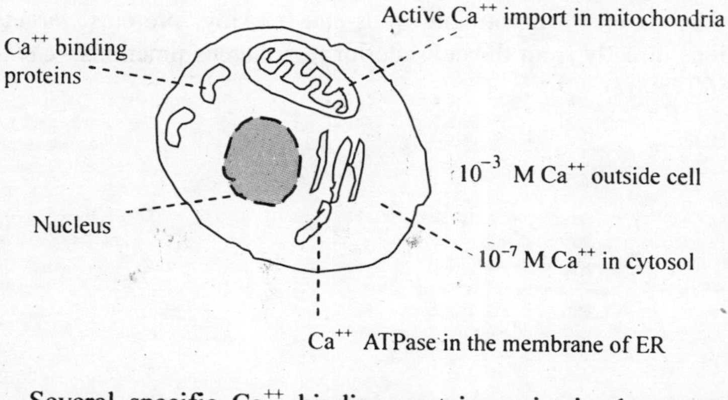

Several specific Ca^{++} binding proteins exist in the cytosol to control Ca^{++} levels. ***Troponine*** is the first protein discovered in the skeletal muscle cells, which binds to Ca^{++} in cells. Another protein binding to Ca^{++} is ***Calmodulin***, which is found in almost all animal-cells.

About 10^7 molecules of calmodulin are present in a cell that constitute approximately 1 % of the total protein present in a cell.

Ca^{++}.activates calmodulin, in a manner similar to cAMP activates A-kinase. Most of the actions of Ca^{++} in the animal cell are mediated by calmodulin dependent protein kinases (also known as ***CAM-kinases***).

Trimeric G-proteins have been known to regulate the activation of various enzymes, changing the concentrations of cyclic nucleotides and Ca^{++} in cytosol. In addition trimeric G-protein can directly activate or deactivate ion channels changing the permeability of plasma membrane of target cell. Indirectly too, trimeric G-protein regulates ion channels through A-kinase or CAM-kinase. G-protein linked receptors are known to be involved in olfactory (perception of smell), visual and gustatory (perception of taste) systems.

Further reading

Hardie, D.G. Biochemical Messengers: Hormones, Neurotransmitters and Growth Factors. Chapman Hall, London (1990).

Molecular Biology of Signal Transduction. *Cold. Spr. Harb. Symp. Quant. Biol. 53*: (1988).

Shaw, R.M., Fay, A.J. Puthenveedu, M.A., Zastrow, M.*v*., Yuh-Nung, J. and Jan, L.Y. Microtubule plus-end-tracking proteins target gap junctions directly from the cell interior to adherens junctions. *Cell, 128*: 547-560 (2007).

CHAPTER 27

Mitochondria

Around one and a half billion ($1.5x10^9$) years ago a primordeal eukaryotic cell probably became host to an aerobic bacterium that evolved to become a mitochondrion and establish a symbiotic relationship with the host cell. The symbiotic relationship has become so strong that .the cell is largely dependent on mitochondria for providing energy to move, contract, produce secretory products and divide. Mitochondria in humans for example import more than 900 proteins and all its lipid requirements from the cell-cytoplasm. Mitochondria are usually similar in size to bacteria 1-10 μm long, but have variable shapes according to the tissue harbouring them.

The architecture of a mitochondrion

Mitochondria are bound by two layers of membranes. Each of these membranes is a phospholipid bilayer with embedded proteins. The *outer membrane* has *porin* protein containing aqueous-channels that allow entry of molecules smaller than 5000 Daltons. The *inner membrane* contains phospholipid *cardiolipin* made of 4 fatty acids and is selectively impermiable to ions and many large molecules. The inner membrane has convoluted folds called *cristae* that project inward. The folded structures of inner membrane enhance the productivity of cellular respiration by greatly increased surface area, which promotes chemical reactions to occur at a higher rate. The innermost zone of mitochondria known as *matrix* contains a mixture of hundreds of enzymes, identical copies of mitochondrial DNA (*mtDNA*), special mitochondrial ribosomes and tRNAs. The *intermembrane space* contains many diffusable *ions* and molecules. Mitochondria are the major organelle in the cell where the energy rich ATP molecules are produced. *ATP molecules are used like a currency by the cell for most types of energy-requiring cell reactions and functions*.

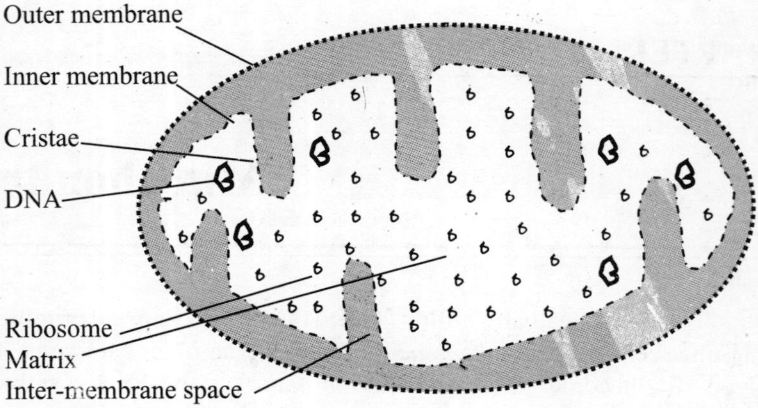

Fig.27.1. A diagram showing the architecture of a mitochondrion.

Mitochondria make a lot of ATP for the cell

Glucose (a six-carbon molecule) is converted to pyruvate (a three-carbon molecule) by glycolysis through anaerobic metabolism in the cell-cytoplasm. Pyruvate enters the mitochondria and it is converted to acetyl Co-A and 1 molecule of CO_2. Acetyl Co-A (cffectively two-carbon compound) plus oxalacetate (a four-carbon compound) produce citric acid (a six-carbon compound), which is at the beginning of the *citric acid cycle* or also known as *Kreb's cycle* of biochemical reactions in the cell.

The H^+ *ions* generated during some of the steps of Kreb's cycle are delivered by NADH* and $FADH_2$* to electron transport pumps, which pump H^+ *ions* out of mitochondrion-matrix. As the H^+ *ion* or proton concentration increases in the inter-membrane space, a strong electrochemical gradient is established across the inner membrane. Protons can come back in the matrix through ATP synthase complex and their energy is used for the synthesis of ATP from ADP and inorganic phosphate Pi. This transport of H^+ across the inner membrane is known as *chemi-osmosis*. Peter Mitchell was awarded Nobel Prize for its discovery.

....

***NAD^+ = nicotinamide adenine dinucleotide; FAD^+ = flavin adenine dinucleotide.**

The H^+ *ions* that are pumped back in to matrix combine with oxygen to make water. Without this is important step, H^+ *ions* would accumulate in the matrix and the concentration gradient meant to run the ATP pumps would not remain sufficient for the pumps to work optimally.

The ATP synthase enzyme converts ADP in to ATP at the surface of the inner membrane by the following reaction:

$$\text{ADP} + \text{Pi} \xrightarrow[\text{By oxidative phosphorylation**}]{\text{ATP synthetase} + H^+} \text{ATP}$$

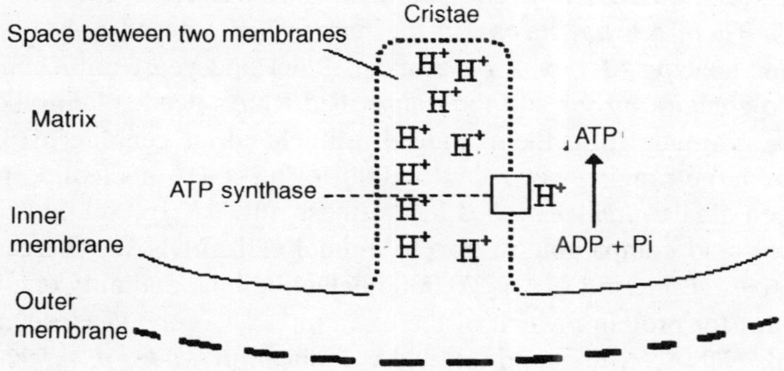

Fig.27.2. Diagram showing the salient features of the synthesis of ATP in mitochondria.

Normally in the absence of oxygen, 4 molecules of ATP are produced by glycolysis for each molecule of glucose utilized in the cell-cytoplasm. ***In the presence of oxygen 24 to 28 ATP molecules are produced out of one glucose molecule in mitochondria.*** So we can get far more energy rich molecules of ATP from one molecule of glucose, if mitochondria are working and oxygen is available.

....

** When H^+ or e^- are taken away from a molecule it gets oxidized. In reverse if H^+ or e^- are given to the molecule it gets reduced. When phosphate group is given to a molecule it is phosphorylated. The *oxidative phosphorylation* means removal of H^+ from one molecule and giving phosphate group to another molecule.

Mitochondrial DNA (*mtDNA*)

Most of the mitochondrial DNA is double stranded except for the *D-loop* (*Cf.* Chapter 19, Replication of DNA) the non-coding region, *which is triple stranded* containing an extra 7S DNA. The triple stranded region is approximately 7% of the circular *mtDNA* molecule. The replication of *mtDNA* starts at O_H on heavy strand (*H*) and proceeds through O_L on light strand (*L*). Each mitochondrion contains 2-10 copies of DNA. Heavy strand (*H*) of *mtDNA* is rich in guanines (*G*) and the light strand (*L*) is rich in cytosines (*C*). Two rRNAs, 14 tRNAs and 10 *polyA RNAs* are transcribed on the *H* strand. The *L* strand transcribes for 8 tRNAs and a small *polyA RNA*. *The poly A* containing RNAs form mitochondrial mRNAs. There are ***no introns*** in the human *mtDNA* and only a small intergenic spacing of 1 or 2 bases exist. Plant and yeast mitochondrial genes do contain *introns* and the transcribed RNAs need splicing before proteins are made from them. Indeed, mitochondrial genome of plants could be large ranging between 150,000 to 2.5 x 10^6 nucleotide pairs. The green alga *Chlamydomonas* has a linear mtDNA 16,000 nucleotide pairs long and comparable in size to animal cell mtDNA. Whereas the yeast *S. cerevisiae* mtDNA is 70,000 nucleotide long and only one-third of it codes for protein. Much of the extra mtDNA in the yeast seems to be `junk' DNA. Mitochondrial DNA replication ***lacks proofreading*** hence the mutation rate is 10 to 100 times higher than nuclear DNA.

Human mitochondria have ~16,600 base pair long circular DNA (*mtDNA*), containing approximately 37 genes. The *mtDNA* encodes for 22 mitochondrial tRNAs and 3 rRNAs of the sizes 16S, 12S and 5S essential for translation of *mtDNA* transcripts. Thirteen mitochondrial genes code for protein subunits of respiratory complexes I, III, IV, and V. Proteins of respiratory complex II are totally coded by host cell nuclear genes. ***In addition, more than 900 proteins coded by nuclear genome are imported in mitochondria. Most of the lipid molecules are imported by mitochondria.***

In mammals 99.99% of *mtDNA* is inherited from mother. Because oocyte contains 100,000 mitochondria and the sperm contains 100 mitochondria in its tail region. Hence less than 0.01% of *mtDNA* is paternal in the fertilized ovum. In addition the paternal mitochondria from sperm containing ubiquitin are selectively degraded. Mitochondrial inheritance in yeast is however biparental when the haploid cells fuse. Yeast strains carrying '*petite*' mutation often cannot perform *oxidative phosphorylation* because of partial loss of DNA.

Mutations including deletions in *mtDNA* may lead to respiratory defects, which could be tissue specific. These mutations are usually maternally inherited from egg to zygote. The paternal mitochondria from sperm containing ubiquitin are selectively degraded. The clinical symptoms of these defects progress with age due to accumulation of defective *mtDNA* in specific tissues. A zygote inheriting a mixture of wild type and mutant genomes is known as heteroplasmic cell and its state is described as heteroplasmy. When heteroplasmic cells divide the

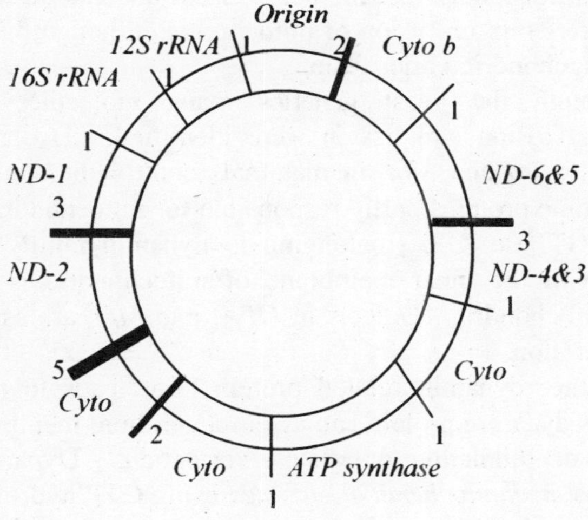

Fig.27.3. Location of some genes on the circular DNA of mitochondria. Radial spokes demarcate the boundary of the gene. The number near the spoke shows the presence of that many *t-RNA* genes. *Cyto* = cytochrome oxidase genes; *Cyto b* = cytochrome b gene ; *ND-1—6* = Dehydrogenase genes.

ratio of wild type and mutant genomes can vary among different tissues and individual cells. As the mutant *mtDNA* load increases (60-90%), the cellular dysfunction becomes apparent beyond a certain threshold of mutant *mtDNA*. Cells with higher proportion of mutant *mtDNA* will have lower respiratory capacity. Ultimately a tissue or cell may inherit only mutant *mtDNA*, a state known as homoplasmy. However, even homoplasmic mitochondrial diseases are also progressive for unclear reasons.

Mitochondrial Fission and Fusion

Mammalian cells may contain hundreds to thousands of mitochondria. Each mitochondrion may have several *mtDNA* clusters. Any particular mitochondrion does not remain a discrete autonomous organelle for long. It may fuse with a neighbouring mitochondrion. The mitochondrial population is usually in a constant flux where mitochondria undergo self-fission as well as fusion with the neighbour.

If cultured mammalian cells are artificially fused to form hybrids, the mitochondrial populations are fully fused in 8 hours, but the functional complementation of gene products occurs after several days only. During mitochondrial fusion outer and inner membranes as well as contents of mitochondria get mixed. It is not understood to what extent *mtDNA* clusters mix on fusion of mitochodria, although they co-habit in the same mitochondrion after fusion.

Through the yeast genetics many molecules involved in mitochondrial fusion and fission were identified. Two mitochondrial fusion genes Mfn_1 and Mfn_2 in mammals control the synthesis of two outer membrane proteins partly responsible for mitochondrial fusion. In addition, a GTPase, OPA_1 belonging to dynamin family GTPase and associated with the inner membrane of mitochondria is essential for fusion of mitochondria. Defects in OPA_1 and Mfn_2 are associated with neurodegeneration.

Another dynamin related protein Drp_1 leads to mitochondrial fission. This dynamin protein can assemble on lipid membranes causing constriction or tubulation or vesicle formation. Dynamins may be considered as *mechanochemical enzymes* using GTP hydrolysis to cause membrane scission. Most of Drp_1 product exists in cytosol of the cell.

Mitochondrial fusion seems to be important for maintenance of mitochondrial function and shape, whereas mitochondrial fission seems to be needed for recruitment of mitochondria to nerve terminals. Fission of mitochondria is also involved in induction of programmed cell death (*apoptosis*). Inhibition of mitochondrial fusion may also facilitate cell death or cells undergoing apoptosis.

Mitochondria and Neurons

Like many other cell types, neurons are susceptible to mitochondrial dysfunction. Time-lapse photography of mitochondrial transport in neurons show a transport rate of 0.1 to 1 μm /sec. Hence a mitochondrion existing within a motor neuron cell body will take approximately 2 weeks to travel to nerve periphery in various limbs.

Synaptic boutons in axons contain abundant mitochondria. It probably indicates the rapid ATP demands of synaptic transmission like fusion and recycling of synaptic vesicles operation of ATP driven pumps to control ionic environment. A number of studies with *Drosophila* mutants have provided genetic evidence for the functional role of synaptic mitochondria. Defects in *Milton*, *Drp1* or *Miro* genes lead to severe loss of mitochondria in specific neuron terminals. The *Milton* gene product is a large coiled-coil protein localized to mitochondria. Milton protein binds to kinesin heavy chain and is believed to mediate the transport of mitochondria up to nerve endings along the microtubules. Absence of Milton product in photoreceptor cells results in total absence of mitochondria and loss of synaptic transmission of photoreceptor cell, otherwise the structure of synapse appears intact.

As mitochondria need to be transported through axonal processes, so they are transported through dendritic spines as well.

Mitochondrial dysfunction has also been used in aging related studies. But how much is the cause and how much is the effect of aging is a bit uncertain. Above all different cells and tissues have different susceptibilities and responses to mitochondrial dysfunction.

Mitochondria help tracing the spread of human population throughout the world

During sexual reproduction in humans the parental genes located on *Y*-chromosome that is derived from father and the genes in mitochondria, which are derived solely from mother, do not undergo shuffling. In a fertilized ovum if a *Y*-chromosome exists (male child), it is in a single copy and inherited from the father. Compared to this an oocyte contains more than 100,000 mitochondria and the sperm has only around 100, which degenerate soon after fertilization of the ovum. Hence all mitochondrial DNA is inherited from the mother. Specific mutations on *Y*-chromosome and mitochondria serve as markers that tie people to a common ancestor. Over long stretches of time as the new mutations build up, they tell the history of a particular species. In a *genographic project* aimed to study human historical migrations, a number of mitochondrial and *Y*- chromosome mutations have been tested from different groups for common ancestors. In this way it has been possible to trace the spread of human populations originating in Africa to the other parts of the world.

In addition the human body is inhabited by a large number of microbes and parasites, which live intimately with humans in space and time over generations and thousands of years. Caufield, PW and colleagues have used tooth decay causing bacteria *Streptococcus mutans* that are transmitted solely from mother to child for human genography. Similarly Achtman, M and coworkers utilized *Helicobactor pylori* bacteria causing stomach ulcer in some people as a marker for tracing movement of human populations in the world. Another team lead by Hoberg, EP relied on a tapeworm *Taenia asiatica* that alternates between humans and pigs to trace the spread of human population in the past. The interesting fact also emerges is that it was humans who infected pigs with tape worm and not the other way round.

Different groups using mutations in mitochondria and Y-chromosome studied migration of human population to the Indian sub-continent. However, the results obtained by different groups are somewhat different. Barnabas Shama and colleagues mapped the whole mtDNA using 14 restriction enzymes and sequenced the non-transcribed HSVI region for deriving the maternal lineages from non-tribal Indians. They concluded that Southern migration brought the haplogroup M while multiple migrations might have brought other haplogroups N and R in India. They also studied 29 mitochondrial genes from 100 individuals belonging to 14 major language-groups in North, South and Central India. They observe that 12 genes are similar to Caucacians. The first to move in sub-continent were the ancestors of Dravidians from Zagros region in Iran-Iraq. The second wave of influx brought speakers of Aryan languages to India. They also highlight the third Southern route of migration emphasizing the view that the supposed Aryan influx in India 3,000-4,000 years ago did not make a big re-shuffle in the human gene pool of Indian sub-continent.

Sahoo and colleagues used 38 single nucleotide polymorphic markers in Y-chromosome and discount the impact of paternal lineages from outside the sub-continent.

Some mutations on the *Y*-chromosome* used for tracing the history of human migration.

Mutation	Years Ago	Characterizing the Event
M45	35,000	Eurasians crossed into Americas. American-Indians and Americans of European descent shared an ancestor in Asia about 35,000 years ago.
M9	40,000	Mutation arose in Central Asian or Middle East human population
M168	50,000	Humans who migrated out of Africa

*A few more useful *Y*-chromosome mutations serving as markers of American Indian population (*M242* and *M3*) and markers for people of European descent (*M207, M 173, M343*).

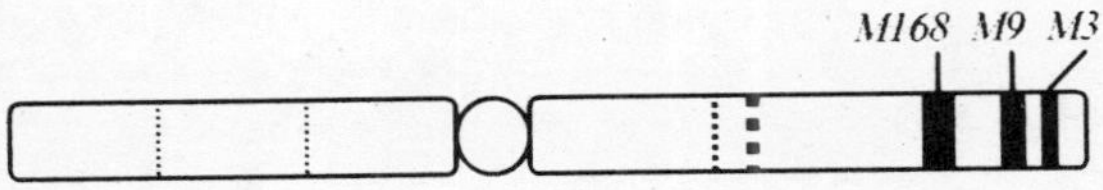

Further reading:

Barnabas, Shama; Souche, Y., and Suresh, C.G. High resolution mtDNA studies of the Indian population: implications for palaeolithic settlement of Indian subcontinent. *Annals of Human Genetics*, *70*:42-58 (2005).

Birky, C.W., Jr. Transmission genetics of mitochondria and chloroplasts. *Annu. Rev. Genet. 12*: 471 (1978).

Caufield, P.W., Saxena, D., Fitch, D. and Li, Y. Population structure of plasmid-containing strains of *Streptococcus mutans*, a member of the human indigenous biota. *J. Bacteriol., 189*: 1238-1243 (2007).

Chan, David.C. (2006). Mitochondria: dynamic organelles in disease, aging and development. *Cell 125*: 1241-1252.

Sahoo, Sanghamitra; Singh, A., Himabindu, G., Banerjee, J., Sitalaximi, T., Gaikwad, S., Trivedi, R., Endicott, P., Kivisild, T., Metspalu, M., Villems, R., and Kashyap, V.K. *Proc. Natl. Acad. Sci.* U.S., *103*: 843-848 (2006).

von Heijne, G. Why mitochondria need a genome? *FEBS Lett. 198*: 1 (1986).

CHAPTER 28

Chloroplasts

Chloroplasts (In Greek *chloros* means green and *plast* meaning entity) are organelles that conduct photosynthesis in plant cells and eukaryotic algae. A plant cell may contain as many as 50 chloroplasts. In the presence of sunlight, water and carbon dioxide, sugar molecules are produced in chloroplasts. Chloroplasts also store energy in the form of energy rich molecule ATP and reduce NADP to NADPH through a set of chemical reactions called photosynthesis. Chloroplasts belong to the category of organelles — plastids. The colourless plastids '*leucoplasts*' synthesize starch, oils and proteins. Yellow or red coloured plastids called '*chromoplasts*' make carotenoids. All plastids develop from tiny organelles *proplastids* found in undifferentiated plant tissue known as '*meristem*'.

Chloroplasts are believed to have originated from the engulfment of a *Cynobacterium* (i.e. blue green algae) by a plant cell or *protista.* Chloroplasts continue to exhibit some prokaryotic traits such as their DNA is circular like prokaryotes and their ribosomes and binary fission are similar to prokaryotes.

The engulfed cynobacterium and the host plant cell developed an endosymbiotic relationship where:

1. Chloroplasts made sugar and ATP molecules through photosynthesis for the host cell.
2. A large number of proteins and enzymes are made by the cell genome in cytosol that are imported by chloroplasts for their use.
3. Chloroplasts have by now only 60 – 120 genes, compared to 1,500 genes of ancestral free living cynobacterium. Many of the genes missing in chloroplasts are instead encoded by nuclear genes of the host cell.
4. Chloroplasts are usually bound by two lipid bilayer membranes (6–8 nm thick) called outer membrane and inner membrane. The inner membrane corresponds to the outer membrane of ancestral cynobacterium. The gap between two membranes (10–20 nm) is known as inter-membrane gap and is the zone where nucleotide phosphorylations are carried out.

Outer membrane is permeable to most ions and metabolites. Whereas inner membrane has selective permeability with embedded transport proteins.

The third membrane system in chloroplasts comprises of *lamellae* or *thylakoids* that are interconnecting flattened (disc-like) membrane compartments. Several thylakoid discs pile or stack over each other to make a *grannum* (singular) and each chloroplast has many *granna* (plural) structures interconnected with each other and anchored to the inner membrane as well. Thylakoids are like a hollow coin, where hollow space is called *lumen*. Groups of *chlorophyll* molecules known as *antenna complex* are embedded in thylakoid membrane. This array arrangement increases the surface area for the capture of light. Two molecules of chlorophyll are ionized to produce an excited electron that participates in photochemical reaction.

Thylakoids contain proteins of electron transport chain and photosynthetic pigments such as chlorophyll α and β, xanthoplylls and carotinoids. Four types of protein assemblies are embedded in thylakoid membrane:

1. Photosystem I
2. Photosystem II
3. Cytochrome b and f
4. ATP synthase.

The fluid filled inside the chloroplast and surrounding granna is called *stroma*. Stroma contains plenty of ribosomes, a few circular DNA molecules and starch granules. The pH of stromal fluid is around 7.8 and that of thylakoid lumen is 5. This in other words is equivalent to 1,000 times more H^+ ion concentration in lumen than stromal fluid. As the H^+ ions flow out from the interior of the thylakoid (lumen) passing down the concentration gradient they give up energy, which is used for conversion of ADP to ATP. by the enzyme ATP synthase.

$$ADP + Pi \longrightarrow ATP$$

The stroma also contains all the enzymes e.g. RUBISCO (ribulose biphosphate carboxylase oxygenase) needed to carry out so called 'dark' reactions of photosynthesis. Most of the reactions of carbon fixation occur in stroma.

The primary reaction of photosynthesis is:

$$2H_2O \rightarrow 4e^- + 4H^+ + O_2$$

The final reaction of photosynthesis through Calvin cycle is:

$$6CO_2 + 12\,H_2O \rightarrow C_6H_{12}O_6 + 6\,H_2O + 6O_2$$

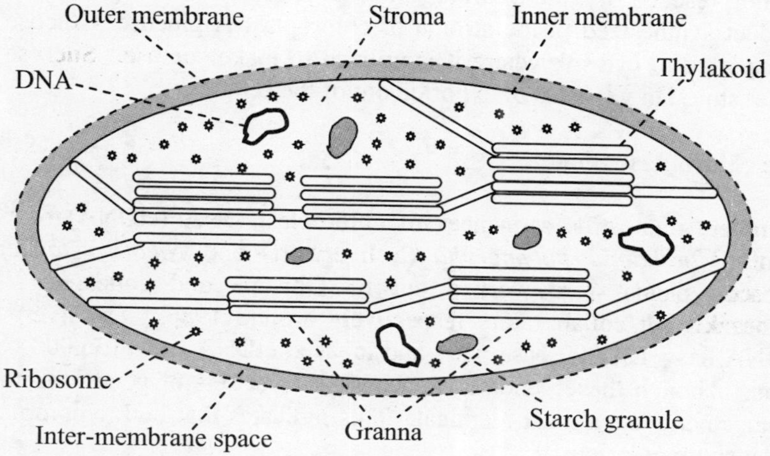

Fig.28.1. Simplified architecture of a chloroplast

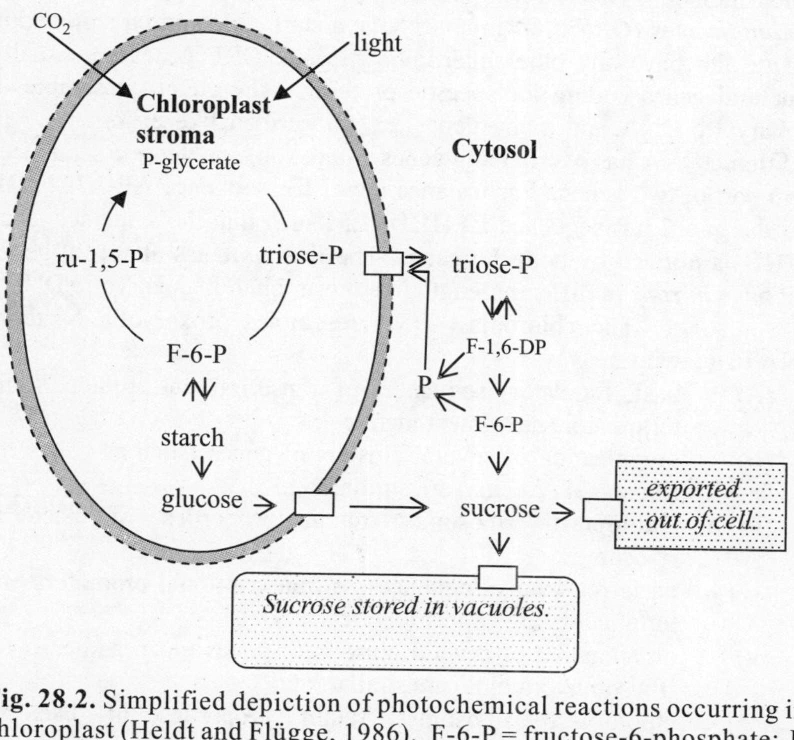

Fig. 28.2. Simplified depiction of photochemical reactions occurring in a chloroplast (Heldt and Flügge, 1986). F-6-P = fructose-6-phosphate; P = phosphate; ru-1,5-P = ribulose - 1,5-biphosphate carboxylase; F-1, 6DP = fructose-1,6-diphosphate;

□ = energy requiring transporter.

In the presence of water, carbon dioxide, phosphate and light the final product synthesized in the stroma of chloroplast is glucose. Glucose is transported to cytosol, where it is utilized to make sucrose. Sucrose is either stored in vacuoles or exported out of the cell.

The chloroplast genome

Complete nucleotide sequences of chloroplast DNA (ctDNA) of two plants *Marchantia polymorpha* (a liverwort) and *Nicotina tabacum* (tobacco plant) were worked out by Ohyama and colleagues and Shinozaki and collaborators respectively around 1986. The liverwort ctDNA has ~121,000 base pairs and tobacco ctDNA has ~156,000 base pairs. Though these genomes differ in size yet sets of genes and their arrangements are almost identical. This indicates that both chloroplasts had a common origin.

Liverwort chloroplast genome has approximately 128 genes which include 4 rRNA genes, 32 tRNA genes and 55 genes with *open reading frames (ORF)*. ORF genes have a start codon and a stop codon and do not have any other interrupting signal. ORF genes are usually structural genes coding for specific proteins. The ctDNA resembles a prokaryotic DNA and many genes are transcribed like an *operon*. In addition ctDNA has overlapping genes where some nucleotide sequences form part of two genes. For instance *gene1* has sequence ABCD**EFGH**, and the *gene2* has sequence **EFGH**IJKLM such that the same sequence **EFGH** is utilized by both the genes. The liverwort has about 20 genes that have *introns* of different length like those found in eukaryotic DNA.

The chloroplast DNA resembles prokaryotic bacterial DNA in a few more ways:

(i) basic regulatory sequences of transcriptional promoters and terminators are almost identical;

(ii) organization of several clusters of genes (such as genes for ribosomal proteins) are similar; and

(iii) chloroplast' ribosomes retain properties of bacterial ribosomes.

(iv) basic regulatory sequences of transcriptional promoters and terminators are almost identical;

(v) organization of several clusters of genes (such as genes for ribosomal proteins) are similar; and

(vi) chloroplast' ribosomes retain properties of bacterial ribosomes.

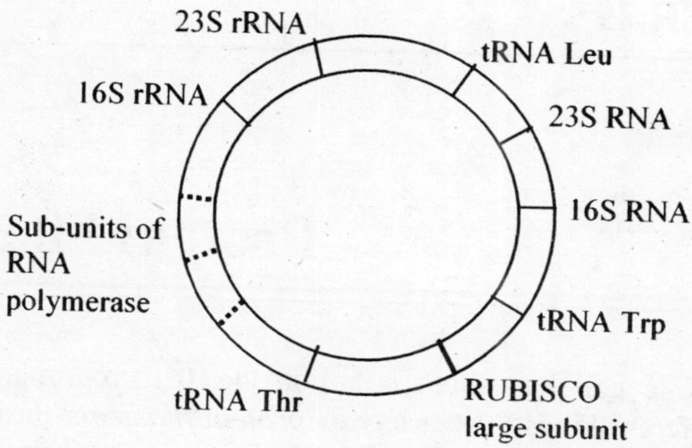

Fig. 28.3. A schematic map of the genome of *Marchantia polymorpha (Bryophyta)*, commonly known as liverwort.

Chloroplast mutants

A large number of chloroplast mutants are known in many different plants. As example, some mutations of chloroplasts known in barley are given here with their phenotypes.

Mutation	Phenotype
xantha-a63	Uncontrolled synthesis of lipid causes formation of honeycombs of membrane.
xantha-b18	Chloroplasts with spheroid membranous granna.
xantha-d31	Thylakoid aggregate to form large granna.
xantha-f60	Mutant unable to arrange thylakoid as grannum. Chlorophyll synthesis inhibited.

Further reading

Alberts, B., Bray, D., Lewis, J., Raff, M., Roberts, K., and Watson, J.D. *Molecular Biology of the Cell*. Garland Publishing Inc., New York, Third Edition, p.1294 (1994).

Heldt, H.W., and Flügge, U.I. Transport of metabolites across the chloroplast envelope. *Method Enzymol.,125*: 705 (1986) also in *Planta 168*: 536 (1986).

CHAPTER 29

Protein Filaments

The eucaryotic cell has about a billion ($1x10^9$) protein molecules of ~10,000 different kinds. A variety of *protein filaments* form a network of scaffold in the cell-cytoplasm. These protein filaments help the cell in contraction, change in shape, and movement on a substrate, transport of intracellular organelles in the cytoplasm and the distribution of chromosomes during meiosis and mitosis.

Mainly three types of protein filaments are found in the cell.

1. *Microtubules* formed by *tubulin* and are primarily organizers of the cell cytoplasm.
2. *Intermediate filaments* formed by a family of fibrous proteins such as *vimantin* and *lamin*. They provide mechanical strength to the cell.
3. *Microfilaments* or *actin filaments* formed by actin molecules and are essential for the movements of the cell.

MICROTUBULES

Microtubules are cylindrical hollow tubes formed from 13 linear proto-filaments each composed of alternative α and β *tubulins* and bunched together with the same polarity so that one end has + and the other end has – (*minus*) polarity. The *plus* polar end is faster growing end than the *minus* end. In the cell the plus end extends ***away*** from the *tubule-nucleating sites* such as *centrosomes, poles of mitotic spindle* or *basal body* of a cilium.

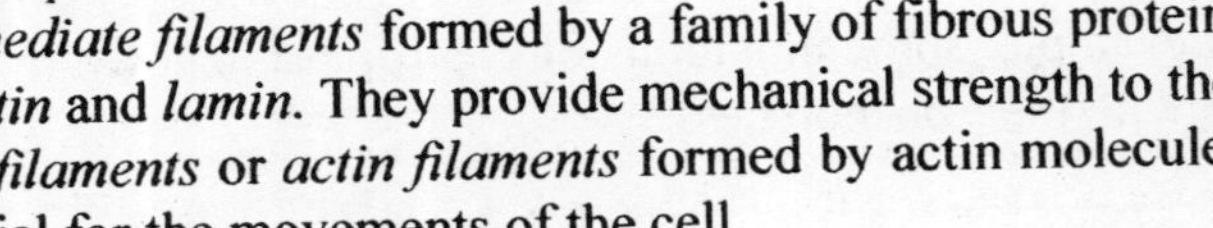

A linear protofilament

Thirteen such *protofilaments* bunch togther in the same polarity and form a hollow cylinder of microtubule. In some organs such as a cilium two microtubules form a fused structure. Then one tubule has 13 and the other has only 11 *protofilaments*.

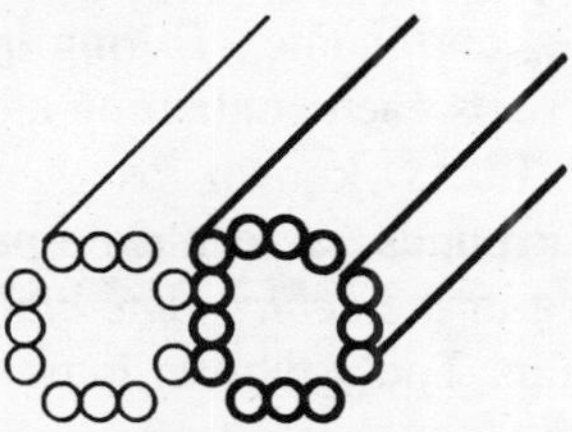

Fig. 29.1. A microtubule doublet having one complete microtubule consisting of 13 protofilaments and another attached partial microtubule made up of 11 protofilaments.

A GTP molecule binds to each α and β tubulin molecules. The α tubulin–GTP bond is more stable than the β tubulin–GTP bond. The heterodimer of β and α tubulins attached with 2 GTP molecules connects to the growing end of a microtubule. The GTP attached to β tubulin hydrolyses and becomes GDP.

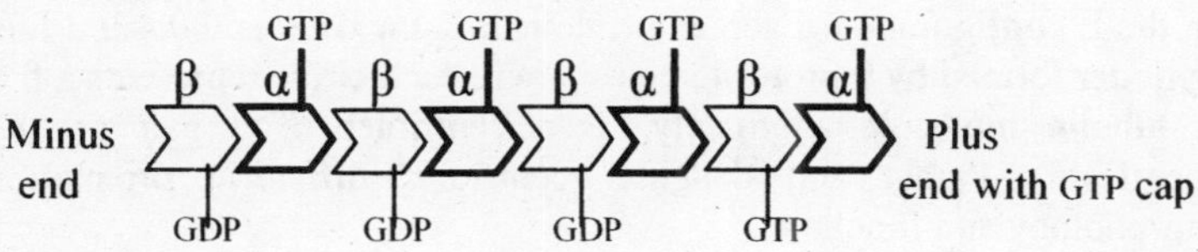

A growing linear protofilament.

Using non-hydrolysable GTP anaglogues it was observed that binding of GTP was needed for microtubule polymerization (growth). However, the binding of GDP weakens the bonds between tubulins and helps the microtubule depolymerization (shrinkage). A collection of GTP molecules at the growing end of microtubule forms a *GTP-Cap* that encourages the growing microtubule to continue growing. On losing the *GTP-Cap* the microtubule depolymerizes and tends to continue shrinking. Polymerization and de-polymerization both seem to be *autocatalytic* phenomena.

Centrioles, Centromeres and Centrosomes

In most of the animal cells centrosome is the major organizing centre for microtubules. During the interphase the centrosome is located close to the outer membrane of the nucleus. A pair of cylindrical structures known as ***centrioles*** is positioned perpendicular to each other in an L-configuration within the centrosome. During interphase the *centrosome* divides in to two equal parts each containing a duplicated *centriole-pair*. A network of small fibres known as *pericentriolar material* or *centrosome matrix* surrounds a centriole-pair. The nucleation of microtubules takes place in the *centrosome matrix* that contains specific proteins such as γ-tubulin. The γ-tubulin may help α- and β-tubulins to polymerize to microtubule.

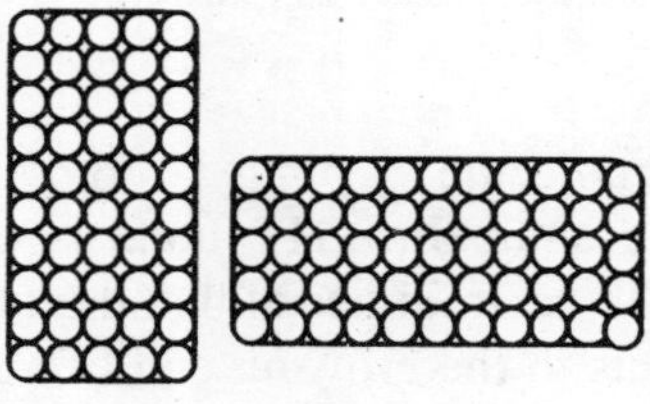

Fig.29.2. A pair of centrioles positioned at perpendicular to each other in the L configuration. Each centriole is 0.2 μm wide and 0.4 μm long cylinder formed by 9 protofilaments where each circle represents a β or α tubulin molecule alternately. Two centrioles of a pair are *not* identical. Parent and daughter centrioles differ in orientation, morphology and function.

Microtubules emanating from a centrosome or from a pole of mitotic spindle often make a star-shaped figure called *aster* in the cytoplasm.

Microtubules present in animal cell cytoplasm tend to radiate out from centrosome. The *minus* ends of microtubules are anchored to centrosome and the *plus* ends radiate towards the cell periphery.

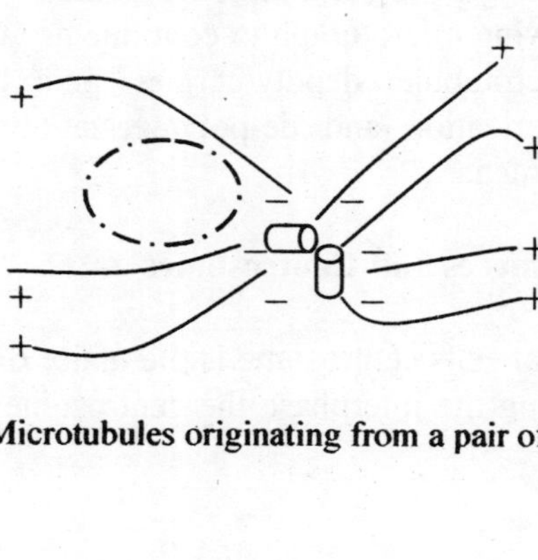

Fig. 29.3. Microtubules originating from a pair of centrioles.

Continuous turnover of microtubules

Microtubules have *dynamic instability*. A microtubule may grow at a regular rate for some time and then shrink suddenly towards the centromere. It may re-grow or fully disappear and get replaced by a new microtubule. The halflife of a tubulin-microtubule in fibroblast cells is around 10 minutes. The tubulin molecule lasts 20 hours before degradation. Hence a tubulin molecule is likely to take part in assembly and dis-assembly of many microtubules.

Many drugs interfere with the assembly of microtubules. *Colchicine* a plant alkaloid binds to tubulin and prevents its polymerisation. However, *colchicine* does not bind to polymerised tubulin that is already attached to a microtubule. Application of *colchicine* or another related drug *colcemid* to dividing cells causes rapid disappearance of mitotic spindle. Similar drugs *vinblastin* and *vincristine*, which temporarily disrupt spindle microtubules are used for killing abnormally dividing cancerous cells.

Another drug *taxol* has an opposite mode of action. *Taxol* stabilizes microtubules by tightly binding to them and arrest dividing cells at *mitosis*.

Stabilization of Microtubules

The tubulin subunits undergo some *slow* modifications after polymerization to microtubule: (a) Acetylation of a lysine residue on α tubulin and (b) removal of a tyrosine molecule from the carboxy terminal of α tubulin. These modifications take several hours for completion. In fibroblasts where the microtubule turnover is rapid such modifications are very few. However, in a nerve axon most of the microtubules are modified and stable.

There are many kinds of *microtubule associated proteins* (**MAPs**). The smaller ones such as *tau* protein have molecular weights around 50,000 Daltons. The large MAP1 or MAP2 have molecular weights around 300,000 Daltons. Both kinds of proteins have a site that binds to the microtubules and another site, which binds to the cell-components. MAPs stabilize the microtubules. Some are the structural components of the cell, while others work as microtubule motors using ATP for energy to transport cell components or organelles.

Motor proteins dynein and kinesin

Movement of organelles and other particles on a single microtubule could be observed in unfixed specimens. Two kinds of microtubule dependent *motor proteins* were identified.

1. Cytoplasmic *dyneins* are responsible for organelle transport, chromosome movement during meiosis and mitosis. They are related to ciliary *dynein motor proteins* of cilia and flagella.

2. *Kinesins* are involved in organnelle transport, meiosis, mitosis, and transport of vesicles along axons.
   Dyneins and kinesins both contain two heavy chains and several light chains of proteins. Each heavy chain has a globular protein as head that binds to ATP. The tail is made of rod-like pieces attached with a string. Both the head regions of the molecule are *ATPase motors* and use the microtubule as a rail for transport.

   Studies *in vitro* as well as with intact nerve axons showed that the organelle transport away from the cell body is carried out by kinesin at approximately 2 μm per second rate. There are some exceptions in kinesins such as a *Drosophila* kinesin *Ncd* involved in meiosis carries out movement in opposite direction at a different rate 0.1 μm per second. In reverse usually the organelle movement from periphery of the cell to centre towards the minus end of microtubule is carried out by *dyneins*. As all proteins are made in the cell soma, the *cytoplasmic dynein* must be carried to nerve terminals in an inactive form prior to begin ferrying organelles back to cell body.

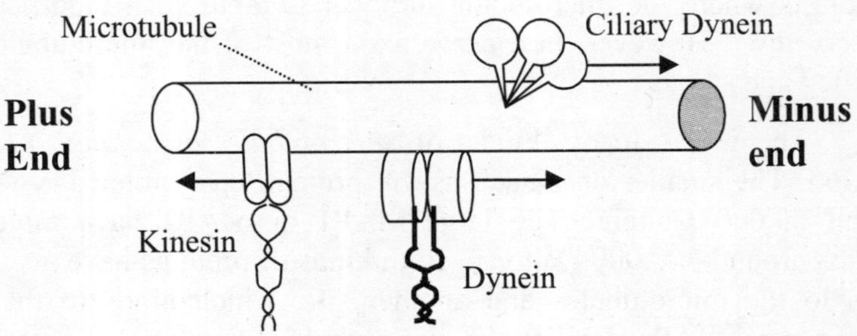

Fig. 29.4. The direction of movement of motor proteins on a microtubule.

Cilia and Flagella

Cilia are 10–100 μm long hair-like structures that grow out from the surface of several types of animal cells, many protozoa and some primitive plants. Their main function is:

(a) to propel fluid around the cell,

(b) to push the eggs down the oviduct and

(c) cilium-like but longer structure called ***flagellum*** provides motility to the sperm and some protozoa.

Along the length of the cilium or flagellum the core called ***axoneme*** contains a very beautifully organized bundle of microtubules and associated proteins. In a cross-sectional view of the *axoneme*, nine fused-doublets of microtubules are arranged in a circle around a pair of singlet microtubules. The fused-doublets are interconnected with protein *nexin*. *Radial spokes* emanating from an inner sheath around the central pair of single microtubules also support them. Each microtubule fused-doublet has *dynein* molecules anchored to them for imparting motion.

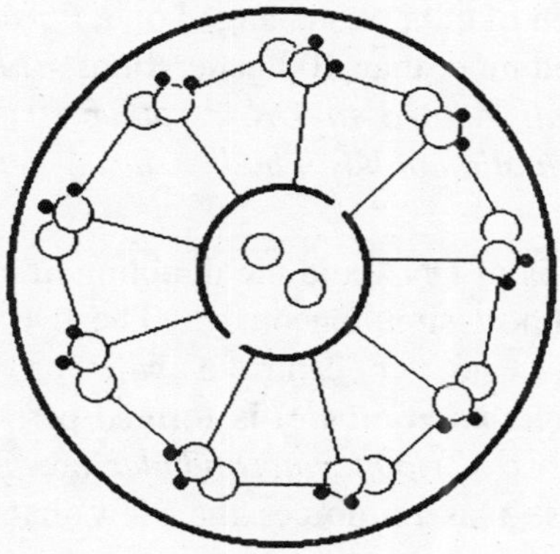

Fig. 29.5. Cross-sectional view of a cilium, where two singlet-microtubules at the centre are surrounded by a sheath and nine sets of doublet microtubules arranged symmetrically near the periphery. These nine doublet microtubules are interconnected with protein *nexin* as well connected with spoke-like structure to the central sheath. Each complete microtubule of the doublet has two molecules of *dynein* protein (·) anchored to it.

Growth of Cilia or flagella

Cilia and flagella grow from basal bodies, which appear similar to centrioles. During mitosis in *Chalmydomonas* the cell absorbs the pair of flagella and the basal bodies migrate into the region of spindle-poles.

One complete microtubule and two partial microtubules fuse to form a triplet microtubule containing 13+11+11 = 35 proto-tubules. Nine such bundles of triplet microtubules arranged in a circle form the core of the basal body. Each basal body forms the lower most portion of the ciliary axoneme. It is not clear how the length of cilia or flagella is determined. However, the paucity of components or the rate of growth does not limit it.

Two centrioles of a pair are not identical. Parent and daughter centrioles differ in orientation, morphology and function. Similar differences exist in basal bodies. Basal bodies replicate in co-ordination with cell duplication. In addition, their orientation in space is maintained during successive duplication, thereby maintaining a particular orientation of a patch of cilia on the body-surface. By surgery the orientation of a patch of cilia was changed on a *Paramecium*. The altered pattern of cilia lasted more than 100 generations. *This form of hereditary change is not at all related to DNA, rather it is dependent on the preservation of orientation of basal bodies during replication.*

The synthesis of DNA and the doubling of centrioles in cultured fibroblasts begin almost simultaneously. The two centrioles of a pair first separate. A daughter centriole with an array of 9 single protofilaments (*singlet-microtubule*) is formed perpendicular to each of the original centrioles. *Triplet- microtubules* are generated from these *singlet-microtubules*. This reinforces the view that *two centrioles of a pair are not identical.*

INTERMEDIATE FILAMENTS

When epithelial cells, muscle cells and neurons with long axons are treated with concentrated salt solutions containing non-ionic detergents, most of the protein filaments dissolve out except the ***intermediate filaments***.

1. The intermediate filaments are located around the cell- nucleus and extend up to plasma membrane where they interact with cell-junctions *desmosomes* (which bond adjacent cells together) or *hemi-desmosomes* (junctions that attach cells to underlying basal lamina) and even with the neighbouring cells' *intermediate filaments*. In addition, intermediate filaments form a basket lining the inside of the *nuclear membrane* envelope.
2. As the name suggests the diameter of the *intermediate filaments* is 10 nm, which lies between mictrotubule's 25 nm and actin filament's 5-9 nm diameters.
3. Unlike microtubules and actin filaments, which are made of *globular proteins*, the *intermediate filaments* are made of *fibrous proteins*.
4. Under a deforming force *microtubules* deform quickly and snap, *actin filaments* deform slowly then snap at greater deforming force. However, the *intermediate filaments* prove quite elastic and do not snap easily.
5. Unlike plant cells that have rigid cell wall, animal cells have flexible plasma membrane. *Intermediate filaments provide tensile strength to animal cells and tissues.*
6. Intermediate filaments in vertebrate cells can be classified into 3 cytoplasmic groups plus a group found in side the nucleus:
   (i) *keratins, cytokeratins* or keratin filaments,
   (ii) *vimantins* and related fibres,
   (iii) *neurofilaments* and
   (iv) *nuclear lamins*.
7. Intermediate filaments are made of long protein molecules that have a head at the *amino*-terminal region. and a tail at the *carboxy*-terminal. The central region consists of *heptad* repeat sequences of amino acids. The *heptad repeats* facilitate formation of *coiled dimers* from two parallel monomers. Similar *coiled dimers* also occur in other proteins namely *myosin* and *tropomyosin*. In the next step of polymerisation of intermediate filaments *two anti-parallel dimers* form a ***tetramer*** that is a non-polarized filament, similar at both ends and symmetrical through the intervening length. *Compared to microtubules and actins which are polarized, intermediate filaments are non-polarized molecules.*

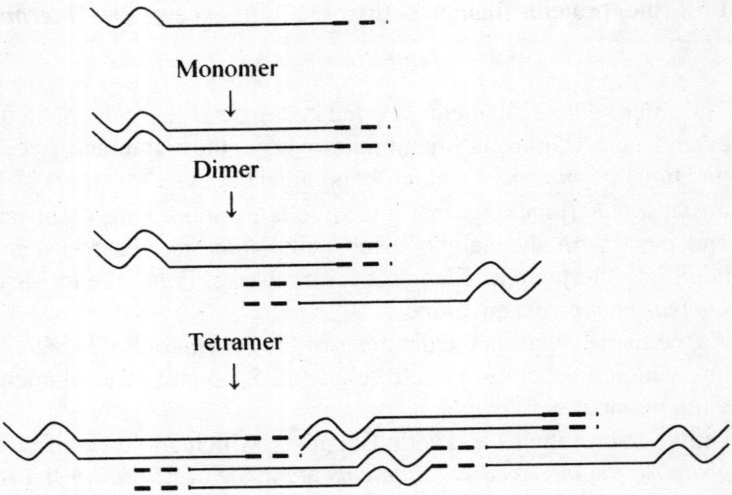

Further polymerization of intermediate filaments takes place by '*bricks in a wall*' type of stacking of tetramers.

Fig. 29.6. Assembly of intermediate filaments.

In a fully polymerized 10nm thick intermediate filament several tetramers are bundled like fibres in a rope

Keratins

On the basis of amino acid sequences, *keratins* may be classified as *type I* (acidic) or *type II* (basic or neutral). *In vitro* experiments show that type I and type II polypeptides can form a heteropolymeric intermediate filament. However, homopolymeric types of filaments usually do *not* from. The embryonic epithelial cells and liver cells have only one type I and type II keratin polypeptides respectively. However, epithelial cells of tongue, sweat glands and bladder contain at least 6 types of keratins.

The most diverse type of intermediate filaments are *α-keratins* numbering more than 20 in human epithelial cells. Eight other *α-types of hard keratins* are found in hair and nails. The diversity of keratins in skin cells is quite useful in diagnosis and treatment of skin carcinomas. A separate type of *β-keratin* is found in the feathers of birds.

Vimantin and Related Proteins

Vimantin is the most important intermediate filament protein in cells of *mesodermal origin*, such as endothelial cells, fibroblasts and white blood cells. Vimantin and related proteins can co-polymerize. Vimantin related *Desmin* is found in cytoplasm of smooth muscle cells and connect together neighbouring myosins. *Glial* intermediate filaments are found in astrocytes in the central nervous system (CNS) and Schwann cells in peripheral nerves.

Neurons contain a variety of *vimantin related intermediate filaments* that express at different stages of development. *Neurofilaments* could be as long as 1 meter and are present throughout the length of an axon and form the main cyto-skeletal support system. Three *neurofilament* proteins are known NF-L, NF-M and NF-H of low, middle and high molecular weight respectively.

Lamins

Lamins differ from other intermediate filament proteins in the following ways:

1. Although like other intermediate filament proteins, lamins are synthesized in cytoplasm yet they are transported to nucleus. Probably the molecule contains a tag 'meant for nucleus'.
2. Lamins form a sieve-like matrix inside the nuclear envelope, possibly in association with other proteins. Nuclear pores are left uncovered for the passage of incoming and outgoing molecules.
3. The sieve –like matrix of lamin is a dynamic structure, which disintegrates at the start of mitosis and forms again at the end of mitosis.
4. Dis-assembly of polymerized lamins is dependent on phosphorylation of many serine residues in lamin. While de-phosphorylation of serine residues promotes polymerisation of lamins.

Phosphorylation ⟶ De-polymerisation.
De-phosphorylation ⟶ Polymerisation.

5. It seems amongst intermediate filament proteins, lamins were the first to evolve. Other intermediate filaments are adaptations of lamins.

In general intermediate filaments are formed in multicellular organisms. Glial cells in CNS that contain myosin do not have intermediate filaments. In cell cultures of fibroblasts, muscle cells or epithelial cells if the intermediate filaments are disrupted the behaviour of cells does not change appreciably. However the major function of cytoplasmic intermediate filaments is to increase resistance of cells to deforming forces.

ACTIN FILAMENTS

About 8 nm wide *actin filament* is composed of uniformly oriented *globular actin* or *G-actin* molecules. The actin filament has a slow growing *minus end* or *pointed end* and a fast growing *plus end* or *barbed end.* Each actin molecule is 375 aminoacids long polypeptide with one ATP molecule attached to it. It is one of the most abundant proteins in eucaryotic cells constituting 5–20% of total proteins. Vertebrate skeletal muscle cells may have up to 20% actin.

Lower eucaryotes like yeast has one actin gene, while higher eucaryotes have a group of genes coding for isoforms of many actins. The α-actins are present in various muscle cells while β- and γ-actins are found in non-muscle cells.

Though the actin filaments are thinner and shorter than microtubules, yet their total length is 30 times greater than microtubules indicating difference in their mode of organization and function in the cell. There are a few similarities too in actin filaments and microtubules.

1. Purified actin requires hydrolysis of ATP in the presence of a monovalent ion like K^+ and a bivalent ion like Mg^{++} for polymerization. The ATP hydrolysis product ADP remains trapped in the actin filament. The rate of polymerization is slower at the minus end than that at plus end.
   The three dimensional structure of actin was worked out by X-ray diffraction. The clam-shaped actin molecule while closing triggers the ATP hydrolysis and traps the ADP molecule inside.
2. The binding of ADP to actin weakens the bonds in the actin filament. Unlike microtubules where tubulin molecule can be re-used rapidly, the de-polymerized actin molecule can be reused for filament assembly only after some delay. This results in higher concentration of ADP bound actin monomer in cytosol that can regulate the rate of actin polymerization.
3. It is noteworthy that actin and tubulin have evolved a similar nucleotide triphosphate hydrolysis mechanism for assembly and dis-assembly. But their amino acid sequences are totally unrelated.

In this context actin is related to enzyme *hexokinase* and tubulin is related to *GTPases* including *heteromeric G-Proteins*.

4. A variety of actin networks existing in eucaryotic cells is due to multiple interactions between actin binding proteins and the actin.

Actin Binding Proteins	**Functions of Actin Binding Proteins**
Tropomyosin	Strengthens filament, encourages α-actin to bind to plus end, binds to myosin II and assembly of contractile actin filaments.
Alpha Actinin, Fimbrin	Bundles filaments by co-linking them.
Filamin	Crosslinks multiple filaments into gel.
Gelsolin	Fragmentation of filaments, which is Ca^{++} dependent
Myosin I	Moves vesicles on filaments.
Myosin II	Slides filaments such as those forming muscles.
Spectrin, Ankyrin	Attaches actin filaments sideways to plasma membrane.
Thymosin	Attaches to individual actin monomer and sequesters them.

5. Unlike microtubules, actin filaments do not show dynamic stability. Rather actin filaments show phenomenon similar to ***treadmilling***, where polymerization of actin takes place at the leading end and depolymerization takes place at the nearby tailing edge. This treadmilling phenomenon of actin filaments can broadly explain many types of cell movements.

   The crawling of animal cells can be sub-divided into three processes: (a) protusion of lamellopodia, filopodia or micro-spikes from the anterior; (b) formation of new attachment sites of cytoskeleton with the substrate and (c) traction, where body of the cell moves forward by de-polymerizing the old attachment sites.

6. Some pathogenic bacteria like *Listeria monocytogenes* that are known to cause food poisoning and *Shigella flexneri* an intra-cellular pathogen causing dysentery can form a brush-like tail from the host cell actin in the cytosol. They become motile and spread to the

adjoining cells using the acquired external actin-tail. *Shigella* is known to secrete a protein similar to protease that breaks down microtubules and clear the path for the pathogen as well as for other bacteria that may follow the same path.

Actin Filaments and Muscles

A vertebrate body for locomotion depends on the skeletal muscles that can contract quickly on the scaffolding of bones. Whereas the involuntary movements within the body such as heart beats and peristalsis of the gut depend on the contraction of cardiac and smooth muscles respectively.

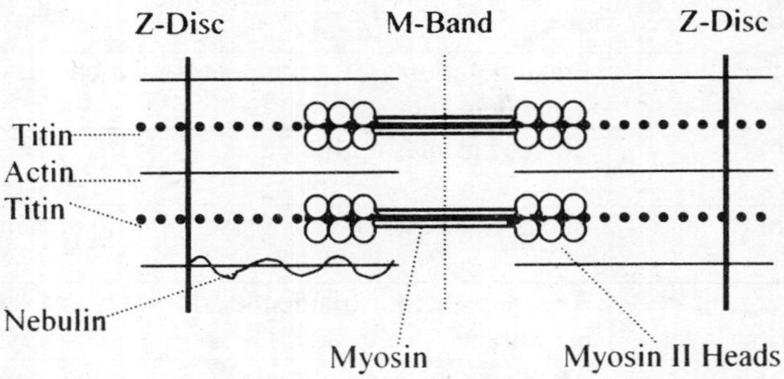

Fig. 29.7. A schematic diagram of a sarcomere, showing the arrangement of actin filaments and myosin along with some of the associated proteins.

Skeletal muscle cells are large cells formed by the fusion of the plasma membranes of several adjacent cells. The nuclei remain separate and are enclosed in a single plasma membrane forming a *syncytium*. More than 60% of the cytoplasm consists of myofibrils. Myofibrils contain a series of contractile units called *sarcomeres*. Each sarcomere contains two major types of parallel and partly overlapping filaments *actin* and *myosin*. In electron micrographs a group of broad light and dark bands are visible in each sarcomere. A dark line at the middle of each light band known as *Z-disc* or *Z-band* forms the boundary of a sarcomere. Thin filaments formed by actin are perpendicularly attached to either of the two Z-discs at the ends of a sarcomere. These actin filaments extend in to the central region of the sarcomere, where a group of six actin filaments surround a thicker myosin filament. Similarly six thick myosin filaments surround a thin actin filament. Both types of filaments form hexagonal patterns in cross section.

Myosin filament has a myosin II head, a 13nm high stub-like structure that makes a labile contact with neighbouring actin filament as well as with an ATP molecule. On the hydrolysis of ATP molecules to ADP and Pi the ***actin filament slides over the myosin heads*** thereby pulling the *adjacent Z-discs closer* resulting in the contraction of the muscle. *The lengths of the myosin fibrils and actin filaments do not change during contraction of the muscle. Actin filaments slide over the myosin heads.*

An accessory rod-shaped protein called *tropomyosin* binds at seven evenly spaced sites to the groove of the actin helix. Another accessory heteromeric protein made up of 3 polypeptides T, I and C is *troponin*. *Troponin T* tail, binds to tropomyosin. *Troponin I* is inhibitory and binds to actin. *Troponin C* binds to four Ca^{++} ions. Troponin C is related to calmodulin that modulates Ca^{++} mediated responses in many cells. *One molecule of troponin-tropomyosin complex binds to seven actin monomers.*

Skeletal muscle cells also contain two very large proteins: *titin* (the largest known peptide of $3x10^6$ Daltons) and *nebulin*. Titin molecules hold myosin filaments in the central region of sarcomere by attaching them to Z-discs on either side. *Nebulin* molecule that has a repeating 35 amino acid binding sequence to actin extends from the *plus end* to *minus end* of actin filament. Myofibrils are bound side by side by *Demin* intermediate filaments. The complete array of *actin-myosin-accessory proteins* is anchored to plasma membrane of muscle cells by several proteins such as actin-binding *Dystrophin*.

Muscle Contraction

The contraction of vertebrate skeletal muscle depends on impulse received from its motor nerve. The signal from the neuromuscular junction generates action potential in the plasma membrane of muscle cell. This external excitation spreads quickly to *transverse tubules*, which are inward extensions of plasma membrane around myofibrils. Large *Ca release channels* exist between transverse tubules and sarcoplasmic reticulum membrane. These channels release Ca^{++} ions. Ca^{++} ions also escape from sarcoplasmic reticulum, where they are stored in high concentration causing more Ca^{++} to enter thereby flooding cytosol with Ca^{++} ions, which initiates the contraction of each myofibril.

Since the signal passes within milliseconds to each sarcomere, all myofibrils contract simultaneously. Abundant *Ca –ATPase enzyme* present on the sarcoplasmic reticulum quickly pumps back the cytosolic Ca^{++} into sarcoplasm, thereby causing muscle to relax within 30 milliseconds.

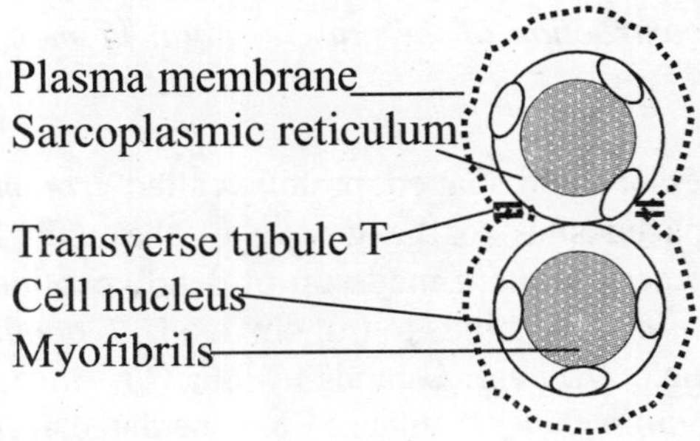

Fig. 29.8. A schematic diagram of sarcoplasmic reticulum

Besides highly organized skeletal muscles there are *myo-epithelial cells* that contract by sliding actin-myosin II filaments. In addition, the following are the two other major types of muscles.

1. The ***cardiac muscles***, which contract about 3 billion times during an average period of human life. Each heart muscle cell has a single nucleus and does not form *syncytium* found in skeletal muscle cells. Heart muscle cells are joined by ***intercalated discs*** through desmosomes connecting actin filaments of adjacent cells and allow rapid spread of action potential between groups of cells synchronizing the heart muscle contraction.

2. The ***smooth muscles*** such as those present in stomach, intestines, uterus and walls of arteries contract slowly for longer durations. The smooth muscle is composed of spindle-shaped elongated cells each having one nucleus. The cells contain myosin II and actin filaments in a loosely aligned manner along the long axis of the cell. Disc-like junctions join adjacent cells, where actin filaments also connect. The contraction of smooth muscle is slow but produces greater degree of shortening thereby causing larger movements.

Further reading

Albers, K., and Fuchs, E. The molecular biology of intermediate filament proteins. *Int. Rev. Cytol. 134*: 243-279 (1992).

Cooke, R. The mechanism of muscle contraction. *CRC Crit. Rev. Biochem. 21*: 53-118 (1986).

Engqvist-Goldstein, Å.E.Y. and Drubin, D.G. Actin assembly and endocytosis: from yeast to mammals. *Annu. Rev. Cell Biol. 19*: 287-332 (2003).

Gelfand, V., and Bershadsky, A.D. Microtubule dynamics: mechanism, regulation and function. *Annu. Rev. Cell Biol. 7:* 93-116 (1991).

Kreis, T.E.,and Vale, R.D. ed. *Guidebook to Cytoskeletal and Motor Proteins*. Oxford, U.K. Oxford University Press (1993).

Vale, D.R. Intracellular transport using micro-tubule-based motors. *Annu. Rev. Cell Biol. 3*: 347-78 (1987).

CHAPTER 30

Vesicular Transport and Protein Recycling

For sustenance and multiplication cells require nutrients, which they derive from surrounding environment. In procaryotic cells some nutrients can diffuse through the plasma membrane, while many others are taken up through *active transport* by *transport-proteins* embedded in plasma membrane. Similar processes of diffusion and active transport are used for discarding or secreting out products of cell metabolism. Eucaryotic cells in addition to diffusion and active transport mechanisms have developed '*endocytosis*', where a region of plasma membrane invaginates and forms a pouch containing external nutrients. The mouth of the pouch is sealed off and a spherical vesicle is formed inside the cell. This internalization of vesicle filled with nutrients or useful molecules is called '*endocytosis*'. The reverse of this process where the plasma membrane buds out a small pouch filled with molecules meant for export. The mouth of the pouch is sealed off by membrane to become a vesicle for export. This process is known as '*exocytosis*'. *Eucaryotic cells use* **vesicles** *not only to import and export molecules but also to transport, process and re-package molecules within the cell.*

Even neuro-transmitters packed in vesicles are released in the synaptic cleft by *exocytosis* and neurotransmitters are re-absorbed after use by *endocytosis*.

A special organelle known as *Golgi apparatus* or *Golgi complex* has evolved in the eucaryotic cells, which is a major location for carbohydrate synthesis as well site for sorting and dispatching the produce of *endoplasmic reticulum* (ER). Golgi apparatus contains stacks of membrane-bound cisternae resembling a stack of plates. A stack is made up of 4-6 cisternae. Animal cells usually contain one or two Golgi complexes while plant-cells have many, though smaller in size. A large number of vesicles are found in the vicinity of Golgi-stacks. These vesicles transport proteins and lipids to and from Golgi cisternae that processes them. The Golgi-stack has an entry side (*cis*- face) and an exit side (*trans*-face).

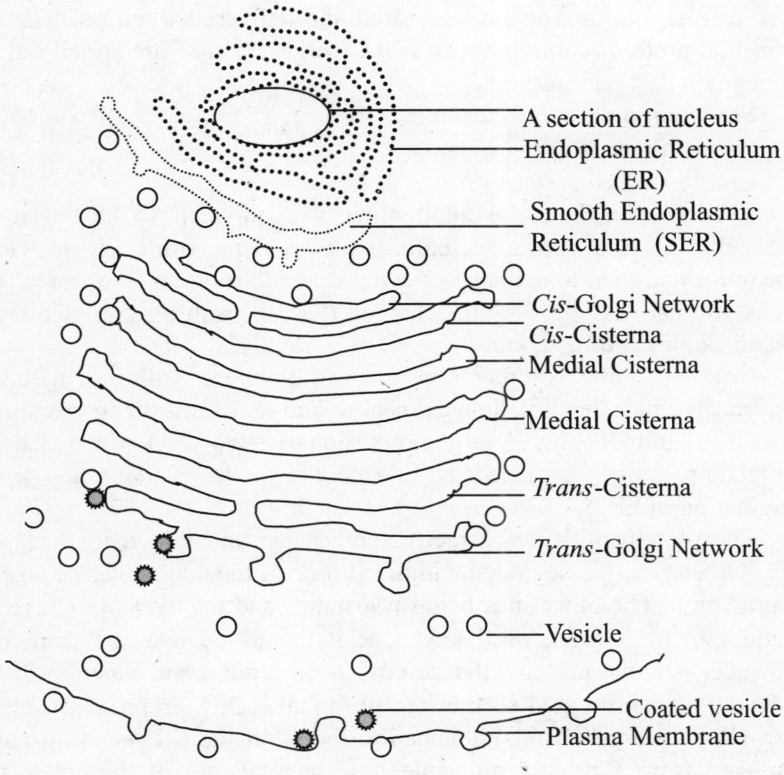

Fig. 30.1. A schematic diagram showing Golgi apparatus in the eucaryotic cell.

The Golgi cisternae are organized in a series of processing compartments where the transport of molecules needing modifications is mainly by exchanging them wrapped up in vesicles.

Goblet cells of the gut that secrete large quantities of polysaccharide-rich mucus have large vesicles loaded with mucus on the *trans*-side of Golgi complex and near the cell surface.

Many of the correctly synthesized proteins need not enter the Golgi complex and can be directly utilized by the cell or sent to plasma membrane. Protein molecules needing modifications enter the *cis*-Golgi network. They either move forward through Golgi apparatus or are returned to ER. Each cisterna processes the protein molecule and sends it out through a vesicle to the next cisterna. Like ways the process continues till the modified protein comes out of the *trans*-Golgi cisternae. Since molecules pass through many individual compartments they can be modified in stages, stored and delivered when needed. The modified proteins coming out of *trans* Golgi cisternae are sorted out for three main destinations:

1. For incorporation in lysosomes.
2. Packed in secretory vesicles or
3. Coasted to cell surface.

The lumen of the Golgi compartments is equivalent to the exterior of the cell. The outward secretory pathway lead from ER to Golgi apparatus and then to cell surface with a branch route to lysosomes. The endocytic pathway moves molecules in the cell from plasma membrane to endosomes and lysosomes.

Golgi apparatus is a major site for carbohydrate synthesis, including polysaccharides, hemi-cellulose, pectin and most of the glcosamino-glycans of animal cells. A large proportion of oligo-saccharides made by Golgi apparatus is attached as side chains to the proteins and lipids originating in ER.

The protein must be correctly synthesized and folded to exit from ER. Otherwise it is degraded within ER, one of the major sites of protein degradation. The other sites being lysosomes and the cytosol. Correctly made proteins do not need any special tag to be released from ER. However, soluble proteins that are meant to remain and function in ER have a four amino acid sorting tag or signal KDEL (representing Lys-Asp-Glu-Leu amino acids) attached to them. If the ER retention tag is removed from a protein molecule it is secreted out of the cell. The reverse is also true, when the retention tag is attached to a secretary protein it is retained within the cell.

The retention signal does ***not*** anchor a protein to the lumen of ER. Retention tag bearing proteins do escape ER sometimes along with other proteins packed in vesicles. However, they are identified in *cis*-Golgi cisternae and sent back with additional tag to ER. In the words of Alberts and co-authors expressed in *Molecular Biology of the Cell*, the ER is compared with an open prison for the resident proteins bearing the tag of four amino acids KDEL. "*There is nothing to stop them leaving but if they leave they are brought back.*"

The transport of proteins amongst the different cisternae is carried out by transport vesicles, which bud out from one cisterna and fuse to the next. Histochemical staining in conjunction with electron microscope showed that the Golgi apparatus is biochemically compartmentalized.

The complex oligosaccharides are created by a combination of trimming of the original oligo- molecule added in ER and by the addition of different sugars. The configuration of protein determines whether it is going to be high in numbers of mannose residues. *If the molecule is more accessible to processing enzymes in Golgi complex it will have fewer mannose otherwise high in mannose residues.*

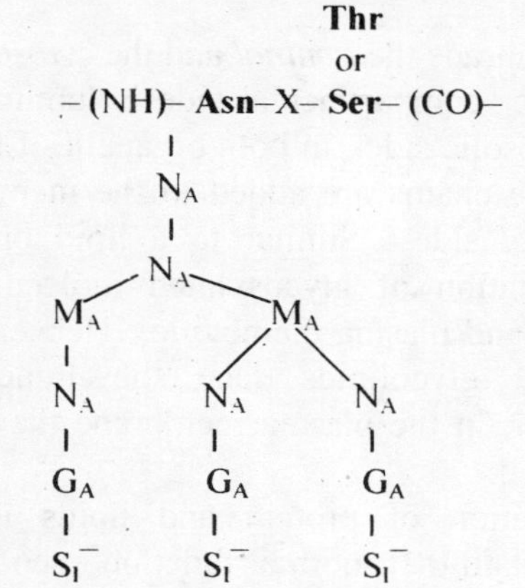

Protein molecule

X = Any amino acid
N_A = N-acetylglucosamine
M_A = Mannose
G_A = Galactose
S_I^- = N-acetylneuraminicacid or NANA or Sialic acid with a negative charge.

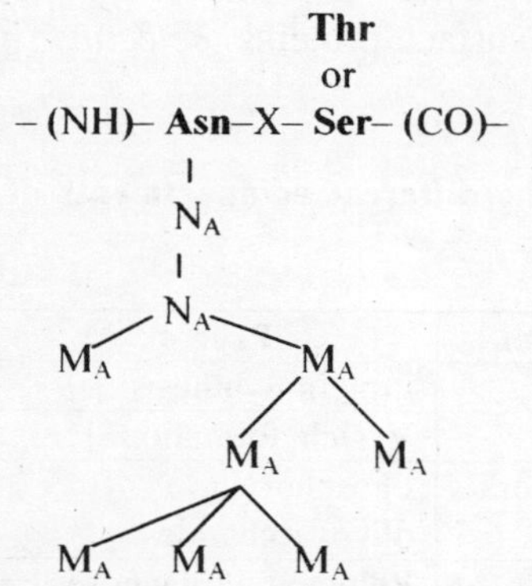

Protein molecule

If a molecule is more accessible to processing enzymes in Golgi complex it will have fewer mannoses otherwise high in mannose residues. NANA or sialic acid (abbreviated here as S_I^-) is of special importance as it is the only sugar in glycoproteins that carries a net negative charge.

Production of Proteoglycans in Golgi

Many proteoglycans form part of (1) plasma membrane, (2) secreted out to become part of extracellular matrix or (3) major component of slimy material e.g. mucus that lubricates the cell-surface. The sugar molecules in proteoglycans are heavily sulfated in Golgi apparatus soon after they are made. This provides them with high negative charge. In addition, *Tyr* residues in protein are also sulfated within the Golgi apparatus. Both reactions depend on sulfate donor 3'-Phosphoadenosine-5'-phosphosulfate (PAPS).

There are two sides of membrane the *luminal* and the *cytosolic* in ER and Golgi cisternae. The inner compartmental side is luminal the other in contact with cytosol is cytosolic side. In both organelles ER and Golgi apparatus all oligosaccharide chains are added to the membrane proteins and lipids on the *luminal* side. Similar to a lipid bi-layer membrane he assymmetric orientation of glycosylated molecules is maintained in vesicles, lysosomes and plasma membrane. Hence sugar molecules of glycoproteins and glycolipids face the lumen of intracellular membranes. However, in the plasma membrane the sugar molecules face the outside of the cell.

The purpose of glycosilation of protein and lipids is not understood fully. Most proteins retain their normal function even in the absence of glycosilation. The resence of oligosaccharide does tend to give glycoproteins a resistance to the action of proteases. In addition oligosaccharides anchored to the cell surface proteins '*selectins*' help in cell to cell adhesion.

Step-wise modification of protein in the different compartments of Golgi apparatus.

Cell Domain	Compartment	Process
ER	Cytosol	Protein Sybthesis. ↓
Smooth ER	Cytosol	Vesicle formation. ↓
Golgi Apparatus	*Cis*-Golgi network	Phosphorylation of oligosaccharides. ↓
	Cis-cisterna	Removal of mannose. ↓
	Medial cisternae	Removal of mannose and addition of N-acetylglucosamine. ↓
	Trans-cisterna	Addition of galactose. ↓
	Trans-Golgi network	Addition of NANA and sorting of proteins. ↓
Cytosol	Cytosol	Endosome. ↓ Lysosomes. ↓ Plasma membrane. Secretory vesicles. ↓

Vesicular Transport and Lysosomes

Eucaryotic cells often take up macromolecules from the external medium by endocytosis. The endocytosed molecules are contained in a vesicle of irregular shape known as *early endosome*. Some molecules are selectively retrieved from earlt endosomes and passed on to the plasma membrane. The early endosome with its remaining cargo becomes *late endosome* with the pH of the interior mildly acidic (pH ~ 6). Hydrolytic digestion of endocytosed molecules occurs initially in late endosomes. ***Mature lysosomes are formed from late endosomes.***

Lysosomes are irregularly shaped ~0.5 μm wide spherical bags containing about 40 hydrolytic enzymes meant for controlled digestion of ingested macromolecules. Lysosomes are usually found in all eucaryotic cells. Fungal and plant cells often contain large fluid-filled spaces called *vacuoles*. Vacuoles contain a variety of hydrolytic enzymes besides nutrients and waste products; help increase the cell size and control turgor (osmotic) pressure of the cell.

Some of the prominent categories of hydrolytic enzymes present in lysosomes are:

1. Nucleases
2. Proteases
3. Glycosidases
4. Lipases
5. Sulfatases
6. Phosphatases and
7. Phospholipases.

All these enzymes are acid hydrolases and work optimally in acidic environment at pH 5.

Pathways delivering material to lysosomes

1. At birth the lysosome receive the material from late endosome to continue digestion by using hydrolytic enzymes.
2. ***Autophagy*** is the process whereby obsolete or defunct components of the cell are degraded. For example the average half-life of a mitochondrion in a liver cell is ~10 days. The defunct mitochondrion is initially surrounded by membrane derived from ER forming an *autophagosome*, which fuses with the *lysosome* or *late endosome*, for further degradation of engulfed material.

3. ***Phagocytosis***: Macrophages and neutrophils engulf microorganism and foreign particles invading a vertebrate body to form ***phagosomes***. This process is known as *phagocytosis*. Phágosome fuses with lysosome to completely digest the engulfed foreign material.
4. Some proteins carry a ***signal sequence*** KFERQ (meaning Lysine – Phenylalanine – Glutamate –Arginine – Glutamine) and they are directly delivered to lysosomes for degradation.

Delivery of lysosomal hydrolases and membrane proteins to lysosomes

The soluble enzymes that are destined for lysosomes are tagged with *mannose-6-phosphate* (*M6P*) in the lumen if *cis*-Golgi network. The trans-Golgi network has a ***trans-membrane M6P receptor protein***. This receptor protein sorts out M6P tagged lysosomal hydrolases and helps in packing them in vesicles that deliver the contents by fusion to the late endosomes. The M6P receptor protein binds specific oligosaccharides at pH 7 in the trans-Golgi network and discharges it at pH 6 in the late endosome. M6P receptors are retrieved from the late endosomes and shipped back to trans-Golgi network.

Pinocytosis, Endocytosis and Exocytosis

Eucaryotic cells continue to ingest tiny portions of their own plasma membrane in the form of *pinocytic vesicles* that are later returned to the cell membrane. This process of internalization of membrane by vesicle formation is called *pinocytosis* and its rate varies from one cell type to another. A macrophage ingests 3% of its plasma membrane every minute or 25% of its own volume- equivalent fluid in 1 hour. Fibroblasts show slower while amoebae show higher rate of *pinocytosis*. As the surface area and volume of the cell does not appreciably change during pinocytosis it is logical to assume that *whatever area of membrane is removed by* ***pinocytosis****, equivalent area is added up in the membrane by* ***exocytosis***. They are interlinked processes and may be considered as *endocytic-exocytic cycle*.

Clathrin coated pits in plasma membrane and coated vesicles

About 2% of the inner surface of plasma membrane has pits coated with electron-dense protein ***clathrin*** and some associated proteins. Within a minute these pits invaginate to form a pouch and then a vesicle, which are called ***clathrin-coated vesicles***. According to a rough estimate 2,500 *clathrin-coated vesicles* form every minute from the plasma membrane of cultured fibroblast cell. Since the extracellular fluid is internalized by clathrin-coated vesicles the process is also know as *fluid-phase endocytosis* or *receptor-mediated endocytosis*. By its selective concentrating mechanism for specific molecules, this process is about 1,000 times more efficient for uptake of certain macromolecules from extracellular fluid. The *receptor-mediated endocytosis* of many different types of molecules utilizes the same clathrin-coated pit pathway. At least 25 different receptors are known to bind in clathrin-coated pit for endocytosis of many more types of molecules.

Cholestrol uptake

Animal cells require cholestrol to make new membrane. If its uptake is blocked, the cholestrol accumulates in the blood and can result in plaque formaytion in blood vessels. The blockage of blood-flow may lead to a stroke or heart attack. The cholestrol is mainly transported through blood in the form of particles called '*low density liporoteins*' (*LDL*).

If a cell needs additional cholestrol to make membrane, it makes receptor protein molecules and embeds them in the plasma membrane as tags. These tags slide in the membrane and align with clathrin-coated pits where LDL particle binds to the receptor protein molecule and are internalized by clathrin coated proteins. This cargo is delivered to endosomes and then to lysosomes. In lysosome the ester bonds of cholestrol are hydrolysed and the released free cholestrol molecules are utilised by the cell. The cholestrol uptake continues until needed by the cell. If it becomes in excess the cell ceases to make or take up cholestrol by shutting the synthesis of LDL uptake *receptor protein*.

The uptake of cholestrol is abnormal in individuals who have genetic defect such that

1. LDL receptor protein is lacking,
2. Defective extracellular binding site for LDL or
3. Defective intracellular binding site that attaches receptor to clathrin coated pit.

In the presence of any of the above mentioned defect LDL particle is not internalized by the cell and it accumulates in the blood.

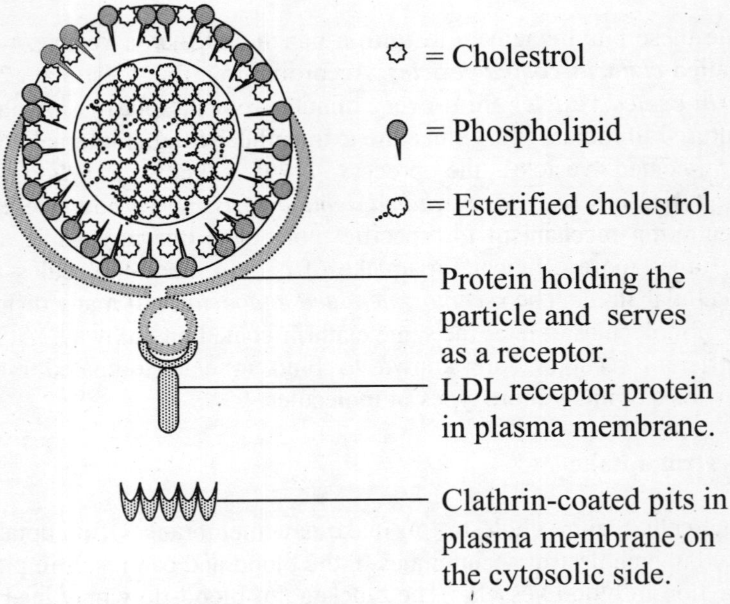

Fig. 30.2. A schematic diagram of the **Low Density Lipoprotein (LDL)** particle ~ 25 nm wide containing at the core about 1,500 cholestrol molecules each attached to a fatty acid tail with ester bond. These molecules are surrounded by a lipid monolayer composed of phospholipids and un-esterified cholestrol molecules. A large protein of 500,000 Daltons organizes the particle and specifically binds to the *cell surface receptor protein.*

Secretory vesicles, secretory granules or dense-core vesicles

When required, some specialized cells secrete rapidly some of their products which could be small molecules like histamine, enkephalins (a five amino acid containing neuropeptide with morphine like activity), digestive enzymes and neurotransmitters etc. Cells make, concentrate and store their products in secretory vesicles or secretory granules or dense-core vesicles as they appear dense in electron microscope. Secretory proteins are first highly aggregated in trans-Golgi network *then packed in clathrin-coated membrane by a process similar to phagocytosis.* Soon after the immature vesicles bud out their *clathrin* coat is removed and the contents are further condensed almost 200 fold compared to concentration in Golgi lumen. The sudden rise in concentration is probably due to increase in the intravesicular H^+ ion concentration caused by ATP driven H^+ pump in the vesicle-membrane.

Proteolytic processing of macromolecules before and after packaging in secretory vesicles

Initially many hydrolytic enzymespolypeptides, hormones and neuropeptides are synthesized as inactive precursors, which are converted to active molecules by appropriate proteolysis. This proteolysis is believed to begin in *trans*-Golgi network and continue in secretory vesicles and even after release in the extracellular fluid. By this delay in activation of hydrolytic enzymes the cell prevents possible damage to self.

Molecular aggregates in mature vesicles are so densely filled that cells can quickly discharge on demand large number of molecules by exocytosis.

Docking of secretory vesicles

Almost mature secretory vesicles are docked near the site of secretion until the signal to secrete arrives. Neurons contain two types of secretory vesicles. In addition to the usual dense-core secretory vesicles, neurons make a different kind of tiny secretory vesicles that are ~50 nm wide and called *synaptic vesicles*. These synaptic vesicles generated by the regional recycling of the plasma membrane and endosomal membrane are docked near the plasma membrane. When an action potential signal reaches the nerve terminal the vesicles release neurotransmitter in the *synaptic cleft* (*cf.* Chapter 30) by exocytosis in less than a millisecond. The components of the exocytosed membrane are rapidly retrieved by endocytosis and delivered to endosomes where vesicles are re-made by budding. ***These newly made synaptic vesicles selectively takeup neurotransmitter in the cytosol***. Once filled, the synaptic vesicles return to the plasma membrane and remain docked there until next stimulus is received through the axon.

Vesicle fusion with the membrane

Docking and fusion of vesicle with the target membrane are two separate processes. While allowing docking to take place, fusion can be prevented by keeping the surrounding Ca^{++} *ion* concentration very low. In the docking process, the proteins protruding from both lipid bilayer membranes need only to interact and adhere. While fusion of membranes requires the membranes to come nearer than 1.5 nm with each other and the intervening water must be displaced from the hydrophilic surface of the membrane. The mechanism of fusion of membrane is still not fully understood. However, in case of coated vesicle fusion with target membrane GTP, ATP, acyl CoA and some proteins are required.

Further reading

Bennett, M.K., and Scheller, R.H. The molecular machinary for secretion is conserved from yeast to neuron. *Proc. Natl. Acad. Sci. (US), 90*: 2559-2563 (1993).

Pryer, N.K., Wuesthube, L.J., and Schekman, R. Vesicle-mediated protein sorting. *Annu. Rev. Biochem., 61*: 471-516 (1992).

CHAPTER 31

Neurons and Nervous Systems

We perceive the world around us through our *sensory organs* such as eyes, ears, nose, tongue and skin, which are capable of receiving physical or chemical stimuli. The *physical stimulus* could be in the form of light, sound, heat, pressure, acceleration, gravity etc. The *chemical stimulus* usually is in the form of molecules and rarely atoms (for example, arsenic) dissolved or suspended in a fluid such as air or water. When the stimulating substance is received *via* air, usually sense of small (olfaction) is involved. The sense of taste (gustation) is involved when the substance dissolved in a fluid is perceived. Similarly, the light is detected by eyes. The sound, acceleration or gravity are perceived by different parts of the ears, while friction, heat and pressure are detected by receptors located in the skin. The basis of detection of all forms of stimuli is a specialized living cell called *neuron*. The *sensory neuron* relays the information to a *ganglion* or the *brain*, where it is processed with the help of a variety of *interneurons* and finally the output signal is relayed through a *motor neuron* or another *interneuron* to the *effector* organ such as muscles or glands. The human nervous system may contain approximately 10^{20} neurons.

Neuron doctrine

Around the end of 19th century the famous Spanish neuro-anatomist *Cajal* (pronounced Kahaal) put forward the *neuron doctrine*, stating that the nerve cell is the structural and functional unit of the nervous system. He *disproved* the then prevalent view that nervous system is a syncytium or reticular or a continuous structure like river and its tributaries. Cajal also proposed that, all neurons are functionally polarized so that excitation can be passed on from the axon of a neuron to the dendrites and soma of the another. However, inside a neuron this excitation passes from dendrites to the axonal end. This *neuron doctrine* and *the law of dynamic polarisation* was supported by experiments done by Sherrington.

Essentially there are four types of neurons:

1. Sensory neurons.
2. Interneurons.
3. Motor neurons or motoneurons.
4. Neurosecretory cells.

Basically, a neuron contains a cell body called *soma* with a nucleus. The cell body usually bears a large number of treelike branches or *dendrites*, which gather information from the surroundings. The various inputs of information impart the cell +ve or –ve charges. The result of the summation of all types of charges in the cell may cause the net accumulation of *negative* charges (***depolarization***) or the *positive* charges (***hyper****polarization*).

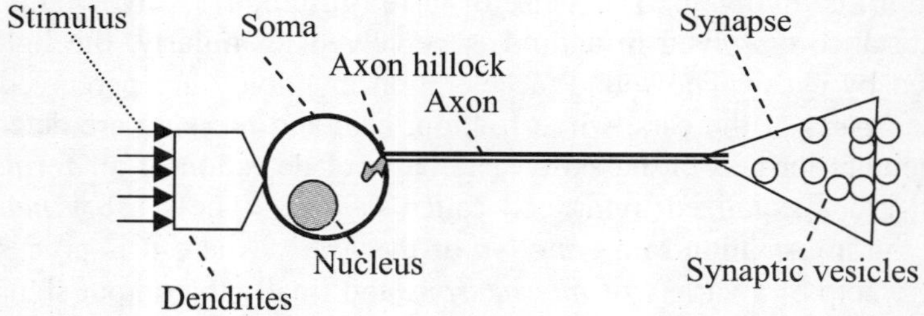

Fig.31.1. A generalized diagram of a neuron.

Compared to the surroundings, there is an excess of K^+ *ions* and deficit of Na^+ *ions* inside the neuron. The membrane surrounding the neuron being permeable to K^+ *ions*, allows some *ions* to leak out of the neuron. The large anions are unable to go out of the neuron, resulting in the accumulation of negative charges in excess over positive ones. This results in the resting membrane potential of a neuron to be around –70 mV.

If the neuron is sufficiently depolarized or in other words the depolarization reaches a *threshold* value, then a signal is transmitted across an *axon hillock* and through a thin fibre called *axon*, usually emanating from soma but can also emanate from a dendrite. This signal

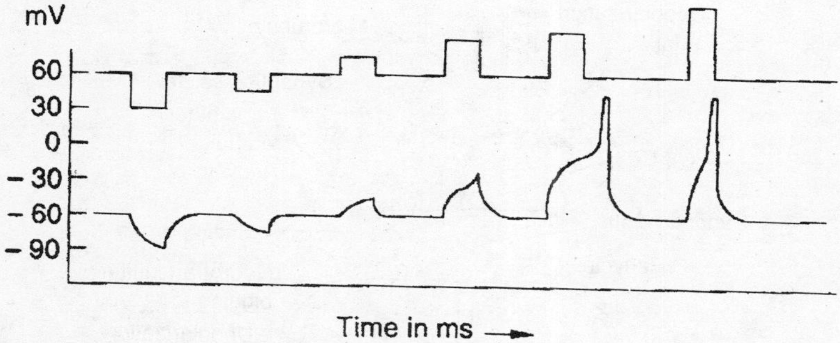

Fig.31.2. The generation of an action potential in a neuron by increasing depolarisation of the membrane potential.

in the form of an *action potential* traverses along the axon *unattenuated.* It is rather all on none phenomenon.

Neurons communicate with each other through specialized contacts called *synapses.* There are two main types of synapses: *chemical synapses* and *electrical synapses.*

Chemical synapses

A *chemical synapse* contains three regions (i) pre-synaptic knob, (ii) synaptic cleft and (iii) post-synaptic membrane region.
The pre-synaptic knob has many sub-cellular components, such as microtubules, mitochondria, vesicles containing neurotransmitter and small ions. Microtubules support the structure of the neuron and facilitate the transport of molecules and organelles in both directions – from soma to the distal end and *vice versa.* Mitochondria supply energy in the form of ATP molecules.

When a train of action potential reaches synaptic knob, the vesicles present in the pre-synaptic knob fuse with the pre-synaptic membrane and deliver the contents, the neurotransmitter in the synaptic cleft. The post-synaptic membrane in the cleft region adsorbs these neurotransmitter molecules and in turn may become depolarized. The depolarization of post-synaptic neuron can further result in generation of its own action potential and the process may continue till the *effector organ* a muscle or gland is reached.

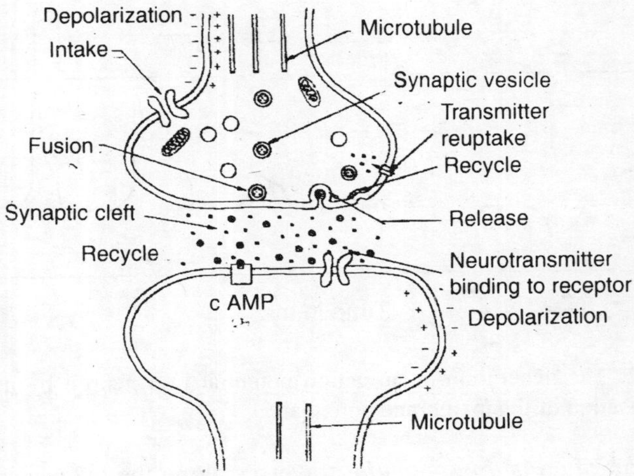

Fig.31.3. A schematic diagram showing the salient features of a chemical synapse, containing the pre-synaptic knob, synaptic cleft and the post-synaptic region of the following neuron .

The neurotransmitter released in the synaptic cleft is partly re-adsorbed by the proximal region of the pre-synaptic knob and recycled by reprocessing, and packaging in the synaptic vesicles.

Neurotransmitters

Neurotransmitter is usually a molecule synthesized by a neuron and released from a *synaptic*, *neuromuscular* or *neuroglandular* junction of a neuron. In addition, it can be present at the terminals of a *neurosecretory* neuron. Often the neurotransmitter is packed in vesicles and released from pre-synaptic neuron by *exocytosis*. The released neurotransmitter combines with specific receptors on the post-synaptic cell, which could be another neuron, a muscle or a gland cell.

In *neurosecretion*, the effector cell responds to neurotransmitter (usually called *neurohormone*) released in the blood stream by a pre-synaptic neuron. Neurotransmitters like somatostatin or vasopressin can behave as a neurotransmitter between two neurons and as a hormone between a neurosecretory cell and target cell.

In a pre-synaptic neuron the neurotransmitter is packaged in membrane-bound synaptic vesicles. A majority of neurons release more than one type of neurotransmitters, which may have quite different actions. However, a particular neuron releases the same neurotransmitter or combination of neurotransmitters. Neurotransmitters are mainly of two types:

1. Low molecular weight neurotransmitters

There are at least a dozen low molecular weight neurotransmitters and they are usually either amino acids or amines except *acetylcholine*.

The amino acid glycine, glutamate, gamma amino butyric acid (GABA), and probably aspartate are neurotransmitters.

Catecholamines — adrenaline, nor-adrenaline, dopamine, serotonin (5-hydroxy tryptamine), histamine and possibly tyramine and octopamine are *bio-amines* and *neurotransmitters*.

2. Neuroactive peptides

A large number of peptides synthesized and released by neurons that can cause excitation or inhibition of other neurons have been identified. Some peptides such as gastrin and secretin were known as hormones. On the basis of structural similarities neuropeptides can be classified into at least seven groups.

1. Insulins.
2. Opioids.
3. Gastrins.
4. Secretins.
5. Somatostatins.
6. Tachy-kinins.
7. Neuro-hypophyseal peptides.

Some main properties of neuropeptides are:

(a) Neuropeptides are synthesized only by neurons and gland cells of nervous tissue origin.

(b) Neuropeptides and the usual neurotransmitter can be present in the same neuron.

(c) More than one neuropeptide may be present in a neuron.

(d) Neuropeptides can modulate the action of neurotransmitters.

(e) Neuropeptides usually have a long-lasting action on the target cells. This long-lasting action may be due to (i) the absence of appropriate enzymes, which can degrade them rapidly, (ii) absence of specific uptake mechanisms in and around the synaptic cleft.

Electrical synapses

In electrical synapses the neurons are in direct electrical contact with each other through minute pores (*gap junctions*). In electrical synapse, the neurons communicate by means of the passage of an electric current formed by the movement of ions. This may have either excitatory or inhibitory effect on the target cell. The excitatory effect can cause depolarisation of the target cell. Whereas, the inhibition may cause any one of the three possibilities: hyperpolarisation, depolarisation or no change in membrane potential, making subsequent depolarisation more difficult. There is hardly any delay in transmission of a signal from one cell to another, through an electrical synapse.

Action Potential

There is an excess of K^+ ions and deficit of Na^+ ions in the protoplasm of a neuron. Normally the +ve charges are balanced by the –ve charges carried by large protein molecules in the neuron-protoplasm. The membrane of the neuron is partly leaky to K^+ ions. Since the concentration of K^+ ions is greater inside than outside, the K^+ ions leak out of the neuron. The negatively charged protein molecules are unable to leak out, because of their size. This results in excess of the –ve charges inside the neuron. The negative charges inside the neuron have a tendency to pull back the K^+ ions. It leads to an equilibrium state i.e. K^+ ions are in electrochemical equilibrium across the membrane. The potential E_K across the membrane is approximately given by *Nernst equation*:

$$E_K = \frac{\mathbf{R}T \log_e}{n\mathbf{F}} \frac{[K^+]_o}{[K^+]_i},$$

where $\mathbf{R}$ = gas constant; n = valence of the ion, in case of K^+ it is 1; $\mathbf{F}$ = Faraday constant; $\log_e$ = natural logarithm; $[K^+]_o$ = concentration of K^+ outside the neuron; $[K^+]_i$ = concentration of K^+ inside the neuron. The equation shows that the potential across the membrane increases when the concentration of K^+ outside increases. At 20°C, by changing $\log_e$ to $\log_{10}$ the equation becomes

$$E_K = 59 \log_{10} \frac{[K^+]_o}{[K^+]_I},$$

However, in addition to K^+ ion usually the cell membrane is permeable to other ions like Na^+ and Cl^-. In such a situation, the membrane potential is more accurately given by the *Goldman, Hodgkin and Katz equation.*

$$Em = \frac{\mathbf{R}T \log_e}{n\mathbf{F}} \quad \frac{P_K [K^+]_o + P_{Na} [Na^+]_o + P_{Cl} [Cl^-]_o}{P_K [K^+]_i + P_{Na} [Na^+]_i + P_{Cl} [Cl^-]_i}$$

where P_K, P_{Na} and P_{Cl} refer to permeabilities of K^+, Na^+ and Cl^- ions respectively. The other symbols used are the same as those in the Nernst equation.

The knowledge about the mechanism of generation of action potential came from the work on squid giant axon. In 1939, using intracellular micro-electrodes Hodgkin and Huxley in the U.K., as well as Curtis and Cole in the U.S.A. found that, during action potential generation a brief reversal of membrane potential occurs. This results in axon becoming approximately 40 mV positive in comparison to the outside.

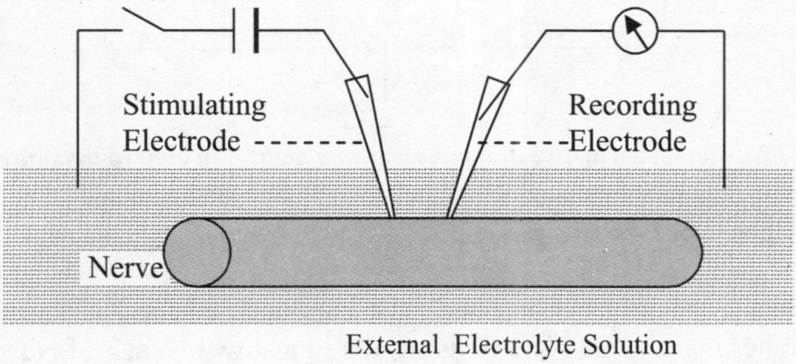

Fig. 31.4. Recordings from squid giant axon with stimulating and recording microelectrodes.

The membrane can be considered to be equivalent to an electrical circuit. A battery equivalent to the resting potential, a resistance (or conductance) in series to the flow of current and a capacitance in parallel with the battery and resistance in circuit. Each ion channel can be represented separately and combined in parallel. For example g_K, g_{Na} and g_{Cl} represent the conductance for the respective ions.

If a potential difference is created between two conducting materials separated by an insulator, then charge can be stored like a capicitor and the capicitance is developed. The cell membrane acts like a leaky insulator separating intra– and extracellular ionic solutions. When potential difference exists across the membrane, it develops capacitance to store charges on its inside and outside surfaces like a capacitor. A neuron-membrane has a capacitance of about 10^{-6} **F/sq.cm.**

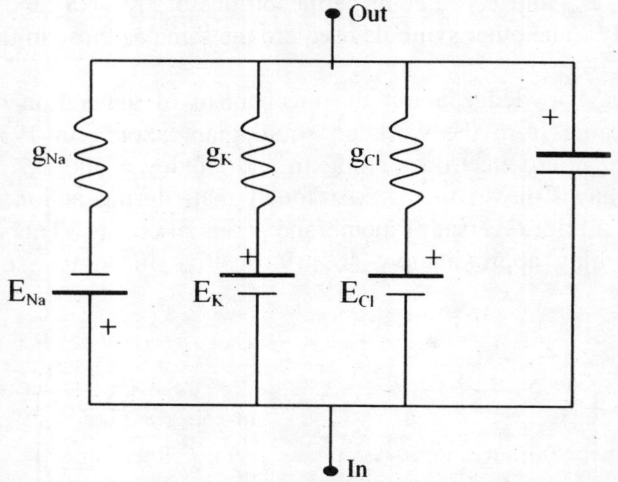

Fig. 31.5. An electrical circuit equivalent to a neuron in electrophysiology.

The sodium— potassium pumps

At the resting membrane potential, the conductance for K^+ is up to 25 times higher that that of Na^+. This results in a slow leakage of Na^+ in the cell, which in turn drives out more K^+ ions. Decrease of membrane potential because of the passive movement of Na^+ and K^+ is checked by active pumping of Na^+ and K^+ ions across the membrane. The sodium—potassium pump needs supply of ATP molecule for energy requirement. The efflux of Na^+ by pump is coupled with influx of K^+. It has been found that ***for every three sodium ions pumped out, two potassium ions are pumped in the neuron.***

The presence of a sodium — potassium pump can be shown by the following experiments.

1. Incorporate radioactive ($^{24}Na^+$) in the neuron and measure its efflux.
2. By cooling the neuron or by the application of drugs such as *digitalis* or *ouabain* which specifically block the Na^+ pump without affecting the oxidative metabolism in the cell.
3. If K^+ is totally removed from the external medium, the Na^+ pump also stops functioning.

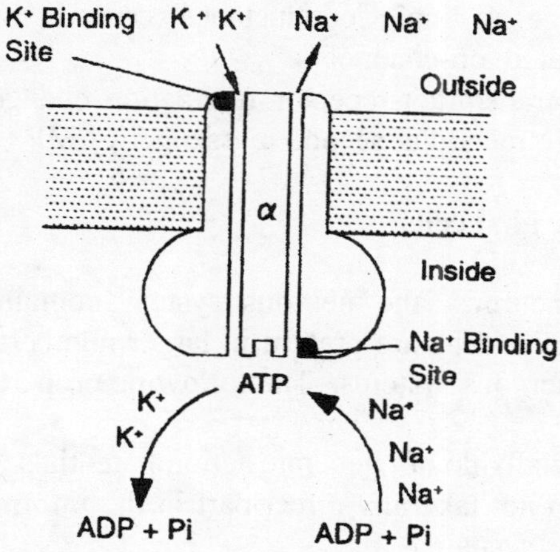

Fig.31.6. A simplified diagram of sodium-potassium pump showing involvement of ATP in pumping out Na^+ and taking in K^+. For every three Na^+ ions pumped out, two K^+ ions are taken in the neuron.

The length of axon affected by a nerve impulse

The length of axon covered by an action potential at a moment can be calculated by the duration of action potential (say 1 milli-second), and the conduction velocity of the action potential (say 100 m / sec or 100 mm/ milli-sec.). This shows that in the duration of 1 milli-sec the action potential covers 100 mm or 10 cm of the nerve. can occupy a greater proportion of the length of the axon, at a particular moment. The length of axon covered by an action potential at a moment will be more in the axon that conducts the axon potential faster.

Post-synaptic receptors

The neurotransmitter released from the pre-synaptic knob diffuses across the synaptic cleft and interacts with the receptors on the membrane of the post-synaptic cell. The neurotransmitter can be excitatory at some synapses (vertebrate skeletal neuromuscular junction), or inhibitory at other synapses (synapse between post-ganglionic parasympathetic neurons and heart muscle cells) or both excitatory and inhibitory at some synapses. The receptors determine the nature of post-synaptic response. Receptors are usually protein molecules, embedded in the membrane structure. There are two main types of post-synaptic receptors.

1. Where change in ionic conductance caused by action on the chemically gated ion-channels.
2. Where neurotransmitter-receptor interaction changes the metabolic rate through intracellular second messenger cAMP.

The neuroglia or glial cells

In addition to neurons, the nervous system contains glial cells or neuroglia. The glial cells are present in larger numbers than neurons in the mammalian nervous systems. The following properties are suggested for glial cells.

1. Glial cells usually do not generate action potentials.
2. Glial cells do not take any direct part in the information processing in the nervous system.
3. Glial cells support the neurons in the nervous system, as the connective tissue supports other parts of the body.
4. Glial cells maintain ionic balance around the neurons and remove transmitter molecules.
5. Glial cells serve as substratum in guiding the tip of growing neuron (*growth cone*) to establish proper connection with other neurons or a target organ.
6. Glial cells often provide an insulating cover for neurons in the form of a sheath.

There are two main categories in the glial cells: *microglia* and *macroglia*. *Microglia are usually involved in phagocytosis*. Macroglia have further subtypes:

(a) *Astrocytes*, which are star shaped and remove excess K^+ ions from the surroundings. They also remove neurotransmitters from the region of synaptic clefts.

(b) *Oligodendrocytes* usually form myelin sheath around axons of the central nervous system. In the peripheral nervous system *Schwann cells* (of different origin than glia) form myelin sheath around neurons.

(c) *Ependymal cells*, line the ventricles and the choroid plexuses of the brain, and help in the formation of the cerebrospinal fluid.

Neural development

The main challenge of neural development is to understand how axons and dendrites grow out and establish contacts with their correct partners so as to form a functional network. Usually the different components of the nervous system — sensory neurons, interneurons, motor neurons as well as muscles develop in separate locations in an embryo. This suggests that each cell develops according to its local program. In the next phase of development an orderly set of connections by axons and dendrites is established provisionally, such as to allow interaction between the components of the network. Finally, these connections are either re-inforced or eliminated depending upon the meaningful electrical signals passing between them.

In all animals the nervous system develops from the *embryonic ectoderm*. In vertebrates, the nervous system originates from two sets of cells.

1. Cells of the *neural tube* are formed by the invagination of ectodermal cells. *Neural tube cells* eventually form brain, spinal cord, retina of the eye and glial cells of the central nervous system (CNS).
2. Cells of the *neural crest*, detach and migrate away from the ectoderm in the embryo. *Neural crest cells* form neurons and the supporting cells of the peripheral nervous system.

   After complete differentiation, the neurons do not usually divide. *The time and position of a differentiated neuron* usually determines the connections it will form. For example in cerebral cortex the early born cells located in the inner layers send axons to the outer regions of the cortex. However, the neurons born late located in the outer layers of the cortex send axons in the region within the cortex.

The positional values of neurons

The projections from the sensory organs map in an orderly manner, in the sensory region of the *central nervous system* (CNS). Outputs from the motor region of CNS project to the muscles. The tip of the growing axon (*growth cone*) takes cue from several sources for making a correct connection with the target cell. The two prominent cues are as under:

1. The substrate on which it is growing.
2. The neurotrophic factor released by the target cell helps to guide the growth cone to reach target cells.

Some model nervous systems

In scientific research often the finding of an appropriate answer to any question is very much dependent upon the system chosen to answer that question. Because of this reason there are many biological systems which have provea to be ideal for researches in neurobiology. Some of them are leeches, snails, zebra fish, the nematode *Caenorhabditis elegans*, fruitfly *Drosophila*, mouse, cat, monkey and human beings. We will discuss the salient aspects of some of them.

Leech *H. medicinalis*

Leech has a head, a tail and 21 sequential ganglia interconnected with the ventral nerve cord. A large number of nerve fibres make the ventral nerve cord.

In an experiment, the ventral nerve cord was cut and allowed to heal. Initially the injured leech was unable to swim for a few days. In a few weeks time the leech learned to swim with an altered gait and style. The healed nerve cord was examined after sectioning, followed by microscopy. It was found that axon fibres though got connected, yet not in the original fashion. For example the severed proximal end of axon fibre number 101 did not get connected to the distal end of the same axon number 101. Instead it got connected to some other axon. In spite of mismatch the leech was able to swim, indicating that the nervous system has sufficient redundancy to meet such a situation.

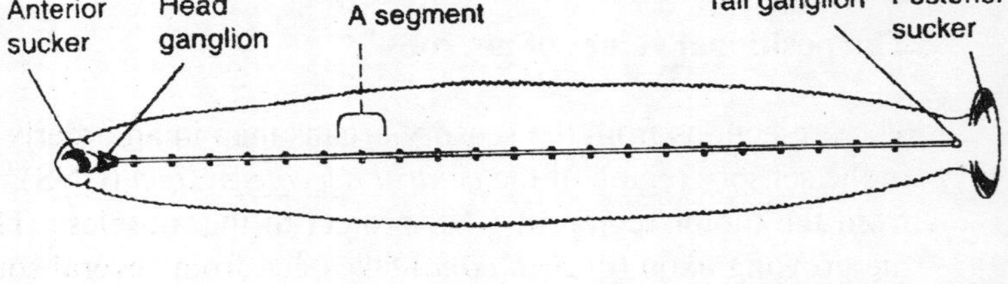

Fig. 31.7. A schematic diagram of a leech with head, tail and 21 abdominal ganglia connected with a ventral nerve cord.

Leech is ideally suited for electrophysiology experiments as it has several sequential ganglia. *Nicholls* and his coworkers have extensively used leech for electrophysiological studies.

Sea snail *Aplysia californica*

This snail has quite large neuronal cells in its ganglia, especially in the abdominal ganglia. The large neuronal cells are favourite system for electrophysiological studies, since glass microelectrode can be accurately impaled in them and electrophysiological recordings made. *Kandel* and his co-workers have done extensive electrophysiological studies with *Aplysia* and investigated some basic mechanisms of learning and memory. For this purpose they studied the reflex withdrawal of 'gill' the respiratory organ and another organ 'siphon', which is used for expelling seawater and waste. Kandel received the coveted Nobel Prize.

Nematode *Caenorhabditis elegans*

The nervous system of this nematode consists of around 700 neurons. The entire nervous system has been extensively analysed by *Brenner* and his co-workers. The cell lineage studies during the development of the ventral nerve cord, carried out by *Sulston* show that programmed cell-death is an essential feature of the development of the nervous system (Cf. Fig. 26.8). In addition a large number of mutations have been identified which affect the behaviour of the nematode. Brenner and Sulston have been awarded Nobel Prize for their work a few years back.

Fruitfly *Drosophila*

Drosophila is popularly known as *Queen of Genetics*. It has been very extensively used for genetic, embryological, developmental, neurobiological, molecular and behavioural studies. *Drosophila* like other *holometabolous* insects develops through egg, larva, pupa and imago (or adult) stages. Indeed, it is like *two animals in one* i.e. larva and adult fly.

Females carrying double mutation for *dorsal,* or other ventraizing mutations such as *cactus*, *torpedo*, *gurken*, *Toll*, *easter* etc., form dorsalized embryos. The formation of ventral structures requires product/s of the *dorsal* locus. The other genes like *Notch* and *Delta* encode for trans-membrane proteins in *Drosophila*.

In some other animals such as cat and monkey the visual system was investigated in detail. In 1962 *Hubel* and *Wiesel* have studied the cat's visual cortex for the analysis of receptive fields, binocular interaction and functional architecture. They also studied in 1977 the functional architecture of the macaque monkey visual cortex.

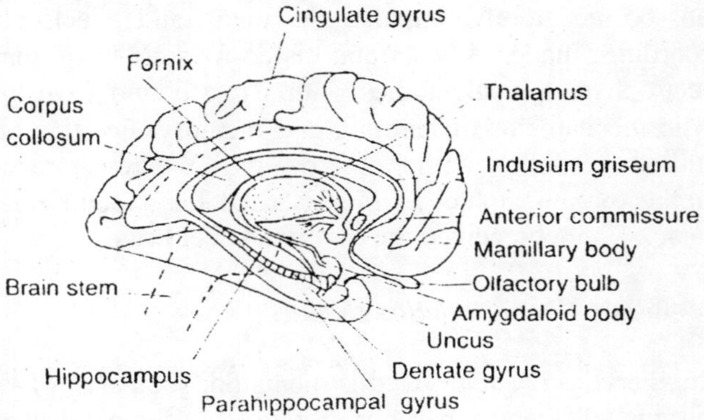

Fig.31.8. A schematic diagram of the medial view of the cerebral hemisphere of human brain showing the prominent parts.

The functioning of human system has been studied in many ways. The main approaches were:

1. Study of persons whose nervous system was abnormal in development.
2. Study of persons whose nervous system was partly ablated for medical reasons.
3. Electrophysiological recording on persons undergoing medical treatment or on volunteers.
4. Study of aging persons.

A Gene governing pain-perception

A 10-year-old Qureshi boy living in Lahore could pierce knife through his limbs or walk barefoot on burning cinder, without feeling pain. The boy died after jumping from the roof of a house just to impress his friends. Dr. C. Geoffrey Woods from Cambridge Institute for Medical Research, England and his colleagues in Pakistan could locate six individuals in three closely related Qureshi families who had never felt pain in any part of their body.

Woods and his team found that all these no pain perceiving individuals had a defect in a sodium channel gene *SCN9a.* This gene is one amongst 11 human genes whose proteins are involved in initiation of nerve signals in the body. They open channels to allow sodium ions to enter the neuron.

The *SCN9a* gene is active in nerves that mediate pain perception, as well as in the nerves of sympathetic nervous system controlling vital functions such as heart rate. However, those individuals not perceiving pain had no symptoms of abnormal sympathetic nervous systems. Dr. Woods found that the boy's mother had one defective copy of the gene *SCN9a* and possibly his father, a first cousin of mother also had defective gene. The father had died of heart attack before he could be examined. The boy possibly inherited two copies of defective gene leading to lack of pain-sensation.

Different proteins embedded in nerve terminals are sensitive to different types of injury such as injury by heat, cut, trauma, corrosive substance etc. These sensor proteins allow a few sodium ions to enter the neuron, occasionally not significant enough to elicit a pain-response. The proteins made by *SCN9a* gene possibly amplify the pain signal by allowing a larger number of sodium ions flow in the neuron, resulting in a larger electrical signal that is interpreted as painful on reaching the brain.

According to Dr. Woods, possibly all pain sensation depends upon the amplification of the signal by *SCN9a* gene protein. Hence all signal eliciting pain are muted when both copies of *SCN9a* gene are defective.

Learning and memory are the important qualities of human beings. From a very large number of studies in these fields it appears that *hippocampus* is involved in declarative learning and short-term memory in human beings. However, in a short time the memory becomes independent of the hippocampus. In addition, it has been found that some protein synthesis is necessary for the short-term memory to establish as a long-term memory.

Further reading

Brown, A.G. Nerve Cells and Nervous Systems: An Introduction to Neuroscience. Narosa Publishing House, New Delhi, pages 265 (1992).

Kandel, E.R., Schwartz, J.H. Principles of Neural Science. Second Edition. Elsevier, New York, (1985).

Katz, B. Nerve, Muscle and Synapse. McGraw-Hill, New York, (1966).

Shepherd, G.H. Neurobiology. Second Edition. Oxford University Press, Oxford, (1988).

Singh, R.N. Neurobiology of the gustatory system of *Drosophila* and some terrestrial insects. *J. Microscopy Research Technique, 39*: 547-563(1997).

CHAPTER 32

Stem Cells

Stem cells are *unspecialized cells* capable of dividing indefinitely and on providing appropriate stimulus have the potential to develop into many different types of cells of the body as insulin producing cells of pancreas, beating cells of the heart, cells forming bones, cells of the lungs, skin and other tissues. Mainly three kinds of stem cells are known to exist in animals and humans.

1. Embryonic stem cells.
2. Adult stem cells.
3. Umbilical cord stem cells.

Embryonic stem cells

Mouse embryonic stem cells have been used for the last 25 years. Whereas the human embryonic stem cells are being used since 1998. Their main source has been the embryos left out from the *in vitro* fertilization procedures and are used with the consent of the donor.

An *in vitro* fertilized, four or five day old human embryo is a microscopic hollow ball of cells known as *blastocyst* comprising of three main regions: *trophoblast* or outer layer of cells; *blastocoel* (pronounced blastoseel) a fluid-filled cavity ; and *inner cells* numbering around 30 clustered in one region of blastocoel.

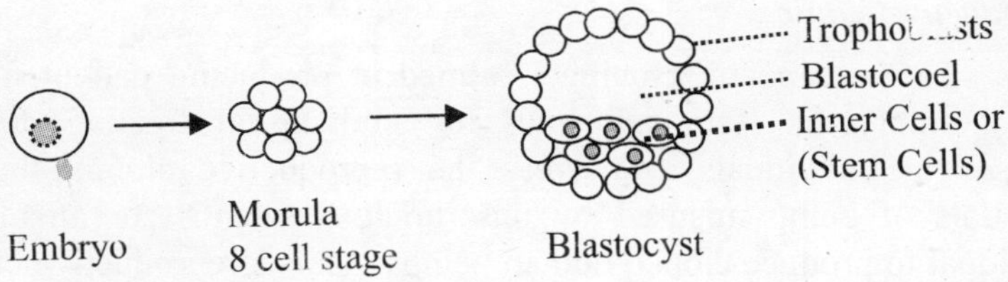

Cell culture

Embryonic stem cells are isolated by picking the inner cell mass with a micro-capillary and transferring it to a culture medium over *a layer of feeder cells* (un-dividing embryonic skin cells). The feeder layer cells supply some nutrients to the dividing embryonic cells as well as provide a substrate for the embryonic cells to adhere.

In several days the embryonic stem cells grow in number. Then they are transferred (*sub-cultured*) gently to A fresh culture medium with feeder cell-layer. Each step of sub-culturing is called *passage* (pronounced pasāāge). In about six months the original 30 embryonic cells yield millions of embryonic stem cells. These cells that have proliferated without differentiation are *pluripotent* (or *totipotent*) and are referred as embryonic stem cell line. Batches of such cells can be frozen and preserved or can be sent to other laboratories for propagation and experimentation.

Dr. James Thomson founder of controversial field of human embryonic stem cell research had said, "*We are asking what's special about these cells, how come they have this potential to form everything in the body, and what are the basic molecules that make them decide to become themselves versus something else?*"

Somatic cell nuclear transfer (SCNT)

The technology exists for removal of the haploid nucleus of an un-fertilized oocyte and replace it with a diploid nucleus from a somatic cell of an individual. The diploid egg so formed by SCNT may be initiated to divide by *parthenogenesis* (by pricking it with a fine needle). If placed in a suitable environment (say in a conditioned uterus), it has the potential to develop into a complete living being. This technology has the potential of being used for (i) *therapeutic cloning* and (ii) *reproductive cloning*.

The therapeutic cloning is aimed at producing patient-specific human embryonic stem cell lines for studying or treating different diseases in individuals. Whereas the reproductive cloning has the potentials of being misused by unscrupulous scientist or an affluent individual to produce cloned human beings. Hence reproductive cloning is banned in many countries.

Adult stem cells

Adult stem cells or *somatic stem cells* are undifferentiated cells found amongst differentiated cell population of a tissue. They are known by the name of the tissue from which they are harvested. There are several types of adult stem cells.

1. Bone marrow stem cells

a. *Hematopoietic stem cells* give rise to all types of blood cells (*cf.* Chapter 24, Fig. 24.1).

b. *Bone marrow stromal cells* (*mesenchymal stem cells*) give rise to a variety of cell types bone cells (osteocytes); cartilage cells (chondrocytes); fat cells (adipocytes); connective tissue cells such as those in tendons.

Bone marrow stem cells can give rise to specialized cell types of other tissues such as *skeletal muscle stem cells* or *hepatocyte stem cells* by a process known as *transdifferentiation* or *plasticity*.

2. Neural stem cells

Brain stem cells are able to generate 3 major cell types: non-neural astrocytes and oligodendrocytes as well as neurons or nerve cells.

3. Epithelial stem cells

Sheets of tightly lined cells forming epidermis, corneal epithelium, linings of digestive, respiratory and uro-genital tracts constitute epithelia. The epithelium not only provides protective envelope to the organ it surrounds but also regulates nutrient uptake, glandular secretions, and water absorption.

Developmentally epithelia may be derived from ectoderm, mesoderm or endoderm and can be either stratified or single layered (such as corneal epithelium). Most epithelia regularly replace damaged or dead cells during the life of animal and this continued cell replacement is known as '*tissue homeostasis*'.

The homeostatic replacement time of epithelial cells varies for different epithelia.

Epithelium type	Self renewal time
Intestine epithelium	~ 5 days
Interfollicular epidermis	~ 4 weeks
Lung epithelium	~ 6 months

4. Skin stem cells

Skin stem cells occur in basal layer of epidermis, which form keratinocytes that migrate to surface of skin and form protective layer. The other set of skin stem cells occur at the base of hair follicles. The follicular stem cells form hair follicle and epidermis.

Interaction between epithelial and mesenchymal cells

A large number of experiments in embryology were done to determine the influence of mesenchymal cell on the fate of epithelial cells. Epithelial cells adopt the cell fate of different mesenchymal tissues with which they are incubated. For example, epithelial lung buds get induced to form gastric glands when placed in contact of stomach mesenchyme. They also form villi epithelium in contact with intestinal mesenchyme or form hepatic cord in association with liver mesenchyme. A large number of similar experiments support the view that *epithelial tissue formation is partly regulated by mesenchymal signals*.

Multipotent and unipotent epithelial cells

Multipotent stem cells can differentiate into all types of epithelial cells. However, epithelial homeostasis in the tissue is usually maintained by *unipotent* progenitor cells that have the capacity to differentiate into one particular cell lineage.

Maintenance of stem cell character

For the life-long maintenance of homeostasis in a tissue stem cells are expected to possess an inexhaustible capacity to self-renew and differentiate. Following every cell division at least one daughter cell must maintain the stem cell character. Wnt / β-catenin signaling pathways have been shown to control the maintenance of stem cell identity, activation and differentiation of stem cells. The regulatory Wnt signals decide if and when the stem cells will self-renew, get activated to proliferate or follow terminal differentiation pathway.

Wnt proteins are cysteine-rich secretory proteins of about 20 different kind in mammals. In the cell most of the β-catenin is localized at intercellular junctions (*adherens*), where it binds to E-cadherin on one side and α-catenin on the other. The cytoplasmic pool of β-catenin is usually phosphorylated and targeted for degradation.

Role of *Notch* gene in epithelial stem cells

It is expected that Wnt signaling is not the only signal transduction pathway that regulates stem cells. For instance the tissue homeostasis and wound repair require epithelial stem cells to follow different pathways of terminal differentiation. For these goals to achieve the stem cells must get their cue from micro-environment around them. In such situation *Notch* gene mediated signaling controls selective cell fate determination in variety of tissues.

Four transmembrane receptors (Notch 1-4) are known to exist in mammals. Notch ligands fall into three sub-families of transmembrane proteins each with several members. *Notch* product after several modifications translocates to nucleus and plays role of *transcriptional activator*. The best characterized Notch target genes are *hairy* enhancer of split (*Hes*) complex.

Notch signaling was also found to promote proliferation and differentiation in mammary epithelium. An over-expression of *Notch* leads to tumorigenesis. *Notch* was considered a tumor suppressor in cornea and epidermis. *Notch-1* deficient skin is more susceptible to induced tumor. Like Wnt signaling, Notch signaling seems to exert its control at multiple steps along the lineage of the epithelial stem cells.

Labelling of stem cells

In principle a single adult stem cell should be able to generate genetically many identical cells called *a clone*, which can give rise to differentiated cell types of the tissue. By labeling a stem cell with a virus it was possible to show that individual stem cell clones have the capacity to repopulate the injured tissue in a living animal.

Unlike other epithelia the existence of a multipotent stem cell in intestine, which could form enterocytes, goblet, Paneth and neuro-endocrine cells is not yet established for lack of suitable cell surface markers. Discovery of suitable cell surface marker could rapidly advance this field in future.

Umbilical cord stem cells

Placenta or the umbilical cord is quite rich in stem cells and a very useful source of hematopoietic stem cells. Cord blood is collected ***after*** the umbilical cord has been detached from the newborn. The umbilical cord blood can be collected by any of the two methods *ex utero* or *in utero after the baby is delivered.* Only *after* the delivery of the baby, the umbilical vein is clamped towards the baby side and placenta is placed in a sterile vessel. The umbilical blood is collected by gravity draining. The usual yield per collection is around 40-150 ml. The collected blood is sent to blood bank immediately where it is screened for any infectious disease or genetic impairment; tissue typed and stored at liquid nitrogen temperature for future use.

Umbilical cord blood stem cells are more proliferative and have a higher chance of acceptance from family members than stem cells from bone marrow. Fathers have 25% chance of matching their children and siblings too have 25% chance of being a perfect match for umbilical cord blood. Since 1988, more than 75 deficiencies are treatable by umbilical cord stem cells.

Applications of stem cells

1. Human epidermal keratinocytes were successfully cultured by the pioneering efforts of Green and colleagues

Although not all cells form human epidermis and show active proliferation, yet some keratinocytes produced large colonies (called *holoclones*) and could be passaged for several hundred generations. Green and colleagues realized the potential of the clinical use for successful treatment of burn patients by using *autologous* (taken from the same person in whom it was grafted again) cultured epidermal cells. Similarly in some cases of eye-injury the limbal stem cells were cultured and then successfully transplants were made from autologous corneal epithelial sheets.

2. Scientists working at Advanced Cell Technology Inc, Worcester, Massachusetts reported a method of producing large number of bipotential progenitor cells known as hemangioblasts from human embryonic stem cells that can lead to formation of blood vessels and blood cells as well as cells of immune system (*Nature Methods*, 2007). These cells when injected into animals with damaged retina due to diabetes or ischemia showed robust repair of damaged vasculature within 48 hours. These cells also showed similar repair capacity in myocardial infarction and restoration of blood flow to near normal level in ischemic limbs. An extension of this technology to humans has the potential to benefit people suffering from vascular diseases.

3. Scientists working at a regenerative medicine company named Aastrom Biosciences Inc., have developed a Tissue Repair Cell (TCR)

Technology that utilizes autologous (cells derived from the same patient) bone marrow stem and progenitor cells to help regenerate vascular, bone, cardiac and neural tissues. Large scale clinical trials are yet to be performed.

4. Stem cells can be used for the treatment of degenerative diseases whether they are genetic or otherwise. For example, it may become feasible to use stem cells by making dopamine producing neurons for treatment of Parkinson's disease (causing tremors, rigidity and decreased mobility). Mouse embryonic stem cells have been induced to differentiate in dopamine producing (DA) neurons by incorporating *Nurr*1 gene in the genome.
5. Stem cells can be used for screening new drugs and toxins.
6. Stem cells can be used for understanding birth defects.
7. Stem cells may be used for cloning of animals.

Scientists, clinicians and the people in general will watch with keen interest, as more and more knowledge emerges about stem cells and more they are used for the benefit of living beings.

Further reading

Artavanis-Tsakonas, S., Rand, M.D. and Lake, R.Y. Notch signaling: cell fate control and signal integration in development. *Science, 284*: 770-776 (1999).

Birchmeier, C., and Birchmeier, W. Molecular aspects of mesenchymal-epithelial interactions. *Annu. Rev. Cell Biol, 9*: 511-540 (1993).

Blanpain, C., Horsley, V., and Fuchs, E. Epithelial stem cells: turning over new leaves. *Cell, 128*: 445-458 (2007).

Logan, C.Y., and Nusse, R. The Wnt signaling pathway in development and disease. *Annu. Rev. Cell Dev. Biol. 20*: 781-810 (2004).

Rheinwald, J.G., and Green, H. Serial cultivation of strains of human epidermal keratinocytes: the formation of keratinizing colonies from single cells. *Cell, 6*: 331-343 (1975).

CHAPTER 33

Chemical Genetics : Confluence of Genetics and Pharmacology

In addition to Biochemistry, the disciplines of Genetics and Pharmacology are two prominent approaches to elucidate the functions of a protein in the cell. A small molecule and a mutation both targeting the same protein have often produced totally different phenotypes.

For instance thiazolidinediones (TZD) are prescribed for the treatment of type II diabetes, a disease mainly caused by obesity. The target of TZD was found to be a nuclear hormone receptor and transcription factor PPARγ that is also a master regulator and promoter of adipogenisis (fat formation). TZD are known to activate PPARγ. On the contrary, the heterozygous deletion of PPARγ gene does improve insulin sensitivity in mice, suggesting that PPARγ inhibitors not activators should be developed for anti-diabetic drug. This contradictory situation was resolved by showing that genetic antagonism and pharmacological agonism of PPARγ, each of them improves glucose utilization through different mechanisms.

In this example TZD exposed the therapeutic potential of PPARγ agonist that was not predicted from genetic analysis. The fact emerges that the small molecules do reveal unexpected properties of their biological targets. The question is how often? In fact less than 5% of proteome (total protein pool) is targeted by potent small molecules. In contrast genes can be efficiently linked to phenotypes through well established genetic methods.

There is no well defined way to pin point the cellular targets of a small molecule. A way to obviate this difficulty would be to use a mutation to impart selectivity on a small molecule, a method which could be called '*Chemical Genetics*'. A few examples in this context are given here.

In the protein kinase super family a single residue known as gatekeeper in the ATP binding pocket, controls sensitivity to a range of small inhibitory molecules. This gatekeeper molecule is a large hydrophobic amino acid common and conserved among many protein kinases. The mutation of gatekeeper to alanine or glycine creates a modified pocket that can be selectively accessed by an analogue of inhibitors. Gate keeper mutation does not impair the mutated kinase. This creates a model kinase system in which wild type kinase has been replaced with the drug sensitive allele, where the effects of selective pharmacological inhibition of kinase can be studied.

A similar strategy has been used to identify allele specific ligands for several protein families such as GTPases, G-protein-coupled receptors, motor proteins, nuclear hormone receptors and phosphatases. For each of these proteins a small molecule binding site was modified so as to bind to a synthetic ligand. This provides with a handle to perform a control experiment where target-less wild type cells are treated with synthetic ligand and thereby confirm that any phenotype needs the drug's target. Such graded target inhibition can be of critical value in estimating clinical efficacy of small molecules.

Small molecules and allosteric interaction

Accumulation of unfolded proteins in the lumen of endoplasmic reticulum of yeast activates production of chaperons. *Ire*1 is an endoplasmic reticulum trans-membrane kinase. Unfolded proteins induce dimerisation of *Ire*1 kinase domains and the attached RNase domains and initiate the '*unfolded protein response*'. Mutations of *Ire*1 that disable kinase also block unfolded protein response. Biochemical mechanism of this kinase is not clear as its substrate is unknown. To understand the mechanism of signalling by wild type *Ire*1, a drug sensitive allele *L745G* was used, which however, is impaired in kinase activity in eliciting unfolded protein response. Surprisingly when impaired *Ire*1 allele was treated with inhibitor 1NM-PP1, the recovery for unfolded protein response was almost complete. Control experiments showed that this recovery was due to specific interactions with 1NM-PP1.

A double mutant was constructed from the drug sensitive mutant *L745G*. This double mutant was drug sensitive but had no detectable kinase activity (*kinase dead*). It was able to bind to inhibitor 1NM-PP1. This double mutant was able to produce unfolded protein response almost equivalent to wild type in the presence of 1NM-PP1. Thus 1NM-PP1 acts as an *Ire*1 activator (agonist) rather than inhibitor (antagonist), although that small molecule binds to *Ire*1 active site and directly blocks its kinase activity.

Indeed, a kinase inhibitor rescued the phenotype of a kinase dead mutation. This reveals a signaling mechanism in *Ire*1 which shuttles between active and inactive configurations upon ligand binding at the ATP site. No other protein kinase is known to signal this way. However, RNase L contains a kinase domain known as *pseudokinase* domain and binding of nucleotides to this domain regulates its RNase activity.

The human genome contains genes for at least 48 pseudokinases. Many of these proteins are for key signalling pathways and are target of amplification and mutation in cancer. The mechanism of pseudokinase signalling is poorly understood. It is likely that many of them may be using allosteric mechanism similar to *Ire*1. Hence it may become possible to inhibit or activate the pseudokinases by developing small molecules that target their vestigial active sites.

Inhibition of kinase activity while keeping protein moiety intact

Small molecules usually do not alter the expression of their protein-target. In contrast knockout of a gene may cause total loss of protein target. Both methods produce different outcomes.

The response of leukocytes to different chemotactic and inflammatory stimuli is mediated by p110γ. Mice lacking p110γ show reduced immune response. This finding has led to look at p110γ inhibitors as anti-inflammatory drugs. It is known that over expression of a kinase-dead p110γ in mice heart muscle protects it from myocardial damage.

However, p110γ knock out mice exhibit increased contractility of cardiac muscle and suffer myocardial damage.

Why the deletion of p110γ produce opposite phenotype to that shown by over expression of kinase dead allele? It was shown in separate experiments that cardiac defect is not due to loss of p110γ kinase activity. Further p110γ allosterically alters an enzyme PDE3B that catalyzes cAMP destruction. Deletion of gene encoding *p110γ* disrupts protein-protein interaction and leads to deleterious accumulation of cAMP and cardiac failure. The regulation of PDE3B by p110γ is independent of kinase activity. Hence it is unaffected by small molecule kinase inhibitors using p110γ target.

The other group of kinases known as Aurora kinases control spindle assembly, chromosome alignment, segregation and cytokinesis during mitosis and meiosis. Many tumors overexpress Aurora kinases. This led to these kinases as potential cancer drug targets. Knock down of Aurora B by RNAi causes a range of undesirable mitotic defects. In contrast use of Aurora kinase inhibitor ZM447439 produced much desirable phenotypes.

Aurora B binds to protein surviving at centromere. Imaging experiments showed that on treatment with RNAi surviving was absent from centromere. Whereas it was localized correctly on treatment with ZM447439. It seems that more drastic phenotype change by RNAi treatment was due to loss of scaffolding function of the kinase.

Whether a protein is targeted by a small molecule inhibitor or by a knock out of the gene, often different phenotypes result. These differences reveal the multiple biological functions of an individual protein. An intermediate path would be to do a saturation mutagenesis of a particular gene of interest and examine all the mutants of different shades for the information of interest. It is a tedious but doable work if absolutely necessary. However, the view that genetics can identify all protein targets for drug development need to be modified and the need for development of appropriate small molecule tools will still remain.

Further reading

Bishop, A., Buzko, O., Heyeck-Dumas, S., Jung, I., Kraybill, B., Liu, Y., Shah, K., Ulrich, S., Witucki, L., Yang, F., *et al. Annu. Rev. Biophys. Biomol. Struct. 29*: 577-606 (2000a).

Bishop, A.C., Ubersax, J.A. Petsch, D.T., Matheos, D.P., Gray, N.S., Blethrow, J., Shimizu, E., Tsien, J.Z., Schultz, P.G., Rose, M.D., *et al. Nature, 407*: 395-401 (2000b).

Knight, Z.A., and Shokat, K.M. Chemical genetics: where genetics and pharmacology meet. *Cell, 128*: 425-430 (2007).

CHAPTER 34

Epigenetics

The roles of nature and nurture have long been recognized in the development of the living being. Gradually the genes were attributed a major role of nature and the environment or upbringing took the role of nurture. Genes usually decide the potential of an organism and nurture decides the extent to which the potential can be achieved. As early as 1908, Garrod identified a metabolic disease 'alkaptonuria' (where urine turns black on keeping in air), to follow Mendelian pattern of inheritance. Since then manv monogenic diseases have been discovered, giving hope that they may be curable by some kind of genetic manipulation or gene therapy. Keeping these views in mind, human diseases may be classified into two broad categories:

1. Diseases determined before fertilization of the egg.

2. Diseases, which occur after fertilization of the egg.

Approximately 2% of the total non-infectious diseases are determined before fertilization and are believed to have genetic origin. In theory, they may be curable in future by genetic engineering if they are monogenic. However, 98% of non-infectious human diseases such as cancer, blood pressure, heart diseases occur after fertilization and majority of them are polygenic, multifactorial diseases. For the manifestation of such diseases genes may be necessary but not a sufficient condition. Usually environment, habits, temperament can affect the manifestation in spite of similar genetic constitution.
epigenetics is an old concept in biology and represents the idea that when many genes control a phenotype, a simple linear analysis is not sufficient for reliable prediction. In multigenic systems environmental inputs and developmental signaling play important roles besides genes, in determining the phenotype. There are quite a few exceptions to the concept that unique genes have unique effects.

Brenner and his colleagues have suggested that this may be due to functional redundancy of genes as well as functional and informational redundancy in cell regulation. More than one gene may specify a particular function in the cell.

Conrad Waddington is credited for coining the word '*epigenetics*' used for, "The branch of biology which studies the casual interactions between genes and their products, which bring the phenotype into being". Waddington also proposed the concept of *epigenetic landscape* where the cell can make different decisions leading to different cell fates by following any of the several available pathways.

Many biological phenomena apparently strange and inexplicable have been grouped under the heading epigenetics. Such phenomena can be broadly classified into two categories: (i) those occurring at cellular level and the (ii) others happening at the organism level.

Epigenetic phenomena at cellular level

Some examples of such phenomenon are:

1. *Paramutation in maize*, where the interaction between two alleles I such that one allele causes heritable changes in the other allele.
2. *Position effect variegation in Drosophila*, where the local environment of the gene determines its expression.
3. *Gene imprinting*, where only a particular paternal or maternal gene is expressed.

In the words of James Watson, "*The major problem, I think is chromatin......, you can inherit something beyond the DNA sequence.*" Here we examine some of the macromolecules as well as small molecules that can influence the expression of genes in chromosomes.

DNA methylation in chromatin

One of the best characterized chromatin modifications is methylation of DNA. Methylation in mammals usually occurs on cytosine residues of CpG dinucleotide sequences. Some regions of chromatin are rich in CpG sequences (known as islands). Methylation of such CpG islands correlates well with transcriptional repressionof the gene. DNa methylation is one of the stable, heritable character of epigenetic regulation.

Histone modifications in chromatin

Correlation is emerging for covalent histone modification in chromatin and epigenetic phenomenon. Charge altering through acetylation and phosphorylation can change properties of chromatin.

Genetic screening for suppressors of position effect variegation (PEV) in *Drosophila* revealed more than 100 genes that encode constituents of heterochromatin. Many of these genes are conserved from flies to humans such as *heterochromatin protein*1 *(HP1)* and *histone H3K9 methyltransferase*.

Two evolutionarily conserved proteins Polycomb group (PcG) and Trithorax group (TrxG) regulate homeotic genes in *Drosophila* during development in almost opposite manner. PcG proteins cause and read methylation as well as facilitate chromatin condensation. Whereas, TrxG protein help methylation and promote transcription of chromatin.

Noncovalent modifications such as chromosome re-modelling. incorporation of histone variants and nucleosome remodeling provide additional ways for variation of chromatin.

Noncoding RNAs and epigenetic phenomena

Role of noncoding RNAs in controlling multiple epigenetic phenomena is becoming clear. These RNAs usually act in conjunction with methylation machinery of DNA and chromatin, for stable silencing of genes.

Post-transcriptional gene silencing (PTGS) RNAs such as microRNAs and siRNAs may not be considered epigenetic. However, transcription gene silencing (TGS) evoking RNAs repeat associated siRNAs, Xist (X inactive specific transcript) RNA and small RNAs in *S. pombe* indeed epigenetic as they can cause long-term gene silencing that can be inherited through cell division. It is also becoming clear that there is appreciable crosstalk between different epigenetic pathways.

Interaction between alleles of genes that cause heritable changes in gene expression is known as ***paramutation***. RNA has emerged as a main mediator of this phenomenoa in maize as well as mice.

A number of mechanisms exist that regulate the stability of phenotypes. Epigenetically inherited phenotypes often show faster variations than genetically inherited traits.

No. generations	Timescale of Epigenetic inheritance		
1	Chromatin		
10			
10^2		Prions	
10^3			DNA methylation
10^4			
10^5			

No. generations	Timescale of Genetic inheritance		
10	Repeat variation		
10^2			
10^3			
10^4		Point mutation	
10^5			
10^6			
10^7			
10^8			Sturdy genes
10^9			
10^{10}			

Epigenetics at organismal level

A number of gene knockout experiments were performed in which in spite of deletion of both copies of a gene in a cell or organism the normal phenotype is retained.

According to Haldane in monogenic diseases that constitute 2% of all infectious diseases, there seems to be a linear connection between a gene and disease.

Gene	Disease
1-------------------------------	1
2-------------------------------	2
3-------------------------------	3

According to Wright the polygenic diseases that constitute 98% of the infectious diseases are controlled by the interaction between many genes and environmental signals.

If say gene 4 is mutant or absent, the result would be difficult to predict. Redundancy at the genome level by a substitute gene may neutralize the effect of change or deletion. The signaling from the environment may change the course of behaviour of network of genes, to compensate the effect of mutation or deletion.

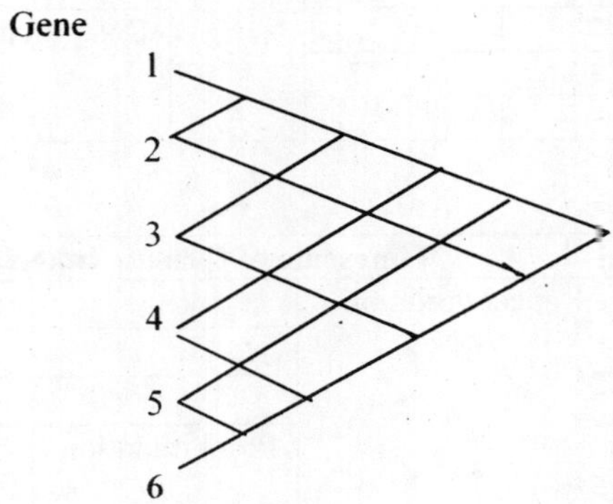

In agriculture, genes and environment have significant interaction. The genetic and environmental effects are not additive rather they are interactive, so that change in environment will have great influence on constant genomes. In the realm of polygenic diseases which fall in the category of highly interactive genetic or epigenetic systems the outcome cannot be predicted from the composition of genes alone.

Hypertension and ACE mutation

Angiotensin converting enzyme (ACE) is responsible for converting rennin → angiotensin protein, which is crucial in the control of blood pressure. Even in ACE mutant rats, which are hypertensive, early developmental changes can nullify the effect of ACE mutation. If the young rats born from ACE $^{-}$ mutant mother, are nurtured by normal mother of a related strain, they show decreased levels of hypertension. However, ACE mutation is not linked to hypertension in humans.

As observed in angiotensin II pathway, a mutant gene itself may be redundant. A single mutation in this pathway does not result in heart disease, as the pathway contains several alternative genetic loci, all of them function similarly.

Myocardial infraction has been linked to ACE mutation in humans. But many individuals harbouring identical ACE mutation have no heart disease. It shows that ACE locus related diseases are most likely to be polygenic, multifactorial diseases. Any particular defective gene or set of defective genes may be necessary but not sufficient for manifestation of heart disease. Perhaps the life style has crucial role in these manifestations.

Resetting of the cellular metabolic network

At times the cellular metabolic network is able to reset it self, in response to external stimuli. The outcome of such a resetting is usually positive but unpredictable. Adaptation of master runners (older persons) to aerobic stress is such an example. Such exercising older persons show regulation of several glycolytic and mitochondrial enzymes resulting in improvement of oxygen utilization. The younger persons achieve the same result through a different pathway. This response of older persons to aerobic exercise involves change in gene expression. Physical activity and electrical stimulations are known to activate or repress genes encoding for isozymes of skeletal muscle cells.

Diseases of the nervous system

Schizophrenia is a mental disease marked by disconnection between thoughts, feelings and actions. Monozygotic identical twins show 50% non-concordance for schizophrenia i.e. amongst identical twins one child may show schizophrenia, the other may not. This clearly shows that genes are not solely responsible for schizophrenia and probably several genes are involved along with epigenetic regulation of schizophrenia expression.

Small changes in the wiring of the nervous system are most probably due to non-genetic causes, such as environmemtal inputs during early development. Unequal sharing of resources in the uterus by identical twins could result in changes in embryonic wiring of the nervous systems affecting the phenotypic outcome of embryos. Indeed, small anatomical changes are present in the schizophrenia affected and unaffected members of the monozygotic twins. Even, hands of schizophrenic persons show micro-anatomical defects.

Bipolar disease causing mental depression is similarly controlled by many genes and with complex epigenetic regulation.

Evidence that environment dominates gene expression in complex phenotypes

1. In the operon theory genes are turned on or off by environmental signals.

2. The multiple forms of cancer have been assigned to the category of multifactorila diseases. Strong evidence exists for a genetic background, which is modulated by congenital and environmental effects. For example, it is known that migration of human populations, results in new patterns of cancer, which is reflective of their new environment. These migrant populations do not exhibit the same diseases occurring to their relatives, who have remained in their home country and with whom they shared the genetic background.

3. Many cancers have been associated with (i) mutation in growth control or (ii) mutation in tumor suppressor genes. These genes usually code for DNA-binding proteins that inhibit or delay cell multiplication. Examples may be given for two such genes *p53* and retinoblastoma. Mice with both alleles of *p53* gene deleted were found normal at birth, and developed normally until adulthood. Only after adulthood a proportion of them developed tumors in excess of control population. It shows that early phases of development are independent of *p53* gene and have redundant pathways in addition to *p53*. The same holds true for adults harbouring *p53* mutation but do not show tumor formation. Even on incorporation of a normal copy of *p53* gene into tumor cell it may not restore normal growth. Further it has been observed that *p53* protein forms *heterodimers* with many cellular proteins. The effect of *p53* gene mutation is modulated by many pieces of genetic or environmental inputs.

Retinoblastoma (*rb*) mutation arises either spontaneously or by inheritance of a deletion or absence of chromosome 13. Only 20-30% of all such genetic anomalies show tumor expression, indicating that other factors too are involved in tumor expression.

Breast cancer

Many mutations have been found in the tissues of later stages of breast-tumors. However, it is not certain that these mutations are cause or effect of non-genetic lesions, which if corrected soon might have prevented the occurrence of tumors. From studies of the family history, an association has been established between 'tendency for cancer' and a locus in chromosome *17q21*. However, only 2.5% of breast tumors are known to be genetic in origin. Expression of tumor may require in addition to this mutation, specific environment, habits, or specific set of other genes.

Cystic fibrosis

Cystic fibrosis, causing pancreatic insufficiency is believed to be a monogenic disease. More than 300 mutations have been found for cystic fibrosis transmembrane regulator (*CFTR*), with a variety of phenotypes. Over 65% of cases of cystic fibrosis are known to have a mutation at locus *F508* in *CFTR* gene. Homozygous mutations at locus *F508* show early pancreatic insufficiency (2 years of age), as well as wide phenotypic variation for pulmonary manifestation. Another mutation at locus *r117h*, when occurs in heterozygous condition with *F508*, shows symptoms similar to F508 homozygous state at a later age (10 years). The *r117h* mutation seems to be prevalent to the extent of 10% among all patients of cystic fibrosis and seems to be responsible for other diseases, in addition to cystic fibrosis. It also appears that the defect in *CFTR* channel may be partly compensated by other channels, indicating involvement of other genes. It is becoming clear that a simple mutation in a complex organism can have multiple interactions and ways of expression not solely determined by genetic constitution alone.

Modification of some simplistic views

Epigenetics as a field was a mere collection of curious and scattered biological phenomena occurring in different organisms. However, in recent times the molecular mechanisms underlying various epigenetic phenomena are being unraveled at a rapid pace, where key players and pathways are being uncovered.

1. The view that genetic inheritance is the only inheritance is an oversimplified view and need to be modified. It is known that in some organisms even the sex determination is influenced by epigenetic factors such as the embryonic temperature (in crocodiles / alligators), or the uterine exposure to hormones.
2. The second assumption that the genetic programmes are the sole script for the phenotype expression, need to be modified. A complex phenotype at present cannot be assigned to a simple set of Mendelian factors (genes). The mechanism by which an organism shows variability of phenotype from isogenic or close to isogenic composition is still not clear.
3. In relation to the genetic constitution of the organism, the role of nurture is equally important. It is becoming clear that the organisms are programmed but the programme is not entirely in the genes. So where is the rest of the programme?

Further reading

Allis, C.D., Jenuwein, T., Reinberg, D., and Caparros, M.-L. Epigenetics. Cold Sprg. Harb. Press, NY, pp. 502 (2007).

Darwin, C. *Origin of Species*. (1859). Reprinted, Penguin, New York (1984).

Goldberg, A.D., Allis, C.D. and Bernstein, E. Epigenetics: a landscape takes shape. *Cell, 128*: 635-638 (2007).

Jablonka, E., and Lamb, M.J. *Epigenetic Inheritance and Evolution. The Lamarkian Dimension.* Oxford University Press, Oxford, p.346 (1995).

Rando, O.J. and Verstrepan, K.J. Time scales of genetic and epigenetic inheritance. *Cell, 128*: 655-668 (2007).

Strohman, R. Epigenesis; The missing beat in biotechnology? *Biotechnology, 12*: 156 (1994).

Waddington, C.H. The Strategy of the Genes: a Discussion of Some Aspects of Theoretical Biology. Allen and Unwin (London), 1957.

Appendix 1

The genetic code inscribed in mRNA. *The amino acid coded by a codon is indicated by its side. The three termination codons signal the end of polypeptide chain synthesis.*

1st base	← 2nd base → U	C	A	G	3rd base
U	UUU phe	UCU ser	UAU tyr	UGU cys	U
	UUC phe	UCC ser	UAC tyr	UGC cys	C
	UUA leu	UCA ser	*UAA* Term	***UGA*** Term	A
	UUG leu	UCG ser	*UAG* Term	UGG trp	G
C	**CUU** leu	CCU pro	CAU his	CGU arg	U
	CUC leu	CCC pro	CAC his	CGC arg	C
	CUA leu	CCA pro	CAA gln	CGA arg	A
	CUG leu	CCG pro	CAG gln	CGG arg	G
A	AUU ile	ACU thr	AAU asn	AGU ser	U
	AUC ile	ACC thr	AAC asn	AGC ser	C
	AUA ile	ACA thr	AAA lys	AGA arg	A
	AUG met	ACG thr	AAG lys	AGG arg	G
G	GUU val	GCU ala	GAU asp	GGU gly	U
	GUC val	GCC ala	GAC asp	GGC gly	C
	GUA val	GCA ala	GAA glu	GGA gly	A
	GUG val	GCG ala	GAG glu	GGG gly	G

A = Adenine; C = Cytosine; G = Guanine; U = Uracil.

Amino acids: ala = alanine; arg = arginine; asn = asparagine; asp = aspartic acid; cys = cysteine; gln = glutamine; glu = glutamic acid; gly = glycine; his = histidine; ile = isoleucine; leu = leucine; lys = lysine; met = methionine; phe = phenyl alanine; pro = proline; ser = serine; thr = threonine; trp = tryptophan; tyr = tyrosine; val = valine.

Term = termination codon;

UAA= Ochre; *UAG*= Amber and *UGA*= Opal.

The genetic code in mitochondria (yeast) is slightly different. The codons **CUU**; **CUC**; **CUA** and **CUG** code for threonine and **UGA** codes for tryptophan.

Appendix 2

The standard ***one letter symbols*** and the ***three letter abbreviations*** of the common 20 amino acids.

A = Ala = Alanine	M = Met = Methionine
C = Cys = Cysteine	N = Asn = Asparagine
D = Asp = Aspartic acid	P = Pro = Proline
E = Glu = Glutamic acid	Q = Gln = Glutamine
F = Phe = Phenyl alanine	R = Arg = Arginine
G = Gly =Glycine	S = Ser = Serine
H = His = Histidine	T = Thr = Threonine
I = Ile = Isoleucine	V = Val = Valine
K = Lys=Lysine	W = Trp = Tryptophan
L = Leu =Leucine	Y = Tyr = Tyrosine

Appendix 3

1. *The Genetics of Bacteria and their Viruses. Studies in Basic Genetics and Molecular Biology.* **W. Hayes**. Blackwel Scientific Publications, Oxford. Fifth Printing, pages 740, 1967.

2. *Cell Biology. R.M. Dowben.* Harper & Row, Publishers, New York. Pages 570, 1971.

3. *Genes*. **B. Lewin**. Wiley Eastern Ltd., New Delhi. Pages 715, 1985.

4. *Molecular Biology of the Gene. General Principles. Vol. I.* **J. D. Watson, N. H. Hopkins, J. W. Roberts, J. A. Steitz and A.M. Weiner.** The Benjamin/ Cummings Publishing Co. Inc. Menlo Park, California. Fourth Edition, pages 744, 1987

5. *An Introduction to Genetic Analysis.* **A.J.F. Griffiths, J.H. Miller, D.T. Suzuki, R.C. Lewonntin, and W.M. Gelbart**. W.H. Freeman Co. New York. Fifth Edition, pages 840, 1993.

6. *Molecular Biology of the Cell.* **B. Alberts, D. Bray, J. Lewis, M. Raff, K. Roberts, and J.D. Watson,**.Garland Publishing Inc., New York, Third Edition, p.1294 (1994).

Index